D1467029

Trust
Functions
and
Services

Second
Edition

Trust
Functions
And
Services

By
Norman A. Wiggins

AMERICAN INSTITUTE OF BANKING
AMERICAN
BANKERS
ASSOCIATION

Copyright © 1978
American Bankers Association
All rights reserved
Second Printing, 1979

050500   Printed in the
                                          United States of America

Contents

Preface

Trust Functions and Services evolved out of the first textbook on trust business issued by the American Institute of Banking and published in 1927, under the title *Trust Functions*. By 1934 trust service had expanded to such an extent that a new textbook became a practical necessity. The 1934 textbook was issued in two volumes, each containing twenty chapters, entitled *Trust Business I* and *Trust Business II*. Ten years later, in 1944, continuing changes in trust business made necessary yet another new edition. In the 1954 revision *Trust Department Services* replaced *Trust Business I,* and in 1955 *Trust Business II* was replaced by *Trust Department Organization.* In 1971 *Trust Department Services* was revised and published under the title *Trust Functions and Services.*

The development of this text over the past 52 years clearly reflects the intention of the American Institute of Banking to give the students of trust business the very best and latest information as they pursue a study of the development of trust business. This volume, like its predecessors, is not a legal treatise. It does not give extensive or detailed treatment of those phases of the law of estates, trusts, and agencies that properly belong to the study of law as contrasted with the study of trust business. Though not a legal treatise, this volume must restate in summary form many of the generally accepted principles of the law of estates, trusts, and agencies as it takes the student on a step-by-step study of trust functions and services that a student would normally take in trying to become familiar with the day-by-day operation of a trust department.

In this, the sixth version, a complete revision has resulted in the addition of new material for the student who is engaged in the settlement of estates, the administration of trusts, and the management of agencies.

Chapters 1 and 2, concerning the development of trust institutions and trust services, are designed to give the student an appreciation of how quickly trust business has developed over a relatively short period of time.

Chapters 3, 4, 5, and 6, dealing with property, property rights, and wills, should enable the student to grasp the principles of the law dealing with property, wills, and intestate succession and the problems involved in the settlement of a decedent's estate.

Chapters 7, 8, 9, and 10, concerning personal trusts, including those funded by insurance, and guardianships, are designed to give the student an overall perspective on the problems surrounding the establishment and administration of trusts.

Chapters 11 and 12, on personal agencies, illustrate some of the fundamental distinctions between a trust and an agency and point up some of the sensitive areas that, if not handled carefully, can result in serious financial liability.

Chapter 13, on charitable trusts and agencies, has for its purpose to distinguish between charitable trusts and agencies. It includes a general, but not very technical, discussion of some of the problems of making gifts, and some brief comments on the taxation of foundations.

Chapter 14, dealing with employee benefit plans, is designed to introduce the student to some of the complexities in one of the most rapidly growing areas of service.

Chapters 15 and 16, concerning the establishment and management of corporate trusts and agencies, are designed primarily, but not exclusively, for the student who wishes to pursue a career in the highly sensitive but very important area of corporate finance. It includes a general discussion of how stocks and bonds are used to finance corporate operations.

Chapters 17 and 18, dealing with investments in both real and personal property, give insight into how investments are selected and, once selected, retained. Particular attention is given to the problems of handling mortgages as trust investments.

Chapters 19 and 20 will help the student understand just how carefully trust business is supervised and the limitations under which the trustee operates.

Chapter 21, on trends in the development of trust business, should enable the student to see that the future for trust business is practically unlimited if corporate fiduciaries continue to conduct their businesses with the welfare of their beneficiaries as their prime consideration.

The appendixes contain illustrative instruments, including a will, a trust agreement, and an investment management agency agreement, that should prove helpful.

For the student who is not familiar with legal and trust terms, a detailed glossary is included.

In the preparation of this edition, the following have contributed suggestions and offered counsel that helped improve it: Rolland D. Ackelson, Senior Vice President, Bank of Pennsylvania; Ronald G. Wilson, Assistant Vice President, Valley National Bank of Arizona, Phoenix, Arizona; August Zinsser, III, Vice President and Trust Officer, Union First National Bank of Washington, Washington, D.C.; and Frank A. McMullen, New York Chapter, American Institute of Banking.

Finally, I wish to express my gratitude to my secretary, Mrs. M. B. Matthews, Jr., who worked diligently and "far beyond the call of duty" in typing the numerous revisions of this text.

Norman Adrian Wiggins
President
Campbell College
Buies Creek, North Carolina

Introduction

The Purposes of This Chapter:

1. To define and explain the trust function—a fiduciary relationship
2. To examine the role of the trust department in the bank and banking system
3. To trace the historical development of trust services and trust institutions

The trust business is a business of rendering service. It involves the obligation to perform certain services faithfully and prudently, in accordance with applicable laws, regulations, and governing instruments.

Anyone can establish a trust. A trust is an arrangement whereby one person transfers legal title to property to another person (a properly licensed bank and trust company is considered a "person" under the law), who manages the property for one or more other persons. The person providing the property to create a trust is called the "trustor," "settlor," or "grantor"; the person holding legal title is called the "trustee"; and the person who derives the benefits from the property is called the "beneficiary."

People and corporations establish trusts for many reasons, but generally the function of a trust is to give the protection and professional investment management that only an experienced trustee can provide. Furthermore, in this unique relation, the trustee is required to administer the trust solely in the interest of the beneficiaries.

The provisions of a trust instrument govern the trust. Typically, the instrument appoints a trustee and names or designates the beneficiaries who will receive the income from the property held in trust and the "remaindermen" or "principal beneficiaries" who will receive the assets upon the termination of the trust. The objectives of a typical trust are to provide a regular income for a surviving wife or husband and to provide for the care and education of children.

The Role of the Trust Department in the Bank— in the Banking System

To understand fully the role of the trust department in the banking system, it is necessary for the student to reflect on the unique characteristics of a commercial bank. It is often said that the business of the bank is the management of funds borrowed from its depositors. It is this special characteristic that distinguishes the commercial bank from the usual business corporation.

There should be no misunderstanding. A banker, like any corporate officer, is accountable to his stockholders. In addition, however, he is accountable for the safety of the depositors' funds. Many people entrust their life savings to the banker, and they expect the funds to be carefully and safely handled. That is why commercial banking has been and will probably always be highly regulated by both the federal and state governments. This near but not complete fiduciary relationship imposes rigorous moral standards on the bank officer.

A trustee has grave responsibilities to the trustor and the beneficiaries. He must not only manage the funds and advise beneficiaries but also invest the assets of the trust estate so as to ensure both safety and income. All must be done without permitting the interests of the trustee or third parties to conflict in any way with the interests of the trust.

Individuals, particularly attorneys, can and do perform trust services. However, most such functions are carried out today by corporate trustees, such as trust departments of commercial banks. Unlike individuals, trust departments do not die, take vacations, or become ill. Furthermore, the financial responsibility of the commercial banks stands behind the management of accounts by the trust department.

In their separate roles, banks and their trust departments supply the capital that enables American industry to produce an endless flow of goods, and they are helping millions of Americans to a richness and security of life not approached by any other people in the world. A complete understanding of present-day trust institutions requires some appreciation of the historical background out of which they evolved.

The History of Trust Services

There are over 80 different types of trust services. Not all of them yield readily to historical treatment. A few have an origin and a development that are of special interest to the student of trust business. They

2

are taken in their chronological order, historically, as follows: wills, trusts, guardianships, and corporate trusteeships.

WILLS

A will is a legally enforceable declaration of a person's instructions as to matters to be attended to after his death; it does not become operative until after the maker dies. It is effective in any society that recognizes the right of the individual property owner to determine who shall succeed to the control of his property upon his death.

Ancient History

A forerunner of the modern will was developed, in a rather limited fashion, in Egypt in 2500 B.C. Three Egyptian wills, each nearly 4,000 years old, have been discovered. One is so modern in form, so plainly expressed, and so properly witnessed that it might almost be granted probate today.

It is interesting to note that the late Professor John Henry Wigmore, in his book *A Panorama of the World's Legal Systems,* quotes a portion of the record of a lawsuit on a will in Mesopotamia that dates back to 2060 B.C.

In the ancient Hebrew law and in the laws of both Greece and Rome, there is ample evidence of some limited right of an individual to dispose of his property by will. The wills developed under Roman law, however, are more similar to ours. For example, during the time of Justinian, the law provided that the testator sign his will and that the witnesses both sign and seal the instrument.

Although the ancient history of wills is interesting, a student of the development of trust services is primarily concerned with the development of the English will and of the office of executor.

Executorships

In nearly all modern English and American wills, an executor is named to carry out the terms of the will. That has not always been the custom, nor does the history of executorships parallel the history of wills. In France the naming of an executor is said to be the exception, not the rule. Some years ago only one of 20 French wills named an executor; that is due, of course, to the influence of Roman law. Unfortunately, no evidence remains to enable the historian to trace the beginning of executorship back to Roman times. If there is any connection between the Roman executor and the English executor, it would seem to be insignificant.

Early English Influences. In England the beginnings of executorship are found as early as the eighth century. In writings of that period, a man on his deathbed distributed by his "last word" a portion of his chattels "to his confessor for the good of his soul." The confessor was the person designated to execute the will of the dying man. In the course of a few centuries, the appointment and duties of an executor became more specific. One early English will reads: "Now I pray Bishop Aelfstan that he protect my widow and the things that I leave her . . . and that he aid that all the things may stand which I have bequeathed."[1]

Wills naming executors were in use by the close of the twelfth century, as evidenced by the will of Henry II. However, even then and for a long time afterward, the position and authority of the executor remained largely undetermined. Wills generally contained no definite statement as to whether the heirs or the executor would represent the decedent; nor did they indicate which of the two was to sue for debts owed to the estate or which might be sued for debts owed by the estate.

In a series of articles on the origin of the office of executor and its early functions, Oliver Wendell Holmes stated that it was customary at first for the executor to receive the testator's assets in his own right and that the English courts did not fully recognize the executor as trustee and not owner of the assets taken over by him until 1802.

Development of English Probate Practice. For several centuries after the middle of the thirteenth century, the office of executor was a church office, and the executor was a bishop or other churchman. As an officer of the church, the executor naturally had no standing in the courts of law with regard to the execution of wills. During the reign of Edward I (1272–1307), however, the executor was granted more and more standing to bring different kinds of actions before the courts. Although no definite date can be assigned, it was probably during Edward's reign that the executor became the recognized personal representative of the decedent—that is, the person who took over the decedent's personal estate, sued and was sued, paid the debts, and distributed whatever remained of the personal property.

With the development and recognition of the office of executor, a recognized probate practice came into being in England. In the thirteenth century, it was established law that the executor had to prove the will in the proper court, usually the court of the bishop of the decedent's diocese and hence an ecclesiastical court. The executor had to give bond and make an inventory of the estate. If he misbehaved, he could be removed from office. Even at that early date, the court (in this instance, an archbishop) issued notice to creditors. For example, the archbishop called on all the creditors of the estate of the Bishop of Exeter to come in and prove their claims or else be barred from the estate.

---

1. Sir Frederick Pollock and William Frederick Maitland, *The History of English Law*, vol. II (London: Cambridge University Press, 1911), p. 319.

PERSONAL TRUSTEESHIPS

There are two schools of thought regarding the origin of the modern trust. One group of scholars claims that the institution of trusteeship is of Roman origin; the other group claims that it is of English origin, with some German influence. Regardless of the merits of these claims to Roman and German ancestry, there is no doubt that the English use, or trust, was the ancestor of the modern trust and that both the use and the trust were essentially English in development, if not in origin. Thus our study will be directed toward the development of the trust under English law.

English Use

Long before the Norman Conquest of England, there appeared instances of conveyance of land to a bishop for the use of the church or for the use of someone who could not under the law of the church own property. The practice of giving property to one person for the use of another created many difficulties. Some owners of property could evade their debts by conveying their property to one person for the use of another, often a kinsman of the property owner.

Statute of Uses

The Statute of Uses, adopted in 1535, was intended to do away with the use altogether by declaring that the beneficial owner of land should also be the legal owner. Thus the holder "for the use of " was to be eliminated. When A conveyed land to B for the use of C, B was to drop out, and C was to become the legal as well as the beneficial owner of the land. But there were four types of conveyances or transfers that the Statute of Uses did not cover. It did not apply:
1. To leaseholds or copyholds of land
2. To instances in which the holder of the legal title had any active duties in connection with the property (for example, to rent and to account for the rent)
3. To chattels
4. To a "use upon a use"

English Trusts

The "use upon a use" was the immediate lineal ancestor of the trust. The fact that the Statute of Uses did not apply to a use upon a use may be illustrated thus: A conveyed land to B for the use of C for the use of D. In this case, the Statute of Uses executed the first use, causing B to drop out; but it did not execute the second one, and C found himself still holding the land for the use of D. This second (unexecuted) use gradually came to be called a "trust." Historians claim that a "use upon a use" was called a trust for the first time in 1634, in the English case of *Sambach*

5

vs. *Dalton*. It was also referred to as a trust in 1715, in *Daw* vs. *Newborough*. And as early as 1442, the Rolls of Parliament referred to a use as an "interest thereyenne, but only upon trust."[2]

GUARDIANSHIPS

Trust departments also serve as guardians to care for the property (and in rare instances the person) of a minor or legal incompetent, such as a mentally or physically incompetent person. The duties of a bank as guardian are similar to those of a trustee.

Guardianship at Common Law

At common law the king, as father of his country, was regarded as the fountain or reservoir of justice and, as such, protector of all infants and incompetents. The king issued letters patent appointing guardians for the infants and incompetents of his realm; but he could not, unaided, select and appoint all the guardians needed. In time the chancellor, as keeper of the king's conscience, became the general guardian of infants and incompetents; but like the king, the chancellor, alone and in person, was unable to serve as guardian for all infants and incompetents or even to select and appoint all the guardians required. Local courts of equity, to which the selection and appointment of guardians were committed, were gradually developed. Thus an infant or an incompetent was first the ward of the king, then the ward of the chancellor, and finally the ward of the local court of equity. Even today an infant or an incompetent is known as a ward of the court.

After the American colonies achieved their independence, the state took the place of the king. The courts of equity of the various states selected and appointed guardians.

Progress in Guardianship

How far society has advanced in the protection of infants and incompetents is shown by a comparison of the plight of the ward in England under the most prevalent kind of guardianship until the reign of Charles II (1660–1685)—guardianship in chivalry—with the infinitely better position of the ward under modern guardianships of the property and of the person.

Guardianship in chivalry was the right of the lord to take charge of the person and property of male infants under 21 and of female infants under 14 (if unmarried) when the lands held from the lord by tenure of

---

2. For a full discussion of the development of English uses and trusts, refer to Austin Wakefield Scott, *The Law of Trusts* (Boston: Little, Brown and Company, 1967), Sections 1 to 1.11, pp. 3–31.

knightly service vested in such infants by descent. Guardianship in chivalry usually proved disastrous for the ward; it was an interest for the profit of the guardian rather than a trust for the benefit of the ward. Like any property interest, the interest was salable and transferable to the highest bidder; furthermore, it was transmissible to the lord's personal representatives. It entitled the guardian to make a sale of his ward's marriage; the female ward was obliged to marry the person tendered by the guardian, under penalty of forfeiting to him the value of the marriage—that is, the amount the guardian might have obtained by a sale to the highest bidder. The male ward who refused the marriage tendered him forfeited double that sum. The guardian in chivalry was not accountable for the profits of his ward's estate but kept them as his private emolument, subject only to the bare maintenance of the ward. It is no wonder that this type of guardianship is referred to as the "most notorious of all guardianships," with "outrageous incidents" that led to its abolishment during the reign of Charles II.

Today, by contrast, the estate of the ward must be well managed for the sole benefit of the ward, and the courts are uncompromising in their determination that the best interests of the ward shall be the primary consideration of the guardian. The English Guardianship of Infants Act (1925) declares that the welfare of the infant is the "first and paramount consideration" in appointing the guardian. Society's provisions for its infants have indeed progressed far during the past 300 years.

In recent years the legislatures of some states have authorized conservatorships in which the powers of the conservator are usually greater than the powers of guardians. This form of administration of property implies that the conservatee is competent but in need of someone to handle his affairs without the declaration of incompetence. Every conservator has the same powers granted to it as a guardian, but the court may grant the conservator additional powers that, when granted in full, give a conservator the same rights as those enjoyed by a trustee with broad powers.

CORPORATE TRUSTEESHIPS

The first recorded instance of a corporate trust indenture or instrument was entered into by the Morris Canal and Banking Company of New Jersey on March 29, 1830. Other early instances of corporate trust indentures were those of the Washington Medical College of Baltimore, which was executed in 1835, and the Philadelphia and Reading Railroad Company, which was executed in 1836. In each instance, the indenture secured a loan, and individuals were named as trustees. As soon as railroads and other corporations began to use the trust indenture in connection with their bond issues, trust institutions began to serve as trustees under the corporate trust indentures. In 1836 the Pennsylvania

Company for Insurance on Lives and Granting Annuities (now the First Pennsylvania Banking and Trust Company) obtained an amendment to its charter of 1812 under which it received authority to accept and execute trusts of "bodies corporate and politic." The original charter of the Girard Life Insurance, Annuity and Trust Company of Philadelphia (now the Girard Trust Bank), granted in 1836, contained similar authority. It was not until 1871, however, that a corporation—the New York Guaranty and Indemnity Company—was first *specifically* authorized to act as "trustee under corporate deeds of trust."

The earliest recorded instance of a trust company's acting as trustee under a corporate trust indenture was in 1839, when the Beaver Meadow Railroad and Coal Company executed a trust indenture with the Girard Life Insurance, Annuity and Trust Company as trustee to secure advances made to the coal company to the extent of $250,000. In 1841 the same trust company was appointed trustee for an issue of bonds by the Tioga Navigation Company. In the same year, the Pennsylvania Company for Insurances on Lives and Granting Annuities was appointed trustee under a trust indenture to protect the creditors of the North American Coal Company. In 1853 the Farmer's Loan and Trust Company of New York was appointed trustee under three railroad bond issues, even though that company had not yet received express power to act as corporate trustee.

Many trust institutions do not perform corporate trust services simply because there is not sufficient business in the community to make it profitable. When such services are rendered, the trust institutions must provide services of the same high quality as in the administration of a personal trust.

CORPORATE AGENCIES

Two types of corporate agencies have traceable historical backgrounds. These are transfer agencies and registrarships.

Transfer Agencies

The immediate cause of the creation of the first corporate stock and bond transfer agencies was a series of tragic events. Before the 1850s, it was the practice of even the largest corporation to serve as its own stock transfer agent, that is, to designate certain officers or employees to act in that capacity. In 1847 the New York and New Haven Railroad Company, which had been incorporated in 1846 with an authorized capital stock of $3 million, appointed its president, Robert Schuyler, transfer agent. He was left by the other officers and directors in absolute and unquestioned control of the stock transfer books. Schuyler began to issue spurious certificates about a year after his appointment and continued this practice for six years; the number of unauthorized shares totaled 19,145.

This was discovered in 1854, and Schuyler resigned as transfer agent.

There followed a series of lawsuits over a period of about ten years. The first was in 1856, when a bank sued the railroad company for refusing to transfer one of the spurious stock certificates or to pay its value. The court held that the certificate was void, that it was not a negotiable instrument, and that the bank had taken it subject to all the equities that the railroad company had against the original holder of the spurious certificate.

In 1858 the railroad company brought suit on behalf of its genuine stockholders against Robert Schuyler and 325 other holders of spurious certificates. The court held that the corporation, while not technically a trustee asking advice for its own benefit, was representative of the genuine stockholders and on their behalf might bring suit against the spurious stockholders. In so holding it overruled the lower court, and the case was sent back for retrial.

In 1865 (nearly 17 years after the first issuance of spurious certificates), upon retrial in accordance with the decision reached by the trial in 1858, the court held that the railroad company was liable for the damage sustained by the innocent holders of the spurious stock certificates. The decision was based on the theory that the transfer agent was the company's agent, that the company had made it possible for Schuyler to issue the spurious certificates, and that by these criteria Schuyler had essentially acted under the direct authority of the company. The court criticized the board of directors for its gross negligence in permitting Schuyler to perpetrate such a fraud.

Aroused by the misfortune that the New York and New Haven Railroad Company had experienced, other corporations hastened to adopt devices that would prevent overissuance of stock certificates. The device generally adopted was that of having a trust company serve as transfer agent. Between 1864 and 1873 no fewer than eight trust companies were organized in New York alone with charter power to serve as agent for transferring and registering stocks and bonds.

Registrarships

The mere naming of an outside transfer agent did not constitute complete protection against overissues. The outside agent, like the inside agent, if it wished and if not carefully supervised, might issue spurious certificates. Logically, the next move was the introduction of a third party—a registrar—whose business would be to prevent overissues.

In January 1869 the New York Stock Exchange adopted a regulation or bylaw requiring that the shares of all active stocks be registered at some agency approved by the exchange. The practice then developed of having as registrar for stock an agency separate from the transfer agency. By the end of the nineteenth century, that practice had become common.

EMPLOYEE BENEFIT TRUSTS

Although the term *employees' trusts* may not apply precisely to all forms of trusts and agencies established to provide pension, profit-sharing, and other benefits to employees of a common enterprise, it is the term usually used to describe the newest form of trust activity, which has grown rapidly in recent years.

Forms of Employees' Trusts

The term *employees* includes officers, nonunion employees, and members of a union that has negotiated a benefit plan with a business enterprise or an entire industry. Forms of employees' trusts include pensions, profit sharing, welfare, stock bonuses, and many other arrangements that provide a share of the growth of a business; deferred compensation; reimbursement for medical, dental, and similar expenses; and disability retirement benefits.

History

Industrial employees' benefit plans were rare before the twentieth century. The American Express Company plan was begun in 1875. In 1880 a second pension plan was started, by the Baltimore and Ohio Railroad Company. By 1930 some 400 plans had been established. At the outset pension plans were rare and were usually found in the railroad, steel, banking, and public utility industries.

The wage stabilization laws of the early 1940s, limiting the compensation that could be paid to certain classes of employees, prompted many companies to turn to deferred benefits as a method of providing their employees with additional rewards. In the latter 1940s, union welfare plans contained pension features. In 1949 it was established under law that pensions were a proper subject for collective bargaining.

The dramatic growth in the number of employee trust plans adopted and in the number of covered participants has come about since 1940. In 1940 there were just over 4 million participants, less than 20 percent of all employees in commerce and industry. By 1975 some 33 million persons were covered, about 44 percent of all employees in commerce and industry. Assets of pension funds are estimated to be $180 billion and growing at a rate of about $14 billion annually.[3]

---

3. Everett T. Allen, Joseph J. Melone, and Jerry S. Rosenbloom, *Pension Planning,* 3rd ed. (Homewood, Ill.: Richard D. Irwin, 1976).

Trust Institutions As Trustees

Trust companies did not actively bid for employee trust business until the early 1940s, although insurance companies offered contracts for pension benefits in the early 1920s. However, the growth of noninsured funds has been quite rapid. Trust funding offers simplicity, flexibility, economy, and investment freedom, as well as the opportunity for independent thought and action in designing and operating a plan and trust for each particular case. Stocks as a proportion of portfolios are increasing, a trend that has advantageous effects on plan costs and benefits. The authorization to pool funds held by trustees for pension, profit-sharing, stock bonus, or other trusts exempt from federal income taxation under the Internal Revenue Code provided trust companies with an additional tool to manage those new trust funds. In addition, pooled funds, unlike common trust funds, are available when a trust company, though not acting as trustee in the accepted sense, is "investment trustee" or "corporate trustee" or, as referred to in Regulation 9 of the Comptroller of the Currency, "agent" for individual trustees.

It is interesting to note that in 1974 banks administered $127 billion in assets for public and private pension, profit-sharing, thrift, and stock bonus plans. Life insurance companies held about $56 billion in private pension assets. About 25 million people are current or future beneficiaries of bank-operated funds. About two-thirds of the assets are invested in common stocks.

The History of Trust Institutions

Although the history of trust institutions in the United States extends over approximately 155 years, recorded instances of various prototypes of the trust institution date far back into antiquity. For example, after the time of Marcus Aurelius (A.D. 161–180), it was customary for Romans to leave gifts by will to fraternities or other corporations, such as professional or trade unions, with instructions as to how the property should be used. In such instances the fraternal or other corporation was, in essence, charged with the administration of a trust.

In Europe during the middle ages, men often left their wills for safekeeping with the church or a monastery and named a representative of the church as executor. The person thus named acted as a representative of the church.

Between 1118 and 1312, the Order of Knights Templars was the most powerful financial organization in Europe and was engaged extensively in the banking business. The treasurers of the order were frequently named as executors of wills, and there is some evidence that they held and invested funds for the payment of annuities. Thus the Knights

11

Templars were in many respects engaged in trust business—that is, making a regular business of settling estates and administering trusts.

It has been suggested that the idea of corporations to handle trust business came to the United States from India. As early as 1774, a public official known as an ecclesiastical registrar was given authority by law to settle the estates of British subjects dying in India. This ecclesiastical registrar was a corporation sole (a one-man corporation). In India there also developed what were called agency houses—concerns somewhat similar to modern corporations that were organized to transact business for trustees and individuals, to receive money on deposit, and to administer estates.

EARLY HISTORY—UNITED STATES

The years from 1820 to 1840 witnessed the beginning of the trust institution in the United States. It was a period of adventure and experimentation in many fields. Among the various undertakings of the period were the introduction of gas for lighting streets, the use of coal instead of wood for heating, the opening of the Erie Canal, and the development of railroad and street railway systems.

It is not surprising that during this period of high adventure the idea of a corporation's engaging in the trust business should have occurred to some enterprising entrepreneur, perhaps suggested to him by his knowledge of the Indian agency houses or other prototypes of the trust institution. It should be noted, however, that much of the so-called trust business at that time was not trust business in the present-day sense but what is now known as investment trust business.

That period was also one when the rural people of the new nation began to move to towns and expand the towns into cities. The situation created a favorable climate for the development of trust institutions, which were initially products of city life.

Still another incentive to the establishment of trust institutions was the change in the nation's wealth from land, livestock, goods, and other tangible properties that have value in and of themselves to stocks and bonds, which are only evidences of value. Before 1800 the wealth of the country consisted almost entirely of land, buildings, ships, agricultural products, fisheries, and commerce. The early 1800s witnessed a transition from a mercantile and agricultural to an industrial society, just as it witnessed a shift of population from rural to urban life. The period marked the beginning of huge individual fortunes.

The change in the form of society produced a change in the form of business organization from sole proprietorships and partnerships to corporations. Although a farm or a store could be financed by one or at most a few persons, manufacturing enterprises and railroads could not. Such enterprises required pooling the available capital of a larger and more widely scattered group; yet people were naturally unwilling to invest their entire estates in industrial ventures in association with strangers. That difficulty, together with the trend toward industrialization, led to the corporate form of business organization. Corporations became the usual rather than the occasional form of organization.

The next step was the creation of corporations to handle the estates of those whose wealth consisted of stocks and bonds. As long as estates consisted of farmlands and merchandise, there was little need for trust services. When a farmer died, his estate was passed on immediately to his heirs and either divided among them or sold for division. Perishable goods could not be held in trust, and there was little point at the time in holding real property in trust. But with the advent of manufacturing as a principal business and the formation of corporations to engage in manufacturing, it became desirable to pass intact from one generation to the next a business that had proved successful. It also became feasible to do so, since only the inheritance of stocks and bonds was involved. Then, as now, there were instances in which it was advisable, because of infancy or dependence or inexperience, to keep property from passing directly into the control and possession of the beneficiary. The result was a growing demand for trusts and trustees. Gradually many American corporations were given the authority to engage in the trust business.

THE GRANTING OF TRUST AUTHORITY TO AMERICAN CORPORATIONS

The first institution specifically chartered to do trust business in the United States was the Farmer's Fire Insurance and Loan Company of 1822 (later the City Bank Farmer's Trust and now the First National City Bank of New York). Some claim that the Massachusetts Hospital Life Insurance Company, which reported $5 million of trust deposits by 1830, was doing trust business even earlier.

Life insurance companies dominated the early trust business, but later trust companies and eventually banks entered the picture. In 1853 the United States Trust Company of New York City became the first institution chartered *purely* to do trust business.

Trust institutions began to act as "transfer agencies" for stocks and bonds to prevent overissuance of securities, particularly after the fraud involving unauthorized stock of the New York and New Haven Railroad.

National banks were prohibited from offering trust services, but many trust companies provided banking services. After prolonged debate, national banks were given authority to do trust business by the Federal Reserve Act of 1913.

In 1916 the Federal Reserve Board issued Regulation F, setting trust industry standards not only for national banks but also for state banks and trust companies that joined the Federal Reserve System. By 1920 some 1,300 national banks were offering trust services.

13

The 1920s were also the golden years of investment banking. Where loans were once the mainstay of bank assets, some banks invested heavily in securities underwriting. When a bank underwrites a security, it sells a stock or bond issue to customers or retains some securities for the bank's own investment portfolio.

In 1933 Congress passed the Glass-Steagall Act. Best-known for creating the Federal Deposit Insurance Corporation to insure customer deposits, the act also put an end to investment banking by commercial banks. Banks were permitted to handle trusts and agencies but prohibited from underwriting corporate securities or engaging in other investment banking activities. Similarly, investment banks were barred from doing commercial banking. Giants like the House of Morgan split in two; what is today the Morgan Guaranty Trust Company continued in commercial banking, and Morgan Stanley and Company carried on investment banking.

In 1962 Congress transferred supervision of national bank trust departments to the Comptroller of the Currency. Regulation 9 replaced Regulation F, but the restrictions of the Glass-Steagall Act remained in force.

PERSONAL TRUST SERVICE

The first corporations granted trust authority were authorized to receive and administer property in trust rather than to settle estates. For example, the 1836 amendment to the charter of the Pennsylvania Company for Insurances on Lives and Granting Annuities mentioned trustee, assignee, receiver, guardian, and committee but not executor or administrator. Those omissions do not prove that the early trust companies could not settle estates; they merely indicate that the companies were created to hold and invest property rather than to settle and distribute estates.

By 1840 there were several instances of trust companies accepting trust deposits and either issuing certificates of deposit against them or setting up investment trusts and issuing certificates of ownership in those trusts. There were also, as already mentioned, a few instances of trust companies serving as guardians, executors, administrators, trustees under will, and trustees by agreement. In fact, before 1840 nearly all the various kinds of personal trust service were performed to some extent by one or another of the trust companies established before that date.

TRUST DEVELOPMENTS BETWEEN 1840 AND 1890

The 50-year period between 1840 and 1890 was characterized by the introduction of corporate trust and corporate agency services. In fact, trust and agency services for corporations developed to such an extent that they threatened to overshadow personal trust business, and it is possible that for a time they retarded the development of such business.

Changing Titles of Trust Companies

The trust companies chartered between 1840 and 1850 that possessed trust authority were named "life insurance and banking company" or "banking and trust company" or some similar title. None of those titles survives today. In the 1850s the use of the word "trust" in corporate titles in combination with such terms as "life insurance" and "annuities" began to disappear, and for a time it appeared that the word "trust" would eventually stand alone in corporate titles.

As industrial corporations developed, however, new trust services were called for. Then, as now, the incorporators of trust companies desired to indicate in the titles of their companies the principal services they were to render. The new titles, therefore, used such phrases as "bank and trust company," "savings and trust company," "safe deposit and trust company," "fidelity trust company," "title guarantee and trust company," and "mortgage guaranty and trust company."

First Reference to Trust Department

An event of historic significance for trust institutions occurred in 1874. In that year the first reported reference to a trust department—that is, to a separate department devoted exclusively to trust business—appeared in an amendment to the charter of the Boston Safe Deposit and Trust Company, as follows:

> All the money or property held in trust, under the third section shall constitute a special deposit, and the accounts thereof shall be kept separate . . . and for the purpose of securing the observance of this proviso, said corporation shall have a trust department, in which all business pertaining to such trust property shall be kept separate and distinct from its general business.[4]

This company, whose trust business is said to outdistance its commercial banking business in size and importance, retains its chartered name.

It is interesting to note that in Great Britain the first separate trust department—that of the Royal Exchange Assurance, a life insurance company in London—was opened only in 1904.

OUTSTANDING DEVELOPMENTS SINCE 1890

The year 1890 has been suggested as the date when the modern trust institution came into existence. Although in that year there were only 63

---

4. *Laws of Massachusetts,* 1874 (June 27, 1874).

trust companies in the United States, many of them had already begun to expand their activities by doing general banking business in addition to offering corporate trust and agency services, keeping and managing trust funds, and engaging in other fiduciary business. In fact, in the early 1890s national banks and savings banks were already feeling the pressure of competition from trust companies.

National Organization of Trust Companies

In 1896 representatives of fifteen trust companies from seven states—Massachusetts, New York, Illinois, Indiana, Missouri, Kentucky, and Colorado—met at a conference to consider the advisability of organizing the trust companies of the country into a section of the American Bankers Association. Seventeen representatives from ten different states met in Saint Louis in September of that year and requested the Association to amend its bylaws to permit the organization of the Trust Company Section (now the Trust Division). The first annual meeting of the section was held in Detroit in 1897, attended by 117 members. Since then membership has grown steadily.

National Banks in the Trust Field

The events of historic significance after 1890 related more directly to trust business than to the trust institutions themselves. The one outstanding exception was the entry of national banks into the trust field—a long and difficult process. An outline of the steps by which national banks finally achieved full and unquestioned trust authority suggests some of the obstacles they had to overcome.

As early as 1906 national banks in some parts of the country were actively seeking trust authority. In that year the New York State Bankers Association adopted a resolution requesting Congress to enact legislation that would permit national banks to exercise trust authority.

In 1908 the Fowler Bill was introduced in Congress to grant trust authority to national banks, but it failed to pass. In 1911 the Secretary of the Treasury recommended that national banks be permitted to do all the things that any bank could legally do, including, at least by implication, carry on trust business.

The right of national banks to engage in trust business was established on December 23, 1913, when Congress created the Federal Reserve Board (now the Board of Governors of the Federal Reserve System). The Federal Reserve Board was authorized to grant by special permit to applying national banks, when not in contravention of state or local law, the right to act in any fiduciary capacity in which state banks, trust companies, or other corporations that come into competition with national banks are permitted to act under the laws of the states in which the national banks are located. This authority was granted to the Federal

16

Reserve Board by Section 11(k) of the Federal Reserve Act. However, it by no means removed the last obstacle faced by national banks before they could actually enter the trust field.

Some of the trust companies in Michigan raised the question whether Congress had the right to authorize the Federal Reserve Board to grant trust authority to national banks. The constitutional question was presented to the Supreme Court of the United States in the case of the *First National Bank of Bay City* v. *Fellows on the Relation of the Union Trust Company et al.,*[5] and the Supreme Court held that Section 11(k) of the Federal Reserve Act was constitutional (Chief Justice White writing the opinion).

The right of a state to keep national banks out of the trust field was finally abolished on September 26, 1918, when Congress amended Section 11(k) of the Federal Reserve Act by providing that, whenever the laws of a state authorize or permit the exercise of trust powers by state banks, trust companies, or other corporations that compete with national banks, the granting to and the exercise of such powers by national banks shall not be deemed to be in contravention of state or local law within the meaning of the Federal Reserve Act. Like Section 11(k) in its original form, this amendment had to be interpreted by the Supreme Court of the United States. The question presented to the Supreme Court, in effect, was this: Can Congress, either directly or indirectly, prevent a state from prohibiting the entrance of a national bank into the trust field? This question was raised in 1924 in the case of the *State of Missouri on the Relation of the Burnes National Bank of St. Joseph* v. *Duncan.*[6] The Supreme Court decided that a state cannot prevent a national bank from engaging in trust business if it holds a permit from the Federal Reserve Board to conduct such business. Justice Holmes, in writing the opinion, referred to the 1918 amendment of Section 11(k) as follows: "This says in a roundabout and polite but unmistakable way that whatever may be the state law, national banks having the permit of the Federal Reserve Board may act as executors if trust companies competing with them have that power." Thus, with the help of the Supreme Court, the last obstacle that national banks had to overcome before being admitted into the fraternity of trust institutions was successfully surmounted.

RECENT GROWTH

The *Trust Fact Book* published in 1976 by the American Bankers Association points out that, although trust services are often thought of as being just for the wealthy, many people of moderate means use such

---

5. 244 U.S. 416, 426 (1913).
6. 265 U.S. 17, 21 (1924).

services. The size of the average trust account established by individuals is generally about $150,000. But in banks that specialize in smaller accounts, the average account is only $40,000.

Today about 14,000 banks are members of the American Bankers Association—about 95 percent of the nation's total. About 4,000 banks—2,000 national and 2,000 state-chartered—have trust powers. The value of trust assets fluctuates, of course, with changes in the investment markets; for example, in 1972, with stock prices booming, trust assets reached a record high of $403 billion, and in 1974, with a decline in the economy, they dropped to $325 billion (see fig. 1). Nevertheless, the number of customers served by trust institutions has risen steadily. From 1969 to 1974 the number of trust accounts rose from 1 million to 1.3 million. Leading the way were employee benefit plans: the number of employee benefit accounts rose from 112,000 to 208,000, and their assets grew from $95 billion to $127 billion. The Employee Retirement Income Security Act of 1974 (ERISA) is expected ultimately to add 40 million workers to the rolls of those covered by pension plans. In light of this prediction, it seems reasonable to conclude that an even larger number of people of moderate means will be the beneficiaries of trust services.

Figure 1

TRUST ASSET GROWTH, 1970-1976

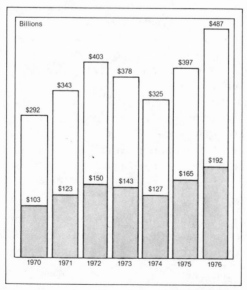

Note: 1975 and 1976 figures are taken from FDIC booklet "Trust Assets of Insured Commercial Banks 1976." Shaded area of bar graph represents value of personal trusts and estates.

Chapter 2   **Trust Department Services**

The Purposes of This Chapter:

1. To classify and describe the various services offered by a trust department
2. To establish a uniform trust terminology to be followed throughout the text
3. To show the great variety of trust services and their adaptability to the requirements of individuals, business organizations, and charitable and other public institutions, organizations, and agencies

In a real sense, the ultimate value of all trust service is to human beings. Corporations, associations, institutions and institutional agencies are, at best, only channels through which human beings are served.[1]

In general, the services of a trust department fall into three main groups:

1. Settlement of estates
2. Administration of trusts and guardianships
3. Performance of agencies

Another activity of increasing importance, a corollary to the main services just mentioned, is financial or estate planning. These services may be provided to individuals, business organizations, and charitable or other institutions or organizations.

Services To Individuals

The services of a trust institution to individuals are considered under five headings. These are settlement of estates, administration of trusts, administration of guardianships, performance of agencies, and financial or estate planning.

---

1. Adapted from Gilbert T. Stephenson, *Reflections of a Trustman* (New York: American Bankers Association, 1960).

SETTLEMENT OF ESTATES

The first main group of services performed for individuals is concerned with the settlement of the estates of deceased persons. In such settlements the trust institution acts either as executor or as administrator. Although it is necessary for the student to distinguish between the powers and duties of executors and administrators, the term *personal representative* is applicable to both executor and administrator and is preferred. Several different kinds of executors and administrators exist, but only those in common use are described here.

An *executor* (*executrix* if a woman) is the one nominated in the will to settle the estate of a person who dies leaving property and a valid will (he is said to die *testate*). The main duties of the executor are to assemble the assets; to pay the administrative expenses, taxes, and debts; and to distribute the net estate in accordance with the will.

When no executor has been named in the will or the one named has died or is unable or unwilling to serve, the court appoints an *administrator* (*administratrix* if a woman) *with the will annexed* (*administrator cum testamento annexo,* often abbreviated to administrator c.t.a.), whose duties are practically the same as those of an executor.

When a person dies leaving property but no valid will, he or she is said to die *intestate*, and the court appoints an administrator to settle the estate.[2]

ADMINISTRATION OF TRUSTS

The second main group of services performed for individuals is the administration of trusts. Such trusts may be divided into three classes: those created under will, those created under agreement or by declaration, and those created by order of court. In administering such trusts, the trust institution acts as trustee under will, trustee under agreement or by declaration, or trustee by order of the court.

When the maker of a will, known as the *testator* or *testatrix,* leaves any portion of his or her estate to an individual or to a trust institution as

---

2. Other types of administrators:

A. *Administrator ad litem* (administrator for the purpose of the suit): An administrator appointed by the court to supply a party to an action at law or in equity in which the decedent or his representative was, or is, a necessary party.

B. *Administrator cum testamento annexo de bonis non* (administrator with the will annexed as to property not yet distributed): An individual or a trust institution appointed by a court to complete the settlement of the estate of a deceased person in accordance with the terms of the will when the executor or the administrator with the will annexed has failed to continue in office.

C. *Administrator de bonis non* (administrator as to property not yet distributed): An individual or a trust institution appointed by a court to complete the settlement of the estate of a person who has died without leaving a valid will when the administrator originally appointed has failed to continue in office.

trustee for someone else instead of leaving it outright to that person, he thereby creates a *trust under will*. That kind of trust, frequently called a testamentary trust, does not become operative until after the death of the testator. It may be made for the benefit of an individual, a corporation, or a charitable institution—in short, for the benefit of anyone capable of taking a gift by will. The trustee receives the trust property from the executor or the administrator with the will annexed, administers it for the benefit of the beneficiaries named in the will, and ultimately distributes it to them.

A *trust under agreement* comes into existence when the creator of the trust (also called settlor, donor, trustor, or grantor) enters into an agreement or a contract with the trustees setting out the terms of the trust. A *trust by declaration* is created when someone declares himself or herself trustee of property for the benefit of someone else. Thus A may declare himself trustee of his own property for the benefit of C; or A may deliver property to B, and B may thereupon declare herself trustee (that is, make a declaration of trust) of that property for the benefit of C.

Into the group of trusts created under agreement or by declaration fall the various living trusts, including insurance trusts. A living, or *inter vivos*, trust is one that becomes operative during the creator's lifetime.[3] Almost every conceivable kind of property may be placed in trust; but the usual kinds of property (and those most readily acceptable by a trust institution under a living trust agreement) are stocks and bonds, notes and mortgages, cash, and real property. Trusteed property may include going businesses with stocks in trade, newspapers, mines and factories, patent rights and licenses to manufacture, and art collections.

Another form of trust under agreement is the insurance trust, which may be unfunded or funded. In an unfunded insurance trust, which is the more common form, a person makes life insurance policies payable to a trust institution as trustee under a trust agreement between the insured and the trust institution. The insured, who continues to pay the premiums, usually retains all his rights under the policies, such as the right to change the beneficiary, the right to borrow on the policies, the right to obtain the cash surrender value, the right to receive dividends, and the right to take back the policies. When the policies mature by death, the proceeds are administered by the trustee in the way specified in the trust agreement.

The funded insurance trust differs from the unfunded trust in that in addition to the policies, cash to be invested or securities (or both) are delivered to the trustee and the income is used by the trustee to pay the

---

3. Living trusts may be further classified as revocable or irrevocable. The terms of a revocable trust may be changed or the trust terminated by the creator; an irrevocable trust cannot be revoked by its creator.

premiums on the policies. An unfunded trust may be converted into a funded trust.

A court of proper jurisdiction may appoint a trust institution to receive property in trust and to administer it for the benefit of someone other than the trustee. Thus some states establish *trustees* (or trusteeships) *by an order of court* for missing persons or for incompetents. In other states a guardianship rather than a trusteeship is established for an incompetent.

A court of proper jurisdiction may also appoint a trust institution as trustee to administer a special trust necessitated by litigation before the court. In divorce proceedings, for instance, payments of alimony may be arranged by means of a trust. In disputes concerning real property, a trustee may be appointed to take over, hold, rent, or dispose of the property and to account to the beneficiaries pending settlement of the controversy.

ADMINISTRATION OF GUARDIANSHIPS

Trustees, except for those appointed by order of court, are guided chiefly by the directions and powers contained in wills or in trust instruments. Those who care for and manage the estates of minors and incompetents, however, ordinarily act under statutory regulations supplemented by special orders of court.

A minor is defined in most states as a person under 18 years of age and is not now regarded by the law as capable of managing property. For example, when a minor becomes entitled to a share of an estate by inheritance, the court appoints a guardian. The guardian's duties are to receive, hold, and manage the property; to make a full accounting to the court; and to make final settlement with the minor when he or she comes of age. A guardian is essentially, though not technically, a trustee appointed by the court to administer the estate of a minor.

In some states there are two kinds of guardians: a guardian of the person and a guardian of the property or estate. A trust institution is not well suited to serve, and in some states cannot serve, as guardian of the person of a minor. In practice the trust institution is usually appointed guardian of the property, and some relative or friend of the minor is appointed guardian of the person. In states where there is only one kind of guardian, however, a trust institution that is appointed guardian may find that it must care for the personal needs of the child as well as for the property.

When a person who holds or acquires property is or becomes mentally incompetent or for other reasons is unable to manage his property, the court appoints a *trustee for the incompetent* (guardian, curator, conservator, or committee—different states have different names for the office), whose duties are to receive, hold, and manage the property for the benefit of the incompetent for the duration of the incompetency.

PERFORMANCE OF AGENCIES

There are many kinds of personal agency services. The principal ones are those in which the trust institution acts as managing agent, attorney in fact, custodian, escrow agent,[4] probate agent or agent for fiduciary, and depositary under order of court.

Another rapidly enlarging area of service is that of employment benefit plans. Under the Employee Retirement Income Security Act of 1974 (ERISA), employees not participating in a qualified pension plan may establish an Individual Retirement Account (IRA). Although the amount is subject to change, employees may contribute $1,500 or 15 percent of their yearly compensation, whichever is less. H.R. 10 plans permit self-employed persons, sole proprietors, and partners to establish retirement plans for themselves and their employees. The annual contribution ceiling is $7,500 or 15 percent of income, whichever is less. A corporate fiduciary often acts as managing agent of the IRA and H.R. 10 plans.

As *managing agent* for investments, a trust institution not only performs the functions of a custodian—receiving and disbursing income—but also analyzes and selects investments for purchase or sale and keeps a customer's investments under continuous supervision. The institution performs these duties either on a full discretionary basis or on a limited advisory basis. In the first instance it carries out the recommendations of its investment supervisory group as soon as they are made, whereas in the latter instance the recommendations are first approved by the principal.

One of the characteristics common to agency services, unlike trust services, is that the trust institution does not take title to the properties—whether securities or real estate—it manages. A nominee designation may, however, be used.[5]

A trust institution becomes an *attorney in fact* when it receives a formally executed power of attorney. By the terms of the power of attorney,

---

4. An *escrow* is defined as money, securities, instruments, or other property or evidences of property deposited by two or more persons with a third person, to be delivered on a certain contingency or on the happening of a certain event. The subject matter of the transaction (the money, securities, instruments, or other property) is the escrow; the terms on which it is deposited with the third person constitute the escrow agreement; and the third person is termed the escrow agent.

5. A nominee is usually defined as a person named for an office, position, or duty; in trust business, usually the person, firm, or corporation in whose name registered securities are held.

it may vote stock, sign proxies, collect debts, endorse notes, convey real property (where permitted by law), transfer personal property, and perform similar services. An attorneyship in fact is usually exercised in connection with some other trust or agency, not as an independent agency. Services rendered by trust institutions under the name of attorneyships in fact in some communities are known as managing agencies in other communities.

When serving in the capacity of *custodian* only, the trust institution ordinarily has no management or advisory duties; its sole duty, except in the case of securities, is to safeguard the property. In the case of securities, the trust institution may collect the income and the principal on the due dates of each; exchange temporary for permanent securities; and notify the owner when bonds are called, when rights to subscribe to additional stock or bonds are offered, when default in payment of interest or principal occurs, or when dividends are passed. It may also buy and sell according to specific directions from the owner.

In its capacity as *escrow agent*, the trust institution acts as a stakeholder. Two or more persons engaged in a business transaction may deem it advisable to deposit with a trust institution (as a disinterested and responsible third party) cash, securities, or documents relating to the transaction. It is the duty of the escrow agent to hold the cash, securities, or documents until certain conditions set forth in the escrow agreement have been fulfilled. It then delivers them in accordance with instructions.

In the capacity of *probate agent* or *agent for fiduciary,* a trust institution acts as agent for an executor or an administrator. The normal managerial steps in the administration of a will are performed by the trust institution in the name of the court-appointed executor or administrator. That executor or administrator has the responsibility of making the decisions required but may make use of the trust institution's recommendations on such matters as what securities should be selected for sale after taxes and other costs have been determined.

A court may order an individual fiduciary to deposit the assets of his fiduciary account with a trust institution as *depositary.* A court frequently does this in lieu of requiring him to give a bond. The trust institution performs the services of a custodian, but it may not deliver the assets to or receive them from anyone except upon an order of court.

Although these are the usual agencies, the trust department's financial and accounting facilities permit it to offer numerous modifications and combinations of them where appropriate.

FINANCIAL OR ESTATE PLANNING

In addition to their services in settling estates, administering trusts and guardianships, and performing agencies, trust institutions help individuals plan their estates. This service is referred to as a corollary rather than an independent service because few, if any, trust institutions offer it as a separate service and most do not charge for it.

The trust institution takes two steps in planning a person's estate. The first is to analyze its component parts, making a detailed study of the holdings of stocks and bonds, life insurance, mortgages, real property, and miscellaneous property. This procedure is sometimes called estate analysis.

The second step is to devise a plan in cooperation with the client's attorney by which those component parts can be rearranged and the property as a whole reorganized so that it will more nearly accomplish the purposes of the owner. That is estate planning proper; estate analysis is a prerequisite to it. The impact of taxes on the transmission of an estate is one of the important considerations in such planning, although it should not be the sole consideration. The plan may involve making a will; creating one or more living trusts, insurance trusts, or agencies; or making present gifts of property either outright or in trust.

In financial planning, the emphasis is frequently on tax saving and reduction. All plans, however, should first take into account the benefits afforded the family or other beneficiary.

While many trust institutions give only general advice on financial planning, some offer extensive financial planning for which they make a charge. This service does not include drafting wills, trust agreements, or other legal documents, which could be construed as the unauthorized practice of law.

Services To Business Organizations or Municipalities

The services provided by a trust institution to business organizations or municipalities fall into four main groups: administration as trustee or agent of pension, profit-sharing, thrift, and other employees' trusts; administration of corporate trusts; performance of corporate agencies; and liquidation of business enterprises.

ADMINISTRATION OF PENSION, PROFIT-SHARING, AND WELFARE TRUSTS

Pension plans are established to provide employees with regular benefits after retirement until death and, in some cases, with disability allowances before retirement. The eligibility of the employee and the promised benefits are outlined in a plan in which a trust is created to finance the plan. A trust institution is the trustee or a co-trustee and may be directed by an administrative committee of employees and management, which makes the decisions necessary in the operation of the plan.

In the early years, many plans were funded only by the purchase of life insurance that provided an annuity after the employee's retirement. By far the greatest increase in pension trusts has occurred in the self-administered type. In other words, contributions as calculated actuarially[6] are placed in the trust, and the trustee purchases investments, manages the portfolio, and issues checks to retired employees according to the provisions of the plan.

Unlike contributions to pension trusts, contributions to a *profit-sharing plan* are not established by an actuary but are made from a certain percentage of the net profits of the corporation and allocated to the participants in accordance with the terms of the plan. Again, the investments are managed by the trust institution, but the funds are less frequently invested in insurance. If the retiring employee's share of the profits and earnings thereon is not distributed as a lump sum, annual payments for a stated number of years will augment the employee's pension or social security benefits. Both pension and profit-sharing plans are usually of the qualified type; that is, they have been approved by the Internal Revenue Service and permit certain tax shelters.

Unions have long recognized the advantages of qualified pension plans, and provisions for increased or new plan benefits frequently constitute part of collective bargaining agreements. Many *union plans* may be of the money-purchase type, in which the benefits are based on the amount paid into the trust by the employer, often at so many cents per hour. Trust institutions are usually co-trustees with union representatives.

The many other plans that provide fringe benefits make a long list. They include thrift plans operating independently and welfare plans providing medical and dental aid. In all such employee stock ownership plans, the trust institution plays an important part both in investment and in general administration.

ADMINISTRATION OF CORPORATE TRUSTS

In the administration of trusts for corporations, the trust institution performs many valuable services. One of the most frequently used is that of securing corporate bond or note issues.

With the advent of the railroads and the subsequent growth in number and size of industrial enterprises, there arose a need for the accumulation of capital from many persons, each requiring satisfactory security for his or her loan, since requirements could no longer be met by wealthy persons or even by single companies. Security was pledged or

---

6. An actuarial cost method is a technique for establishing the amounts and incidence of the normal costs and supplemental costs pertaining to benefits of a pension plan.

mortgaged by the borrower to be held in trust by a responsible, disinterested trustee. Lenders were given notes or bonds, each identified as one of a particular issue. If those obligations were met promptly when due, the trustee released the property to the borrower. If the borrower defaulted on the payment of any of the obligations, the trustee might enforce the rights of the bondholders against the borrower and against the security.

That arrangement was an outstanding factor in the rapid industrial development of the United States and, in general, was a great boon both to industry and to investors. For a time individuals served as trustees, but gradually the practice of appointing corporate trustees arose. Today all stock exchanges require that a corporate trustee be appointed if the bonds constituting a new issue are to be listed for trading.

Frequently a partnership or a close corporation insures the lives of the key men in the organization to offset, as far as possible, the loss that would be sustained in the event of their deaths. The proceeds of the insurance are paid into the treasury of the company for general business purposes or made payable to a trustee to meet certain commitments made by the company because of the insured's connection with the business.

The primary purpose of a business liquidation insurance trust is to provide for the orderly liquidation of a deceased partner's or a deceased shareholder's interest in a business by sale at his death to the survivors, who are obligated to buy it. The insurance on the life of each partner or shareholder is trusteed to provide immediate funds for the purchase of his interest at the time of his death.

In some states owners of real property may convey the legal title to certain land to a trust institution under a trust agreement that reserves to themselves all powers to deal with the property. These trusts are frequently referred to as "dry" or "naked" real estate title holding trusts. The principal purpose of such a trust is to keep the actual or beneficial ownership of land undisclosed on the public records and avoid title complications arising from the death of the owner. The trustee deals with the property only according to the written directions of the owner or as provided in the trust agreement.

Trust institutions in large cities sometimes serve as trustees for foreign insurance companies. To do business in the United States, such companies must maintain in U.S. trust institutions adequate reserve funds for the protection of their policyholders and creditors. In connection with this service, the trust institution must make frequent reports to the foreign insurance company or to its manager in the United States of the exact condition of the fund. When properly authorized by the company or by its U.S. manager, the trustee may use the fund to pay the claims of policyholders and creditors, and it may make such delivery of cash and securities to banks and to state insurance departments as may be required for proper conduct of the company's business.

Some states require that out-of-state corporations offering investment certificates for sale maintain a deposit of securities with a trustee located in the state in order to protect the certificate holders residing in that state. In those cases a trust institution is usually designated as trustee, with duties similar to those of a trustee for a foreign insurance company.

PERFORMANCE OF CORPORATE AGENCIES

Among the well-known functions of a trust institution are the corporate agency services that it performs. As agent for a corporation, a trust institution may serve in any number of the following capacities: transfer agent for stock, registrar of stock, transfer agent for registered bonds, fiscal or paying agent, and depositary.

When a corporation is relatively small and its stockholders are comparatively few, an officer of the company may easily maintain a record of the stockholders and acts as a *transfer agent for stock* as required. As a corporation grows, the number of stockholders and the number of transfers also increase, and keeping accurate records becomes burdensome. A trust institution is usually appointed to serve as transfer agent for a larger corporation. The trust institution, which generally has a special department or division for handling such work, can usually effect transfers more efficiently, safely, and cheaply than the company itself. It also protects both the company and the stockholders against improper transfers of stock, failure to effect transfers, and other errors.

As *registrar of stock,* a trust institution performs the important duty of guarding against overissuance of stock. In addition to checking original issues, it checks each transfer made by the transfer agent to ensure the genuineness of the certificates presented for transfer, to make certain that the old certificates are canceled, and to see that the number of shares represented by the new certificates does not exceed the number represented by the certificates presented for transfer. It is a requirement of stock exchanges that all stock listed be registered by a corporation that is entirely independent of the issuing company. Moreover, no single institution may serve as both registrar and transfer agent for a listed issue.

Almost all bond issues provide for registration of bonds as to principal, and many provide for registration as to both principal and interest. Although only a small proportion of the bonds issued are registered—in contrast to stock certificates, which must be listed in the stock register and stock transfer books—there is a growing interest on the part of trust institutions in registering more and more bond holdings to simplify the collection of interest. The duties of the *transfer agent for registered bonds,* usually referred to as the registrar of bonds, are substantially the same as its duties with respect to the transfer of stock. The registrar of bonds keeps a record of the registered bondholders, effects transfers, and passes on the legality and genuineness of such transfers from one owner to another. Usually the registrar of bonds is the same institution that serves as trustee for the bond issue.

In its capacity as *fiscal* or *paying agent for bonds,* a trust institution makes interest payments on coupon bonds as the coupons are presented and pays off maturing bonds and notes. It files ownership certificates with the government and may also make out and mail interest checks. A fiscal agent is often referred to as a disbursing agent, an interest-disbursing agent, a coupon- and bond-paying agent, or a similar name indicative of its special duties.

Trust institutions are frequently called on to serve as *depositaries* in the event of defaults and in connection with mergers, consolidations, reorganizations, and other transactions in which it is necessary that such items as outstanding bonds, notes, or stocks be deposited with a responsible and disinterested party. The depositary may also receive and record the claims of creditors.

A special kind of depositaryship is created under a voting trust agreement. If all or a majority of the stockholders of a corporation desire to continue a particular business policy over a period of years, they may resort to a voting trust. The stock of those desiring to enter into the arrangement is deposited with a trust institution acting as depositary under a voting trust agreement. The agreement provides for the appointment of specified stockholders or other designated persons as voting trustees. Deposit receipts or voting trust certificates are issued by the depositary in exchange for the deposited stock. Those certificates, which are evidences of stock ownership but do not carry the right to vote the stock, may be listed on the stock exchange. If they are so listed, the depositary acts as transfer agent for the certificates, and there must also be a registrar. The registrar, as stated previously, must be an institution other than the transfer agent.

LIQUIDATION OF BUSINESS ENTERPRISES

The liquidation of business enterprises is analogous to the settlement of estates for individuals; but whereas the settlement of estates is the best known service of a trust institution to individuals, the liquidation of business enterprises is perhaps the least known and least attractive service that is rendered. Liquidations of business enterprises are of two kinds: voluntary and involuntary. They are performed by a trust institution acting in the following capacities:

First, when a business concern gets into financial difficulties but is not actually insolvent, it may place its assets in the hands of a trust institution as *assignee for the benefit of creditors.* The advantage of this procedure is that it allows time for the orderly sale of assets and for the settlement of claims in such a way as to protect the interests of both creditors and owners.

Second, if a concern that is in financial difficulty can effect no compromise with its creditors, the court may appoint a *receiver*. It is the duty of the receiver to operate the business, if he is authorized by the court to do so, until such time as the assets can be liquidated or it is evident that bankruptcy cannot be averted.

Third, the duty of the *trustee in bankruptcy* is to realize as much cash as possible from the assets of the bankrupt business and, under the direction of the court, to apply the amount thus realized to the claims of creditors. Few trust institutions accept trusteeships in bankruptcy, since most business of this kind is both undesirable and unprofitable. The organization of a special division of the trust department to handle bankruptcies is seldom justified unless the trust institution has some assurance that it will be appointed trustee in bankruptcy in most of the bankruptcy cases that arise in its district.

Services to Charitable and Other Organizations

Trust institutions also perform services for charitable and other organizations and institutions for the benefit of groups of persons. Those services are the administration of trusts and the performance of agencies.

ADMINISTRATION OF TRUSTS

In recent years educational, social, recreational, religious, and charitable foundations and institutions have had a tendency to separate from their main activities the business and financial management of their endowment funds. This trend has been illustrated by the development of the community trust and by the increasing use of trust and agency services by colleges, churches, hospitals, and charitable organizations. The distinction between trust and agency services should be kept clearly in mind.

The need for some method that could ensure safe and efficient administration of long-term gifts for philanthropic purposes and effective use for the public good under constantly changing conditions brought about the creation of the first *community trust* (or foundation) in Cleveland, Ohio, in 1914. Under the community trust plan, gifts of public-spirited citizens for the benefit of the public are placed in a trust, the funds being pooled and deposited in one or more trust institutions that serve as trustees and are responsible for the safety, investment, and management of the funds entrusted to their care. The income from those funds and, under certain conditions, portions of the principal (or even all of it) are distributed under the direction of a committee or a board of directors composed of a number of citizens in the community elected or appointed in a manner prescribed by the trust instrument. By means of this plan, donors are assured that both the principal and the income of their gifts will be the objects of responsible and competent business management.

Persons who desire to contribute to the *endowments* of colleges, hospitals, churches, and charitable organizations are to an increasing extent using the services of trust institutions as trustees for the funds. By this means the managers or the trustees of such organizations are relieved of the burdensome and time-consuming duties involved in the management of endowments and thus are able to devote their entire attention to the main objectives of their organizations.

PERFORMANCE OF AGENCIES

A trust institution may serve a charitable or other organization or institution created for a social welfare purpose in many of the agency capacities described in connection with services to businesses. Only three of the many types of agencies are mentioned here.

In some instances gifts are made directly to a college or similar body in trust, and it is not always possible for the college to pass on the trusteeship to another institution. In such cases the college may appoint a trust institution as its *agent for endowments* to handle the funds. It obtains the advantage of trained and responsible management without actually surrendering title to the property.

A trust institution may serve as *agent for the financial secretary or treasurer* of corporations, firms, and organizations of various kinds. In that capacity it may keep minute books and account books, receive and disburse funds, and prepare and render financial statements.

In connection with the flotation of bond and note issues for city and state governments and their subdivisions, a trust institution may provide some of the agency services that are performed for business corporations under similar circumstances. These were discussed earlier in this chapter.

GIFTS TO CHARITIES—TAXES

As a general rule, the limit on a deduction for a gift to a public charity is 50 percent of the taxpayer's adjusted gross income. Under the 1969 Tax Reform Act, a donor who gives appreciated property to charity is allowed a deduction for the full appreciated value of the property, but the deduction is limited to 30 percent of his or her adjusted gross income; if, however, the taxpayer elects to bypass that deduction and have the amount of his gifts reduced by one-half of the appreciation, the

31

limit is 50 percent of adjusted gross income.

The deduction for gifts to private foundations is limited to 20 percent of the taxpayer's adjusted gross income. Corporations are entitled to a deduction for contributions made to charitable organizations that is limited to 5 percent of the corporation's taxable income.

The Tax Reform Act of 1969 restricts the activities of private foundations. For example, the act imposes an excise tax usually of 4 percent on the net investment income of a private foundation and an additional excise tax on its accumulated income.

Chapter 3

**Property
and
Property
Rights**

The Purposes of This Chapter:

1. To distinguish between property and rights in property as the subject matter of trust business
2. To classify and describe the different estates and interests in property
3. To discuss methods of acquiring and disposing of property

"A trust is a fiduciary relationship in which one person (the trustee) is the holder of the legal title to property (trust property) subject to an equitable obligation (an obligation enforceable in a court of equity) to keep or use the property for the benefit of another person (the beneficiary)." [1]

Since trust business is essentially the care and management of property, a study of it logically includes a study of property as the subject matter of estates, trusts, and agencies, that is, a study of those elements and incidents of property and property rights that a person employed in a trust department is likely to encounter in the course of a day's work.

Classification of Property

Property, as used in this text, means anything that may be owned, such as land, buildings, automobiles, money, shares of stock, bonds, or patent rights. It is classified as movables and immovables; lands and chattels; real property and personal property; and tangible personal property and intangible personal property.

REAL AND PERSONAL PROPERTY

According to modern classifications, all property is divided into two main groups: real property and personal property. The usual distinc-

---

1. *Glossary of Fiduciary Terms* (Washington, D.C.: American Bankers Association, 1976).

tion between the two, which is adequate for practical purposes, is that real property is land and anything attached to the land with the intention that the attachment shall become a fixture, whereas personal property is all property except real property.

Since land is immovable, it has always been possible to bring an action at law to recover land, that is, the thing itself. The Latin word for thing is *res*, from which the word *real* is derived. Actions for the recovery of land hence came to be known as real actions, and the property that was the subject of such actions became known as real property. Real property, therefore, meant property that, because of its immovability, might itself be recovered in an action. In the case of other property, which was movable and destructible, an action could be brought not for the recovery of the property itself, which might have been removed or destroyed, but for damages from the person who might have removed or destroyed it. Such an action was called a personal action, that is, an action against the person who might have removed or destroyed the property, and the property that was the subject of the action was called personal property. Even today, when the historical basis for the distinction between real and personal property has lost its meaning (actions may now be brought for damages to real property and for recovery of personal property), the classification of all property into real and personal property and the concept of land as real property and goods as personal property survive.

Real property includes not only the surface of the earth but also things of a permanent nature attached to it and improvements of a permanent character placed on it with the intention that they become fixtures. It includes the natural products or growth of the land. It includes buildings, fences, party walls, and bridges. There are, however, certain interests in land (described later) that are regarded as personal property.

Personal property includes all objects and rights that are capable of being owned except freehold estates and certain lesser interests arising out of such estates. A person has no difficulty in recognizing money, goods, and chattels as personal property, because such objects can be seen, touched, or realized with the senses. He knows at once that they are not real property because they are not permanently attached to land. It is much more difficult to recognize the intangible (untouchable) forms of personal property.

The distinction between real and personal property is of practical importance for the student of trust business. For example, when a person dies intestate, in many states his real property descends at once to his heirs, whereas his personal property passes to the administrator of his estate, who pays the debts and distributes the residue among the distributees under the governing statute. The heirs and the distributees may be different persons. Furthermore, the personal property is primarily liable for the debts of the decedent. The trust institution as administrator, therefore, must know what part of the estate is real property to be left in the hands of the heirs and what part is personal property to be taken over and administered.

TANGIBLE AND INTANGIBLE PERSONAL PROPERTY

"Tangible personal property," as the term implies, is property that can be touched, has physical substance, and is not a mere evidence of value but has value in and of itself. "Intangible personal property" is property that cannot be touched or realized with the senses. A certificate of stock is classified as intangible because, although the certificate as a piece of paper is a tangible thing, it is only an evidence of a right. The right is the stockholder's claim on the profits and assets of the company. If the certificate were lost, destroyed, or stolen, the stockholder would not lose his right; but he would have to take certain prescribed steps to prove that right. The same holds for notes, bonds, and other evidences of debt; they are valuable not in and of themselves but only as evidences of rights. It should be stated, however, that laws have been enacted that treat bonds, notes, certificates of stock, and the like as if they were tangible personal property. That is particularly true of tax laws.

Real Property

In common practice, "real property" and "real estate" are used as if they were synonymous. Throughout this text, however, a distinction between the two is observed. "Property," as used here, refers to the thing itself (land or buildings), and "estate" refers to the right, title, or interest one has in such property. It is entirely accurate to refer to a person's interest in real property as an estate.

FREEHOLD ESTATES

The three legal estates in land are fee simple estates, fee tail estates, and life estates. These three estates are known as freehold estates and in the eyes of the law constitute real property.

A *fee simple estate* is the largest estate that one may have in land. A person who holds land in fee simple holds it to himself and his heirs forever. If he dies without leaving a will, the land goes to his heirs. If he has no heirs, the land escheats[2] to the state. A conveyance of land by deed "to A and his heirs" is a conveyance of a fee simple estate provided that the grantor himself had a fee simple estate. Under the statutes of most states, conveyance of land "to A," even though the words "and his heirs" are omitted, is sufficient to convey a fee simple estate.

---

2. *Escheat* signifies a reversion of property to the state or federal government when under the law there is no person competent to inherit it.

A *fee tail estate* is an estate that on the death of the owner, called the tenant in tail, descends to the heirs of his body—that is, to children begotten by him or to their issue—whether or not he leaves a will. If the tenant in tail has no heirs of his body, the land reverts to the original grantor, on the theory that the grantor who had granted the fee tail is still the fee simple owner of the remainder.

A *life estate* may be one of two kinds: an estate for the life of the tenant or an estate for the life or lives of some person or persons other than the tenant. For example, A may convey land to B for the life of B, or he may grant land to B for the life of C.

OTHER TENANCIES IN REAL PROPERTY

There are other interests in land that represent lesser degrees of ownership than freehold estates, the most common of which is a tenancy for years. A tenancy for years is a tenancy for a time certain (a definite period of time); it may be a day, a week, a year, or 99 years. As long as it is a tenancy for a definite period of time, it is a tenancy for years. The instrument creating such an interest is frequently called a lease, and the interest itself is known as a leasehold.

Undivided Interests

There are three well-recognized kinds of undivided interests in property: tenancies in common, joint tenancies, and tenancies by the entirety. It should be noted that, although we usually think of an undivided interest in real property, there can be undivided interests in personal property, such as joint bank accounts.

TENANTS IN COMMON

When two or more persons own property in which each has an interest and that interest does not pass to the survivors or survivor upon the death of one or more of the owners, these persons are said to be holding the property as *tenants in common*. Each is said to have an undivided interest in the property. A, for example, devises Greenacre Farms to B and C (who are not husband and wife). B and C take possession as tenants in common. Upon B's death his undivided interest in Greenacre passes to his heirs or devisees and not to C.

JOINT TENANTS

When property passes to two or more persons and to the survivor or survivors of them, they hold the property as joint tenants. For example, in his will A devises Greenacre Farms to B and C and to the survivor of them, or, to use the more modern phraseology, he devises Greenacre to B and C as *joint tenants with right of survivorship*. Upon the death of either

B or C, Greenacre becomes the property of the survivor, and thereafter the survivor holds it as a tenant in severalty. At common law a conveyance to two or more persons, without the addition of other words, created a joint tenancy; but the modern rule by statute is that unless the intention to create a joint tenancy is expressed, which in many states requires only the words "as joint tenants," a conveyance to two or more persons creates a tenancy in common.

TENANTS BY THE ENTIRETY

When real property is conveyed to a husband and wife, they hold it as *tenants by the entirety* in states in which this form of tenancy is recognized. In such states, when title to real property is taken in the name of "A and B," who are husband and wife, or in the name of "A and his wife," or in the name of "B and her husband," even without naming the wife or the husband, A and his wife, or B and her husband, are tenants by the entirety. If one of them dies, the property goes to the survivor. Except in concert with the other, neither husband nor wife has a disposable interest in the property during the lifetime of the other.

Tenancies by the entirety[3] are usually limited to real property, although some states recognize estates by the entirety in personal property. That is to say, in states where estates by the entirety are still recognized, if *land* were devised to A and B (husband and wife), they would take possession as tenants by the entirety; upon the death of either, the land would go to the survivor. If, however, a *bond* were bequeathed to A and B, they might take possession of it as tenants in common even though they were husband and wife; each of them would have an undivided interest in the bond, which on his or her death would pass to his or her legatee or distributees.

It is usual for a person to own personal property in severalty, but it is possible for each of two or more persons to have an undivided interest in personal property; this situation is analogous to their being tenants in common. It is also possible for two or more persons to own personal property jointly, with the provision that upon the death of one the entire property is to become the property of the survivor or survivors; this situation is analogous to their being joint tenants with right of survivorship. Except in a state that recognizes estates by the entirety in personal property, it is doubtful that a gift of personal property made to a husband and wife without any reference to survivorship would vest in them the ownership of the property as tenants by the entirety and carry

3. Tenancy by the entirety, where recognized, is confined to husband and wife. It cannot be terminated except by consent of both parties. Property owned by way of tenancies by the entirety is usually not subject to debts of the spouse first to die. In other words, the surviving spouse receives the property free and clear of the claims of the creditors of the deceased spouse.

with it the right of the surviving wife or husband to take all of the property.

Other undivided interests in property have resulted from a form of registration authorized for the issuance of U.S. savings bonds. Co-ownership of bonds exists when bonds are registered in a co-ownership form, such as "John Jones or Ellen Jones." In discussing the effect of this form of registration, the U.S. Treasury Department has stated that bonds so registered may be redeemed on presentation by either owner and that upon the death of one co-owner they become the sole and absolute property of the survivor.

An undivided interest in money deposited in a bank is created by the opening of an account in a form such as "John Jones or Ellen Jones, either or the survivor." Each depositor in whose name the account is opened has the right to withdraw all or any portion of the balance in that account. Upon the death of one of the joint depositors, the entire balance in the account becomes payable to the survivor. By signing the bank's signature card, both parties enter into a contract with the bank authorizing it to honor withdrawals by either of them and, upon the death of one, to deliver the balance in the account to the survivor. Such accounts are in common use in states that recognize the rights of the parties established through their mutual agreement at the opening of their joint account. In some states, however, additional evidence is required to establish the ownership of each depositor's interest in the balance held in the joint account.

Conversion of Property

In some instances the form or character of property may be changed from personal property to real property, or from real property to personal property, by an act of the owner or some other person. A standing tree in a forest is real property; a log is personal property. The owner of the woodland may sell the standing trees and, for practical purposes, convert them into personal property before the trees are actually severed from the land. Again, a person who dies intestate may not leave enough personal property to pay his debts, and the administrator may have to sell some of the real property in order to obtain sufficient cash to pay the debts. In some cases all the real property may be sold, leaving a surplus of cash after the debts have been paid. Although it is in the form of cash, such a surplus is regarded as real property for purposes of descent; it therefore goes to the decedent's heirs rather than to his distributees.

Property Rights

"Property rights," as the term is employed here, are the rights that a person has with respect to property that he owns or in which he has an interest. Naturally, those rights depend on the kind or degree of ownership. An absolute owner is one who has the exclusive rights of possessing, using, enjoying, and disposing of property. Those rights are called the incidents of absolute ownership. In a limited ownership one or more of those rights are either absent or reduced. Property rights are classified in two ways: legal ownership and equitable ownership; and interests and estates.

LEGAL OWNERSHIP AND EQUITABLE OWNERSHIP

The most interesting and practical classification of property rights is that of legal ownership and equitable ownership. It is a frequent practice in the United States, England, and other common-law countries to split the ownership of property into two parts and to vest the legal ownership in one person and the equitable ownership in another.

For example, A transfers stock to B (as trustee), who holds it and collects the dividends, pays the income to C during C's lifetime, and transfers the stock to D at C's death. This is easily recognized as a common type of trust; yet it illustrates the two kinds of ownership. A, the original owner, parts with his legal right, title, and interest in the stock when he transfers the shares to B; and B therefore becomes the legal owner of the stock. On the company's books, the stock is transferred to B's name. He can attend the stockholders' meetings and vote the stock; he receives the dividends and has the right to sell, trade, or otherwise dispose of the stock. As owner of the stock, he can sue or be sued in his own name, just as A could have sued or been sued before the transfer was made.

Even though B becomes the legal owner of the stock, he does not thereby become entitled to enjoy or to use the dividends for his own purposes. C is entitled to receive the income during his lifetime, and D is entitled to receive the stock itself after C's death. Although B is the legal owner, he does not receive the benefits of his ownership; although neither C nor D has the legal ownership, one of them has the right to receive the income and the other has the right to receive the principal eventually. In recognition of this fundamental difference between B on the one hand and C and D on the other, B is referred to as the legal owner of the stock, and C and D are referred to as the equitable owners of the stock.

The preceding example also illustrates two kinds of equitable ownership. C is the equitable owner of the income, and D is the equitable owner of the principal. C and D together are referred to as the beneficial owners or beneficiaries. To distinguish between the one who is entitled to the income and the one who is entitled to the principal, C is referred to as the income beneficiary and D is referred to as the principal (or ultimate) beneficiary or, commonly, the remainderman.

Both real property and personal property are divisible into legal ownership and equitable ownership. That is, A may convey real property or he may deliver or transfer personal property to B to hold in trust for C and D, and in each case B will become the legal owner and C and D the equitable owners.

PRESENT AND FUTURE INTERESTS

Rights in property may be either present interests or future interests. For instance, if property is left to A for life and after A's death to B, A's rights in the property are present interests and B's rights are future interests.

VESTED AND CONTINGENT INTERESTS

Rights in property may be either vested interests or contingent interests. An interest is vested when the owner has a present fixed proprietary right to present or future enjoyment; it is contingent if the realization of the right depends on some future, uncertain event. For example, property is left to A for life and after A's death to B if B outlives A, but to C if B does not outlive A. A's interests are vested in that they are already determined, B's interests are contingent in that they are conditional on his outliving A, and C's interests also are contingent in that they are conditional on B's not outliving A. If the property is left to A for life and after A's death to B or B's estate, B's interests, as well as A's, are vested. In order to determine the rights of beneficiaries under wills and trust agreements, a person engaged in trust work must ascertain whether their interests in the property are vested or contingent.

DOWER, CURTESY, AND COMMUNITY PROPERTY

There are three principal property rights arising from the marital relation. They are the right of dower, the right of curtesy, and the right in community property. They may be defined as follows:

Curtesy: the life estate of a widower in the real property of his wife. At common law curtesy took effect only if a child capable of inheriting the property had been born of the marriage.

Dower: the life estate of a widow in the real property of her husband. At common law a wife had a life estate in one-third (in value) of the real property of her husband who died without leaving a valid will or from whose will she dissented. In many states common-law dower has been abolished by statute or has never been recognized.

Community property: property in which both a husband and a wife have an undivided one-half interest by reason of their marital status. It is recognized in all civil law countries and in certain states of the Southwest and Pacific Coast areas of the United States.

In many states common-law dower and curtesy have been abolished, and the husband and wife are placed on an equal footing in their rights to inherit property from each other's estate. Usually, but not always, the surviving husband or wife is entitled to inherit at least a one-third share of the deceased spouse's estate.

RIGHTS TO THE USE OF PROPERTY

It is possible for a person to have a right to the use of property, real or personal, without owning the property. The gift of a use may, in general, serve the same purpose as a trust, although it is not the same as a trust. The next few examples show how rights to the use of property may arise.

A may give B the use of land for B's life, for C's life, for a stated time, or until the occurrence of a certain event. B will have what is the equivalent of a life estate or a tenancy for a briefer period, under which he will be entitled to receive all the rents and profits of the land.

A may give B the use of household furniture or other tangible personal property for life, for years, or until the occurrence of a certain event. B will have the right to use the property for the period named and will then be required to pass it on to the eventual owner.

A may give B the use of stocks, bonds, or notes for life or for years. B will be entitled to receive the dividends or interest for the stated period and will then be required to pass the property on to the eventual owner.

A may give B the use of certain goods, clothes, or other perishable products that are consumed in the using. The gift of the use of such articles is equivalent to an absolute gift, to the extent that they are consumed in the using.

POWER TO DISPOSE OF PROPERTY

A person may be given the power to use and to dispose of property. Thus A may give his household furniture to B, his wife, to use or to dispose of as she sees fit during her lifetime, with the provision that what remains at her death, if anything, will be divided among their children. In that case B has the right, if she sees fit, to dispose of the whole gift during her lifetime; but if she does not use or dispose of it entirely, whatever is left goes to their children.

A may give B the use of the property for life, at the same time giving B the power to provide for the disposition of that property after B's death. This is a power of appointment. A may direct that B shall dispose of the property only by will or among a certain class of persons, thus giving B a limited or special power of appointment; or A may direct that the property shall be disposed of by B in any way and distributed as B sees fit, thus giving B a general power of appointment.

Methods of Acquisition and Disposition of Property

The acquisition and the disposition of property may be treated together, for they are, in a sense, reciprocal. There are many methods of

41

acquiring or disposing of property other than by buying or selling it. The principal ones are by:

1. Gift between living persons
2. Gift because of approaching death
3. Deed of trust or trust agreement
4. Declaration of trust
5. Survivorship under joint tenancy
6. Intestacy
7. Will

A *gift between living persons* is a gift actually made during the lifetime of the donor, and all that is necessary to complete the title of the donee of personal property is effective delivery of the subject matter. The gift of a watch by a father to his son during the father's lifetime, without reference to his death, is an example of a gift between living persons.

If A, conscious of approaching death, gives personal property (such as household and personal articles, money, securities, or the like) to members of his family, he thereby makes *gifts because of approaching death.* This term applies to personal property only; there must be actual or symbolic delivery of the property, and it must be made in expectation of death. The gift is revoked if the donor recovers from the illness or condition that was expected to result in his death.

A, during his lifetime, conveys property to B by a deed of trust or by a trust agreement in which he states the terms on which the property is to be held by B, the trustee, and to whom the income and the principal shall be paid, delivered, or conveyed. If real property is conveyed, the instrument should be a *deed of trust;* if only personal property is conveyed, a *trust agreement* may suffice.

A declares himself trustee of property for the benefit of C. His declaration that he is holding the property in trust may be as effective a method of disposing of property as a deed of trust or a trust agreement under which B, a third person, is called upon to serve as trustee. By prearrangement, A may deliver property to B and B may make a *declaration of trust* for the benefit of C.

When the law permits *survivorship under joint tenancy,* A may have property conveyed or transferred to B and C "as joint tenants" or "as joint tenants with right of survivorship and not as tenants in common," or words to that effect. At the death of B, the property passes to C as the surviving joint tenant.

When a person dies without leaving a will, he is said to die *intestate.* His real property descends according to the laws of descent in the state where it is located, and his personal property is distributed by the administrator according to the laws of distribution in the state where the decedent had his residence. In some states the distinctions between real and personal property with respect to descent and distribution have

42

been largely abolished, and all property passes according to certain rules that apply to real and personal property alike. The estate of the heirs in the real property and the interest of the distributees in the personal property are subject to the rights of the surviving spouse. The laws of the states vary so widely that the student of trust business should study the laws of his own state and those of any state or country in which he is interested, keeping in mind the fact that they are frequently changed by legislative bodies.

The most important means of disposing of property is by *will*. Though not an inherent or inalienable right, since it was granted by the legislature and may be taken away by the legislature, the statutory right to dispose of property by will exists in almost every country. That right does not necessarily extend to all property that a person owns at the time of his death. For instance, in states that have community property, a husband or wife cannot by will dispose of more than his or her half of the community property. In most states a husband cannot dispose of all his property by will to the exclusion of his wife's rights if she objects, and in some states a wife cannot dispose of her property by will to the exclusion of her husband's rights if he objects. In most states a parent cannot dispose of his or her property by will to the exclusion of the rights of children born after the making of the will (known as pretermitted children) for whom no provision has been made. Thus in numerous ways the legislature asserts anew, by limiting or extending the right, that the right to dispose of property by will is a statutory and not an inherent or inalienable right.

Limitations on the Exercise of Property Rights

There are certain limitations on the exercise of property rights other than those already mentioned. They include restraints on the alienation of property, restraints on contingent interests in property, restraints on accumulation of income, and restraints on the duration of private trusts.

RESTRAINTS ON THE ALIENATION OF PROPERTY

To what extent may a person dispose of property by gift between living persons, by deed of trust or trust agreement, by declaration of trust, by will, or in any other way and yet limit the right of the person receiving the property to dispose of it? Limitations on the right to dispose of property are referred to as restraints on the alienation of property.

In general, if A gives property to B outright and unconditionally, A cannot limit B in the disposition of that property. An unconditional conveyance of real property transfers a fee simple title that carries with it the rights of absolute ownership, including freedom from restraints on the alienation of the property. Similarly, a restraint on the alienation of an absolute legal interest in personal property is invalid.

If A conveys property to B in trust for C, can A put any effective restraints on C's right to dispose of C's interest in the income or in the principal of the trust property? Most states, by statute or by judicial decision, provide that by an appropriate clause in the will or in the trust agreement, A may restrain C from disposing of his right to the income or to the principal (or to both) as long as the property remains in the hands of the trustee. This is known as a spendthrift trust provision. Some states, by statute, provide that the right of a beneficiary to income shall not be assignable by him and that his creditors cannot have access to the amount necessary for his education and support. Such statutes are applicable even though the trust instrument has no provision restraining alienation.

In England, A may provide in his will or in a trust agreement that if C undertakes to dispose of his interest in the trust property, his interest therein shall cease and someone else shall receive the principal or the income. Such a provision is known as a protective trust provision.

Thus through the instrumentality of a spendthrift trust or a protective trust, restraints may be imposed on the alienation of property. The law regarding spendthrift trusts varies greatly in the different states.

RESTRAINTS ON CONTINGENT INTERESTS IN PROPERTY AND ON ACCUMULATION OF INCOME

The rule against perpetuities as defined at common law states that no interest in property is good unless it must vest, if at all, not later than 21 years after some life in being at the creation of the interest. If there is a possibility that such an interest may not vest within the time prescribed, the gift of the property is void. The practical effect of the rule is that the creator of a valid trust must make all interests under or following his trust vest (that is, must cause the beneficiary to receive a present fixed proprietary right to present or future enjoyment) not later than 21 years after the end of some designated life in being at the time the will or the trust agreement goes into effect.

In some states there are also limitations on accumulation of income. If A creates a trust and directs the trustee to accumulate the income and add it to the principal of the trust estate, for how long a period may A effectively direct the accumulation of income? Usually, where the rule against accumulations is in effect, the income must not be accumulated longer than lives in being plus 21 years.

It should be noted that the law makes a distinction between private and charitable trusts. The rule against perpetuities and the rule against accumulations do not usually apply to charitable and employee trusts.

44

Chapter 4　**Wills**

The Purposes of This Chapter:

1. To describe the will as the underlying document in the settlement of a majority of estates by trust institutions
2. To outline the essential steps taken in the execution of the attested will and to describe briefly other kinds of wills

"A will is a legally enforceable declaration of a person's wishes in writing regarding matters to be attended to after his death and inoperative until his death. A will usually, but not always, relates to the testator's property, is revocable (or amendable by means of a codicil) up to the time of his death, and is applicable to the situation which exists at the time of his death." [1]

Since the settlement of estates under wills constitutes a large part of a trust department's business, it is essential for a person interested in trust business to acquire a clear understanding of wills. The definition set forth accurately describes the will as a legal declaration of a person's wishes regarding matters he may request or require to be attended to after his death, which is not operative until his death.

Power of Distribution by Will

In the case of *Magoun* v. *Illinois Trust and Savings Bank*,[2] the United States Supreme Court noted that "the right to take property by devise [by will] or descent [by way of intestate succession] is the creature of the law and not a natural right—a privilege—and, therefore, the authority which confers it may impose conditions upon it."

The statement of the Supreme Court notwithstanding, one of the characteristics of the United States and other common-law countries is

---

1. *Glossary of Fiduciary Terms* (Washington, D.C.: American Bankers Association, 1976).

2. 170 U.S. 283, 18 Sup. Ct. 594, 42 L.Ed. 1037 (1897).

the power they give their citizens to distribute their property by will. It would be quite a reckless legislator who would attempt to abolish an institution that has become so deeply imbedded in our jurisprudence that it hardly needs protection for its existence.

Since the right to dispose of property is so firmly imbedded in the common law, one might assume that every property owner would zealously exercise that highly treasured right. Yet the sad fact is that, for the country as a whole, probably no more than 15 to 20 percent of property owners make wills. The vast majority of Americans die intestate (without having made a will), leaving it to the law to dispose of their property.

The failure of a property owner to make a will means that at his or her death the law steps in and, through a probate court and administrator, passes the property on to the heirs and next of kin without any provision, other than what the general law provides, for the administration of the property or its adaptation to the special needs of those who receive it.

Not only is the privilege of making a will neglected, it is often abused. Why so many property owners, even those with sizable estates, write their own wills or have them written by lay persons instead of lawyers remains one the great unsolved mysteries.

Equally disturbing are the cases in which the property owner writes a will but nominates an inexperienced person to serve as executor or executrix. There is perhaps nothing more confusing to the members of the property owner's family or costly to the estate than administration by one who lacks either the experience or the knowledge to discharge the task.

Fortunately banks and trust companies have the right and probably the duty to inform people about the importance of making wills and the settlement of estates by qualified persons.

Kinds of Wills

Wills are generally of two kinds, written and oral. Written wills are divided into two classes—those attested to by witnesses, called attested wills, and those that require no witnesses. The will that needs no attesting witnesses is called a holographic will. The states that recognize holographic wills generally require that such a will be entirely in the handwriting of the deceased, be signed by the deceased, and be either found among his or her valuable papers and effects or in the hands of some person or corporation with whom, or with which, it was deposited by the deceased for safekeeping. Oral wills, where recognized, are called nuncupative wills. A nuncupative will is one spoken during the testator's last illness, before a designated number of witnesses, and reduced to writing within the time prescribed by law.

In addition to the customary wills, there are other kinds. For example,

46

some states make special provisions for a will executed by a person while in the armed forces of the United States or the merchant marine. The obvious purpose of such laws is to make special provision for wills of persons who may not be able to comply with the usual provisions of the law at the time of execution.

Provision is sometimes made for "joint wills," a term used to describe the same testamentary instrument executed by two or more persons as their separate wills. Some states recognize "mutual wills," which are separate wills of two or more persons in which the provisions made by each are reciprocal or substantially identical with those made by the other or others. Because of the infrequency of their use, no further attention will be given to these special kinds of wills.

Last Will and Testament

The word "will" is derived from the Anglo-Saxon. At an earlier time, it was applied to an instrument disposing of real property, and the word "testament" was used for an instrument disposing of personal property. The phrase "last will and testament" was used in those wills in which the owner disposed of both real and personal property. Although many good draftsmen continue to use the phrase "last will and testament," the words "last will" are sufficient to dispose of both real and personal property, and good draftsmanship would seem to dictate their use.

Testamentary Capacity

Generally, in the United States any man or woman who is 18 years of age and of sound mind may make a valid will. What constitutes a sound mind and by what standards soundness of mind may be established are questions that have been variously interpreted by the courts. Although each state has its own standards for determining testamentary capacity, in most states a person is regarded as having the capacity to make a will if he or she can do the following:

1. Comprehend the fact that he or she is making a will
2. Recollect the property that he or she possesses
3. Remember the persons (objects of his or her bounty) who will normally be supposed to receive his or her property
4. Comprehend the manner in which the instrument will distribute the property among the objects of his or her bounty

A condition of mind due to physical causes or to outside influence that made it practically impossible for a person to exercise his rational judgment in dealing with his property would, if clearly proved, prompt the court, on proper application, to set aside the will of such a person on the ground of lack of testamentary capacity.

Ordinary Will

An ordinary will, which is by far the most common kind in the United States and England, may be either handwritten or typewritten. Whether the writing is done by the testator or by someone else is of no consequence. The will may be written with pencil, pen, typewriter, or any other means of writing and in any language. However, it must clearly show that it is intended to be a will. It must be signed by the testator or by someone for him at his direction. For example, if the testator cannot write, if he is blind, or if for any other reason he is unable to sign his name, he may sign by making his mark or may have someone sign for him in the following manner: "John Doe, by the hand of Richard Roe." If the testator is illiterate or blind or for any reason is unable at the time to read the will, it should be read aloud to him in the presence of the witnesses. He should then state or indicate in some unmistakable way that the will has been read to him and that it expresses his desires.

An ordinary will must be witnessed by at least two persons; in some states it must be witnessed by no fewer than three persons. Although most states require two subscribing witnesses, it is generally advisable to have three. A will having only two witnesses, though valid in the state where the testator lived, may not be valid to pass the title to real property located in a state that requires three witnesses.

In most states the testator must sign the will in the presence of the witnesses or, having signed it previously, acknowledge in their presence that the signature is his own and declare that the instrument is his will. In those states the witnesses, in turn, must sign in the testator's presence. If the testator is blind, the witnesses must sign while standing or sitting in such relation to him that he could see them in the act of signing if he were not blind. In some states the witnesses must also sign in the presence of one another. Although not all states have that requirement, it is a good practice in every state to have the witnesses sign in one another's presence and to have the testator and the witnesses satisfy all the other requirements set forth in the attestation clause shown in the specimen will in Appendix A.

Subscribing and Attesting Witnesses

Some states make a distinction between subscribing witnesses and attesting witnesses. A subscribing witness is one who sees the will signed or hears the signature acknowledged by the testator and subscribes (signs) his own name to the document as a witness. An attesting witness is one who testifies or gives evidence that the will was signed by the testator but has not necessarily subscribed his name to the instrument. Such a witness may not have seen the testator sign the will; he may base his testimony entirely on his knowledge of the testator's handwriting. Most states require subscribing witnesses, but in some states attesting witnesses are sufficient. Pennsylvania, for example, requires only that a will be proved by the oath or affirmation of two or more competent witnesses who need not have subscribed their names to the will or even have seen the testator sign it.

Selection of Witnesses

The laws of the various states differ widely as to the requirements for witnesses to a will. The subscribing witnesses should not be financially interested in the estate. For example, a testator should not have his will witnessed by his spouse or child, by any member of his immediate family, or by any near relative. In some states such a witness would be penalized by being deprived of a share in the estate, even though the will would stand in every other respect. There have been court decisions that an officer of a trust institution should not witness a will in which the institution is named executor, because of its financial interest in the executor's compensation. If a will should be contested on the ground of fraud or undue influence, the relationship of a witness to the testator or the financial interest of a witness in the outcome of the contest might have an important bearing on the matter.

Both the selection of witnesses and the act of witnessing a will are matters of great importance. Trust officers, who frequently are called on to witness wills, should know the requirements with respect to these matters not only in their own state but also in states in which the testator is likely to own real property.

Codicils

A codicil, which is an amendment or supplement to a will, must be executed with the same formalities as the will itself. As a rule, a codicil should be used only to make slight changes in a will. Suppose that a testator executes a long, carefully drawn instrument that meets his desires in every respect; later he wishes to increase a particular gift or to make a new gift. Since it seems unnecessary to write a new will, he has a codicil prepared, signs it, and has it witnessed.

Two practical points about codicils should be mentioned. First, in the case of a testator who was admittedly in full possession of his faculties at the time his will was originally executed but may be of doubtful testamentary capacity when he desires to make a change in the will, a codicil, even though long and involved, is preferable to a new will because it avoids the possibility of questions being raised as to the validity of the appointment of the executor or the exercise of the express powers contained in the original will. Second, if a testator wishes to eliminate or reduce certain gifts made in the original will, it is often preferable for him to execute a new will rather than a codicil, for there will then be no cause for hard feelings on the part of those who would learn from the reading of the original will what they might have received if the codicil had not been appended.

The ease with which codicils may be added to wills often leads to overuse of them. Sometimes not one or two but many codicils are added. Since it is difficult for a testator to add numerous codicils without creating inconsistencies, he should generally have his will rewritten if he desires to make many or major changes.

Revocation of a Will

A will or a codicil may be revoked (recalled or rescinded) in two ways. These are (1) intentionally by an act of the testator and (2) unintentionally (as far as the testator is concerned) by operation of law.

A testator may revoke his will or codicil by tearing, burning, mutilating, or otherwise physically destroying the instrument with the intention of revoking it. In some states he may execute with all the formalities of a will an instrument that expressly revokes his will or codicil, or he may make a new will that expressly revokes all former wills and codicils. However, the execution of a later will, unless it expressly revokes all former wills, does not revoke such wills except to the extent that they are inconsistent with the last will.

A will may also be revoked by operation of law. In some states the marriage of a testator or a testatrix after making his or her will revokes it. In other states the subsequent marriage of a man does not revoke his will, but the subsequent marriage of a woman revokes hers. In some states subsequent marriage *and* birth of a child revoke the will, whereas the marriage alone or the birth alone would not revoke it. In still other states, the birth of a first child revokes the parent's will, but the birth of a second or a later child does not. The effect of marriage and birth on a preexisting will varies from state to state.[3]

Contest of a Will

Probate is the act of proving before a court having competent jurisdiction that a document offered for official recognition is the valid last will and testament of a deceased person. In American law, probate is now a general term applied to all matters over which the probate court has jurisdiction. That process is treated in more detail in the chapter on estate settlement.

After a will has been offered for probate, it may be contested, that is,

---

3. The student is advised to study the laws of his or her own state on the execution and revocation of wills.

objections may be filed against the probate of the will. A will may be contested on one or more of six grounds:

1. The will or codicil was not duly executed.
2. The decedent did not have testamentary capacity at the time he executed the instrument.
3. The execution of the instrument was procured by undue influence.
4. The execution of the instrument was procured by fraud.
5. The instrument is a forgery.
6. The instrument has been revoked.

A will is not considered duly executed if it is not properly signed by the testator or by the required number of subscribing witnesses in states that require subscribing witnesses or if the witnesses do not sign the will in the presence of the testator. In some states a will is not duly executed if the witnesses do not sign in one another's presence.

The evidence required as to testimentary capacity has already been stated. Undue influence is pressure exerted over the testator to the extent of destroying his free agency in the making of his will.

A will is procured by fraud when it is made on the strength of false representations that actually mislead the testator into making a will different from the will he would otherwise make.

A will that is forged is not the will of the testator. It is possible for a will to be genuine in part and forged in part. In that case the genuine part may be admitted to probate, but the forged part will be denied probate.

If a will was revoked by an act of the testator or by operation of law in any of the ways previously mentioned, the instrument, even though still in existence and offered for probate, is not considered to be the testator's will. Each state has its own statute of limitations that specifies the time within which a will may be contested. Some states permit contests both before and after probate with limitations in each instance. The records of the probate courts of the United States show that a very small percentage of wills are contested. In only a small proportion of those instances are the contests successful.

Contents of a Will

The opening paragraph of a will should give the maker's name and place of residence. It is advisable, though not necessary, for the testator to use his or her full name. If generally known by some nickname, he or she should give that as an additional means of identification. Although the testator's place of residence may always be substantiated by testimony, a statement of the residence incorporated into the will itself may serve to identify the testator further and establish what he regarded as his domicile.

REVOCATION OF FORMER WILLS

Most wills contain the statement that all previous wills are revoked. That statement need not be a separate item of the will; the phrase "hereby revoking any will or codicil previously made by me" is frequently appended to the first sentence of the will and is regarded as sufficient. Whether the old will or codicil should be preserved or destroyed depends on the circumstances of the case. If it should ever become desirable to show the continuity of the testator's intention as to the disposition of his property, the existence of former wills and codicils might prove helpful. The revocation of a later will may in some states have the effect of reviving a former will still physically in existence.

DECLARATION OF SOUND MIND

Often a will begins with a declaration that the testator is of "sound mind and disposing memory." That phrase may make the testator feel better, but it does not add to the validity of the will.

PAYMENT OF DEBTS

Since debts must be paid, it is not legally necessary that the will contain a statement that they shall be paid, although most wills contain such a statement. It is essential, however, for the testator to let the executor know about any debts that require special treatment. For example, if the testator knows that a claim has been or is likely to be made against his estate that he wishes his executor to contest, he should not only call the matter to the executor's attention, either in the will itself or in a letter to the executor (such as is described later in this chapter), but also state where the best possible evidence can be obtained to support the executor's contest of the claim.

Directing the payment of funeral expenses is also unnecessary, except in a jurisdiction where a husband is obligated to pay his wife's funeral expenses or where there is a limit on the amount of funeral expenses. In such jurisdictions a direction in a wife's will for the payment of funeral expenses will make those expenses deductible in computing her inheritance and estate taxes; a direction that the executor may pay the funeral expenses without regard to the limits of local law will avoid financial problems for the person contracting for the funeral and will allow a deduction on estate and inheritance tax returns.

If the testator has what he regards as a moral rather than a legal obligation, such as a debt that has been barred by the statute of limitations or a promise to contribute to a specific charity for which he has not yet signed a pledge card or other binding obligation, he should make some reference to it in his will. In the absence of a specific reference, it may not be incumbent on the executor to meet the obligation.

DISPOSITION OF PERSONAL EFFECTS AND OTHER TANGIBLES

With surprising frequency, family discord results from the testator's failure to spell out the disposition of heirlooms and other articles that are worth relatively little in dollars and cents but are of great sentimental value. Tangible personal property should not be thrown into a residuary trust, obligating the trustee to sell it (usually for very little) and invest the proceeds. Specific bequests of articles of sentimental value or substantial monetary value are generally desirable.

An omnibus clause making outright gifts of assorted chattels of dissimilar character in equal shares among a designated group, such as the testator's children, may cause practical difficulties. Of course, if the testamentary donees will execute a joint receipt and make the division themselves, there is no problem from the executor's point of view. Another possibility is to allow the donees to make their selections, article by article, in rotation, in order of seniority, or by lot. Still another device is to divide the appraised value of the tangible personal property by the number of donees and credit each donee with his share. The chattels are then auctioned off to the donees until each exhausts his credit.

Outright bequests of tangible personal property to a designated person accompanied by nonmandatory directions about eventual distribution are occasionally made. Precatory words, expressing merely a "wish" or "hope," give that person the right but do not require him to carry out the testator's desires. If the values are substantial, this device may subject the testamentary donee to gift and death tax liability, even though he is under no legal obligation to make the ultimate distribution contemplated by the testator. Occasionally the testator incorporates by reference a separate list disposing of chattels. Generally, however, such incorporation by reference is an unwise practice, and some states require attestation of the incorporated instrument. The list may be lost, or the testator may yield to the temptation to add to or delete from it after the will is executed and thus violate the rule that only existing writings can be incorporated.

KINDS OF OUTRIGHT GIFTS

Wills record an almost endless variety of outright gifts. Technically a gift of real property is a devise, and a gift of personal property is a legacy or a bequest. Courts are not particular about the name used, as long as they can interpret fairly and accurately the real intention of the testator. Although different kinds of legacies and devises are called by different names, the substance of the gift is the important factor. It is well, however, to know the technical names for gifts.

A gift is *general* when it is not the gift of a particular thing as distinguished from all others of the same kind. A bequest of $1,000 or of 100 bushels of wheat is a general gift in that it does not refer to any particular money or wheat.

A gift is *specific* when it refers specifically to some one thing belonging to the testator as distinguished from everything else of the same kind. A devise of real property is almost always a specific gift in that it refers to a particular tract of land. A legacy of some article of household furniture or of a specifically described mortgage bond or other security is a specific gift. If the specifically described property is no longer owned by the testator at the time of his death, the donee of the specific gift receives nothing.

A *demonstrative* gift is usually a gift of a specified sum of money to be paid from a designated fund, the testator clearly indicating his intention that if the designated fund fails or proves insufficient, the gift or the portion remaining unpaid shall be satisfied out of the general estate. A legacy of $1,000 payable from the proceeds of a certain insurance policy or from a certain bank deposit is a demonstrative gift. Demonstrative gifts should be discouraged except under unusual circumstances, especially if they involve property other than specific sums of money.

A *residuary* gift is a gift of the property remaining after all general, specific, and demonstrative gifts have been made.

Gifts That Lapse

When a person who is named in the will to receive an outright gift dies before the death of the testator, under common law the gift is said to lapse, and the property goes into the residue. Statutes in most states have modified the common-law rule by providing that in the absence of other disposition, the property shall go to persons designated in the law as substituted legatees or devisees. In some states the statute applies only if the legatee or devisee is a near relative of the testator; in others, only if the legatee or devisee left issue surviving. These statutes are called lapse or antilapse statutes.

Since the statute might not bring about the result desired by the testator and might at any time be changed by the legislature, it is generally preferable for the testator to make a gift contingent on the donee's surviving him or her and name alternatives or in some other way indicate by the express terms of his will the disposition he desires to be made of each outright gift in the event that the person for whom he originally intended it does not survive him.

Gifts That Abate

When the testator dies, his assets are subject to all debts, taxes, charges, and claims that constitute his legal obligations or those of his estate. If there is not enough property to satisfy all the gifts after the legal obligations have been met, the residuary gifts usually fail first, then the general gifts, next the demonstrative gifts, and last of all the specific gifts. Moreover, the general rule is that in case of a deficiency of assets, all gifts of the same class shall abate (be reduced) proportionately.

Gifts to Charity

Testators frequently desire to leave gifts to charitable institutions. Most states do not impose a limit on the amount a person may leave to charity so long as the statutory provisions relating to the wife's or husband's or after-born child's share of the estate have been complied with. Other states place limits on the amount of such gifts. In some cases the gift, to be effective, must have been directed in a will made a given length of time before the testator's death; in others the gift cannot constitute more than a specified fraction of the estate.

Gifts of Designated Amounts

Since material changes in the size of a person's estate may take place between the time he makes his will and the time of his death, it is often inadvisable to make substantial gifts of designated amounts. At the time of the testator's death the amounts designated may constitute a much larger part of his estate than he had intended to leave in such legacies. This also applies to gifts of dollar amounts to be paid in kind, or property, from assets of the testator's estate. In view of this possibility, it is frequently advisable to express all but the smallest legacies as gifts of fractional shares of the residuary estate, rather than as gifts of a designated number of dollars.

UPKEEP OF THE CEMETERY LOT

One person may direct that his body be cremated; another may leave specific directions not only about the preservation of his body but also about the upkeep of the cemetery lot in which it is to be buried. Sometimes a fund is left with a trust institution in perpetual trust for the upkeep of the cemetery lot, but more often such a fund is left to the cemetery association. The latter plan is preferable, since in some states cemetery lot upkeep trusts are not valid. The care of numerous cemetery trusts, each differing from the other in minor details of services required, will prove burdensome, sometimes unaccomplishable, and definitely unprofitable to a trust institution.

RESIDUARY ESTATE

The property that remains after the testator has made provision out of his net estate for specific, demonstrative, and general gifts is called the residuary estate. When the disposition of any gifts that may lapse is not taken care of by statute or by the express terms of the will, lapsed gifts of personal property become part of the residuary estate. In most states that is also true of lapsed gifts of real property, but in some states such lapsed devises go to the heirs as intestate property.

The residuary estate is usually given to those in whom the testator is primarily interested—spouse, children, grandchildren, parents, brothers, and sisters. Sometimes beneficiaries who receive portions of the residuary estate also receive gifts of specific sums that the testator particularly desires them to have. Generally, however, gifts of designated amounts, whether made outright or in trust, that are provided for before the residuary estate is disposed of go to beneficiaries in whom the testator's interest is secondary. Consequently the testator and his advisers should be careful to see that such gifts do not absorb so much of the estate, particularly if estate and inheritance taxes are to be paid out of the residuary estate, that little or nothing is left for those in whom the testator is primarily interested. It is usually better to avoid substantial gifts of designated amounts (except when the testator desires to give priority to such gifts) and to prefer gifts of fractional shares of the residuary estate for all beneficiaries who are to receive substantial portions of the testator's property.

When the residuary estate is to be left outright to one person, it is usually advisable for the express terms of the will to indicate one or more alternates to receive the property if the person for whom the estate is intended does not survive the testator. When the residuary estate is left outright to several persons, originally or as alternates, it is equally important for the provisions disposing of the residuary estate to set forth clearly the desired disposition of the share of each person in case he or she should not survive the testator.

The nature and amount of the residuary estate can never be exactly predetermined, for no person can predict exactly what he will own on the day of his death. It is well to remember, particularly with respect to the residuary estate, that a will is construed as if it had been made just before the death of the testator and that it covers all property then owned, even though such property, or some of it, was acquired after the date of the will. It is for this reason that a will is said to "speak as of the date of the testator's death."

TRUSTS UNDER WILL

Gifts of property of all kinds, whether specific, demonstrative, general, or residuary, may be made either outright or in trust. Since the trust provisions in wills are almost the same as those in instruments creating living trusts, they are discussed in later chapters.

NAMING THE EXECUTOR

In many cases the testator's main purpose in making a will is to name the executor or executors that he has chosen as most acceptable to him and his beneficiaries as the person or persons best equipped to settle his estate. There have even been unusual instances in which a will did nothing more than name the executor, leaving the property to be disposed of according to the laws of descent and distribution.

EXECUTOR'S POWERS

Another important purpose of a will is to give the executor ample powers. In the absence of powers expressly conferred by the will, the person or trust institution appointed to settle an estate has only the somewhat limited powers that belong to all executors and administrators by virtue of traditional statutes or court decisions. For the reasons presented in Chapter 9, broad powers, clearly and definitely expressed in the will, enable the executor to proceed without uncertainty, delay, or undue expense. Well-drawn wills therefore always contain an adequate grant of powers, even though a number of states have recently enacted broad statutory powers for executors and in some cases trustees.

When the residuary estate is left outright to an adult or to a small group of adults, none of whom is under a legal incapacity such as minority or incompetency, it is sometimes possible for them, by agreement with the executor, to avoid the ill effects of inadequate executor's powers. That cannot be done when minors or other persons under legal disability are involved or when there are trusts under the will; in such cases an express grant of adequate powers is especially important. Numerous express powers are frequently conferred upon both the executor and the trustee without differentiation, particularly if the executor and the trustee are identical. In such cases certain powers intended to be exercised primarily by the trustee may likewise be exercised, under appropriate circumstances, by the executor.

PAYMENT OF ESTATE AND INHERITANCE TAXES

Unless the will states specifically how estate, succession, transfer, and inheritance taxes shall be paid, the federal estate tax is ordinarily paid out of the residuary estate, although statutes in many states provide that, in the absence of other instructions in the will, the federal estate tax must be apportioned among the recipients of the taxed property. In the absence of other instructions in the will, most state death taxes (whether they are called estate, succession, transfer, or inheritance taxes) are assessed against the individual gifts.

The testator may desire to have each gift bear its share of all such taxes; but if he wishes the beneficiaries to receive the full amounts designated, he should provide that taxes imposed on property passing under the will shall be paid out of the residuary estate, not deducted from the individual gifts. Although it is advantageous to the specific and general legatees and devisees to have these taxes paid out of the residuary estate, it may be disadvantageous to the residuary beneficiaries (who may be the chief subjects of the testator's care), since the residuary estate may be overloaded and depleted if all death taxes, state and federal, on property passing under the will are charged against it. Consequently, the problem of how those taxes are to be paid should have the testator's thoughtful attention during the preparation of his will.

Certain death taxes are imposed on life insurance proceeds, on property passing under nonexempt powers of appointment, on the decedent's contribution to joint tenancy property, and on larger gifts made before death. Therefore, great care must be exercised in the planning stage to determine whether the testator wishes those taxes, imposed on taxable property that does not come into the hands of the executor, to be paid by the recipients of the property or wishes all such taxes to be paid by the executor out of the residuary estate.

EXECUTOR'S COMPENSATION

In the United States it is generally unnecessary for wills to cover the matter of the executor's compensation, since the courts in each state will usually allow the executor what they regard as reasonable compensation. In many states the ceiling on compensation is fixed by statute. Unless unusual circumstances make it advisable to specify in the will that the executor is to be allowed a given amount or percentage, in most states it is preferable to specify that the executor receive compensation at the usual rates allowed for the services of executors at the time such compensation becomes payable.

CLOSING OF THE WILL

Wills ordinarily close with wording such as "In witness whereof, I have hereunto set my hand and affixed my seal, this_____ day of_____, 19___." Another suggested clause is "I subscribe my name to this will this_____ day of_____, 19___, at_____, _____." The signature of the testator follows.

ATTESTATION CLAUSE

The attestation clause generally follows the testator's signature. It is phrased somewhat like this: "Signed, sealed, published, and declared by the said_____ as his last will in the presence of us, who, at his request, in his presence, and in the presence of one another, have hereunto subscribed our names as witnesses."

Unless the witnesses are well known in the community, their printed names and addresses should also be given; otherwise they may be difficult to identify and to locate when the will is offered for probate. In states that require the addresses of witnesses—for example, New York—failure to provide those addresses would not invalidate the will. It is well to have younger persons and persons who are permanent residents of the community as witnesses rather than older persons or persons whose addresses are likely to change.

SPECIAL PROVISIONS

Occasionally a testator desires to make special provisions to take care of certain rights or wishes. To be effective, some of these provisions must appear in the will itself. Although other special provisions that merely contain information or expressions of wishes that are not to be legally binding on the executor are sometimes included in the will, it is preferable that they be put in a letter of information and advice to the executor.

Exercise of Power of Appointment

If A leaves property in trust for B with the provision that upon B's death the property is to be disposed of according to directions contained in B's will, B is thus given what is termed a "power of appointment." When B directs how the property is to be disposed of in his will, he exercises his power of appointment. B may make a will disposing of his own property without exercising his power of appointment with respect to the property held in trust. In some states B's disposition of his residuary estate will be construed as an exercise of the power of appointment, even though the power is not specifically mentioned in B's will. In other states B's power of appointment is deemed not to be exercised unless B's will contains express reference to the instrument under which his power of appointment was given. In some cases the manner of exercise is outlined in the instrument granting the power. Exercise of the power of appointment may require a separate instrument or specific reference to the power by a provision in a will in which the power is exercised. In view of this difference in the law and of the possibility that B may change his residence between the date of the making of his will and the date of his death, the only safe course for him to follow is to refer specifically to his power of appointment and state whether or not he is exercising it.

Disputing the Will

As a precautionary measure, a testator may provide in his will that any heir or beneficiary who contests it or tries to set it aside shall lose his portion of the estate. In some states, however, such a provision will be effective only if a gift of the property forfeited by the contest is expressly made to someone else.

Bequests to heirs of nominal amounts under the mistaken belief that they must receive something are undesirable. They often prompt disputes that might otherwise have been avoided.

Statements Concerning Property of Others

If coupon bonds or other indistinguishable property belonging to others—the testator's spouse or parents or children, for example—are kept in the testator's safe at home or in his safe deposit box, it is desirable that the ownership of those securities or other property be definitely indicated. Moreover, if such items are to remain in the safe or safe deposit box for any length of time, they should be mentioned in the will or in a letter to the executor so as to avoid embarrassment on the part of the executor in the event that a member of the family or a friend should lay claim to securities or other property found among the possessions of the decedent.

Letters of Information and Advice

Certain matters may be covered to better advantage in a letter of information and advice than in the will itself. Some of these matters, such as statements concerning the property of others and information about unjustified claims that may be filed against the estate, have already been mentioned; others include the following.

INFORMATION ABOUT PROPERTY AND FAMILY

Statements concerning property owned by the testator that the executor might not otherwise easily discover—such as a savings account in a distant state—and information about the testator's family may be very helpful to the executor. It is frequently advisable for the testator to furnish the executor with the names, ages, and places of residence of his children and provide other information about them. That information is especially important if there are two or more sets of children, if there are adopted children, or if any of the children have not been heard from for several years.

FUNERAL DIRECTIONS

When burial instructions or directions about cremation or other funeral arrangements appear only in the testator's will, there is a danger that the funeral may take place before the will is read. Therefore an expression of the testator's wishes concerning these matters should be included in a letter or letters immediately accessible to both the executor and the family on the death of the testator.

RECOMMENDING LEGAL SERVICE

The testator may desire to suggest the name of the lawyer whom he would like to have serve as attorney for his executor or to render any legal service necessary in connection with the settlement of the estate. It should be understood, however, that the testator cannot require his executor to employ any particular attorney. If the testator names a lawyer in his will and later changes his attorney without making a new will, the executor may be placed in an embarrassing position. Therefore suggestions about legal service should be made in a letter.

In view of the customary policy of trust institutions to retain as the executor's attorney the attorney who drew the will, a provision recommending an attorney may not be necessary. An unapproved statement in the will that the executor will retain the services of the draftsman is not only ineffective but also raises serious ethical questions.

ADVICE, SUGGESTIONS, AND RECOMMENDATIONS

Letters of advice and suggestions from the testator to the executor, possibly filed in the same envelope as the will, are also generally preferable to the inclusion of such advice and suggestions in the will itself. Such letters may provide the names of possible advisers on problems that may arise in connection with specific business interests or personal problems of certain members of the family. They may also contain confidential advice from the testator on such matters as the comparative business ability or judgment of various members of the family, employees, or business associates. Such letters may also outline plans that the testator had hoped to carry out during his lifetime and would like his executor and trustee to follow as far as possible.

Discretionary powers, authorizations, directions, and other provisions that are mandatory must, of course, appear in the will itself in order to be effective. But expressions of wishes and preferences that are not mandatory, as well as information, suggestions, and advice, can often be covered to better advantage in confidential and informal letters to the executor, greatly assisting the executor and benefiting the testator's family.

The testator should be advised that requests or expressions of wishes to executors outside the will concerning the making of gifts to friends or servants cannot be carried out inasmuch as they constitute a disposition of property for which the will provides no direction.

The Safekeeping of Wills

Where to keep a will is a major concern of the property owner. A bank may keep a will in its vault, often free of charge, when the bank is named executor or co-executor.

In some states there is a statutory provision for the filing and safekeeping of wills in the office of the probate court. Many states have adopted what is sometimes referred to as "self-proving" or "living probate" of the will, which enables the will to be put on record during the lifetime of the testator. That solves the problem of the safekeeping of wills of living persons.

Drawing Wills and Trust Agreements

Banks do not draw wills, trust agreements, or other legal documents. They have learned from long experience that the testator is usually better off if his or her family lawyer drafts his will. Both the testator and the executor and trustee can reap the benefit of the lawyer's knowledge and experience of the testator's estate and, often, the surviving members of the family. Even if trust institutions wanted to draft wills and trust agreements (and they usually prefer not to do so), they could not, inasmuch as the drafting of such instruments is in many states considered the practice of law.

Chapter 5   **Intestate Succession**

The Purposes of This Chapter:

1. To study some of the history of the development of the law of intestate succession
2. To study an illustrative order of intestate succession
3. To consider some of the difficulties that surround the inheritance of an intestate's property by surviving wives, husbands, and adopted children

"The law establishing the succession to intestates' estates is founded on the presumed will of the deceased, that if he had made a provision in his lifetime, it would be such as the law prescribes—that he would have done that which is equally prompted by natural inclination and duty; and it is one of the first duties, that we take due care for the maintenance of those whom nature teaches us to cherish with a peculiar affection."[1]

"Intestate" is the term used to describe a person who dies without leaving a valid will. "Intestate succession" is the phrase used to describe the descent of real property and the distribution of personal property of an intestate according to the method provided by the law of a particular state.

In all countries that recognize the institution of private property, the law must provide a way to distribute the property of one who dies intestate. Our original laws of intestate succession were, for the most part, inherited from England, where they were part of the common law. Such laws exist throughout the common-law world and, to some extent, in many other countries. Were it not for our laws of intestate succession, when a person died intestate or partially intestate, his or her property would escheat to the state or to some agency of the state, such as a hospital or educational institution. Inasmuch as each state has its own

---

1. Kimbrough v. Davis, 16 N.C. 71, 76 (1826).

laws of intestate succession, it is suggested that the student study the laws of his or her own state.

The Distinction Between Real and Personal Property

In the early history of the United States, land was the chief source of wealth, and it was natural for land to descend in accordance with laws (called the canons of descent) of the state in which it was located—the law of the situs. Personal property was distributed in accordance with laws (called statutes of distribution) of the state in which the owner was domiciled at his or her death (the place he or she regarded as permanent home).

Inasmuch as there were two systems governing the distribution of the intestate's property, the same persons did not always receive both the real and personal property. Real property descended to the intestate's heirs. Personal property was distributed among the next of kin.

In many states the canons of descent and the statutes of distribution have been replaced by a uniform rule designed to distribute the intestate's property to one class of heirs without regard to whether the property is real or personal. The more recent intestate succession acts are discussed later in this chapter.

The death of one who is intestate can present multiple and complex family problems. The intestate may be survived by a wife or husband, children—natural born and adopted, legitimate and illegitimate— grandchildren, parents, brothers and sisters both of the whole and of the half blood, uncles, aunts, and cousins.

As a general principle, the intestate law of every state tries to distribute the intestate's property to those people to whom the decedent would most likely have distributed it had he or she made a will. It doesn't require much imagination to realize that no matter how carefully the law provides for heirs of the intestate, no law of intestate succession is an adequate substitute for a carefully planned and well-drawn will.

It should be noted that husbands and wives, through an antenuptial or postnuptial agreement, can relinquish their rights in each other's property. In those instances the husband or wife is held by law to have waived his or her intestate share of the deceased's estate.

In addition, either a husband or a wife may enter into a contract with a third party to give up any interest such as dower and curtesy (discussed later in this chapter) in the estate of the deceased. For example, if the husband secures a loan giving a mortgage on his real property as collateral, the lender will require that the wife sign the note and the mortgage, thereby waiving her dower interest. Likewise, if the husband or wife conveys real property to a third person, the purchaser will, if he is properly advised, require the wife or the husband to join in the execution of the deed, thereby waiving her or his dower or curtesy interest in that property.

An Order of Intestate Succession

Under the common law, the personal property of a person dying intestate descended to his or her "next of kin," who were determined by a statute of distribution. The intestate's realty descended directly to his "heirs," who were determined by the canons of descent. Today the canons of descent and the statutes of distribution have generally been replaced by one uniform rule that distributes the intestate's property to one class of heirs without regard to whether the property is real or personal.

In order that there be no misunderstanding as to the intention of the law to abolish the distinction between real and personal property, it is usually provided that the "share" of intestate property that any person is entitled to receive is defined to include both a fractional share of the personal property and an undivided fractional interest in the real property. To help the student understand better the distribution of property of one who dies intestate, the Intestate Succession Act of North Carolina is set forth below:

The shares of the husband and the wife in each other's estates are the same. For purposes of illustration, let us assume that the husband or wife dies without a will.

If he or she leaves:
1. a spouse and one child or the lineal descendant or descendants of one child, the spouse takes one-half of the estate;
2. a spouse and two or more children or descendants of deceased children, the spouse takes one-third of the estate;
3. a spouse, no child or descendant of a deceased child, but one or both parents, the spouse takes one-half of the real property, the first $10,000 of personal property, and one-half of the remainder of the personal property;
4. a spouse but no child, descendant of deceased child, or parent, the spouse takes all of the estate.

After the deduction of the surviving spouse's share or if the spouse predeceased the decedent, the rest of the estate is distributed as follows:

If he or she leaves:
1. one child or descendants of one child, the child or the descendants take all the estate;
2. two or more children or descendants of deceased children, the estate is divided among the children and the descendants.
3. no child or descendants of a deceased child but one or both par-

ents, the estate is divided between the parents or goes to the surviving parent;

4. no child, descendant of a deceased child, or parent but brothers and sisters or descendants of deceased brothers or sisters, the estate goes to the brothers and sisters and descendants of deceased brothers and sisters.

5. no child, descendant of deceased child, parent, brother or sister, or descendant of deceased brother or sister but one or more grandparents, one-half of the estate goes to the paternal grandparents or surviving grandparent or their descendants and the other half to the maternal grandparents or surviving grandparent or their descendants.

Although not covered in this discussion, the statute goes on to state the circumstances under which other persons may inherit the intestate's property. Again, the student is urged to go to the statutes of his or her state and study the order of intestate succession.

Homestead and Family Allowances

When a husband or a wife dies with or without a will, the law attempts to free certain items of property from the claims of the deceased's creditors. The purpose of doing so is to furnish the members of the deceased's family with a measure of security during the period of administration and settlement of the estate. The property is generally referred to as the homestead and the widow's and children's allowances. In some states the allowance is limited to a surviving widow. In others it is available to either the widow or the widower and to children formerly part of the decedent's household.

The property set aside to meet the everyday needs of food and lodging of the family pending distribution of the decedent's estate is not part of the decedent's distributable estate. The allowance usually consists of a small amount of cash or personal property.

Today, by constitution or statute, a property owner is entitled to have, in almost every state, real property and, in some states, personal property set aside as a homestead. For example, the constitution of one state provides that personal property not exceeding $500 and real property not exceeding $1,000 are exempt from the claims of creditors.

There is no uniformity of treatment of the homestead on the death of the property owner. In some states it passes to the owner's family still free of the claims of creditors. In others, if a husband entitled to a homestead dies without having it allotted, his minor children or widow can have it set aside. Some states provide that if the widow or children fail to have the homestead laid off and the personal representative has to resort to realty for the payment of the decedent's debts, the court is required to see that the property constituting the homestead is set aside.

66

The laws on homesteads and family allowances vary from state to state and are, of course, subject to change from time to time.[2]

Special Problems in the Inheritance of Property

ADOPTED CHILDREN

Although there is evidence that adoption was known to the Babylonian, Hebrew, Egyptian, and other early societies, it was unknown to the early common law. England did not recognize legal adoption until 1926. Today an adopted child is generally given the same status as a natural legitimate child of the adoptive parent. He or she is entitled to inherit from the adoptive parents and their heirs, and they are entitled to inherit from him or her. The adopted child usually becomes eligible to inherit as soon as the final order of adoption is entered in the records of the court.

To be eligible to inherit a share of property, a child must be formally adopted. Informal adoption is not sufficient to sever the relation between a child and his natural parents.

ILLEGITIMATE CHILDREN

At early common law, an illegitimate child could inherit from no one, and no one but a surviving husband or wife and children could inherit from him. Later an illegitimate child was permitted to inherit both real and personal property from his mother but could not inherit property from the heirs of his mother.

Today the more modern intestate succession laws treat an illegitimate child, for the purposes of intestate succession, as if he were legitimate.

POSTHUMOUS HEIRS

A posthumous child is one born after the father's death. An after-born child is one born after the making of a parent's will. The general rule is that a child born within "ten lunar months" (nine calendar months) after the death of the intestate inherits along with the other children of the deceased.

INHERITANCE BY CHILDREN OF THE HALF BLOOD

At common law children of the half blood[3] were excluded from inheriting property by way of intestate succession. In the determination

---

[2]See *Estate Planning—Wills, Estates, Trusts* (Englewood Cliffs, N.J.: Prentice-Hall), Sec. 2734.

3. Half blood is a legal term describing the degree of relationship that exists between persons having the same mother *or* father but not the same mother *and* father. Children of the whole blood are children who have both parents in common.

of those persons who take property when one dies intestate, the trend today is to abolish the distinction between relations of the whole and of the half blood. One can still find, however, statutes that limit the share of collateral relatives of the half blood to half as much of the intestate's property as those of the whole blood. Some states will not permit a child of the half blood to inherit property that the stepparent inherited from his relatives.

INHERITANCE BY ALIENS

At common law an alien could not inherit real property. The exclusion of the alien was usually predicated on the theory that he possessed no "inheritable blood" or that, if unlimited inheritance rights were given to aliens, the nation might eventually be unduly subject to foreign influence.

Notwithstanding the limitation on the inheritance of real property, at common law the alien could inherit and transmit inheritance to personal property. That indulgence was, however, limited to alien friends. An alien enemy could not, without special permission of the king, inherit and transmit inheritance to personal property.

At present in the United States, the law tends to permit aliens to acquire, hold, inherit, and pass on both real and personal property, as for example, in Arkansas: "*Aliens.* No person is disqualified to inherit or transmit by inheritance, real or personal property because he is or has been an alien. . . ."[4]

DOWER, CURTESY, AND STATUTORY SUBSTITUTES

A student of trust business should be acquainted with the estates of dower and curtesy or their statutory substitutes, as discussed in Chapter 3. In all states today in the intestate distribution of property, it is necessary to lay off the widow's dower, the husband's curtesy, or the statutory substitute for dower and curtesy. It is suggested that the student study the law of his or her own state setting forth the procedure to be followed in the allocation of those interests.

Misconduct—Barring Property Rights

DIVORCE

In both testate and intestate distribution of property, the question sometimes arises whether the conduct of the beneficiary toward the decedent was such as to make it wrong to allow him to inherit the deceased's property. Unfortunately the question frequently arises in the

---

4. Arkansas Statutes, 61-143: *Estate Planning—Wills, Estate, Trusts* (Englewood Cliffs, N.J.: Prentice-Hall), Sec. 2742.

case of divorce. Although one cannot generalize about the effect of divorce on the right of the husband and wife to inherit from each other, the trend seems to be toward handling the problem as it is handled in Iowa: When a divorce is decreed, the guilty party forfeits all rights acquired by marriage.[5]

Usually the law also provides that marital property rights, including the right to an intestate share of the deceased husband's or wife's estate, are lost when a marriage is annulled, when the surviving husband or wife knowingly contracted a bigamous marriage, or when the husband or wife obtains a divorce recognized as valid in the state where the parties were domiciled.

ABANDONMENT

The states provide, as a general rule, that a parent who abandons a child to whom he or she owes the duty of support cannot inherit from the child if the child dies intestate. The law often recognizes exceptions to the general rule. For example, if the parent resumed care and maintenance one year (or some other stipulated time) before the death of the child, or if the parent was deprived of the custody of the child by an order of the court with which the parent has complied, the parent's right to inherit from the child is reestablished or, in the second example, not disturbed.

CRIME

The law will generally not permit one person to murder another and then claim to be the rightful owner of the deceased's property. The statutes of the various states differ in wording. The following illustration from the Illinois statutes should, however, be helpful: "A person who is convicted of the murder of another shall not inherit from the murdered person . . . but the estate of the decedent descends and shall be distributed in the same manner as if the person who murdered the decedent died before the decedent."[6]

Advancements

An advancement is usually defined as an irrevocable *inter vivos* gift (a gift made during life) of property, made by an intestate donor to any person who would be his or her heir or one of the heirs upon his death and intended by the donor to enable the donee to anticipate his or her inheritance to the extent of the gift. Often a gift is not considered an

---

5. Iowa Statutes, 598-16; *Estate Planning—Wills, Estates, Trusts* (Englewood Cliffs, N.J.: Prentice-Hall), Sec. 2714.

6. Illinois Statutes, 2-6, Probate Act of 1975; *Estate Planning—Wills, Estates, Trusts* (Englewood Cliffs, N.J.: Prentice-Hall), Sec. 2741.

advancement unless it is so designated by the intestate donor in a writing signed by him at the time of the gift.

In recognizing a gift as an advancement, the law is attempting to bring about an equality of division of the intestate's estate. The presumption is that, in the absence of a will, the intestate would have desired that all the heirs receive an equal share of the estate: "If a person dies intestate as to all his estate, property which he gave in his lifetime to an heir is treated as an advancement . . . only if declared in a contemporaneous writing by the decedent or acknowledged in writing by the heir to be an advancement. . . ."[7]

Renunciation

At common law an heir could not disclaim or renounce property that descended to him or her through intestate succession since the title was said to be vested in him or her by operation of law. If the law recognized the right to renounce at all, the right extended only to personal property. Today several states permit the heir to execute, within a stipulated time after the death of the intestate, a court-approved renunciation, which usually must be signed and acknowledged before a judge. When an effective renunciation is made, the property is treated as if it had never been inherited by heirs.

Escheat

Sometimes a person dies leaving no heirs entitled to inherit his property. In that instance, the property is said to "escheat" to the state.

As might be suspected, there are those who specialize in finding heirs. Although the law sets forth the procedure for notifying known heirs and generally does not require the personal representative to resort to an "heir finder," the student should study the statutes of his or her state to determine what, if any, additional responsibilities are imposed on the personal representative to find the intestate's heirs.

---

7. Delaware Statutes, 12, 509: *Estate Planning—Wills, Estates, Trusts* (Englewood Cliffs, N.J.: Prentice-Hall), Sec. 2751.

Chapter 6

Management of Estate Settlements

The Purposes of This Chapter:

1. To trace the steps usually taken by a trust institution in settling an estate as executor or administrator
2. To explain some of the details that must be attended to in the settlement of an estate
3. To show that personal services are essential to the proper settlement of an estate

"Every property owner of legal age and mental competence has the option either of saying himself by will how his property shall be disposed of at his death. . . . This is one of our distinctive and should be one of our cherished privileges. . . . The full impact of the [this] enduring value of trust service will not be felt until property owners turn to their banks and trust companies to settle their estates habitually as they now turn to them for bank service."[1]

In the settlement of an estate, a trust institution acts in one of four capacities: as executor, as administrator with the will annexed, as administrator of the estate of an intestate decedent, or as administrator to complete the settlement of the estate. Executors and administrators are commonly known as personal representatives of decedents. Throughout this text the term "personal representative" is used to apply to both the executor and the administrator.

Unless an estate is negligible in amount or within the limits of the provisions of summary administration statutes in the particular state, it must be settled by an executor or an administrator. In either case it is settled under the supervision of the court.

There is a difference between the settlement and the administration of an estate. To settle an estate is to close it out and distribute the property. To administer an estate is to keep it intact, care for it, and

---

1. Gilbert T. Stephenson, *Reflections of A Trustman* (New York: American Bankers Association, 1960), p. 22.

manage the property. Settlement is primarily the function of an executor or an administrator, administration of a trustee or a guardian. In settling an estate, the personal representative is often required to administer it as well, but only to the extent necessary to perform his primary function.

In some states real property may not enter into the settlement of an estate unless the will gives the executor the power to sell or mortgage it or the personal property is insufficient to pay the administration expenses, debts (including estate, inheritance, and other taxes), and cash legacies, so that the real property must be sold by order of court for that purpose. In other states, however, real and personal property may be used in exactly the same manner, there being no distinction as to which may be sold to obtain the cash necessary to settle the estate.

The practical steps that the personal representative must take in the settlement of an estate may be classified into six main groups:

1. Obtaining court appointment
2. Assembling the assets
3. Safeguarding the assets
4. Paying administration expenses and debts
5. Settling all tax obligations
6. Distributing the net estate, accounting to the court, and, as may be required by a particular state, obtaining releases or a discharge

In the performance of these duties, the personal representative is frequently required to render certain personal services to members of the family and others financially interested in the estate.[2]

Although a few states have adopted the Uniform Probate Code in an effort to make less formal the court-supervised administration of decedents' estates, the vast majority of states continue to follow more traditional methods of settling estates. The discussion focuses on those procedural steps that the student will usually find in his or her state.

Obtaining Court Authority

Obtaining court authority to settle an estate implies probate of the will and appointment of the executor if the decedent died testate. If the decedent died intestate, an administrator must be appointed.

---

2. The Uniform Probate Code was originally promulgated by the National Conference of Commissioners of Uniform State Laws in 1969. From time to time, there are amendments to the code. The assumption is that the interested parties to the settlement of an estate will seek legal assistance and court relief if needed. The following states have enacted essentially the provisions of the code: Alaska, Arizona, Colorado, Idaho, Montana, Nebraska, and North Dakota. For a discussion of the Uniform Probate Code, see *Estate Planning—Wills, Estates, Trusts* (Englewood Cliffs, N.J.: Prentice-Hall), Para. 71.

PROBATE OF THE WILL

If the decedent leaves a will, the executor's first step is to probate the will and to obtain from the proper court a certificate of authority to settle the estate, known in most states as letters testamentary. In different states the court is variously called the probate court, the surrogate's court, the orphan's court, the ordinary court, or the register of wills. Throughout this textbook "probate court" is used to designate the court having jurisdiction over estates of decedents.

The word "probate" means proof. The probate of a will means proof that it is the will of the deceased person in the manner required by law. The following procedure is known as *probate in common form.*

The will must first, of course, be located and taken from the place where it has been kept—a safe deposit box, the vault of the trust department, the private safe of the testator, or elsewhere. Delays that may occur in removing a will from a safe deposit box furnish a strong argument for the deposit of the will itself or a copy of it in a place immediately accessible to the executor, particularly if the will contains burial instructions. In some states a safe deposit box may be opened only in the presence of representatives of the state taxing authorities; in others a box may be opened without such representation to remove the will.

When the will has been found, it must be filed with the probate court of the county or city that has jurisdiction—generally the probate court of the county or city in which the testator had his residence at the time of his death. In a number of states, however, the probate of the will of a nonresident is permitted if any of his assets are found to be in the state or if he died in the state. A formal petition for probate of the will and for the grant of letters testamentary to the executor must usually be filed in addition to the will.

In some states the will offered for probate must remain on file for a specified number of days to allow time for other possible wills to be filed or for possible objections to the will to be presented. Some states may also require that the heirs or legatees or both be notified that the will has been submitted for probate. At the end of this period, or as soon as possible if no period of waiting is required by law, the witnesses to the will (or one of them) must appear in court for the purpose of proving the will. In a state where subscribing witnesses are necessary, they must swear that all the requirements of the law of that particular state were met. They may have to swear, for example, that the testator signed the will in their presence, that he (or she) declared it to be his will, that they witnessed his signature in his presence and in the presence of one another, and that the testator signed the will voluntarily and when in his right mind.

The procedure just described is the one necessary to probate a will and to obtain letters testamentary in the great majority of cases. It may be, however, that two wills are found or that the capacity of the testator to make a will or his freedom from undue influence in making his will is called into question. Heirs, legatees, and devisees are formally notified of the proceedings to probate the will and are given an opportunity to present evidence as to whether or not it should be probated.

As a rule, these formal proceedings are conducted by the judge of the probate court, but testimony may be heard or affidavits examined by commissioners appointed by the court. The witnesses are formally examined, and complete records of the hearings are kept. Counsel may be heard for and against the probate of the will; usually a jury passes on all questions of fact, and the judge passes on points of law and renders a decree or judgment either admitting the will to probate or denying it. This procedure is known as *probate in solemn form.* In some states probate in solemn form is the only recognized procedure for probating a will; in others probate in common form is the usual procedure, and the solemn form is seldom used.

While the hearings are in progress, the executor named in the will but not yet appointed by the court can do nothing; he must await the settlement of the issue. In the meantime the affairs of the estate may be placed in the hands of a temporary administrator, receiver, collector, or curator designated by the court to assemble and preserve the property until the personal representative is formally appointed.

The details of proving the will differ greatly from one state to another and are governed by local statutes and practices. But those statutes and practices are all designed to establish beyond any reasonable doubt that the will offered is the valid last will of the decedent.

LETTERS OF ADMINISTRATION

The certificate of authority of an administrator is known as letters of administration. The procedure for obtaining letters of administration on the estate of a person who has died intestate is somewhat different from the procedure for obtaining letters testamentary.

In the event of intestacy, the law prescribes the persons (usually the near relatives of the decedent in a certain order of priority) who are entitled to letters of administration on the estate. In some states the person entitled, according to the order of priority, to receive letters of administration may renounce that right and request the court to appoint another person or a trust institution instead. In all states the interested parties (kin or creditors) may agree on an administrator. If there is a disagreement or if the person designated is unsuitable, the court names a suitable person or a trust institution, and the one selected is given an opportunity to qualify. In some states, when no individual of the classes of persons authorized by statute qualifies, a public officer, known as the public administrator, receives letters of administration.

CERTIFICATES OF QUALIFICATION

In some states the original letters testamentary or letters of administration are retained by the court for its files, and the executor or administrator receives a certified copy or copies. In other states the executor or administrator receives a "short" certificate, which is a brief statement that on a certain date the person or trust institution designated in the certificate duly qualified as executor under the will or as administrator of the estate of a named decedent.

If the executor or administrator has certain duties to perform in another state—for instance, to effect a transfer of stock—it must obtain, for use in that other state, a "long" certificate, or an exemplified copy of the letters testamentary or letters of administration. This requirement means that, in addition to the certification of the clerk of the court, the certificate or letters must bear a certification by the judge that the certifying clerk holds the office of clerk and another certification that the certifying judge holds the office of judge. Under the Constitution of the United States, a certificate of qualification or a certified copy of letters so exemplified must be recognized by the authorities of another state as legal evidence of the authority of the personal representative to act on behalf of the estate, although the right of the personal representative to act in another state is generally determined by the laws of that state.

NECESSITY OF AUTHORIZATION

The personal representative has no authority whatsoever with regard to the estate until the letters are granted. That does not particularly concern the person who expects to be appointed administrator, for he knows that his only source of authority is the appointment of the court, which is evidenced by the letters. It does, however, concern the nominated executor, for he knows that he is named in the will and that those who are interested in the estate are depending on him to settle it as expeditiously as possible.

It is of the utmost importance that the personal representative take no steps with respect to the affairs of the estate, except to assemble information, until the letters are actually granted. The facts that the trust institution is known to be named in the will as executor and that the creditors or members of the family are pressing for action afford no justification for action. To be sure, interference may be excused if the letters are granted later; but if the will is not admitted to probate or the nominated executor is not appointed, any action taken by a person toward the settlement of the estate will render that person liable for his wrongdoing. The court, naturally, is reasonable and generally approves action taken with regard to perishable assets, such as fruit and vegetable crops, that require immediate attention for their preservation, even though such action is unauthorized. The payment of taxes that become due in the interim and the renewal of insurance that will expire also constitute justifiable exceptions to the general rule. Other steps to safeguard the assets may be justifiable but must be taken with extreme care. The only safe course for the personal representative to pursue is to take no other steps with respect to the affairs of the estate until the letters are granted. Many corporate fiduciaries have arranged for blanket insurance coverage that will protect the estate from loss if the assets should be destroyed by fire between the death of the testator and the appointment of the executor.

QUALIFICATION OF THE EXECUTOR AND ADMINISTRATOR

When the will has been proved, the executor named in it goes to the probate court to qualify. The executor must swear that he or she (or it) will settle the estate of the decedent in accordance with the law and with the terms of the will. In some states an individual serving as executor is not required to give bond unless the will requires it; in other states he is required to give bond with surety unless the will expressly relieves him of doing so; in still other states the testator may not relieve the executor of giving bond to protect the creditors of the estate but may relieve the executor of giving bond to protect the legatees. The amount of the bond for the protection of creditors is sometimes fixed at twice the estimated amount of the debts. If a bond is also required for the protection of legatees, the amount is always in excess of the estimated value of the personal property and is sometimes fixed at twice that value. The surety on the bond, whether it consists of one or more individuals or a surety company, must be approved by the court.

The expression "give bond" is in common use, but there is a distinction between giving bond and giving bond with surety. When an individual is required to give bond, surety on the bond is always required unless the will specifically directs or requests that no surety be required and the laws of the state permit that practice.

When a trust institution is required to give bond, its own substantial capital and surplus are behind the bond. In some states a deposit of securities with the state treasurer, based on the capital and surplus of the institution, is required. According to the laws of most states, no surety is required when the trust institution is to serve under the jurisdiction of a probate court in the state in which the institution is located. Surety is sometimes required when the trust institution is to serve under the jurisdiction of a court in a different state or under the jurisdiction of a federal court.

When the executor has qualified and been appointed by the court, letters testamentary are granted by the court. Those letters serve as the executor's passport into all the business affairs of the testator.

Qualification of an administrator, like qualification of an executor, means taking the prescribed oath and executing the prescribed bond. The amount of the bond is often twice the estimated value of the personal property belonging to the estate. Even in states where the laws permit an individual executor to be relieved of giving bond with surety, an individual administrator is not relieved of that requirement. A trust institution, on the contrary, is generally not required to give surety on its bond unless it is qualifying as administrator in a state other than that in which it is located.[3]

NOTICE TO CREDITORS

As the first step after the letters are granted, the personal representative should publish the fact of its appointment and give public notice to anyone having a claim against the estate that the claim must be presented within a specified time. The period varies from two months to a year, according to state laws. In some states the notice must also direct that anyone indebted to the estate make prompt payment to the executor. Not all states require public notice, but some that do not require it provide that the period of settlement may be shortened by publication of notice to creditors.

The importance of the notice to creditors should not be overlooked. Some state statutes require that if a claim is to be barred, the personal representative must forward to the claimant a statement by certified or registered mail that the claim must be presented in the time and manner required by law.

Assembling the Assets

When the personal representative has received its letters and published notice of its appointment (if required to do so), its next main objective is to assemble the assets of the estate. These may include bank accounts, brokerage accounts, contents of safe deposit boxes, life insurance, out-of-state property, real property, business interests, open accounts, household furniture, collections, and goods in storage.

BANK ACCOUNTS

The first act in assembling the assets usually relates to the decedent's bank accounts. He or she may have carried several kinds of accounts, such as checking, savings, certificates of deposit, individual, joint, personal, and business. The personal representative may write a letter to each bank with which the decedent is presumed to have done business to inquire whether the decedent had an account of any kind with that bank.

---

3. It should be noted that if a bond backed by a surety company should be necessary, the premium is paid by the estate, not by the personal representative.

Later, when going over the decedent's papers, the personal representative may find deposit slips, passbooks, maturity notices, or interest notices of other banks and may then address similar letters to them.

All bank balances belonging to the estate should be transferred to the estate account of the personal representative as soon as they are discovered and earmarked to indicate that they do not belong to the personal representative itself. Such transfers sometimes involve legal questions. For example, there may be a joint account in the name of the decedent *and* his wife or an account in the name of the decedent *or* his wife *or* the survivor. The question at once arises whether the entire balance belongs to the estate or to the wife, or half to each, or portions to each according to the amounts deposited by husband and wife. In the case of a savings account, the question arises whether the personal representative should let the balance stand to draw interest or transfer the balance to the estate's checking account, which draws no interest. In addition, the personal representative should determine whether the Federal Deposit Insurance Corporation adequately protects the accounts. The answers to such questions depend on the facts of the case and on the law of the jurisdiction.

BROKERAGE ACCOUNTS

The brokerage accounts of the decedent must be closed out as promptly as the bank accounts. It is the duty of the personal representative to communicate, by telephone, letter, or personal visit, with every local and out-of-town investment house in which there is any evidence that the decedent may have had a trading account. As soon as such an account is located, the personal representative should close it out and take over the cash and securities, unless the will expressly authorizes the executor to keep the account open for a stated period of time.

In this matter the personal representative cannot act too promptly for its own protection. If it does not act promptly and a loss is incurred through a fall in the price of securities, the personal representative itself may be liable. Brokerage accounts are often highly speculative, especially if they are operated on margin, and the personal representative may not speculate with the property of the estate. If the account is a margin account (one involving a loan for the purchase of securities), the margin loan will have to be paid before the securities will be released.

SAFE DEPOSIT BOXES

Another step in assembling the assets is the opening of the decedent's safe deposit box or boxes. The location of one box in a particular bank or safe deposit company does not preclude the possibility of finding another box in the same or another bank or safe deposit company. The number and location of boxes must be ascertained through prompt inquiry of every safe deposit department or company where the decedent might have had a box.

After satisfying the requirements of the bank or safe deposit company as to authorization and, if necessary, making arrangements with the state taxing authorities to be represented at the opening, the personal representative should open the box—in the presence of one or more responsible members of the decedent's family, if possible, but in all events in the presence of two persons. An itemized list should be made of the contents of the box and signed by everyone present at the opening. Notations should be made on the list of any items specifically labeled as belonging to someone other than the decedent and of any items claimed by members of the decedent's family as their property. The personal representative should not, however, distribute the contents of the box until such claims have been considered and approved. The contents of the box, to the last scrap of paper, should be preserved. Although a scrap of paper may appear worthless at the time, it may later serve to throw light on some fact or transaction that might otherwise be obscure.

LIFE INSURANCE

The decedent's life insurance policies require the attention of the personal representative. If the policies are payable not to the estate but to a named beneficiary (for example, spouse, son, daughter, or trustee under an insurance trust agreement), the personal representative has no legal obligation with respect to these policies except to report them for tax purposes. It may also want to keep in mind any taxes that may be allocated to such insurance. Nevertheless, the representative may have a moral or social obligation to assist the beneficiary in preparing the proofs of death and forwarding the claims to the insurance companies for payment.

If the policies are payable to the estate of the decedent, the personal representative has a definite legal obligation, as soon as its letters are obtained, to prepare the proofs of death and forward the claims to the insurance companies for payment. Normally an insurance company settles such a claim without delay. Sometimes, however, the right to the insurance proceeds is disputed or contested by claimants other than the estate. If there are conflicting claims, the company usually pays the money into court, and the claimants litigate the matter.

OUT-OF-STATE PROPERTY

Possibly the most difficult detail requiring the personal representative's attention is to locate out-of-state property of the decedent. Bank balances, brokerage accounts, or safe deposit boxes may be found in two or more states. Ancillary administration proceedings (that is, local and subordinate administration proceedings) may be required in some cases, especially when the decedent left real property located outside the state. Some states permit the release of personal property to the personal representative in another state on the publication of notice within the state where the property is located. The prescribed form is, in effect, a notice to creditors.

REAL PROPERTY

Except in states where real and personal property are treated alike for administration purposes, the personal representative should not assume any duties with respect to the real property unless authorized to do so by the court or by the will. Often the will imposes on the executor certain duties with regard to the real property, or the personal representative is required (in accordance with the laws of some states) to use rents to pay debts; hence the personal representative frequently finds itself actively involved with real as well as personal property in the process of assembling the assets. In such cases leases must be attended to, rents on business or residential property must be collected, the sufficiency of existing insurance must be checked, expiring insurance must be renewed, and buildings under construction or repair must be supervised. In the case of farm property, there may be growing crops to be cultivated and harvested, livestock to be fed, perishable property to be protected, and a multitude of other things that must be cared for promptly.

BUSINESS INTERESTS

The decedent's business interests require immediate attention. Sometimes a direction or a recommendation to continue is contained in the will; but in the absence of special authority, the personal representative can continue the decedent's business only until it has had a reasonable time in which to dispose of that business. It must sell or liquidate the business as soon as a fair value can be realized. Frequently a business cannot be closed pending a sale without the risk of its losing much of its value as a going concern. In the case of a continuance, a court order is frequently obtained so as to protect the personal representative.

If the decedent was a member of a partnership, usually the terms for the liquidation of the decedent's interest by the surviving partners are prescribed by the partnership agreement or by statute. If he or she was the sole proprietor or the controlling stockholder, the personal representative may be under the practical necessity of continuing business operations and providing competent management until a fair value can be realized or every reasonable possibility of doing so has been exhausted.

OPEN ACCOUNTS

Awaiting the attention of the personal representative are the claims owned by the estate—open book accounts with customers, clients, and others, and notes and mortgages held in the name of the decedent. Although the personal representative may, by law, be allowed a specified period of time in which to make collections, it should make them as soon as possible.

The personal representative usually encounters many problems in collecting accounts. Open accounts, particularly those of long standing, may be disputed. Customers may claim credits not shown on the books of the decedent. The personal representative knows that some of these contentions are valid, some may be questionable, and some may constitute flagrant attempts to take advantage of the decedent. Although the personal representative is expected by the creditors and the beneficiaries of the estate to collect all outstanding obligations, it is not justified in expending the estate's money to litigate worthless claims. In some states the statutes specify the procedure to be followed in the compromise of doubtful or worthless claims held by the decedent's estate.

HOUSEHOLD FURNITURE

Still another step in assembling the assets is the listing and, on rare occasions—such as when the estate may be insolvent—the actual taking over of the household furniture and other tangible personal property located in or about the family residence. The manner in which this very delicate duty is handled may affect all future relations between the personal representative and the family. In handling furniture and personal effects it is vitally important that the personal representative be sympathetic, understanding, and patient, yet at the same time businesslike, firm, and impartial, and keep in mind that for the family household furnishings have a value far beyond their intrinsic worth.

Safeguarding the Assets

To some extent the work of safeguarding the assets proceeds simultaneously with the work of assembling them. Safeguarding the assets includes taking an inventory, making an appraisal, disposing of perishable goods, protecting valuable chattels, dealing with the decedent's business, and transferring and managing his securities. Close attention must also be given to compromising and adjusting claims and to raising cash for paying administration expenses and debts.

PREPARATION OF THE INVENTORY

As fast as the assets are assembled, the personal representative must prepare a detailed inventory, which, when completed, is filed with the court. This inventory should be an itemized list of specific assets rather than a list of assets by groups. The items must be designated accurately and described so clearly that they can be easily identified by the appraisers and by others who are interested.

The inventory serves to put the estate assets under accounting control. The personal representative charges itself with each item appearing in the inventory and must account for each item in the final settlement of the estate. It is sometimes necessary to include in the inventory an item for which an adverse claim has been made, but ordinarily the adjustment of conficting claims before the inventory is taken will facilitate the settlement of the estate.

APPRAISAL OF THE ASSETS

Another step in safeguarding the assets consists of fixing the value of the items listed in the inventory. In some states appraisers are selected by the personal representative, and their report is subject to later check by the court or by the taxing authorities; in other states appraisers are appointed by the court.

The appraisal of an estate is an important and highly technical matter. In addition to the usual holdings of corporate or municipal bonds, listed stocks, and real estate, many different kinds of property may require valuation—for example, unlisted stocks and bonds, open accounts, unsecured notes, stocks of raw materials and merchandise, household furniture, antiques, and heirlooms. The appraisers should be experienced in fixing reasonable values for such items or, as in the case of valuable jewelry, should obtain the advice of specialists. Overvaluation of the property would be as unfair to the beneficiaries of the estate as undervaluation would be to the taxing authorities.

DISPOSAL OF PERISHABLE GOODS

While the inventory is being prepared and the assets are being appraised, prompt action must be taken to protect the perishable goods of the estate, by sale or other means. As previously stated, this is a matter in which the personal representative cannot wait for court authority to act. In some states, pending qualification and appointment of the executor or administrator, a temporary administrator may be appointed by the court to take over and dispose of perishable goods, just as a temporary administrator may be appointed to protect a going business.

PHYSICAL PROTECTION OF VALUABLES

During the period of settlement, valuable chattels, such as paintings, bronzes, tapestries, and furniture, should receive the special attention of the personal representative. If they are not in storage or under the protection of responsible members of the family, the personal representative may have to place a caretaker in charge of the residence where the valuables are located until they can be delivered to the legatees. Jewelry and other small articles of value not in the hands of responsible members of the family should be placed in a safe deposit vault.

INSURANCE

The personal representative must also give prompt attention to obtaining adequate insurance on the estate property. Blanket policies providing for immediate, automatic coverage of all such property are available to personal representatives.

HANDLING THE DECEDENT'S BUSINESS

A real test of the quality of the personal representative's service is the handling of the decedent's business. It must do everything in its power to provide for successful operation to preserve the value of the business as a going concern, for there is danger that much of the value may be lost if earnings decline sharply after the decedent's death.

If the business must be sold, the personal representative must determine the timing of the sale and the terms that will be acceptable. In making a sale, the personal representative should obtain the approval of the court and, if possible, of the beneficiaries. If the personal representative merely closes the business and sells the assets at auction, it may sacrifice much of their value and cause irreparable damage to the estate. The proceeds obtained from the sale of the business depend largely on the efforts made by the personal representative to find a buyer, its resourcefulness in promoting a sale, and its skill in negotiating satisfactory terms. Intelligent planning of a businessman's estate should include consideration of the many problems involved in conserving the value of his business in his estate, the continuance or sale, and the training of his successors in management skills.

TRANSFER AND DISPOSITION OF SECURITIES

One of the first steps in safeguarding the assets is giving notice of death to the transfer agent of the decedent's registered bonds and stocks, with the request that interest and dividend checks be remitted to the personal representative. Since it is necessary to file proof of the appointment and authority of the personal representative with each transfer agent, many trust institutions, instead of merely giving notice of death, proceed immediately with the transfer of the decedent's registered bonds and stocks to the name of the personal representative or to the name of its nominee. Other trust institutions, after giving notice to the transfer agent, prefer to hold the registered bonds and stocks in the name of the decedent and to have them transferred directly to the names of the legatees or distributees when the estate is ready for distribution. Of these two procedures, prompt transfer from the name of the decedent is preferable, for it definitely disposes of state inheritance tax waivers, avoids delays in distribution, and establishes the right of the personal representative to vote the stock.

While the transfer of securities requires technical knowledge rather than the exercise of business judgment, the decision about what to do with the security holdings during the estate settlement period calls for investment judgment of a high quality. Definite action must be taken with respect to the securities. The personal representative cannot merely hold them without attention throughout the period of settlement in the form in which they were received and then distribute them to the ultimate owners. When the estate is to pass outright, it is usually desirable and proper to ascertain whether the legatees wish to accept particular securities or have them disposed of. The question whether the securities belonging to the estate should be retained or sold requires a prompt decision based on sound investment information and experience, on the cash needs of the estate, on the needs of the beneficiaries, and on the personal representative's powers under the will and under the law.

REAL PROPERTY

When the personal representative, either under the law or under the will, has active duties with respect to real property, close attention to that property may be required throughout the period of settlement. In such a case, all buildings must be kept insured, repaired, and tenanted, if possible. Farms may have to be rented or tenanted. The decedent may have died when he or she was engaged in developing real property and making subdivisions. That activity must go on; otherwise the estate may lose all that has been put into the development. Property that is suitable for long-term lease may have to be re-leased during the period of settlement. Real property may have to be sold to obtain cash for the payment of debts and expenses, and sale of the property may involve advertising, bargaining, and other forms of promotion and development.

COMPROMISE AND ADJUSTMENT OF CLAIMS

The collection of open accounts, notes, and mortgages due the estate (often a long-drawn-out process) was discussed earlier, and it was pointed out that the assets of the estate should not be wasted in vain attempts to collect worthless or outlawed claims. Although the personal representative must endeavor to collect every dollar that is due the estate, in certain cases it should be satisfied with partial collection of an obligation rather than risk spending too much money in a useless effort to collect the entire claim.

RAISING CASH

In the settlement of an estate, cash is usually needed to pay administration expenses, debts (including taxes), and legacies. Early in the settlement of an estate, the personal representative should make a cash analysis to determine whether there is sufficient cash to meet all requirements. If cash is not available from life insurance or other sources during the period of settlement, the personal representative must sell enough assets to raise the necessary money.

A number of problems arise in connection with the raising of cash: which assets should be sold first and when such sales should be made in the best interests of the beneficiaries; whether, instead of selling assets at a sacrifice in a depressed market, the wiser course would be to borrow on them; and whether, if it is deemed wiser to borrow, the will gives the executor the power to borrow. These are only a few of the difficulties that confront the personal representative in determining the best method of raising the necessary cash without impoverishing the estate. Ordinarily the personal representative cannot borrow money on the credit of the estate in the absence of an express power in the will or an order of court. If the executor has been given ample powers in the will, the work of safeguarding the assets will be facilitated.

In states that prescribe the order in which property shall be sold for the payment of debts, some of the real property—or even all of it—must be resorted to if the personal property is insufficient to provide the required cash. In the absence of power under the will to mortgage, lease, or sell real property, the personal representative must show the court that it is necessary to use the real property for the payment of debts and must obtain an order of court to mortgage, lease, or sell the real property for that purpose. In states that do not prescribe the order in which property shall be sold to satisfy the debts, real property may be sold first, even though ample personal property is available.

Paying Administration Expenses and Debts

Another important step in the settlement of an estate is the payment of charges against the estate. Those charges may be classified into three general groups—administration expenses, family allowances, and debts—and they must be paid before the amount of the net estate can be determined and distributed.

ADMINISTRATION EXPENSES

Administration expenses include appraisers' fees, attorneys' compensation, court costs, the executor's or administrator's allowance, and the disbursements made by the executor or administrator in carrying out its duties. As a rule these expenses do not present many problems. Although they may vary considerably in different jurisdictions, in general they are fixed by custom, by statute, by court decision, or by contract and are subject to court approval.

The compensation of the attorney for the estate may be fixed by the will or by the court. Any understanding between the personal representative and the attorney regarding compensation is always subject to the approval of the court.

Various methods of fixing the executor's or administrator's allowance are followed in different states. In some states the allowance is based on the value of the entire estate; in others it is based on the value of the personal estate alone. Sometimes it is figured on the basis of the total of receipts and disbursements. Gains and losses computed on the basis of the appraised value may be taken into account in the calculation of the allowance.

All court costs are fixed by law or by practice and are assessed by the probate court. Those costs cover probating the will, issuing the letters, recording the will, receiving and filing the inventory, appraising when done by court appraisers, and receiving, auditing, and recording the accounts and settlements. Although they are negligible in themselves, they are nevertheless a prior claim against the estate.

FAMILY ALLOWANCES

As noted in the discussion of the law of intestate succession, one of the important steps in the settlement and distribution of an estate is the allocation of the family allowances—sometimes referred to as the widow's and children's allowances or the widow's year's support—set aside for the surviving widow or widower (if the law makes provision for the widower) and the children. The statute is designed to give the family support and maintenance for a limited period of time after the death of one of the parents.

The allowances are usually given preference over all other obligations of the estate except funeral expenses, expenses of the last illness, and administration expenses. The nature and duration of the allowance and the degree of preference vary in different states. All statutes, however, are designed to give a measure of financial protection to the family as the estate is being settled.

DEBTS

A third group of charges against the estate includes taxes due from decedent, debts proper, funeral expenses, and expenses of the last illness of the decedent.

Two sets of the same kinds of taxes may have to be paid during the period of settlement, one set assessed against the decedent but unpaid by him during his lifetime and the other assessed against the personal representative. For example, at the time of the decedent's death, his last year's local or state tax based on the value of his real property or of his intangible personal property may be due and unpaid; if so, the personal representative must pay that tax as well as a similar tax for the current year. If the death occurs early in the year, the previous year's federal and state income tax returns may not have been made; this task must be attended to, and the taxes must be paid. Moreover, separate federal and state income tax returns may have to be made for the portion of the year during which the decedent was living and for the portion remaining after his death. There may also be gift tax returns to be prepared and gift taxes to be paid for gifts made by the decedent shortly before his death.

Included in debts proper are open accounts, unsecured notes, mortgage debts, and unliquidated claims. In many states those debts must be proved according to law. This requirement usually means that open accounts, such as store accounts and doctors' bills, must be itemized, sworn to, and filed within the period allowed by law for proving claims. Unsecured notes are usually proved by filing verified copies of them. Although a secured creditor may be required to file his claim, he can nevertheless, at his option, realize on his security just as if the debtor were still alive.

Unliquidated claims against the estate—unfinished jobs, claims for damages, and many kinds of disputed and contested claims—may be difficult to handle. The decedent may have left an inadequate record of the basis of such claims, or he may have left no record at all. There may be little evidence on which a proper defense can be based. Furthermore, unless by law or by the terms of the will the executor is given full authority to compromise, adjust, and settle claims against the estate, it may find itself at a costly disadvantage in negotiating with creditors.

Funeral expenses are mentioned separately from other debts because, as a rule, they have a special standing in the order of payment of debts. Expenses of the last illness of the decedent are also mentioned separately, mainly in order to call attention to the fact that in most states they likewise take priority over ordinary debts.

If the estate is solvent, all administration expenses and debts will in due course be paid in full by the personal representative; but if the estate is insolvent, not all such expenses and debts can be paid in full; some must take priority over others. Such priority is fixed by statute in each state. Although the statutes vary greatly, the following order of payment is typical:[4]

1. Debts constituting a specific lien on property not exceeding the value of the property
2. Reasonable funeral expenses not to exceed a stipulated amount, such as $600 or $900
3. Taxes assessed on the estate of the decedent before his or her death
4. Dues to the United States and to the state

4. It should be noted that the family allowance usually takes priority over items 3–7.

5. A judgment docketed against the decedent during his or her life-time
6. Wages due a servant or laborer employed by the decedent
7. All other demands

Taxation

It is not the purpose of this text to discuss in detail tax matters that must be considered in the settlement of estates. Any statement concerning taxes should be reviewed by the student with the knowledge that the entire area is in a continual state of change and any statement may be out of date and misleading.

ESTATE AND INHERITANCE TAXES DISTINGUISHED

The federal estate tax is a tax on the transfer of property. It is levied on the right to transfer property and is measured by the size of the estate.

An inheritance tax is usually imposed by the state in which the decedent made his home at the time of death. The tax is levied on the right of the recipient to receive property and is usually measured by the amount of the property received by a beneficiary and his or her proximity of kinship to the deceased.

In addition to the inheritance tax, many states impose an estate tax on the transfer of the net estate of every decedent when the inheritance tax is less than the maximum credit allowed by the federal estate tax law. In such instances the inheritance tax is increased by an estate tax on the net estate such that the aggregate amount of tax due the state will equal the maximum amount of credit allowed under the federal estate tax law. If, because of exemptions, no state inheritance tax is due but a federal estate tax is due, an estate tax equal to the maximum amount of the credit will usually be due to the state.

FEDERAL ESTATE TAX

Before January 1, 1977, the date on which the 1976 Tax Reform Act became effective, the estate of each decedent was entitled to a specific exemption. The Tax Reform Act of 1976 repeals the specific exemption and instead allows a "unified credit" against the gross estate.

A UNIFIED TAX AND CREDIT SYSTEM

The elimination of separate gift and estate tax schedules with exemptions of $30,000 and $60,000 and the substitution of a new unified rate schedule for taxable estates of less than $6 million and of a new unified tax credit that will by 1981 reach $175,625 introduce far-reaching and fundamental changes into the system of estate and gift taxation. Notwithstanding the impact of the new law on the planning and settlement of estates and the administration of trusts, it does not bring new substantive concepts to the gift and estate areas. The "unified tax system" will have to be studied, however, and the student will have to keep in mind that the estate and gift tax systems remain separate but operate in the context of a single rate structure and a single credit against the unified taxes on gratuitous transfers.

The unified credit as set forth in the Internal Revenue Code (IRC) Section 2010, provides:

For Decedents Dying:	*Credit*	*Exemption Equivalent*
In 1977	$30,000	$120,666
In 1978	$34,000	$134,000
In 1979	$38,000	$147,333
In 1980	$42,500	$161,563
Thereafter	$47,000	$175,625

The credit will be reduced by 20 percent of any specific gift tax exemption allowed on gifts made after September 8, 1976, and before January 1, 1977.

By 1981 there will thus be no tax liability for cumulative gratuitous transfers during life or death of up to $175,625. (See IRC Section 2010.)

The unified rate schedule is a table of higher marginal tax rates, graduated from 10 percent on transfers not exceeding $10,000 to 70 percent on transfers greater than $5 million. A brief comparison of the former and present liabilities is revealing:

Estate Tax

Taxable Estate	*Former Law*	*New Law*
$ 100,000	$ 4,800	$ 0
250,000	47,700	23,800
500,000	126,500	108,800
1,000,000	303,500	298,800
2,000,000	726,200	733,800

Gift Tax

Taxable Gift	*Former Law*	*New Law*
$ 100,000	$ 9,225	$ 0
250,000	42,525	23,800
500,000	102,075	108,800
1,000,000	235,950	298,800
2,000,000	554,775	733,800

There are four credits in addition to the unified tax credit. They are:
1. Credit for state death taxes (IRC Section 2011).

2. Gift tax credit (IRC Section 2012). This is repealed as to past 1976 transfers.
3. Credit for tax on prior transfers (IRC Section 2013).
4. Foreign death tax credit (IRC Section 2014).

Gift Taxes and the Unified Tax Credit

Under the former gift tax law, the specific exemption was elective, and it operated to reduce the tax base. The unified tax credit operates directly to reduce the tax liability. Under the specific exemption of $30,000, the donor could elect whether to use any portion or all of the exemption when he or she made a gift. Under the 1976 act, the amount of the credit is reduced by the sum of the amounts *allowable* as a credit for previous gifts. (See IRC Section 2505(a).)

Conclusion

Complex in its application, the unified tax and credit system eliminates the tax savings that under the former law could be achieved by lifetime transfers of property. Fortunately, however, the annual exclusion of $3,000 remains available to the donor. In addition, any appreciation in value of the property given is not taxable to the donor.

CARRYOVER BASIS PROPERTY

Before the adoption of the 1976 Tax Reform Act, the basis of property acquired from a decedent was its fair market value at the date of death or at the date the property was valued for estate tax purposes if the executor elected the alternative valuation date (currently six months after death). If the property had appreciated in value after having been received by the decedent, the resulting gain would not be taxed since the legatees or devisees received a "stepped-up basis" in the property. (See former IRC Section 1014.)

Property received by way of gift from a donor during his or her lifetime had the same basis in the hands of the donee that it had had in the hands of the donor plus any gift tax paid. In other words, the donor's adjusted basis carried over.

Section 1023(a)(1) provides that the time for determining the basis in carryover basis property is "immediately before the death of the decedent," in effect, the date of death. Thus electing the alternative valuation date does not directly affect the carryover basis. Section 1023(b) exempts a number of items from the carryover basis rules, including income in respect of a decedent,[5] life insurance proceeds, and personal and household effects not exceeding $10,000 in value if elected by the

---

5. Income in respect of decedents is defined in Section 691 of the Internal Revenue Code. It provides for determining to whom income received before death shall be taxable.

personal representative, a joint and survivorship annuity where the surviving annuitant was taxable under Section 72, and payments under a deferred compensation plan.

Additional property is excluded if disposed of before the decedent's death in a transaction where gain or loss is recognized: property that was the subject matter of a gift made in contemplation of death (within three years before death), property over which the decedent held a power of revocation or a general power of appointment, stock or stock options to the extent the income in respect to the option is includable in gross income, and stock in a foreign personal holding company.

All property acquired from a decedent that is not excluded is carryover basis property.

It should be noted that the carryover basis may be increased by certain adjustments. The adjustments will not be permitted to increase the basis of the asset above its estate tax value. Briefly stated, the adjustments come as the result of:

1. payment of death taxes by the decedent's estate
2. a guarantee of a minimum carryover basis of $60,000
3. an increase on account of inheritance tax paid

The new law also permits the adjusted basis of any marketable bond or security to be stepped up to its fair market value on December 31, 1976, for the purpose of determining gain.

It should be noted that property qualifying for the marital or charitable deduction is not subject to adjustment, i.e., does not get a stepped-up basis. The state estate and inheritance tax adjustments are not made for property not actually subject to such taxes.

There is perhaps no more troublesome area in the settlement of estates than the valuation of property for estate tax purposes. What is set forth here is only a brief introduction to the carryover basis property; it is enough, however, to make anyone learned in the field realize that the new carryover basis property rules set the stage for difficult controversies. If proof of future problems is needed, one need only mention that under Section 6039A of the Internal Revenue Code, the executor is required to furnish information with respect to carryover basis property as required by the regulations. Failure to furnish the information required without reasonable cause will result in a penalty, which could be as much as $5,000. In addition, the failure to furnish in writing to each person acquiring property the adjusted basis of each item can result in a penalty of $50 for each failure, the total amount not to exceed $2,500.

FIDUCIARY INCOME TAX

At the death of the property owner, his or her liability for income tax ceases, and the liability of his or her estate for income tax during the period of the settlement of the estate begins. That tax is commonly referred to as the "fiduciary income tax." In other words, during the period of settlement and before the distribution of the property to the beneficiaries, an estate is a taxpayer, and the personal representative must file a special return reporting the income the estate has received during the taxable year.

OTHER TAXES

In addition to estate, inheritance, and income taxes, the personal representative must be mindful of and knowledgeable about property taxes or, as they are commonly called, ad valorem taxes; gift taxes on gifts made by the decedent during life; and the tax on intangibles.

Ad valorem taxes are taxes imposed by states, counties, cities, towns, school districts, or other taxing units on the assessed value of real property. When such a tax is imposed on personal property, cash on hand or in the bank, and other intangible personal property, it is sometimes known as an intangible tax.

POST MORTEM ESTATE PLANNING

One cannot study the problems surrounding the settlement of an estate without realizing the complexities of the task and the need for skillful planning both before and after death. The planning and settlement of estates are not tasks for the unwary.

The selection of property for the payment of taxes, the handling of the redemption of stock needed for the payment of taxes and administration expenses, and the handling of such matters as retirement and pension plan benefits and carryover basis property make it virtually certain that the public will turn more and more to the corporate trustee for the planning and settlement of estates.

Distributing the Net Estate

Having assembled and safeguarded the assets throughout the period of settlement and having paid all administration expenses and debts, the personal representative is ready to make a final accounting to the court and to distribute the net estate. That is done after the time required for notice to creditors has passed.

FINAL ACCOUNTING

The procedure for making a final accounting and distributing the net estate varies widely from one state to another. In some states the personal representative prepares and files the account without a formal procedure. In others the procedure is formal; the account is filed (together with vouchers covering all disbursements), a date for a hearing is fixed, and all parties interested in the estate are notified so that they may appear if they wish to do so. If those parties object to any phase of the account, they have an opportunity to be heard. When the court has heard all the parties that care to be heard, it approves, or modifies and approves, the final account. The personal representative is then free to distribute the net estate.

The purpose of both the informal and the formal procedures is to place on permanent record with the court a statement by the personal representative showing clearly all the assets received and all the amounts paid out, itemized so that the accounts can be checked item by item. If the estate is unusually complicated and more than the customary time is required to collect debts, conclude business ventures, or complete lawsuits, the settlement may be drawn out. In that case it is often desirable to render to the court one or more intermediate accountings, even in states where such accountings are not mandatory. If the intermediate accountings are approved, the period covered by them may be considered settled, and the personal representative may proceed along the lines previously pursued with greater assurance of receiving the court's ultimate approval.

SCHEDULE OF DISTRIBUTION

A schedule of distribution must be prepared before the distribution can be made. In some states that schedule, together with the final accounting, must be filed with the court for approval.

If the will directs the distribution of the estate, item by item, to named beneficiaries, another beneficiary taking the residue, and if all the beneficiaries are alive, the preparation of the schedule of distribution may be easy. It may be difficult, however, when the amounts of the distributive shares must be determined through the application of a formula. It may also be difficult if there is no will, and allocated tax liabilities may have to be taken into consideration if there are numerous kin in varying degrees of relationship—for example, brothers and sisters, half-brothers and half-sisters, uncles and aunts, children of deceased uncles and aunts, and adopted children (the legality of whose adoption must be investigated). In such cases the preparation of the schedule of distribution calls for a thorough knowledge of the laws of intestate succession in the state(s) in which the decedent lived and in which he or she owned property, as well as for a careful investigation of the kinship of the various relatives.

RELEASES AND FINAL DISTRIBUTION

In some states it is possible to dispense with a formal schedule of distribution and to close the estate by making distribution and receiving a release from each of the beneficiaries. Such a release, which may or may not be recorded in the court, serves as a receipt for the distribution and frees the personal representative from further liability to the legatee who signed it.

In certain states it is customary to include in the release what is known as a refunding bond. By the terms of that bond, the legatee promises that, if the personal representative is required to pay any additional (but at the moment unknown) taxes or debts, the legatee will reimburse the personal representative from the legacy, even if he has to repay the full amount of the legacy. In most states, however, the personal representative would be well advised to retain a reserve to meet possible claims for additional taxes until all tax matters have been settled.

When the personal representative is finally ready to distribute the net estate, it makes the distribution according to the terms of the will, if there is one. If the decedent died intestate, the personal property is distributed to the spouse and next of kin as determined by the laws of distribution in the state of domicile, the real property descending to the heirs according to the laws of descent in the state where the real property is located.

With ample property of the right kinds available to pay all the legacies and make all the devises, the distribution is simple. If the will calls for gifts in money and the property is chiefly in the form of securities or real property, some of the property must be sold. But if there is not sufficient property to satisfy all the gifts, the problem is more difficult, and the personal representative must determine, under the applicable rules of law, whether some of the beneficiaries will take their shares in full while others get nothing; whether the shares of all will be scaled down ratably; or whether the persons mentioned first in the will will have some preference over those named later. If the personal representative is under bond with surety, a court accounting and releases or a discharge are necessary to discharge the surety.

Personal Services

No description of the practical steps to be taken in the settlement of an estate is complete without a reference to the personal services required of the personal representative by the family of the decedent or by others. These include funeral arrangements, providing for the immediate cash needs of the family, and advisory services.

FUNERAL ARRANGEMENTS

Although a trust institution as executor usually takes no active part in funeral arrangements, it must do so if no immediate member of the decedent's family is available or if the family wants it to make these arrangements. Each case must be handled on its merits. In some instances the family might resent as an intrusion on its privacy any activity of the trust institution on behalf of the family until after the funeral. In other instances the family might regard as neglect and indifference the failure of a representative of the trust institution to call immediately at the home to pay his or her respects and tender the services of the trust institution. The representative may even have to take charge in such private matters as the selection of the burial lot and the casket and the arrangement of the funeral services.

IMMEDIATE CASH NEEDS

After the funeral (and sometimes before), the first service of the personal representative to the family of the decedent is to arrange for the family's immediate cash needs. The impression that the representative of the trust institution makes on the family during those first meetings often affects the entire settlement of the estate. Tact is of the utmost importance.

If the decedent has provided for the immediate needs of the family through life insurance or if the surviving spouse has an independent estate on which he or she may draw, the immediate need for cash may not arise. But if—as is frequently the case—no such resources are available, the personal representative may have to make cash advances to the family. If the estate is solvent, that is the proper course to follow; if it is insolvent, such advances will be made at the risk of the personal representative. The personal representative, therefore, must familiarize itself with the estate as soon and as completely as possible so that it may be able to decide to what extent it can make advances to the family with reasonable safety.

ADVISORY SERVICES

An executorship or administratorship may last only a few months or, at most, a few years. A trusteeship may extend throughout one or more lifetimes. The first year or two after the death of a parent is a critical period, and the personal services rendered during that time may have as telling an effect on the family's attitude toward the trust institution as the services rendered during the longer period of trusteeship. The personal representative must step into the breach caused by the death, advise the members of the family during the period of readjustment, and keep them apprised of the progress of the estate settlement.

The trust officer, representing the trust institution as executor or administrator, must develop patience and sympathy for the family and dependents from the beginning to the end of the settlement of the estate. He or she must prove a friend to every member of the family. He or she is dealing with people who are grief-stricken and sensitive; then, if ever, they should find in the trust officer a real friend and adviser.

Chapter 7 **Personal Trusts**

The Purposes of This Chapter:

1. To present personal trusts as a primary source of trust business
2. To show how personal trusts are created and the purposes they serve
3. To present some of the factors that should be considered in deciding whether a trust should be created and how long it should continue

"If an experienced and thoughtful man were asked, 'What after all, is the greatest, most worthwhile, most enduring service that trustmen and their institutions now are rendering to Americans and to other English-speaking people?' I should be surprised if the answer would not be, 'Administering personal trusts.'"[1]

As noted in Chapter 1, banks through their trust departments currently administer about $487 billion of assets for the benefit of more than 1.3 million trust customers and millions more beneficiaries. Of the $487 billion, approximately $192 billion is in personal trusts and estates of individuals. This chapter focuses primarily on testamentary trusts, which are established under the terms of a will and take effect upon the death of the testator, and living trusts, which are established and come into operation during the life of the creator.

Although once the insurance policies mature the trust of the proceeds is a personal trust, insurance trusts are sufficiently distinctive to merit separate treatment. They are covered in Chapter 8.

A trust is frequently defined as a person's obligation arising out of confidence reposed in him or her to apply property faithfully according to that confidence. It is also defined as a fiduciary relationship in which one person is the holder of the title to property subject to an equitable

---

1. Gilbert T. Stephenson, *Reflections of a Trustman* (New York: American Bankers Association, 1960), p. 24.

obligation to keep or use it for the benefit of another person. In simpler terms, a trust exists when the legal title to and the management of property are in one person and the beneficial interest is in another.

Essential Elements of a Trust

The definitions given indicate the essential elements of a trust. These are the creator of the trust, the trustee, the beneficiary, the trust property, and the trust terms.

First there must be someone who reposes confidence. That person is the *creator of the trust.* If he (or she) reposes confidence through a will, he is known as the testator; if he does so through a trust agreement, he is called the settlor, trustor, or donor; if he does so through a deed of trust, he is known as the grantor. In practice, "settlor," "trustor," "donor," and "grantor" are used interchangeably. Throughout this textbook "settlor" is employed to designate a person who creates a trust either by a trust agreement or by a deed of trust.

Next there must be someone in whom confidence is reposed. In English-speaking countries that person is generally known as the *trustee*. If an existing trust has no trustee to administer it and no provision has been made for appointing one, the court appoints a trustee. No valid trust is permitted to fail for want of a trustee.

There must also be someone for whose benefit confidence is reposed. That person is generally known as the *beneficiary.*

There cannot be a trust, at least in the sense in which the term is used in this textbook, except with regard to property. The property that is the subject matter of the trust is known as the *res,* the trust estate, the trust property, or the trust fund.

In one form or another, the *trust terms* must exist (that is, the purposes for which and the terms on which confidence is reposed in one person for the benefit of another with regard to property); otherwise the trustee will have no way of knowing its duties or the beneficiary his or her rights. Depending on the type of trust, the terms are found in wills, in written trust agreements or deeds of trust, in declarations of trust, in orders of court, in statutory provisions, or in oral statements.

Classification of Personal Trusts

Because of their similarity, this discussion includes personal trusts and insurance trusts that provide personal benefits. Personal trusts may be classified in three ways:
1. According to the duties of the trustee
2. According to the character of the trust instrument
3. According to the method of creation of the trust

DUTIES OF THE TRUSTEE

Classified according to the duties of the trustee, trusts are active or passive. An *active trust* is one that requires the trustee to perform some active duty. A transfers securities to B in trust so that B may hold, analyze, review, and reinvest the trust property and pay the income to C. This is an active trust in that B cannot do his duty as a trustee without performing active services with regard to the securities.

A *passive trust* (sometimes called a dry trust) is one that requires the trustee to serve only as a titleholder. He has no active duties to perform; he merely permits the beneficiary to do something. A conveys land to B in trust to let C use, occupy, and receive the rents from it. During the continuance of the trust, B has no active duty; at the termination of the trust, he has only the duty of passing on the legal title in accordance with the directions contained in the trust instrument. Until the death of the insured, unfunded insurance trusts are usually passive, whereas funded insurance trusts are active in light of the obligation to manage property, the income usually being applied to the payment of premiums.

CHARACTER OF THE TRUST INSTRUMENT

Classification by the character of the trust instrument is most common in trust business. On this basis there are four kinds of personal trusts: trusts under will, trusts under agreement (trust agreement or deed of trust), trusts by declaration, and trusts by order of court.

A *trust under will* is created when a testator leaves property to a trustee, including in the will instructions to the trustee to hold and administer the property and to apply its benefits to some person or persons other than the trustee.

A *trust under agreement* is created when an owner of property delivers, transfers, or conveys property to a trustee in accordance with an agreement or contract. Under the terms of the contract, the trustee agrees to hold the property in trust and to administer it for the benefit of some person or persons other than the trustee.

A *trust by declaration* is created when an owner of property makes a declaration that he or she holds the property as trustee for the benefit of someone else. Instead of declaring himself trustee, the owner may deliver the property to a trust institution, which then makes a declaration of trust. In other words, a trust institution sometimes takes title to property outright on the condition that it immediately declare itself trustee of the property for the benefit of some designated person or persons. Trusts under agreement and trusts by declaration are also known as living trusts.

A *trust by order of court* is created when a court of proper jurisdiction appoints either an individual or a trust institution to receive property in trust and to administer it for the benefit of someone other than the trustee. Such trusts usually arise from litigation before the court, as in payment of alimony resulting from divorce proceedings or a dispute over real property. In a few states trustees for incompetent or incapacitated persons are appointed by order of court.

METHOD OF CREATION

Classified according to the method of creation, trusts are express, implied, constructive, or resulting. An *express trust* is one that is stated orally or in writing, with the terms of the trust definitely prescribed. It is the type created by the act of parties who, fully aware of what they are doing, intend to create a trust.

An *implied trust* is one that is created when the nature of the transaction and the words used are such as to cause the court to infer that it was the intention of the parties to create a trust, although the trust is not directly or expressly declared. Such trusts frequently arise in connection with homemade wills drawn by the testators. Thus A bequeaths property to B with the request that B use it for the education of A's daughter, C. If, on the basis of the entire transaction and the nature of the instrument, the court is convinced that A meant to leave the property in trust for the education of C, it will enforce the trust just as it would if technical trust terms had been used by either or both parties.[2]

Although a trust institution may occasionally accept a passive trust, the trusts administered by such institutions are nearly always active and express trusts.

Trusts Under Will

A testator has the choice of leaving property outright to the contemplated beneficiaries or leaving it in trust for them. A large group of personal trusts consists of trusts under will.

BENEFICIARIES OF TRUSTS UNDER WILL

Except for limits imposed in some states on gifts for charitable purposes, a testator may create a trust under will for the benefit of any person, corporation, association, or institution that is capable of owning property. The legal or actual inability of a person to manage property in

---

2. Two other types of trust about which the student should have some general information are (1) a constructive trust—a trust imposed by a court of equity as a means of doing justice, without regard to the intention of the parties, in a situation in which a person who holds title to property is under a duty to convey it to another person; and (2) a resulting trust—a trust that results in law from the acts of the parties, regardless of whether they intend to create a trust, as when a person disposes of property under circumstances that raise the inference that he does not intend the person taking or holding the property to have the beneficial interest in it.

no way affects the right of a testator to create a trust for the benefit of that person; in fact, among the chief beneficiaries of trusts under will are minors, who are legally, if not actually, incapable of managing property, and incompetents, who are both legally and actually incapable of managing it.

In most instances a trust under will is created for the benefit of the immediate members of the testator's family and his or her dependents—in other words, for the testator's spouse, children, grandchildren, parents, grandparents, brothers, and sisters. A trust is not usually created for a distant relative or a friend unless that relative or friend is in some way dependent on the testator; when such a trust is created, the testator generally has the double purpose of providing for that beneficiary and preserving the principal for an ultimate beneficiary.

PURPOSES OF TRUSTS UNDER WILL

Many property owners have become aware of the tax reduction advantages provided by trusts under the present tax laws and regulations. Beginning in 1977, a trust operating through several generations (in which the restraints of the rule against perpetutites and the rule against accumulation do not apply) will, except to a limited extent, be subject to tax on the death of each generation benefiting from the trust. The present exclusion, which is subject to change, is limited to $250,000 per child for property passing to the testator's children. The tax is substantially equivalent to the estate tax that would have been imposed if the property had actually been transferred outright to successive generations.

Although tax savings can be justified as the reason for creating a trust only in special cases, a larger estate resulting from tax savings can provide additional benefits for family, dependents, or others for whom a trust benefit is contemplated.

The usual purposes for which trusts under will are created include the following:

1. To hold the family intact
2. To meet the special requirements of children
3. To avoid the necessity for guardianships of the property of minor beneficiaries
4. To bestow the benefits of property without imposing its burdens

Keeping the Family Intact

From both the personal and the social points of view, one of the beneficial purposes served by trusts under will is that of keeping the family intact. That goal is achieved by preserving the family home, by relieving the survivors of responsibilities connected with investments

101

and other property, and by supplying the income needed to maintain the family's normal standard of living.

For the purpose of preserving the family home, a testator may leave his or her residence outright to his or her spouse, to the spouse for life and then to the children, or in trust as a family home for the spouse and children. In the first case, if the residence is costly and constitutes a considerable part of the estate, it may be too expensive to maintain. If it is sold, investment management and preservation of the proceeds of the sale may be difficult and burdensome.

In the second case, the residence cannot be sold except with the joinder of the testator's spouse and all of the children. If one of the children is a minor, that child can act only through a guardian, and the guardian can join in a sale only on an order of court.

If the testator chooses the third alternative, the residence, large or small, may be left in trust under terms and provisions that will make possible its use as a home in the best interests of the family. For example, the will may make any one or more of the following provisions: that the testator's residence at the time of his or her death be held in trust as long as the surviving spouse desires to retain it as a family home; that the expense of upkeep be borne by the trustee as a general expense of the trust estate; that if the spouse later desires to give up the residence as a family home, the trustee may sell the residence publicly or privately and, according to the spouse's wishes, either purchase another residence or add the proceeds of the sale to the general trust estate. Such elastic trust provisions as these enable the trustee and the spouse to retain the residence as a family home as long as it is needed and then dispose of it to the best advantage. An impartial yet sympathetic and understanding viewpoint can be particularly helpful in the exercise of discretion over distributions of income and permitted invasions of principal with varying impact on different family members. The impartial trustee can make those decisions free from the resentments and frictions that can occur when a member of the family must make such determinations.

If the testator leaves his or her estate in trust, the trustee assumes full responsibility for safeguarding and managing the property and either pays all the available income to the beneficiaries or applies it for their benefit. To the extent that the estate is ample, the family is thus relieved of business and financial responsibilities.

For the purpose of supplying the income necessary to maintain the family's normal standard of living, a testator may leave his or her entire estate to the surviving spouse. In that case the family income is reduced only by the amount of the personal wages, salary, or professional income of the decedent and by the amount of the income yield on the part of the estate that has been used to pay estate and inheritance taxes and the costs of settling the estate.

A testator who does not create a trust is more likely to leave his or her spouse what he considers a fair share of the estate and divide the residue equally among the children. The estate is thus divided into as many portions as there are members of the family, each member receiving his or her portion outright. The portion of any child who has left the family circle, through marriage or otherwise, is at once withdrawn from the family estate. The portion of any minor is kept separate by the guardian and used exclusively for that child's benefit. Thus an estate that, if handled as a unit, would have been ample for the requirements of the family as a group becomes inadequate when split up and used for the separate requirements of its various members.

The testator may, however, trustee his (or her) residuary estate. He or she may provide that his or her spouse shall receive all the income for the maintenance of the home, for his or her own support, and for the support and education of the children during the spouse's lifetime and that in the event of the death of the spouse, the trustee shall apply the income from the whole estate for the support and education of the children until the youngest child is of age and has completed his or her education. The testator may also provide that if the income of the estate is inadequate for these purposes, the trustee may use the principal to the extent necessary.

Meeting Special Requirements of Children

The second main purpose served by trusts under will is that of meeting the special requirements of children as members of society as well as members of a family. If, under the will, the spouse receives all of the income, the spouse (not the trustee) is responsible for meeting the special requirements of the children. In the absence of a parent, the trustee may have to do its best to take the parent's place in this respect, whether the requirements of the children are financial or personal.

If all children could be fitted into a given pattern and made to adhere to a rule-of-thumb procedure, trusts under will for their benefit would not be necessary. Each child, however, is different from every other child, and the needs and development of each are unpredictable.

The best that a testator can do in providing for his or her immature children in the absence of a surviving parent is to place a trustee in charge of the property of each child and empower the trustee to use the property to the best of its judgment in meeting the special requirements of the child as they arise. The terms of the trust may be made so elastic that, apart from the trustee's limitations, the child's portion of the estate may be used effectively for his or her special requirements. The trustee may be authorized to advance or withhold income, to use principal, to advance or withhold principal, or to apply income or principal for the benefit of the child instead of paying it directly to him.

Avoiding Guardianships of Property

Another main purpose for which testators create trusts under will is to avoid the necessity for guardianships of the property of minor beneficiaries. Under the law a guardian must settle with his or her ward when the ward reaches legal age, which is usually 18 years. A trustee may be authorized to continue the trust until the beneficiary reaches a more mature age or meets the requirements specified by the testator. In most states a trust is more economical than a guardianship; and in all states a trustee can be given wider powers than those of a guardian, particularly powers with respect to investments and the use of principal for the benefit of the minor. The flexibility that can be provided through such powers is one of the great advantages of a trust over a guardianship for the management of the property of a minor beneficiary, whether a child, a grandchild, a niece, a nephew, or any other minor for whom the testator desires to make provision.

Bestowing the Benefits of Property Without Its Burdens

Another main purpose for which trusts under will are created is to bestow the benefits of property without imposing its burdens. A daughter, for example, wishing to have her aged or infirm parent receive the full benefit of a gift by will without the responsibility of managing or investing the property and without running the risk of losing it through neglect or poor management, creates a trust under will for the benefit of her parent. Such a trust may also be created for an aged or infirm relative or friend, an incapable or irresponsible brother, sister, son, or daughter, or one who, though not incapable, is nevertheless not business minded. By trusteeing a gift to any of those persons, the testator bestows the full benefits of property without imposing its burdens.

Two types of trusts designed for the protection of the beneficiary, which in the law of trusts have acquired special names, are *trusts for support* and *discretionary trusts*. A trust for support is one that provides that the trustee shall pay or apply only so much of the income and principal, or either, as in its judgment is *necessary* for the support or education of the beneficiary. A discretionary trust is one that entitles the beneficiary to only so much of the income or principal, or either, as the trustee in its *uncontrolled discretion* shall see fit to give him or to apply for his use. Trusts under will are created for various other purposes, some of which are considered in the discussion of living trusts, since such purposes may be carried out through either a living trust or a trust under will.

Living Trusts

Living (*inter vivos*) trusts are also called voluntary trusts and, occasionally, immediate trusts. All three designations are correct and may be

104

used to emphasize different points. Someone who speaks of a living trust means to emphasize that the trust becomes operative during the lifetime of the settlor. When he speaks of a voluntary trust, he means to emphasize that the trust has been established voluntarily and not by operation of law. When he speaks of an immediate trust, he calls attention to the fact that the trust becomes operative at once and not at some later date, for example, after the settlor's death. The term "living trust," which is perhaps the best known, is generally used in this text.

Insurance trusts and trusts with a nominal *res* that are intended as a device to receive insurance proceeds or other property at some future time (frequently at the death of the settlor), while not immediate trusts in the context of the previous paragraph, are nevertheless living trusts.

CREATION OF LIVING TRUSTS

A living trust may be created in various ways. An owner of property may transfer the property to a trustee to hold in trust and administer for the benefit of someone other than the trustee, or the owner may declare himself trustee of the property for the benefit of someone else, or the owner may transfer the property to a second party who, though apparently receiving it outright, immediately declares himself trustee of the property for the benefit of someone other than himself in accordance with the terms of an agreement between the second party and the owner. The first and third methods are those that concern trust institutions.

In the first method, A, the owner, delivers cash, transfers stocks, or conveys real property to B, a trust institution, to hold in trust for the benefit of either A or C, a third party. The terms and conditions on which the property is to be held in trust by B are expressed in the trust agreement or, if real property is involved, in the deed of trust. The trust agreement or the deed of trust is commonly referred to as the trust instrument.

In the third method, A, the owner, transfers property outright to B, a trust institution. To all appearances B thus becomes the absolute owner of the property; but in accordance with an agreement between B and A, B immediately declares itself trustee of the property for the benefit of A or of someone other than the trust institution itself. B does so by executing a declaration of trust that contains all the terms and conditions on which B is to administer the trust. It is not necessary, as it is in the case of a trust agreement or a deed of trust, that A join in the declaration of trust. Consequently, a living trust consisting only of personal property can be created without the beneficiaries ever knowing the identity of the creator of the trust. If real property were involved, the identity of the grantor would be revealed because the deed to B would have to be recorded.

BENEFICIARIES OF LIVING TRUSTS

An owner of property may create a living trust for his or her own benefit. A, the owner, transfers property to B, a trust institution, to be held in trust for the benefit of A during A's lifetime and then to be handed over to someone else to be continued in trust for the benefit of that person.

Frequently an owner of property may create a living trust for the benefit of a third party. A transfers property to B to hold in trust for the benefit of C, who may be a person, a corporation, a public institution, or any organization or association legally and actually capable of receiving the benefits of property.

One cannot be trustee for himself alone. A cannot trustee property to B for the benefit of B alone. If A attempts to do so, B becomes the holder of both the legal title and the equitable title. B is then the absolute owner of the property and hence is discharged of the attempted trust. A may, however, trustee property to B and C for the benefit of B or to B for the benefit of B and C; in neither case are the holder of the legal title and the holder of the equitable title identical.

REVOCABLE AND IRREVOCABLE LIVING TRUSTS

Classified according to the rights reserved by the creator, living trusts are either revocable or irrevocable. It is important to know the differences between revocable and irrevocable living trusts with respect to both their purposes and their effects.

A revocable living trust is one under which the creator has reserved the power of revocation. He may have reserved the right to have the trust property transferred back to him, discharged of all trust, at any time he chooses, whereupon he once more becomes its legal owner. Instead of reserving this right to himself alone, he may have reserved to himself the power of revocation but only with the consent or approval of one or more persons; or he may have given this right to one or more specified persons other than himself. When the revocation is subject to the consent or approval of one or more other persons, the trust should be referred to as a revocable trust with consent or approval.

An irrevocable living trust is one under which the creator or a person designated by him does not possess the power of revocation either alone or jointly with another person. However, the settlor may make a living trust irrevocable for a period of one, three, or five years or for any other stated period and revocable after that time. He may make it revocable for a stated period and provide that if he does not revoke it within that time, it shall be irrevocable thereafter. He may make it revocable until the occurrence of a certain event and provide that it shall be irrevocable thereafter. Finally, he may make it irrevocable until the occurrence of a certain event and provide that it shall be revocable thereafter.

106

When the creation of the trust is evidenced by a written instrument that purports to include the terms of the trust and makes no provision that expressly or impliedly reserves to the settlor the power to revoke it, the trust is in most states irrevocable. However, in some states the trust can be revoked unless it is expressly irrevocable.

A trust institution should exercise great care in accepting an irrevocable trust, for if such a trust is accepted and the settlor later desires to revoke it, he is likely to feel that he was not properly advised concerning the inflexibility of the plan. Some trust institutions are opposed to accepting an irrevocable trust unless the complete instrument has been in the hands of the settlor for some time before it is executed by him, so that he will have had ample opportunity to think through all the phases of the step he is about to take. Other trust institutions will not accept an irrevocable trust unless the attorney for the settlor is present at the time the trust instrument is executed. Some trust institutions even require the settlor to sign a separate declaration of irrevocability.

In all irrevocable trusts and in revocable trusts in which consent to revocation is required, there may be important tax considerations. Tax returns may have to be filed and taxes paid. Therefore the settlor should also seek competent tax advice.

POWER TO REVOKE AND POWER TO AMEND

A distinction should be made between the power to revoke a trust and the power to amend a trust agreement; the two are frequently confused. The power to revoke a trust is the power to terminate it, whereas the power to amend a trust agreement is the power to change the terms of the trust either generally or within specified limits. Even in the case of an irrevocable trust, the settlor may reserve the power to amend the trust agreement. For example, the creator of the trust may make it irrevocable but reserve the right to add property to the trust, to change the beneficiaries, to change the relative proportions of the property given to the beneficiaries, or to change the terms of distribution. Although the settlor may change the terms of the trust in one of these vital ways, he can never resume control of the trust property. The tax effect of reserving the right to amend an irrevocable trust is, of course, a primary consideration.

PURPOSES OF LIVING TRUSTS

Some of the principal purposes of living trusts, as distinguished from trusts under will, are the following:

1. To obtain specialized property management and investment service
2. To hold a separate estate
3. To eliminate interruptions, delays, court procedures, and publicity at death

4. To use the trustee as a go-between
5. To test the trustee's administration
6. To obtain tax savings

Obtaining Property Management and Investment Service

A common objective of men and women who create living trusts is to obtain specialized property management and investment services. By means of such trusts, they keep the benefits of property and shift its burdens to others. Active business men and women realize that if they devote the greater part of their time and attention to business, they may be unable to devote sufficient attention to the management of property that is dissociated from the business or to exercise sound judgment in the investment of personal funds. By creating living trusts, they place on the trustees the responsibility of managing their personal investments and other property.

Professional men and women find that living trusts relieve them of property management and investment problems and leave them free to devote themselves to their professions. Likewise a soldier, an explorer, an artist, a musician, a writer, or a scientist may be relieved of investment responsibilities through creation of a living trust.

Retired business men and women create living trusts to be free to enjoy the benefits of their estates. In doing so they seek and obtain continuous skilled property management and investment service.

Holding a Separate Estate

Active business and professional men and women create living trusts to hold for themselves or for their dependents estates that are separate and distinct from their businesses or professions. Building an estate that is independent of one's business profits or professional income, to be drawn on in later life, is an objective of many young men and women as well as of older people.

Business men and women have learned that it is not wise to invest all their earnings in their businesses, because a business may become unprofitable and the capital invested in it unproductive. Therefore, as soon as they have funds that are not needed to meet the requirements of their businesses, they place those funds in living trusts. They begin with a certain amount of cash or securities or both and from time to time add surplus funds derived from the business. Sometimes, by leaving the income from the trust estate to be reinvested (provided that the rule against accumulation of income does not interfere), they are able to make their separate estates grow at a surprising rate. With the same objective in view, professional people, realizing that their professional incomes depend on their mental and physical health and on the demand for their services, create living trusts and from time to time add funds not needed for professional and living expenses.

Eliminating Interruptions, Delays, Court Procedures, and Publicity

A trust created by will cannot go into full operation immediately upon the death of the testator. The personal property must pass through the process of administration, and a period of time (from four months to several years) may elapse before the personal representative completes distribution to the trustee. Property in a living trust, however, need not become part of the settlor's estate at his or her death but can continue, without interruption, to provide for the requirements of the beneficiaries of the trust.

The settlor may make himself the beneficiary during his lifetime and provide that after his death the trust shall continue for the benefit of his family, or he may provide that other persons shall receive the income from the beginning. In either case, since the trust property has already been invested in accordance with the terms of the trust and income is being received and remitted by the trustee, the trust continues in full operation when the settlor dies.

Moreover, since a living trust agreement, unlike a will, is seldom made a matter of public record, the size of the trust and provisions of the trust instrument do not become matters of general knowledge. All information about the living trust is held in confidence, and the beneficiaries are thereby spared publicity when the testator dies.

Another advantage of a living trust is that it often reduces expenses at the time of the settlor's death. Even though the amount of inheritance and estate taxes payable at that time may be the same as for a trust under will, the property in a living trust is free from certain court costs and accounting fees to which property that passes through an estate into a trust under will is subject.

Using the Trustee as a Go-Between

Many living trusts are created primarily for the purpose of having the trustee act as an intermediary between the creator of the trust and the beneficiary. Illustrations of such trusts follow.

A daughter creates a trust for the benefit of her aged parent not only to provide for the parent but also to avoid offending the parent's sensibilities. To be sure, each month the daughter might donate or pay directly to the parent the same amount that the parent would receive from the trustee. In the one case, however, the payment would be a direct gift, possibly subjecting the parent to embarrassment; in the other, it would be the trustee's regular monthly or quarterly voucher and would look like an interest or a dividend check representing the return to the parent from an investment.

109

In a similar spirit, a settlor creates a living trust for the benefit of a distant relative, a friend, a former associate, or a benefactor. Instances are known in which aged and retired teachers, ministers, and nurses, with no sacrifice of pride or self-respect, have gratefully received the benefits of a trust when they would have refused an outright donation.

A husband creates a living trust to provide his wife with a regular and dependable income for her household and personal expenses. The trust property is separate from the property of his business or profession, and the trustee assumes all the investment and accounting responsibilities. The settlor's wife is thus enabled to systematize and regulate her personal and household expenses and handle them in a businesslike way. Parents create a living trust for their child, often a minor, with the objective of teaching that child how to handle money matters and of bringing him or her into contact with a financial institution selected by the parents.

Testing the Trustee's Administration

Property owners, particularly those who possess large estates, frequently create living trusts partly to make a preliminary test of the trustee's administration. It is not easy for a person to select as executor and trustee a trust institution with which he has never done any trust business and commit to it the administration of his entire estate and the financial care and protection of his family. Thus, when a property owner creates a living trust and states that the primary purpose is to test the trustee while he is still alive, the trust institution selected as trustee should not construe the act as indicating a lack of confidence. As a rule, a person who creates a living trust for this purpose is eager to help the trustee administer the trust successfully. He will usually give the trustee the benefit of his own judgment and experience with respect to all business, financial, and investment problems that arise in the administration of the trust. Furthermore, he will arrange for contacts between the trust officer and the beneficiaries and pave the way for harmonious relations between them later on.

Obtaining Tax Savings

Sometimes living trusts are created primarily to reduce taxes. Two popular types are trusts for minors and short-term trusts. A trust for a minor drawn to conform to the tax laws is an exception to the gift tax laws, which do not allow exclusions for gifts of future interests. A trust established for a period of at least ten years—whereupon it usually reverts to the settlor—may shift to the beneficiary the obligation to pay tax on the income. Although other tax effects must be considered, such trusts have been effective in providing more tax-free income in certain support situations.

It should be understood that the creation of a living trust for the chief purpose of saving taxes (the good of the beneficiaries being an incidental consideration) is not only questionable from a social point of view but may in fact prove ineffectual as a tax-saving device. The changes in tax laws and regulations are so frequent and so substantial that a person who creates a living trust has no assurance that a tax-saving plan that is clearly within the law today will still be so tomorrow.

Duration of Trusts

The problem of the duration of trusts, whether trusts under will or living trusts, raises two questions: For how long a period *may* a trust continue? And for how long a period *should* a trust continue?

How long a trust *may* continue is a legal question based on statutory limits or exemptions from them. The ordinary limitation is the rule against perpetuities, which is dealt with in some statutes in terms of rules against suspending the absolute ownership or suspending the absolute power of alienation. Because of variations in laws and decisions, the law of the state where a trust is to be established or a will drawn must be referred to.

How long a trust *should* continue is a question of trust business and trust service (and sometimes of public policy), and the answer depends entirely on the facts in each case. A trust for a spouse, a parent, or any other adult is ordinarily designed to continue throughout the lifetime of the beneficiary. Many problems arise, however, in providing for a minor, both before and after he or she reaches legal age, and in providing for an incompetent. Different considerations as to the duration of a trust may come into play, for example, when a testator or a settlor is providing for a minor or an incompetent and when he is providing for a person after that person's minority.

PROVIDING FOR A MINOR OR AN INCOMPETENT

The property of a minor should be continued in trust until he or she comes of legal age; it would be vain and futile for the testator or the settlor to provide for the termination of such a trust before that time, only to have the court set up a guardianship for the minor during the remainder of his or her minority. Likewise, a trust for an incompetent should be continued as long as the incompetency lasts.

PROVIDING FOR A PERSON AFTER HIS OR HER MINORITY

When providing for the period after a person comes of legal age, the testator or the settlor must consider this question: Should the beneficiary be given his property outright, discharged of all trusts, when he or she attains the age of majority, or should the distribution be postponed until the age of 25, 30, 35, or 40? No answers to this question will apply in all cases. The trust instruments of those who have created trusts for sons and daughters, and the experience of trust officers who have administered such trusts, may be drawn on for suggestions as to the advantages and the disadvantages of different ages and terms of distribution.

In many instances the instrument provides that the trust shall terminate when the child attains the age of 21. The advantage of this plan is that the child has working capital available on the day he or she was traditionally legally capable of engaging in a business or profession. Its disadvantage is that the child may not actually be capable of handling capital at that time or may still be attending school.

Other parents provide for the property to be held in trust until the child is 25, 28, 30, or even 35 years old. The advantage of such an arrangement is that the child will have a longer period of preparation for the management of the property; its disadvantage is that he or she may get too late a start in business or professional life or may be inclined to loiter until the inheritance is received.

Still other parents provide that the child's share shall be delivered in instalments—for example, one-third at 25, one-half of what remains at 30, and the rest at 35 years of age. The advantage of this plan is that if the child is unfortunate and loses the first instalment, he or she has another chance with the next. The disadvantage is that the child, knowing that there is more property to come, may dissipate the first instalment and even the second, acquiring habits of extravagance and recklessness in money matters.

From the foregoing discussion it is clear that there can be no standard answer to the question of how long a trust should continue. In general, a trust should continue only as long as there is a need to have the legal title to and the management of the property in one person and the beneficial interest in another. For beneficiaries who are mature at the time the trust is created, the separation of the legal title and the beneficial interest will normally continue during their lifetimes. But for growing children who in a few years may reveal characteristics and talents (and possibly weaknesses) that are unknown at the time the trust is created or the will is made, the best course open to a parent is to select a trustee with great care and give the trustee broad discretionary powers. Moreover, in the case of a trust under a parent's will or a revocable living trust established by a parent, the terms of the trust should be reviewed from time to time and modified if modification seems desirable.

Chapter 8   Essential Features of Personal Insurance Trusts

The Purposes of This Chapter:

1. To present those features of trusts that are peculiar to insurance trusts
2. To show the adaptability of insurance trusts to both personal and business needs
3. To discuss the technical feature of insurance trust agreements
4. To consider some special problems of business insurance trusts

"The life insurance trust is a method of settlement especially to be considered in the following situations:

1. When flexibility of administration and the exercise of discretionary powers are needed to meet situations which cannot be foreseen or requirements of beneficiaries that cannot be provided for beforehand;

2. When, in connection with business insurance, there is need for an impartial and responsible third party to carry on the plan under which the insurance was effected;

3. When the immaturity, inexperience, or incompetence of the beneficiaries creates a need for the services of an experienced and objective financial advisor;

4. When the primary purpose of the insurance is to safeguard the estate against complications and shrinkage due to debts, taxes and administration expenses."[1]

Since the administration of the proceeds of life insurance policies that are held in trust differs very little from the administration of other funds received by a trustee, this chapter is limited to a discussion of the distinctive features of trusteed life insurance policies that require consideration during the lifetime of the policyholder.

A life insurance policyholder may provide for the trusteeing of the

---

1. "Principles for Relationships Between Life Underwriters and Trustmen (1968)," *Trust Principles and Policies* (Washington, D.C.: American Bankers Association, 1973), p.8.

proceeds of his or her insurance policies either under an insurance trust agreement or under his will. During his lifetime he may have the policies made payable to a trustee under an insurance trust agreement in which he directs that the proceeds be held in trust and administered as specified in the instrument. His policies may be made payable to his estate; then the total net probate estate, including the insurance, will become the corpus, or principal, of any trust created by his will. He can also, by agreement with the company, have his insurance made payable directly to the trustee named in his will. Under such an arrangement, the proceeds are not part of the probate estate and thus not subject to estate costs and creditors' claims. Changes of residence, new wills, and new trustee designations require conforming changes in the beneficiary designation.

Although an insurance trust may provide that the proceeds be merged with a testamentary trust, thereby preserving a state insurance exemption and facilitating administration, the more usual arrangement is to add the probate estate to the insurance trust. Many states have adopted statutes designed to permit such additions, or pour-overs, and to clarify the freedom from court supervision considered desirable. There was considerable concern in the past over the effect of a provision in a will describing a trust when the trust was later amended, but this problem can be solved either by carefully coordinating revisions in the will and the trust or by referring to the trust "as amended." Legal justification, if not covered by statute, has been discussed by writers on the concept of "incorporation by reference" and on the doctrine of "independent significance"; these are subjects not included in this textbook.

Classification of Insurance Trusts

Classified according to their main purpose, insurance trusts are personal or business. Classified according to their provisions for the payment of premiums, they are funded or unfunded.

PERSONAL AND BUSINESS INSURANCE TRUSTS

A personal insurance trust is one created by a person for the benefit of other persons, for example, when a person in his or her capacity as spouse, parent, child, or kinsman creates a trust for the benefit of his or her spouse, child, parent, or other relative. Personal insurance trusts are essentially the same as other personal trusts and are created for similar purposes.

A business insurance trust is a trust created in connection with a business enterprise. One type of business insurance trust is created for the purpose of liquidating the business interest of a deceased partner or stockholder or, more rarely, of a deceased sole proprietor. For example, a trust is created by two partners, each of whom effects insurance on the life of the other, making the policy payable to a trustee under a trust agreement providing that the insurance proceeds, when collected, be used for the purchase of the deceased partner's interest in the business. As another illustration, two stockholders of a corporation effect insurance on each other's lives, each policy being made payable to a trustee under a trust agreement providing that the insurance proceeds be used for the purchase of the policyholder's stock in the company in the event of his death. Such trusts, like personal insurance trusts, benefit the surviving policyholders and the business enterprises.

Other types of business insurance trusts are the trust created to strengthen the credit of a business enterprise by the addition of new money at the death of the policyholder and the trust created to replace at his or her death, as far as possible, the money value to the business of the man or woman on whose life the insurance is carried. This type of insurance is often referred to as "key man insurance," i.e., insurance on one of the most important leaders of the company.

A partnership, for example, may effect insurance on the life of one of the partners and have the policy made payable to a trustee, to be administered in a specified way for the benefit of the business. An example would be the payment under an agreement of a guaranteed income to the spouse of a deceased partner for a number of years. Likewise, a corporation may effect insurance on the life of a key person in the business and have the policy made payable to a trustee to be administered in a specified way for the benefit of the corporation.

UNFUNDED AND FUNDED INSURANCE TRUSTS

An unfunded insurance trust is one in which only the life insurance policies are trusteed, the trustee having no duty or responsibility whatever with respect to the payment of premiums. A funded insurance trust is created when a person trustees life insurance policies and, in the same or in a supplementary trust instrument, trustees cash, securities, or other property to provide sufficient income for the payment of premiums, at the same time charging the trustee with the duty of paying the premiums out of the income. If the income from the trust estate will be more than sufficient to pay the premiums, the creator of the trust may provide that the surplus income:

1. Be paid to him or her or to someone else
2. Be allowed to accumulate and be invested
3. Be held subject to his or her order

At the death of the creator, the trust estate consists of the insurance proceeds and the property that has been placed in the trust to provide for the payment of premiums.

Reasons for Trusteeing Personal Life Insurance

Not all personal life insurance should be trusteed. Some insurance might accomplish its purpose more effectively if paid in a lump sum to a named beneficiary or to the estate of the insured. When the purpose of the insurance is to provide funds to meet the needs of the insured's beneficiaries over a long period, the insurance proceeds may either be left with the insurance company for distribution under one of its optional modes of settlement or be trusteed by means of an insurance trust. The insurance trust has many advantages, however, including flexibility in distributing income and principal, which is not provided by optional settlements.

It is generally agreed that the insurance trust is the mode of settlement especially to be considered when the primary purpose of the insurance is to safeguard the estate against complications and shrinkage due to death taxes and administration expenses; when the immaturity, inexperience, or incompetence of the beneficiaries creates a need for the services of a local, experienced, and impartial financial adviser; and when flexibility of administration and the exercise of discretionary powers are needed to meet emergencies that cannot be foreseen or requirements of beneficiaries that cannot be provided for in advance. It is also used when a *pour-over* arrangement offers particular advantages or when it is important that a desired long-term investment program be established.

READY CASH FOR ESTATE REQUIREMENTS

One of the most troublesome problems of an executor in the settlement of an estate, especially a large estate, is that of raising the ready money with which to pay administration expenses and debts, since persons of large estate often keep their funds fully invested and have relatively little cash on hand. The problem is further complicated by the fact that increasingly large amounts of cash are needed for estate and inheritance taxes.

One method of providing immediate cash that might naturally suggest itself would be to have life insurance made payable directly to the estate.[2] That arrangement is objectionable, however, because the proceeds of the insurance would become part of the decedent's general estate and would therefore be subject to all administration expenses, claims of creditors, and debts, including estate and inheritance taxes.

---

2. Although at an earlier time life insurance was exempt from federal taxation and some state taxation, proceeds of insurance receivable by the executor, proceeds payable to the insured's estate, or proceeds over which the insured held any "incidents of ownership," such as control of almost any type, are now generally taxable to the estate, and cash for estate requirements is thereby reduced.

116

A better method is the insurance trust agreement, which offers two means of raising the necessary cash without sacrificing the integrity of either the general estate or the trust estate. An insurance trust may enable the trustee of the insurance estate to purchase assets from the general estate or make loans to the general estate using the estate assets as collateral.

SPECIAL REQUIREMENTS OF BENEFICIARY

When those for whose benefit the life insurance was effected are immature or inexperienced or legally incompetent, a local experienced and impartial trustee is needed to administer the insurance proceeds. To meet the special requirements of each beneficiary, the trustee must be given broad discretion as to the allocation of income and principal. Provisions in settlement options of life insurance companies permitting withdrawals of principal can afford a degree of flexibility, but they are no match for an experienced corporate trustee with a full range of discretionary powers.

Insurance Features of Insurance Trust Agreements

The essential features of all personal trust instruments are discussed in Chapter 9, but some mention of the insurance features peculiar to insurance trust agreements should be made here.

METHODS OF MAKING INSURANCE PROCEEDS
PAYABLE TO THE TRUSTEE

In most cases the proceeds of a life insurance policy should be made payable to the trustee through a form of change of beneficiary rather than through a form of assignment. An assignment is the transfer of property or of an interest by one person to another. A change of beneficiary is merely the exercise of a person's right to specify who shall receive the proceeds of his policy when they become payable in accordance with the terms of his policy contract.

If an insurance trust is to be irrevocable, the policyholder desiring to part irrevocably with all his right, title, and interest in the policy, there can be no objection to assigning the policy to the trustee if such assignment is contemplated and provided for in the trust agreement. But if he wishes to retain control of the policy during his lifetime and to enjoy the policyholder's benefits under the contract, he should make the policy payable to the trustee through a form of change of beneficiary. If he assigns the policy to the trustee and at the same time makes a revocable trust for the benefit of contingent, undetermined, or minor beneficiaries, difficulties may arise later, for the assignment included in the trust agreement and the right to change the beneficiary reserved in the policy

117

are inconsistent provisions and may prevent the policyholder from exercising the rights reserved under the policy if he should subsequently desire to do so without terminating the trust and having the policies reassigned to him.

INSURANCE ON LIFE OF ANOTHER

In most cases the creator of a personal insurance trust trustees policies on his own life. Occasionally, however, a husband may trustee policies on the life of his wife, a wife may trustee policies on the life of her husband, a father may do so on the life of his daughter, or a son may trustee policies on the life of his mother, with appropriate changes in the trust agreement.

TRUSTEE'S DUTIES AS TO COLLECTION OF POLICY PROCEEDS

Life insurance companies are prompt in the settlement of claims in all clear cases, but sometimes a question arises as to the validity of a claim. Has the policy lapsed? Has it become incontestable? Is an assignment to the trustee or creditors or a change of beneficiary valid? Are there several disputing claimants? The beneficiaries of the trust may be disposed to insist on the trustee's pushing a disputed or contested claim but may not offer to protect the trustee against loss if the claim is disallowed. Therefore, the trust agreement should give the trustee the right to demand indemnity before incurring expense in prosecuting a contested claim.[3]

CUSTODY OF POLICIES

A receipt for the insurance policies is usually incorporated in the trust agreement or attached to it. In the case of a funded insurance trust, there is also a receipt for the property trusteed. The question naturally arises, Is it necessary for the trustee to take over and retain possession of the policies? The answer to this question is that during the lifetime of the policyholder it is no more *necessary* for the trustee to have possession of the policies than it is for the executor to have possession of the will, but it is highly *desirable*.

The rights of the parties are determined not by the physical possession of the policies but by the terms of the contracts (the policies and the trust agreement) under which the parties are operating. Nevertheless, by having possession of the policies, the trustee is able to move promptly toward the collection of the insurance proceeds and the establishment of the trust. If the policies are in the possession of the policyholder or someone other than the trustee, they may be difficult to locate, and the

---

3. See Appendix D for a typical section of an insurance trust agreement setting forth the duties of the trustee as to the collection of insurance.

collection of the proceeds may be delayed. Another practical advantage of the trustee's having custody of the policies is that it enables the trustee to know the extent of the insurance estate and to know when changes are made, for the policies must, as a rule, be withdrawn from the possession of the trustee if the policyholder wishes to change the beneficiary, obtain a loan, or get the surrender value of the policies.

RIGHTS RESERVED BY THE POLICYHOLDER

In a revocable insurance trust agreement, the policyholder usually reserves to himself all his rights under the policy. Life insurance companies have raised the question whether the general power (reserved in the trust agreement) to exercise all rights of every nature accruing solely to the policyholder includes the right to borrow on the policies. Because insurance companies vary in their interpretation of this provision, the policyholder should protect himself by enumerating, among the rights reserved, the specific rights to borrow, to receive dividends, to take maturities, and to withdraw policies from and add policies to the trust.[4]

PAYMENT OF PREMIUMS

In an unfunded insurance trust, the full responsibility for the payment of the premiums, assessments, and other charges on the trusteed policies rests on the creator of the trust, and the trust agreement should expressly relieve the trustee of any responsibility in this respect.[5]

In a funded insurance trust, the trustee is responsible for paying the premiums, assessments, and other charges on the policies. If the income from the funded portion of the trust is more than sufficient to pay the premiums, the trustee has the duty to apply the surplus income as directed in the trust instrument. If the fund (both principal and income) for the payment of premiums has been exhausted, how can the trustee relieve itself of liability with regard to the policies? It is highly important that the trust instrument clearly define the trustee's duties under all possible circumstances.[6]

---

4. See Appendix D for a provision reserving the insured's rights.

5. See Appendix D for a provision for the payment of premiums of an unfunded trust.

6. See Appendix D for a provision for handling the payment of premiums of a funded trust.

Chapter 9

Essential Features of Personal Trust Instruments

The Purposes of This Chapter:

1. To suggest some of the administrative powers that should be incorporated into the trust instrument
2. To explain some of the provisions of trust instruments that facilitate the administration of trusts

"Many forms of conduct permissible in a workaday world for those acting at arm's length, are forbidden to those bound by fiduciary ties. A trustee is held to something stricter than the morals of the marketplace. Not honesty alone but the punctilio of an honor the most sensitive is then the standard of behavior. . . ."[1]

The principal instruments under which personal trusts are administered are wills, declarations of trusts, deeds of trust, trust agreements, and orders of court. The essential features of those instruments are discussed in this chapter except for the features peculiar to insurance trust agreements, which are covered in Chapter 8, and the distinctive features of court orders creating personal trusts, which may be found in any of several legal treatises.

Trusts Created by Will

At the outset, the student should recognize that there is a sharp line of demarcation between personal trusts created by will and personal trusts created by agreement. A will is usually a well-drawn blueprint for the settlement of the testator's estate. Many of its provisions concern only the handling of the estate by the executor. The trust features of the will, however, have some similarity to the essential features of other personal trust instruments. An analysis of the essential features of a typical living trust instrument will serve to bring out most features of personal trust

---

1. Meinhard v. Salmon, 249 N.Y. 454, 464; 164 N.C. 545, 546 (1928).

instruments. The student should remember that in a will the wording of the trust provisions would be slightly different.

Appendix B sets forth a trust agreement containing many of the provisions usually found in such agreements. The following provisions are typical:

1. The names of the parties
2. The property trusteed
3. The powers of the trustee

Inasmuch as the success or failure of the trust depends on the powers given to the trustee and its ability to exercise them prudently, the student should carefully examine some of the more critical and sensitive powers, the absence of which from the trust agreement can make administration of the trust extremely difficult.

Express Powers of the Trustee

Experience has shown that, if the trust is to be administered efficiently and economically, the trustee should be given broad powers of administration. Even though powers may be clearly inherent or implied, they should be expressly stated in the trust instrument so that the trustee may have no doubt or hesitancy in exercising them. A failure to include such powers may bring about uncertainty and delay, impair investment performance, and prevent the trustee from taking action that it considers to be in the best interests of the beneficiaries.

The Uniform Trustees' Powers Act was approved by the Commissioners on Uniform State Laws at their annual conference in August 1964. The terms of the act confer broad powers of administration on trustees. In states where the act has been adopted, a trustee has the power, without the need to obtain court authorization, to perform every act a prudent man would perform in the administration of a trust. In some states—North Carolina, for example—a testator of a will or settlor of a trust may incorporate by reference any or all of the powers set forth in the statute.

The effect of the Uniform Trustees' Powers Act is to make unnecessary the insertion in a will or trust instrument of a long list of specific detailed powers. Where the act or some modification of it has not been adopted, however, the draftsman has no choice but to include elaborate provisions as to the powers of the trustee.[2]

POWER TO RETAIN ORIGINAL INVESTMENTS

The purpose of a provision that original trust property may be retained is to prevent the sacrifice of trust property (usually stocks and

---

2. See Appendix B for a typical section of a trust agreement setting forth the powers of the trustee.

bonds) that the settlor may have accumulated. If the trust instrument limits the trustee to statutory trust investments or otherwise specifies what the trust investments shall be and the original property received in trust does not meet those requirements, the trustee will in many states be obliged to dispose of the original property within a reasonable time and invest the proceeds in property that meets the investment requirements of the statute or of the trust instrument. Further, in the absence of such a provision, a trust institution may have to dispose of property that it would not normally hold because of its value in relation to the total value of the trust or because of a lack of investment information about the particular property.

A provision for the retention of original investments should be included in all trust instruments (wills as well as trust agreements) when the original trust property includes investments that may not satisfy the investment provisions of the trust instrument or of the statutes or conform to court decisions in the particular state but that the creator of the trust wants the trustee to retain. The provision should also be included when such investments are likely to be added to the trust property.

A grant of power to retain does not attempt to relieve the trustee of liability for its negligence. It recognizes the possibility that the retention of original property may result in lack of proper diversification of the trust investments. It provides for retention of unproductive property and for ultimate apportionment of the proceeds of the sale of such property between income and principal in such a way as to be fair to both the income beneficiaries and the principal beneficiaries. The provision for apportionment of the proceeds of the sale of unproductive property between income and principal may be very important in a state in which apportionment is not covered by statute.

POWER TO INVEST

If the trust instrument is silent on the subject of investments, the trustee will be limited, as a rule, to statutory trust investments (in a state that has either a mandatory or a permissive legal list) or to investments that a prudent man would make. If the terms of the investment provisions are general or indefinite—for instance, if they state that the trustee shall invest in safe, income-producing or interest-bearing securities—the prudent trustee, as a matter of practice, will limit its investments to those expressly authorized by law. If the settlor or testator wants the trustee to invest trust funds in a special class of securities or in participations in common trust funds, he should leave the trustee in no doubt about what kind of investments he wants or about the authority of the trustee to make such investments. The power to invest should be as broad as possible.

A provision to purchase from or lend to the general estate may not be appropriate for a will but is usually included in living trust agreements and insurance trust agreements. Clothed with this authority, the trustee may purchase securities or other property from the executor or administrator of the deceased settlor, even though they are not statutorily or otherwise authorized trust investments, and thus supply the executor or administrator with funds for the payment of administration expenses, debts (including death taxes), and legacies and obviate the necessity of selling the securities or other property in the market at a possible sacrifice. Inasmuch as the trust under the will is frequently designed for the same beneficiaries as the trust under the agreement, the terms of the two trusts being almost identical, the beneficiaries are not greatly concerned with the question of whether the assets are held under the will or under the trust agreement. In states that have adopted the Uniform Testamentary Additions to Trusts Act, the assets of the estate and the trust may, of course, be merged by a pour-over provision in the will.

A provision giving the trustee power to exercise options and rights may settle beyond question the trustee's right to exercise options, rights, and privileges arising in connection with securities or other property as freely and as promptly as an absolute owner. The trustee is likely to find in its possession stocks and bonds of corporations that must go through liquidation, reorganization, merger, consolidation, or other financial readjustments. The trust estate may have a large stake in those corporations, and the ultimate value of the stocks and bonds held may depend on the success of the process through which a corporation is going. A provision permitting the trustee to participate in reorganizations is intended to authorize the trustee to become active in the affairs of the corporation and take the steps it considers necessary to protect the trust investment, instead of waiting while others work out the corporation's problems.

POWER TO SELL

The purpose of a provision authorizing the trustee to sell property is to give the trustee the same power of sale that an absolute owner possesses and to relieve a purchaser from the trustee of any responsibility for following the proceeds of the sale. The trustee already has certain inherent or implied powers of sale, and the purchaser is seldom required to follow the proceeds of the sale. Nevertheless, broad powers of sale may give the trustee some advantage and the purchaser greater assurance in dealing with the trustee.

POWER TO LEASE BEYOND PERIOD OF TRUST

The purpose of a provision to lease property beyond the duration of the trust is to meet a situation that is likely to arise in a long-term trust containing real property. In some states the rule is that a trustee may not lease real property beyond the duration of the trust, but usually that rule may be altered by an express power.

For example, a trust is to terminate when the named beneficiary reaches the age of 25. Since the beneficiary is now 23, the trust has only two years more to run. The trust estate consists partly of real property. A prospective lessee offers to lease the property and to make extensive improvements and alterations at his own expense if he can obtain a long-term lease, but he declines to take the lease unless he can be assured of having the property for more than two years. In the absence of a lease provision in the trust instrument, the trustee might be unable to lease the property for as short a period as two years. Clothed with the authority contained in such a provision and having had confirmation that the beneficiary approves, the trustee may properly make the desired lease, even though it extends beyond the duration of the trust, and thus handle the property in the same businesslike way as an absolute owner.

An express lease provision of this kind is advantageous to the principal beneficiary, as well as to the income beneficiary, because it means that he will receive the trust property advantageously leased instead of vacant and perhaps unrentable. Such a provision is a practical necessity for a trust that is to terminate at the death of a beneficiary or, as in the illustration cited, a trust that is to terminate when a beneficiary reaches a specified age.

POWER TO SET UP RESERVES

The cost of upkeep of property is not constant. A building may stand for several years without putting the owner to any appreciable expense and then in a short space of time require repairs that cost almost as much as rebuilding. If a building is trusteed and the income beneficiary periodically receives the full net rent without any deductions for setting up reserves, any extensive repairs that are needed will consume the rent for a considerable period, and the income beneficiary will be embarrassed and perhaps not provided for adequately.

A provision for setting up reserves for the upkeep and maintenance of buildings and other property is desirable both for the trustee and for the beneficiaries. In setting up such reserves, however, care must always be taken not to violate any local law against accumulation. In some states no reserves can or need be established unless authorized or directed in the instrument.

POWER TO BORROW

The trustee may have to pay heavy income, estate, or inheritance taxes; or it may have to make cash distributions at a time when selling securities to raise money would mean a sacrifice to the estate. Sometimes the trustee has to improve real property, exercise rights, or pay expenses of foreclosures. In all such instances, an express power to borrow and to give security may be used by the trustee to the advantage both of the trust estate and of the beneficiaries. Since under the laws of most states a trustee cannot borrow money on the credit of the trust estate unless authorized to do so by the terms of the trust or unless borrowing is necessary to accomplish the purposes of the trust, it is essential that the settlor give the trustee express power to borrow money for the benefit of the trust estate. A power to borrow from itself could be of considerable assistance when the trustee is a trust department of a commerical bank. The trustee bank must, of course, pay no more than the prevailing rate of interest, borrow no more than needed, and repay to stop interest as soon as funds for repayment are available, cautionary practices that also apply to individual trustees.

POWER TO COMPROMISE CLAIMS

The right of an executor or administrator to compromise, arbitrate, abandon, or adjust claims is referred to in Chapter 6. Even though the personal representative has the inherent power to do these things, the authority should be expressed in the will. Although a trustee is called on less frequently than an executor or administrator to deal with claims in favor of or against an estate, occasions arise when the trustee must present and prosecute, accept and pay, or otherwise pass on claims; on such occasions the trustee given express power in the instrument to compromise, arbitrate, abandon, or otherwise adjust claims has an advantage over a trustee lacking that express power.

POWER TO VOTE BY PROXY

Although the law seems to be tending in the direction of permitting a trustee to vote shares of stock by proxy if a man of ordinary prudence would do so under similar circumstances, it is still unsettled and therefore uncertain, except in the few states where the point is covered by statute. In some cases in which a question of judgment or discretion in the interest of the trust is involved, it has been held that the delegation by proxy can extend only to recording the vote in a manner previously decided on. The objection to voting trusteed stock by general proxy is that it involves too great a delegation of duty by the trustee. There are many instances, however, in which shares of stock in trust accounts should be voted for one reason or another; yet it may not be practical for the trustee to vote the shares in person or to direct how they shall be voted. A prudent man under similar circumstances would vote the stock by general proxy; hence it seems logical that a trustee should have express power to vote in that way.

POWER TO HOLD SECURITIES IN NAME OF NOMINEE

A trustee may have a certificate of stock that it holds in trust issued to itself in its fiduciary capacity. In such a case, the trustee may have to furnish the issuing corporation or its transfer agent with a certified copy of the will or trust agreement and other documents to obtain a transfer.

Another plan is for the trustee to carry stock in the name of a nominee. Both the trustee and the beneficiaries are protected by a contract between the nominee and the trustee, which strictly limits the rights of the nominee and shows that the nominee has no beneficial interest whatsoever in the stock. The main reason for using a nominee is to make prompt sales and deliveries possible. Some states have specific statutes authorizing trust companies to register corporate securities in the name of a nominee.

Carrying trusteed stock in the name of a nominee is a standard practice of many trust institutions; it is sometimes done even in the absence of express authority in the trust instrument, on the grounds that the beneficiary cannot be injured thereby. However, since the practice is subject to criticism when no express authority is given, the settlor should make specific provision in the trust instrument if he wants the trustee to carry stock in the name of a nominee. A nominee may be an individual or, more frequently, a partnership of officers of the trust company who, by resolution or bylaw, are authorized to sign. It is generally considered inadvisable to hold in the name of a nominee securities that are subject to assessment, such as stock that is not fully paid for or that is subject to double liability.

POWER TO ALLOCATE OR APPORTION

A common provision dealing with the power to allocate or apportion stock dividends is to the effect that all dividends payable in securities of any class shall be considered principal of the trust estate and not income. From the standpoint of the trustee, such a specific direction may be easier to administer, and many persons establishing trusts prefer to give directions about the allocation of various types of stock dividends and other extraordinary dividends. Such a mandatory provision, however, may result in an injustice to the income beneficiaries in that dividends, even though payable in stock, may nevertheless represent current earnings of the company and therefore may rightfully be classified as income. The more equitable provision in many cases would be to authorize the trustee to allocate or apportion stock dividends and other extraordinary dividends at its own discretion. Such a broad power imposes a greater responsibility on the trustee, but it is one that the trustee may be obliged to assume if it is to do justice in all cases both to the income beneficiaries and to the principal beneficiaries.

For many years there has been a difference of opinion, particularly in the Massachusetts and New York courts, as to whether capital gain distributions by investment companies constitute income or principal. This diversity is being solved by the Revised Principal and Income Act (where it has been enacted in full), which provides that capital gains are principal, or by specific statute.

When a trustee purchases a bond at a premium (for instance, when it purchases for $1,100 a $1,000 bond that matures in five years), to which account—income or principal—is the $100 premium to be charged? If it is charged to principal, the principal beneficiaries will receive for their accounts only $1,000 when the bond matures; that procedure may be unfair to them. If the premium is charged to income, the income beneficiaries suffer a reduction of $100 in their incomes; that may be unjust to them. In a number of states, the point is covered by statute; but even in those states, the settlor may provide instructions as to how he wants such premiums handled, and those instructions will control. Or the settlor may confer on the trustee full discretionary power (as in the specimen provision in Appendix B), enabling the trustee to deal with unusual situations, such as the purchase of a high-coupon, long-term municipal bond at a very high premium, in a different way from that in which it might deal with the purchase of other bonds at a few points above or below par.

A trustee is, of course, entitled to reimbursement for actual expenses incurred in connection with the trust estate. Frequently it does not know, and cannot ascertain with any certainty, whether an expense should be charged against principal or against income or should be divided. For example, repairs to buildings may be required. They may be for the benefit partly of the income beneficiaries and partly of the principal beneficiaries, but it is impossible to determine with absolute accuracy the proportionate share chargeable to each. The express power to allocate or apportion merely gives the trustee authority to use its best judgment in dividing expenses equitably between principal and income.

POWER REGARDING ACCRUED INCOME

The settlor may provide that, at the death of any beneficiary who is receiving net income, income that has accrued and that would have been distributed to such beneficiary if living be paid to the beneficiary entitled to the next successive estate. The purpose of such a provision is to eliminate the necessity of accounting to the personal representative of the estate of the deceased beneficiary for the income accrued as of the date of his death. Under certain circumstances, however, tax laws may make the use of this provision inadvisable.

POWER TO DISTRIBUTE

A frequently used provision authorizes the trustee to exercise its judgment in making distributions in cash or in kind, taking into consideration the best interests of all the beneficiaries. In the absence of such a provision, the trustee might have to sell securities at a sacrifice to raise funds with which to make distributions.

A trustee should not be required to distribute the principal ratably but should be permitted to make distributions of equal value. Parts of trust property are frequently not susceptible to equal division, and the trustee will be saved much embarrassment if it has the authority to make a division on the basis of equal value.

OTHER EXPRESS POWERS

The powers of the trustee (as enumerated in the illustrative trust instrument in Appendix B) are by no means all the express powers to be found in trust instruments. Among additional powers that may be found, some of them duties of the trustee in any case, are the following: to bid in mortgaged property at public sale; to grant options; to perfect titles; to insure titles; to make exchanges; to repair property; to insure property; to develop real property; and to continue, sell, or liquidate businesses. The trustee may also be empowered to delegate ministerial powers; to execute papers; to employ agents, brokers, attorneys, and assistants; to employ and reimburse experts in other fields; to keep property in trust in other jurisdictions; and, in general, "to do any and all things determined by the trustee to be necessary and proper to carry out any of the express powers by this instrument conferred or declared, including the execution, acknowledgment, and delivery of instruments of writing, sealed or unsealed." The quoted provision is a recognition of the existence of implied powers and an expression of the intention of the settlor that the trustee exercise all appropriate powers, whether express or implied.

Distribution Provisions

The distribution provisions—that is, the portion of the trust instrument that contains instructions to the trustee regarding the distribution of income and ultimately of principal—are the core of the instrument. All the other provisions may be more or less standardized, but the distribution provisions must be specially drafted for each trust. (The distribution provisions of a living agreement in Appendix B—also applicable to personal insurance trusts—for the benefit of the settlor's wife, children, and grandchildren are offered as illustrative and not as model provisions, since in practice these particular provisions would not meet the requirements of every person who desired to create a living trust of this type.)

DISTRIBUTION OF INCOME

Although a typical provision may suggest that the income be paid to the settlor's spouse monthly or quarterly, it usually gives the trustee authority to change the time for making payments and even to make the payments at irregular intervals. The phrase "but at least once a year" is included only to prevent a trustee from withholding the income for an undue length of time.

By stating that the income shall be paid to his or her spouse for the support of that spouse and the support and education of the minor children or grandchildren, the settlor clearly indicates that the income shall be used for family purposes, that the spouse shall not use it exclusively for himself or herself, and that the needs of minor children or grandchildren shall not be overlooked. Such a provision is adaptable to the requirements of a harmonious family, but it might lead to dissension in a family in which the children were disposed to claim that a parent deprived them of a fair share of the income for their support and education.

DISTRIBUTION OF PRINCIPAL

At the death of the settlor's spouse (assuming that she or he survives the settlor), each child who is then living and has attained the age of 21 receives his or her share outright under the terms of the provision just outlined. The shares of minor children who are then living are at once set apart for them but are not paid over to them until they, in turn, reach the age of 21. The share of any child who is not living at the time but who has left descendants then living is set apart for those descendants, but the part of that child's share that is set apart for each descendant is not paid over to him or her until he or she reaches the age of 21. (As pointed out earlier, the property of a minor beneficiary should be continued in trust until he or she comes of legal age, but outright distribution is often postponed for practical reasons until the beneficiary is older.)

One advantage of the provision illustrated in Appendix B, especially when it is part of the distribution provisions of a trust agreement as distinguished from those of a will, is that at the death of the settlor's spouse (or at the death of the settlor if the spouse has predeceased him or her), the interests of the children who are then living and the interests of the living descendants of deceased children vest in them immediately. Therefore, even though some of those children or descendants may have been born after the execution of the trust agreement, there is no violation of the common-law rule generally referred to as the rule against perpetuities (sometimes referred to as the rule against remoteness of vesting). In any specific case, of course, the local applicable state law should be checked, both as to the rule against perpetuities and as to when the statute goes into effect.

Another advantage of this illustrative provision is that the shares of living children and the shares of deceased children set apart for descendants of those deceased children are all set apart at the same time and are therefore equal in value. When property that will ultimately go to several children is held together after the spouse's death under a provision that requires a child's share to be paid over outright to each child as he or she attains the age of 21, the share paid over to one child at a time when market prices are high is sometimes so much larger than the share paid over to another at a time when market prices are low that the children may incorrectly, but understandably, feel that they have not received equal treatment.

The possibility that all the settlor's children may predecease his spouse and that none of them may leave descendants surviving to take the trust estate at the spouse's death should be covered in the trust instrument, especially when it is a trust agreement rather than a will. The instrument shown provides that in such a case the estate shall go to a named university. A settlor might prefer to have the estate go to named individuals or to those who would receive his estate under the laws of descent and distribution in force in a specified state.

When the family includes several young children (especially when there is no great difference in their ages), it is sometimes advantageous for the trust instrument to provide that the trust property be held together after the death of the settlor and the settlor's spouse and that the trustee apply the income (and the principal if necessary) in varying amounts to meet the needs of the children, without being obliged to see that each child receives the same amount as every other child even though his or her needs may not be the same. In such a case, it is generally preferable to have the trust property held together until the youngest child who lives to attain the age of 21 attains that age—or a later age when higher education will probably have been completed—and at the same time to divide and set apart for the children then living and for the then living descendants of any deceased children their shares of the trust property. In such cases and also when it is desired to postpone distribution to children beyond the time when they attain the age of 18, care must be taken to avoid any violation of the prevailing rule against perpetuities.

DISCRETIONARY POWER TO USE PRINCIPAL

Expressed in different ways, broad provisions for the use of principal, without limitation to need, are found in many—perhaps most—modern trust instruments and are advisable whenever the primary motive of the settlor in creating the trust is the good of the immediate beneficiaries. If, however, the settlor's primary motive is to hold the estate intact for the ultimate beneficiaries, he should not give his trustee such broad authority to use principal for the benefit of the immediate beneficiaries.

The provision shown authorizes the trustee to take into account the other resources of the beneficiary and does not sanction depletion of the trust estate if there are ample funds available from other sources. That limitation is useful in cases where there may be a disposition on the part of the beneficiary to consume the trust to avoid using other property owned outright. Whether the use of principal is justifiable is determined by the judgment of the trustee and not by the desire of the beneficiary. If the beneficiary were authorized to declare that a misfortune or an emergency existed, a trust for an extravagant or improvident person would soon be depleted.

Authority granted to the trustee to use principal "on account of diminution of income yield" even when no other emergency exists is not only a convenience but almost a necessity in a trust for a family being administered during a period of depression, when income from dividends and interest is diminishing while living and school expenses are continuing, or during times of inflation. For the settlor merely to authorize the use of principal for education without specifying the type of education is to leave the trustee in doubt how far it may go in using principal for higher or technical education if some members of the family object to others' taking advanced courses.

The suggested provision that the trustee obtain the consent of the settlor's spouse, unless he or she is incapable of giving such consent (for example, if the spouse has been injured in the same accident in which a child has also been injured), before using principal for the benefit of a child and thus depleting the amount from which the spouse will thereafter receive income is a requirement that the settlor may desire to make in fairness to the spouse and to fortify the spouse's parental authority. The last sentence in the suggested provision clearly shows that it is the settlor's desire that, despite the provision that the trust property be held together during his spouse's lifetime, payments or expenditures for the benefit of a particular child to meet such needs as the expenses of a serious illness or the expenses of that child's college education are to be charged against the trust property as a whole and not against the child's share when that share is ultimately set aside.

The trustee may be given extremely broad power to use principal to augment a beneficiary's income in cases in which tax laws do not make this action inadvisable. For example, the settlor may authorize the trustee to make payments of principal to the spouse whenever the trustee deems such payments necessary to maintain his or her customary standard of living or to provide for his or her comfort or pleasure. Such a provision, unlimited except to the exercise of sound discretion, in effect makes the spouse a preferred beneficiary. The ultimate beneficiary's interest is thereby reduced to the mere right to receive, at the termination of the spouse's interest, whatever property remains in the trust.

Strictly speaking, a decedent's "debts" include only those obligations owing at the time of death. Such items as funeral expenses, costs of administration, and estate and inheritance taxes do not constitute debts of the decedent, but they are usually classified as debts by the debt-payment statute of a state and made a charge on the assets in the hands of the executor. To avoid difficulty in the administration of an income beneficiary estate, consideration should be given to authorizing the trustee to pay the expenses of the last illness and the funeral.

Except when tax laws are a consideration, it is not unusual for the settlor to fix an amount of principal that his spouse, or a child after attaining a specified age, may withdraw as a matter of right whether the trustee approves such withdrawal or not. In trusts with the withdrawal privilege, it is advisable to conform to any tax-free privileges in the tax laws as well as to state in every case whether a periodic right is cumulative or noncumulative.

PROTECTIVE AND SPENDTHRIFT PROVISIONS

A protective provision must be distinguished from a spendthrift trust provision. A spendthrift trust is a trust created to set up a fund for the maintenance of a beneficiary and to secure it against his own improvidence or incapacity. It provides, in effect, that the beneficiary's interest in the income or principal or both shall not be disposed of by the beneficiary or reached by his creditors through legal process before he receives it. A protective provision directs that something else shall be done with the income if a beneficiary attempts to dispose of his interest in the trust property or his creditors attempt to reach it. The provision suggested is modeled on the English protective trust. It may have tax disadvantages in certain cases.

Some states have express statutory provisions governing the creation of spendthrift trusts; in those states the terms of the statute must be followed. In other states the courts have sanctioned a form of spendthrift trust that, if followed, will be effective. In some states a mere provision in the trust instrument to the effect that the trust income or principal shall not be assignable or transferable will suffice; in others the trust instrument must provide for a gift to a secondary beneficiary—as in the illustrative protective provision—to make the provision effective. In some states such a provision is effective as to income but not as to principal. In no state can a settlor create a valid spendthrift trust in his own favor. Because of the differences in state laws, the student should become familiar with the form of provision that is enforceable in his own state.

Not all trust instruments contain a protective provision. In fact, many lawyers and trust men regard it as unwise under normal circumstances. Nevertheless, even those who are opposed to a protective provision or to a spendthrift clause in the normal case are in favor of it in special cases. There are instances when a beneficiary should be protected from his own extravagance or improvidence; in such cases the very purpose for which the trust was created will be defeated if the beneficiary is permitted to assign, transfer, or encumber his interest in the trust. If the trust itself is needed, the terms of the trust should be such as to give assurance that its main purpose will be carried out.

Other Provisions

It is necessary to include in trust agreements provisions relating to the rights reserved by the settlor, such as the right to terminate the trust, which determines whether the trust is revocable or irrevocable. In the evolution of trust agreements, additional provisions have been developed; some of them often appear in wills creating testamentary trusts, whereas others appear in such wills only occasionally. Among these provisions are those relating to:

1. The right of the trustee to resign
2. Successor trusteeship
3. Accounting by the trustee
4. The trustee's compensation
5. Construction of the trust instrument

REVOCABLE TRUSTS

A fundamental right usually reserved by the settlor is the right to revoke the agreement. If he has reserved that right, he may terminate the trust at any time and create a new trust in accordance with his changed plans. If he has not reserved the right to revoke the trust, he may find himself unable to carry out his revised plans, no matter what other rights he may have reserved.

IRREVOCABLE TRUSTS

Experienced trust officers exercise great care in accepting irrevocable trusts, knowing that the conditions and desires of settlors change and that an arrangement that may be ideal at the moment may be totally undesirable not long afterward. No single feature of a trust instrument is more important in practice than its revocability or irrevocability. If the settlor, after obtaining competent advice, desires to create an irrevocable trust, a provision declaring the trust irrevocable (as shown in Appendix B) should be included.

RESIGNATION

There seems to be no question that, if the settlor has the right to revoke the trust in its entirety and thereby terminate a relationship that may have proved unsatisfactory, the trustee should have the corresponding right to resign and thereby terminate a relationship that may have proved unsatisfactory to it. There is a real question, however, what right of resignation the trustee should have after the death of the settlor.

Those who are opposed to requiring the trustee to go to court to obtain its release from an undesirable trusteeship maintain that ample safeguards against hasty resignation will be established if the trustee is required to obtain the consent to its resignation of all the beneficiaries who are not under legal disability and if the beneficiaries themselves, without the intervention of the court, are authorized to name a successor trustee. In their opinion, an unwilling trustee is less likely to be an efficient or a satisfactory one; for this reason, if for no other, a trustee should ordinarily be permitted to resign at will. But if there is a provision permitting the trustee to resign at will, there should be a corresponding provision permitting the beneficiaries, by majority action, to remove the trustee and name a successor trustee. (A provision appropriate for this purpose is shown in Article V of Appendix B.)

Although this provision gives the beneficiaries who are not under legal disability the right to appoint a successor trustee, it limits them to the appointment of a bank or a trust company having a specified capital and surplus and doing business in a specified trade area. It also gives the beneficiaries the right to acquit and discharge the original trustee. Whether such acquittal and discharge would be binding on the beneficiaries under legal disability is determined by the law of the particular jurisdiction.

SUCCESSOR TRUSTEE

In view of the possibility of changes in the organization of trust institutions—state banks becoming national banks, national banks becoming state banks, mergers, the formation of holding companies, consolidations, and reorganizations—a provision outlining the method of selecting a successor trustee is highly desirable so that the settlor may be assured of continuity of administration.

ACCOUNTING

Another suggested provision fixes the accounting on an annual basis and designates who is to receive a copy of the account. In a state in which the trustee must make an accounting to the court, the settlor may, by an appropriate provision, relieve the trustee of the court accounting unless the terms of the statute provide otherwise.

COMPENSATION

A provision for compensation contemplates that the trustee has published schedules of compensation for normal services, but it also takes into consideration the fact that the trustee may not have published such schedules. In the latter case, the trustee will receive the usual compensation received by trustees at that time for the type of service rendered.

Needless to say, the bases for compensation vary throughout the country; special charges are made for special services, and schedules are changed as cost studies of trust business increase in accuracy. Some trust companies have considered an additional charge based on the growing trend that places greater discretionary decisions in the hands of trustees. Time spent by seasoned, competent administrators, with greater responsibilities, should be paid for.

In all states a trustee is entitled to reasonable compensation even if there is no statutory provision and the instrument is silent on the subject. In the event of disagreement between the trustee and the beneficiaries, the court is the judge of what constitutes reasonable compensation. If there is a co-trustee with the trust institution, the trust instrument should contain a specific provision that the trust institution shall have custody of the books and records and receive compensation for its services as if it were acting alone.

CONSTRUCTION OF THE INSTRUMENT

If the settlor is a resident of one state, the trustee of another, and the beneficiaries of still others, it is desirable to specify the state whose laws shall control in all matters concerning the validity and construction of the trust instrument. That should also be done with respect to the administration of the trust.

Signatures of the Parties

There is nothing distinctive about the closing paragraph of a trust agreement; it is like the conclusion of any other contract. The agreement is executed by the trust institution in the manner required by law for corporations. The signatures of the parties follow in the usual way. Whether the signatures should be acknowledged before a notary public or some other officer authorized to take acknowledgments depends on whether the trust instrument is to be recorded. If it is to be recorded immediately after execution or may need to be recorded at some future date, the execution should be acknowledged; if not, there is no need to take this step. The matter is largely determined by local practice.

Schedules

Attached to the trust instrument and incorporated into it by reference is the schedule containing a list of the securities or other property trusteed, properly identified by the signatures of the settlor and the trustee. There may be other schedules, similarly identified, such as a list of the policies in an insurance trust. These schedules, however, may with equal legal effect be written into the body of the instrument.

Chapter 10

Management of Personal Trusts and Guardianships

The Purposes of This Chapter:

1. To study the steps that must be taken by the trustee for a proper administration of the trust estate
2. To study the differences between business and personal services
3. To study the problems surrounding the distribution of income and principal
4. To distinguish guardianships from other personal trusts
5. To describe the duties, powers, and responsibilities of a guardian as compared with those of a trustee

"In the administration of its personal trust business, a trust institution should strive at all times to render unexceptionable business and financial service, but it should also be careful to render equally good personal service to beneficiaries. The first duty of a trust institution is to carry out the wishes of the creator of a trust as expressed in the instrument. Sympathetic, tactful, personal relationships with immediate beneficiaries are essential to the performance of this duty, keeping in mind also the interests of the ultimate beneficiaries."[1]

The practical steps required of a personal representative in the settlement of estates are described in Chapter 6. The aim of this chapter is to describe the practical steps taken by a trustee in the administration of personal trusts. Whether they are trusts under will, trusts under agreement, insurance trusts, trusts by declaration, or trusts by order of court, the trustee has two kinds of services of equal importance to perform—those of a purely business character and those of a distinctly personal nature. The settlor expects the trustee to exercise good business management and to act as a friend and counselor to the beneficiaries.

---

1. "A Statement of Principles of Trust Institutions (1933)," *Trust Principles and Policies* (Washington, D.C.: American Bankers Association, 1973), p. 3.

The Business Side of Trust Administration

The business side of the administration of personal trusts includes the following activities:

1. Preservation of the trust property
2. Management of the trust property
3. Distribution of the income and the principal
4. Recording of and accounting for each step of administration

PRESERVATION OF TRUST PROPERTY

The trustee is primarily concerned with preserving and safeguarding the trust estate, which may consist of the following classes of property: cash; real property; intangible personal property, such as stocks, bonds, and mortgages; tangible personal property, such as art objects, household furniture, and jewelry; and a going business.

Frequently a considerable amount of *cash* is received in the trust estate, particularly in an insurance trust. During the period, however brief, when the trustee is determining the best form of investment for the cash or, as in a business insurance trust, waiting to distribute the cash, the preservation of the funds must be given special attention. Whether this uninvested cash is to be deposited in the trustee's own banking department or in another banking institution is a question to be decided by the trustee in accordance with the laws of the state in which it operates. If the trustee deposits the cash in another institution, it must do so only after it has made a careful investigation of the bank's solvency. Since the establishment of the Federal Deposit Insurance Corporation, it has been prudent for a trustee to limit the amounts of its deposits in outside banking institutions to the amounts that are insured.

The *real property,* including buildings and other improvements, must be given attention as soon as a trust containing such property is received. Safeguarding the real property may include such activities as having the title searched and the title ownership effectively established and recorded, settling disputes over boundaries, and completing unfinished developments. If the real property is outside the state in which the trust institution is located, the trustee must ascertain whether state laws permit it to hold the property in trust or whether a trustee who is a resident of the state in which the property is situated must be appointed. The trustee must determine whether the property is insured and, if it is, whether the premiums are fully paid. The trustee must take out additional insurance if the property is underinsured and must maintain the insurance. Insurance protection, depending on circumstances, would include not only fire insurance but also liability insurance.

Buildings and other improvements must be kept in repair. Reasonable demands of tenants for alterations should, as a rule, be complied with. In brief, preservation of the real property means that it must be kept in rentable and salable condition as long as possible.

The property that is often of the greatest concern to the trustee in its efforts to preserve the trust estate is *intangible personal property,* which consists of the stocks and bonds transferred to the trustee by the executor, by the court, or by the creator of the trust when the trust is created. Unless prompt and skillful attention is given to these original investments at the outset, the trust estate may suffer serious losses.

The trustee must, of course, look into the trust instrument and the statutes to ascertain its powers with respect to original investments. Whether the trustee's powers are broad or limited—and even if no course of action regarding the original investments is specifically pre-scribed in either the trust instrument or the statutes—the trustee, in deciding which securities (if any) shall be sold, must exercise the judg-ment of an ordinarily prudent man in handling similar property under the same circumstances. If the decision is to sell the securities or some of them, the trustee must decide whether to sell them at once or to hold them for a reasonable time to obtain a better price, even though by doing so it runs the risk of being forced to sell in a lower market.

The subject of trust investments is considered more fully in Chapters 17 and 18. It is sufficient here to point out that the trustee's action in holding or selling original investments and its continuous management of the trust investments during the life of the trust are important to the preservation of the trust estate and involve burdensome and inescapable duties and responsibilities.

On rare occasions valuable *tangible personal property*—such as tapes-tries, jewelry, furniture, and miscellaneous art objects—is received by a trust institution as trustee. The trustee may be charged with the duty of safeguarding and preserving such property until it is sold or otherwise disposed of. Seldom would it be the normal function of a trustee merely to preserve tangible property for an indefinite time. If preservation alone were required and the property were not perishable or subject to depreciation from natural causes, the services of a trustee would not be required. It is chiefly when preservation requires activity that a trustee is needed.

A trustee is sometimes charged with the duty of preserving a *going business* in its existing condition. That occurs, for example, when the maker of the trust desires to protect a business pending the attainment of majority by a minor beneficiary. In such a case, although the trustee is not expected to make major policy changes concerning the long-range improvement of the business, it must at least endeavor to preserve the credit, goodwill, and physical property of the enterprise. To that end, accounts receivable must be collected and accounts payable satisifed;

appropriate arrangements must be worked out with banks and creditors; commitments to manufacturers, wholesale houses, and customers must be fulfilled; raw materials (for a factory) and stocks of goods (for a store) must be periodically replenished. In brief, the trustee must give such attention to the business as would any prudent man under the same circumstances.

In many states the operation of a going business by a trustee involves special problems and risks for the trustee, since the proper course may be to dispose of the business and invest the proceeds in proper trust investments. The trustee, therefore, should be sure that clear authority to carry on a going business is conferred by statute, by court order, or by the terms of the trust instrument.

Temporary Investment of Trust Funds

When a trustee comes into possession of the trust assets, it is not always immediately possible for it to invest all the assets in more permanent investments. So long as the funds are not invested for an undue length of time, the trustee can consider its own savings department. Furthermore, the trustee may want to consider short-term certificates of deposits or other short-term obligations of its own institution. An investment in the obligations of its bank for a period longer than a year could raise the question of self-dealing. Thus short-term investments should be considered carefully to avoid even the appearance of a conflict of interest.

MANAGEMENT OF TRUST PROPERTY

Following the steps taken by the trustee to preserve the trust estate are those to be taken in managing it. These include management of real property and intangible personal property, providing for payment of taxes, and other management activities. If the powers of the trustee with regard to real property are limited or are not expressly stated in the trust instrument or the statutes, there is not much the trustee can do in managing the real property except lease it to the best possible advantage. But if the creator of the trust intended that the trustee manage the real property so as to make it as profitable as possible and if the trust instrument gives definite authority for such management, the activities of the trustee may be many and varied. In developing and improving the real property, the trustee may exchange all of it (or part of it) for other property; subdivide large tracts of land into smaller plots and sell the individual plots; tear down or modernize old, unprofitable buildings; and supervise the construction of new buildings.

Instead of managing the real property, the trustee may decide, in the best interests of the trust, to sell it. The procedure will then depend on the powers granted in the trust instrument. According to its authority, the trustee may sell the property at private or public sale; grant options to buy the property to prospective purchasers; sell the property for cash or for credit secured by a mortgage or a deed of trust; or grant leases that include purchase options and covenants providing for the erection of buildings by the lessees.

In perhaps the majority of personal trusts, the management of stocks, bonds, notes, and other intangible personal property occupies most of the time and attention of the trustee. Management of such intangible property includes analysis and review of investments, both those received with the trust and those acquired later by the trustee; investment of cash received with the trust; and investment of funds arising from the sale of securities or other trust property, from called bonds, or from matured bonds, notes, or mortgages.

It may be necessary for the trustee, either in person or by proxy, to vote the stocks in which trust funds are invested. The trustee may be required to pay assessments, calls, and other charges on account of stocks, bonds, debentures, and other corporate securities held in the trust; to sell or to exercise stock or subscription rights; to participate in foreclosures, reorganizations, consolidations, mergers, liquidations, pooling agreements, and voting trusts; to assent to corporate sales, leases, and encumbrances; or to deposit stocks, bonds, or other securities with protective or similar committees. (Chapter 17 indicates the extent to which a trustee may be required to go and the many and varied steps it may be obliged to take in efficiently managing the intangible property in the trust estate.)

The trustee must also give close attention to tax matters. It must ascertain the various taxes for which the trust estate is liable, the amounts and the dates of such taxes, and the discounts allowed for early payment. It must obtain and set aside ready cash to pay the taxes when due, and it must take advantage of all possible discounts and avoid interest charges and penalties; otherwise it may be liable for any losses suffered by the trust estate.

There are many other management activities that the trustee may perform in the best interests of the trust. For example, the trustee may deem it necessary to set up reserves out of the trust income to provide for amortization of such trust assets as unrecoverable premiums on bonds purchased or obsolescence of income-producing real estate. The trustee may have to borrow money to fulfill the requirements of the beneficiaries or of the trust and, as security for the loan, to mortgage or otherwise encumber or pledge trust property, future income, or principal. The trustee itself may be called on to advance money needed for the protection of the trust estate. The extent to which the trustee may safely go in such matters depends on the powers granted by the trust instrument and by the law.

DISTRIBUTION OF INCOME AND PRINCIPAL

The third main activity of the trustee in the administration of a trust is that of distributing the trust property. The phrase "distribution of the trust property" is used here to cover more than payment of the principal to the beneficiaries at the termination of the trust; it includes payment of income to, or application of income for the benefit of, the beneficiaries during the life of the trust and determining which among certain extraordinary receipts to allocate to income and which to principal.

The income of the trust estate is usually received at irregular intervals, in varying amounts, and from various sources. The trustee may be required to pay the income to the beneficiaries as it is received. In some cases, however, the trustee equalizes the income; that is, it makes payments to the beneficiaries not as the income is received but in equal stated amounts and at such periods as may best meet the needs of the beneficiaries, any necessary adjustments being made at the end of the year. Unless the amount and the time of payments have been definitely and unalterably fixed in the trust instrument, the trustee uses its discretion with regard to these matters, holding itself ready to assist the beneficiaries in any emergencies that may arise. Frequently the trustee is authorized to pay the income monthly or quarterly or as often as the needs of the beneficiaries, in the trustee's judgment, require; in that case the trustee may equalize the income.

Payments for the benefit of minors who will soon reach their majority or of abnormal beneficiaries who have not been formally declared incompetent frequently present a serious problem. Considerable pressure is often brought to bear on the trustee by such beneficiaries to have the payments made directly to them.

The court in most states allows reasonable spending money to be paid directly to a minor approaching his or her majority. In some states trust instruments sometimes provide that minor beneficiaries may receive their payments directly, at the discretion of the trustee; otherwise the trustee must make the payments to the guardian of the minor or apply the payments for the beneficiary, paying school bills, board bills, and other personal expenses, even though the minor is fully capable of managing the money himself. Moreover, even if it is authorized to make payments directly, the trustee should not rely on such a provision as furnishing complete immunity in the absence of a supporting legal opinion based on local law.

The case of an abnormal beneficiary who has not been declared incompetent by the court is somewhat different. Although there is no general rule to hold the trustee negligent for making payments directly to such a beneficiary, no trustee worthy of its office would make payments if it is aware that the money might be wasted or lost. To do so would be to commit a moral, if not a legal, breach of duty.

In deciding how to apportion a receipt or an expense between principal and income or whether to allocate it to principal or to income, the trustee encounters some of the most difficult problems it has to face in the administration of personal trusts. To apportion an item of receipt or expense means to divide it on some basis, not necessarily equally, between principal and income and to charge or credit the item partly to principal and partly to income. To allocate an item of receipt or expense means to charge or credit the item wholly to principal or wholly to income.

The law varies so widely in the different states that no rule on any given point relating to apportionment or allocation is universally applicable. Where the Uniform or the Revised Principal and Income Act has been adopted, the subject is covered, but this act, although it is called uniform, is not the same in all the states that have adopted it. It is therefore necessary to ascertain from the statutes and the judicial decisions of each state the local rules on apportionment and allocation.

Among the types of receipts often encountered, including those that may be especially difficult for the trustee to apportion or allocate, are the following:

1. Ordinary cash dividends (at a time when there is a change of income beneficiaries)
2. Accumulated dividends on preferred stocks
3. Extraordinary dividends, including those paid in cash, those paid in shares of the corporation itself, and those paid in shares, other securities, or obligations of another corporation
4. Liquidating dividends
5. Rights to subscribe
6. Receipts from property subject to depletion, including mineral, oil, and gas royalties
7. Proceeds realized from delayed conversion of unproductive property
8. Capital gain distributions of investment companies.

Questions as to the apportionment or allocation of such receipts may arise under state law. (In the case of real property, the law of the state in which the property is located may be the law that controls.) Such questions may also arise under the terms of individual trust instruments.

A problem that arises with respect to bonds purchased at a price greater than their face value (frequently referred to as bonds purchased at a premium) is whether all the interest received on the bonds shall be treated as income. That is a controversial subject, with definite variations in practice from state to state. A similar problem with respect to bonds purchased at a price less than their face value (frequently referred to as bonds purchased at a discount) is whether only the actual interest received shall be treated as income or whether the income beneficiary is also entitled to benefit from the appreciation that takes place when the full face amount of the bond is collected at maturity. On this question there is more uniformity; the prevailing opinion is that in the case of bonds that pay interest currently (as distinguished from bonds like U.S. savings bonds on which there are fixed maturity and redemption values that include interest), no part of the proceeds at maturity is allocable to income.

The types of expenses that must frequently be apportioned or allocated include the following:

1. Regularly recurring taxes
2. Water rents
3. Premiums on insurance
4. Interest on mortgages on trust property
5. Ordinary repairs
6. Trustee's compensation
7. Attorneys' fees and other costs incurred in maintaining or defending legal actions
8. Costs of or assessments for improvements to property forming part of the principal

Although the rules for the apportionment or allocation of expenses are fairly uniform in the different states, a trustee often encounters practical difficulties. It may, for example, have trouble determining whether a given expense is for an ordinary repair or is, as a whole or in part, for a permanent addition to or improvement of the trust property.

Besides learning the local rules as to apportionment and allocation, those who seek a better understanding of the administration of personal trusts will generally find it advantageous to learn the theory behind the rules known as the Massachusetts rule, the Pennsylvania rule, and the Kentucky rule and, when these rules are in conflict, to know which rule was adopted in the Uniform or the Revised Principal and Income Act and which applies in his own state.[2]

Regardless of the rules as to apportionment and allocation found in the statutes and in the judicial decisions of the state, the creator of a trust, by express provisions in the trust instrument, may establish different rules or confer on the trustee discretionary power to apportion or to allocate receipts or expenditures or both.

Exercising Discretion

It is customary to vest a trustee, especially an experienced corporate trustee, with the power to determine the allocation of income and

---

2. These subjects are dealt with at length in textbooks on the law of trusts and in looseleaf services such as those published by Prentice-Hall and by Commerce Clearing House. The statutes in force in the various states also appear in these looseleaf services.

principal to the beneficiaries. There is no complete road map to guide the trust officer in making such decisions. The creator will generally think of the trust as a "family trust." His desire will be to put the trustee in a position to deal with the family much as he would have done had he survived.

In determining whether all the income shall be paid to the surviving parent for himself and the children, the trust officer needs to have full knowledge of the personal characteristics and the financial affairs of all members of the family. Ordinarily all income is paid to the surviving parent, who uses it as his or her own judgment dictates as between himself and the children and as among the children. That is the ideal arrangement. However, if there are undesirable tax consequences or the surviving spouse is not a responsible parent, the trustee may have to pay the income directly to, or apply it for the benefit of, the beneficiaries other than the parent.

ACCOUNTS AND RECORDS OF ADMINISTRATION

Simultaneously with its work of preserving, managing, and distributing the trust property, the trustee must keep complete and accurate accounts and records of every step taken in its administration and of all facts essential to a complete understanding of the trust. It may be required to have its records and accounts audited by certified public accountants if requested by the beneficiaries or ordered by the court. It must render statements to beneficiaries. In the case of court trusts, it must render such reports and accountings to the court as are required by the order of the court or by the law of the jurisdiction. It must make all required tax reports and returns on behalf of the trust.

Trusts often run for many years, and the ultimate beneficiaries have as much right as the immediate beneficiaries to inspect the trustee's accounts at any reasonable time and for any period between the beginning of the trust and its termination. The trustee's accounts and records, therefore, must be permanent and durable and so clear and complete that they will serve to justify, in or out of court, every decision and action of the trustee over a period of years.

Sooner or later a trust institution will receive in trust almost every kind of property that exists in its community, and since personal trusts may and frequently do continue for a generation or more, it is apparent that administration by a trustee is fully as extensive and varied as administration by the owner of similar kinds of property. In practice, a trustee does everything an owner does in administering his own property, except that the trustee must never use the trust property for its own benefit. That is the fundamental difference between the owner and the trustee.

147

Termination and Distribution

A trustee has the duty to keep and render accounts during the administration of the trust. In addition to rendering accounts to the beneficiaries, a trustee under will must usually account to the probate court. In some states, unless relieved by the terms of the instrument, a trustee under a living trust or insurance trust is required to account to the court as well as to the beneficiary.

At the termination of the trust, the trustee must file its final account, containing a schedule of receipts, disbursements, and distributions. In some instances, in lieu of having its account examined and settled, the trustee can negotiate a nonjudicial release of liability with the interested parties. Although the agreement to approve the account and release the trustee would not be binding on the court, it would, in the absence of fraud, be binding on the parties who are legally competent to enter a contract.

Usually the instrument provides that the trustee can make distributions in cash or in kind in valuations determined to be fair by the executor or trustee. In the absence of fraud or bad faith, the decision of the trustee will be conclusive.

With the enactment of the 1976 Tax Reform Act, the trustee has additional responsibilities with respect to generation-skipping transfers. Trusts established after a certain date and other trusts under certain circumstances that provide for generation-skipping transfers are subject to tax, with certain exceptions, at the time the interest is transferred to a younger generation. When the transfer is in the nature of a "taxable termination," the trustee is liable for the tax and should be very careful to make provisions for its payment.

The Personal Side of Trust Administration

Often the personal problems of the beneficiaries occupy as much of the trust officer's time and attention as business aspects of the trust. In fact, the business side of trust administration often cannot be adequately performed unless full justice is done to the personal factors. The personal side of trust administration includes maintenance of an active personal acquaintance with the beneficiaries, as far as possible; performance of active personal services for beneficiaries; and performance of advisory services for beneficiaries, on request, in connection with their individual problems—which are sometimes financial and sometimes intimately personal.

ROLE OF THE TRUST OFFICER

In this discussion of the personal side of trust administration, the trust officer is referred to more frequently than the trust institution or the

148

trust department because of his or her importance in the personal aspects of trust administration. The representative of the trust department who deals directly with the beneficiary in the administration of the trust is the embodiment of the trustee. To the beneficiary that representative *is* the trust institution.

The tendency to identify the trust officer with his institution has two consequences. First, it helps make the administration of personal trusts by a trust institution as personal as trust service rendered by an individual. Second, personal qualities such as sympathy, patience, tact, and human understanding are given due emphasis by trust institutions in the selection of trust officers.

It stands to reason, however, that only in the smaller trust departments can the executive or administrative head handle all personal dealings with beneficiaries. As the trust department grows, the personal trust officer will call on other officers, such as the tax officer, investment officer, and real estate officer, for support as he or she makes important decisions relating to the management of the trust estate.

Relations with beneficiaries constitute perhaps the most fascinating and perhaps the most difficult of the trust officer's activities. To be successful, he must be able to communicate with the beneficiaries, i.e., he must be able to use plain English in talking with and writing to customers, beneficiaries, and fellow employees. In conversing with customers and beneficiaries, he should be careful to use nontechnical and nonprofessional terminology. The trust officer who can combine these attributes with patience and with empathy for his customers and beneficiaries will probably find his relations with them his greatest joy and ultimate satisfaction.

PERSONAL ACQUAINTANCE WITH BENEFICIARIES

An active personal acquaintance with the beneficiaries of a trust is particularly advantageous in connection with equalizing income payments and making decisions about advances from principal. Lacking close personal contact with a beneficiary and familiarity with his life, habits, tastes, associates, and prospects, the trustee may be at a disadvantage in performing its duty to pay the income to the beneficiary at certain intervals. A provision that is frequently expressed in trust instruments is the direction to disburse funds "monthly or quarterly or as often as in the judgment of the trustee his needs shall require, but at least once a year."

If it is not acquainted with the beneficiaries, the trustee may experience difficulty in acquiring the necessary information on which to base its decisions concerning such questions as these: Shall the amounts and kinds of income payments originally agreed upon be changed to meet new conditions? Is the income more than the beneficiary actually needs, so that the surplus should be withheld and invested (if such accumulation of income is authorized by the trust instrument and not forbidden by the law of the state)? Is the income inadequate? Should it be supplemented by payments from principal when, as some trust instruments provide, such use of principal is authorized if the income is not sufficient to support the beneficiaries comfortably and to educate the children according to the standards to which they have been accustomed? The trustee must have a thorough knowledge of the ability and habits of a son or a daughter if it is to judge whether a portion of the principal shall be used to provide additional capital for that son or daughter, since the trust instrument sometimes provides that the trustee may do so at its discretion.

Sometimes moral courage, as well as a thorough knowledge of the ability and habits of a beneficiary, is required of the trustee. An example would be when, under a spendthrift or a protective provision, the trustee is called on to decide whether to withhold income or principal from an improvident beneficiary and apply it to the use of another designated person, as the trustee is authorized to do if, in its opinion, the facts of the case justify such a drastic course of action.

PERFORMANCE OF PERSONAL SERVICES

Next in importance to maintaining an active acquaintance with the beneficiaries is rendering personal services to them. The trustee must frequently stand *in loco parentis;* that is, it must, as far as possible, do for a minor beneficiary exactly what a parent would do for that child if the parent were living. In some cases the trustee must find a suitable home for a child and must see that not only his physical welfare but also his mental and spiritual welfare is properly cared for. Sometimes the trustee must select a suitable school and arrange for vacations, taking into consideration the child's tastes, aptitudes, and financial resources. If the trustee has reason to suspect that the child is not getting the full benefit of the payments made to the person in charge of the child, the trustee must observe the situation closely and see that the child's interests are fully protected. When no competent members of the family are available, the trustee must arrange for medical or surgical treatment and for hospital or other institutional care needed by the beneficiary. Upon completion of the beneficiary's education, the trustee must often help him get started in a business or profession.

PERSONAL ADVISORY SERVICES

In addition to the active personal services rendered to beneficiaries, trustees are constantly called upon for advice in connection with personal problems. These include not only financial but also family or personal problems.

Upon the death of a parent, a family frequently finds its income sharply reduced and does not know how to meet its living expenses. The advice of the trust officer is sought in planning a new personal and household budget so that the family may live within its income. Whether trips may be taken, a summer house kept up, or a new automobile, new furniture, or furnishings purchased are matters in which the family often consults the trust officer who, in view of his detailed knowledge of the family's financial resources, may be the only person competent to give the needed advice.

One of the most difficult problems confronting the trust officer with regard to the living expenses of the beneficiaries of different trusts is that of determining their varying requirements on the basis of their respective standards of living. For instance, the normal and reasonable requirements of the members of a family accustomed to an income of $50,000 a year are different from those of a family used to an income of $10,000. Expenditures that would be reasonable in the former case might be extravagant in the latter. The natural inclination of the trust officer is to apply his own standard of living to the requirements of the beneficiaries, but that may be entirely unfair to the beneficiaries. The understanding trust officer must shift his point of view for each set of beneficiaries and apply a flexible standard.

In many cases the trust officer must help revise educational plans that have been made for the children. Expensive schools and college courses that may have been planned while the parent was alive may be entirely out of the question. The family must be encouraged to make plans that will permit education of the children within the family's means.

In helping a minor beneficiary choose a vocation, the trust officer must do his best to take the place of the parent. Often his advice is sought about the choice of a vocation, the location of an office or a business, or how to make the proper business connections.

A widow with a separate estate or any ambitious and mature beneficiary who wishes to conserve or build up an estate often seeks the advice of the trust officer about the best way of accomplishing this objective. Among the problems placed before the trust officer are the following: Should the surplus money be put in a savings account or invested? What investments should be made? Should life insurance be taken out and, if so, how much and of what kind?

Trust officers do not habitually or voluntarily offer service or advice on matters completely unrelated to the trust account. Yet, as these illustrations amply demonstrate, matters connected with the trust account—particularly with the terms of the trust as to the distribution of income and principal—lead trust officers sooner or later and in one way or another into practically every phase of personal service and advice.

151

Guardianships

"The administration of a guardianship when compared to the administration of a properly planned trust is cumbersome, inflexible and expensive. In almost every jurisdiction, the guardian is limited in the investments of the property and severely limited in the use of such property for the benefit of the ward."[3]

PERSONS REQUIRING GUARDIANS

For the purpose of this discussion, persons requiring guardians are grouped into three general classes: infants; insane or otherwise mentally incompetent persons; and persons legally declared incapable or incapacitated.

In this section the term "guardian" is used to designate all guardians, regardless of the term—committee, conservator, trustee, or curator—in use in any particular state. The term "ward," as used here, applies alike to infants or minors, to insane or otherwise mentally incompetent persons, and to others legally declared incapable of taking care of themselves or managing their property. The term "incompetent" covers all kinds of wards except infants.

Recognizing that there is sometimes a stigma attached to guardianships for insane or mentally deficient persons that should not attach to guardianships for persons whose incapacity is due to old age or infirmity or service in the armed forces, the statutes in a number of states designate the special type of guardianship provided for such incapacitated persons by a different term from that used when the guardianship is for an insane person. "Conservator" is one such term. This is done in an effort to overcome a natural reluctance on the part of the family of an incapacitated person who is not insane to seek through the court the protection of such statutes.

A guardian of the property is one who has been lawfully invested with the power of caring for and managing the property of an infant or incompetent. A guardian of the person is one who has been lawfully invested with the power of caring for the person of an infant. In most states an insane or other incompetent person who is not also an infant does not have a separate guardian of the person.

Guardianship of the property and guardianship of the person are classified here as two kinds of guardianships because in some states the guardianship of an infant or of an incompetent may be divided, one person being appointed guardian of the property and another guardian of the person. Although the two offices are separable in those states, one person may nevertheless be appointed to both.

---

3. Norman A. Wiggins, *Wills and Administration of Estates*, (Atlanta: Harrison Co., 1964), p. 928.

In nearly all states a trust institution, either by charter or by statute, may be appointed guardian of the property. In some states a trust institution cannot serve as guardian of the person, and in no state where the two offices are separable would a trust institution seek appointment as guardian of the person except under extraordinary conditions.

Although the general rule is that there is to be a guardian of the property of every minor and incompetent person, it is common knowledge that many minors reach their majority and many incompetents live out their lives without ever having had a guardian.

The guardian appointed is often a member or friend of the family who has had no practical experience in the management of property or the administration of a guardianship. Incompetent mismanagement by an inexperienced guardian frequently results in the loss of some or all of the property. Rather than embarrass the guardian, the ward loses his property in silence.

It is because of unfortunate experiences with inexperienced and incompetent guardians that there is a growing tendency for the courts to appoint corporate fiduciaries to serve as guardians. Courts have found that banks and trust companies are experienced and will follow the law in carrying out their duties of administration.

DUTIES

A guardianship is not a trust, although it contains many elements of a trust. The main distinction between a guardianship and a trust is that a guardian, unlike a trustee, does not, except in a few states, have title to the ward's property. The ward normally has the legal title to the property as well as the beneficial interest in it, and the guardian has only certain powers and duties with respect to the property for the benefit of the ward. The beneficiary of a trust has an equitable interest in the trust property but does not have legal title to it. The relation between a guardian and a ward is fully as confidential and fiduciary as the relation between a trustee and a beneficiary; but a guardian, although he can correctly be described as a fiduciary, is not technically a trustee.

Many duties of a guardian are the same as those of a personal representative, and most are the same as those of an active trustee. The duties of a guardian are:

1. To assemble the property of the ward
2. To conserve the property
3. To manage the property
4. To use the property for the benefit of the ward
5. To make proper accounting of the administration
6. To deliver the property to the ward (or to his or her personal representative if he or she is deceased) at the termination of the guardianship

The distinctive duty of a guardian is the duty to use the property for the benefit of the ward—that is, for the maintenance and education of a ward who is an infant or for the maintenance of a ward who is an incompetent (and sometimes of the ward's dependents).

To Assemble the Property

As soon as possible after it has qualified, the guardian collects, assembles, takes over, and assumes charge of the ward's property of every kind located within the jurisdiction of the court making the appointment. Assembling the property of an infant is easier for a guardian than assembling the property of a decedent is for a personal representative, since the property of an infant has in most cases already been assembled by the executor, administrator, or trustee from whom the guardian takes it over.

The property of an incompetent, on the other hand, may be as miscellaneous, widely scattered, involved, or encumbered as that of a decedent. The guardian may experience great difficulty in untangling the situations created by irrational acts of the incompetent that took place before his incompetency was legally declared.

Assembling the property of an infant or incompetent also includes making an inventory and an appraisal of the property and filing them with the court. The inventory and the appraisal form the basis of the guardian's accountability and responsibility.

To Conserve the Property

There is no fundamental difference between the conservation of the property of a ward by a guardian and the conservation of the property of a beneficiary by a trustee. In special cases, however, the relationship between a guardian and a ward imposes on the guardian additional duties with respect to the conservation of the ward's property—duties less frequently required of a trustee. The guardian of an infant, for example, is often charged with the duty of conserving and keeping intact tangible personal property (furniture, portraits, jewelry, books, antiques, and heirlooms of all sorts) and delivering it to the infant when he attains his majority. The guardian of an incompetent—if there is a probability that his competency may be restored and that the guardianship may therefore be temporary—may feel an even greater obligation than usual to keep the property in its original state, as far as possible, so that it may be returned to the ward when his competency is restored.

To Manage the Property

Guardianship also parallels trusteeship with respect to the management of the ward's property. A guardian is appointed not only to care for, safeguard, and conserve the property but also to manage it in such a

154

way as to make it reasonably productive and profitable. Consequently the guardian's management of property involves every function involved in property management by an owner or a trustee.

To Use the Property for the Benefit of the Ward

Assembling, conserving, and managing property are means to an end—the welfare of the ward. In the case of an infant, this duty means applying the income from the property to his maintenance and education. In some states a guardian may apply the income without an order of court; in others it may not. Principal, however, may not be used without a court order.

Although the law does not impose on the guardian of the property the supervision of the guardian of the person, it does require the guardian of the property to be diligent and conscientious in the use of the property for the infant's benefit. If, for instance, the guardian of the property has reason to believe that the guardian of the person, even though he is the child's parent, is using the income for his own benefit rather than the benefit of the ward and is neglecting the ward, the guardian of the property would not be justified in continuing to make payments to the guardian of the person. Its duty would be to call the situation to the attention of the court or, on its own initiative, to make a better arrangement. If the parent is financially able to support and educate his child adequately without using the child's property, he has an obligation to do so in most states. It then becomes the duty of the guardian of the property to conserve the property by reinvesting the income.

The guardian of an incompetent has the duty of seeing to the maintenance of the incompetent; sometimes this duty extends to the maintenance of his dependents as well. Maintenance of an incompetent often means providing for hospital or other institutional services. If there is a chance that the incompetent may recover, the guardian must be vigilant in taking steps to promote his recovery. If there is no chance of recovery, the guardian must be equally diligent in arranging for the incompetent's comfort.

Allowances for the incompetent's dependents would need court approval, of course; but some states, on court approval, will direct that surplus income be paid to the incompetent's dependents or will allow gifts to be made from the incompetent's property, depending on what he would probably do in similar circumstances if he were competent.

Another general rule is that the guardian must make the payment of income *for* the ward and not *to* him, although this rule is not to be followed to an extreme that is not in the best interests of the ward. For example, if a minor ward is in school or college, the guardian must pay all bills for tuition and other regular school expenses, but it may also pay directly to the ward a reasonable amount of spending money. On such practical matters as these, the court takes a commonsense view and expects the guardian to do likewise.

To Make Proper Accounting

A guardian must make two kinds of accounting. One is the periodic accounting to the court alone; the other is its final accounting both to the court and to the ward. The former, usually called "annual" even though in some states it is made less frequently, is made directly to the court and is intended solely to keep the court informed about the administration of the guardianship. The object of such periodic or intermediate accountings is not so much to adjudicate the respective rights and liabilities of the guardian and the ward as to compel the guardian to furnish evidence to the court and to the public respecting the condition of the estate, its liabilities and resources, the propriety of orders with regard to investment of the ward's funds, the sufficiency of the bond, the necessity of selling personal or real property, and other valuable information concerning the safety of the ward's estate.

The final accounting to the court and to the ward is more formal and conclusive than the intermediate accountings to the court. In some states it involves a formal hearing at which the ward is present or represented. Errors made in the periodic accountings may be corrected in the final accounting. On the basis of the final accounting, the guardian settles with the ward, with the successor guardian if there is to be a change of guardians, or with the personal representative of the estate if the ward is deceased.

To Deliver the Property

When an infant ward attains his majority, he is entitled to receive his property. Similarly, when an incompetent ward recovers his competency and has been formally discharged by the court, he is entitled to receive his property and to resume management of it. If the incompetent dies without recovering his mental faculties, the guardian must deliver his property to the ward's personal representative. If the ward made a will after he attained his majority and while he was still competent, that will may still be good; in that case the guardian settles with the executor or the administrator with the will annexed. If, as is more often the case, an incompetent ward was never competent to make a will, the guardian must settle with the ward's administrator. The points to be noted are that guardianship and executorship (or administratorship) are different functions, that the estate of an infant or an incompetent must be settled in the usual way, and that the guardian does not become the administrator unless appointed to that office by the court.

156

POWERS

General Powers

Because of the nature of the relationship, a guardian has the power to take all necessary or appropriate steps to obtain possession of and to manage the ward's property, both real and personal. The general rule is that a guardian has the power to sell the ward's personal property without an order of court. The sale must, of course, be for the ward's benefit, and the guardian must use the care and skill of an ordinarily prudent man in making it. A guardian does not usually have the power to sell the ward's real property without an order of court. As a rule, the real property may not be leased for a term that extends beyond the duration of the guardianship. If it is so leased, however, the lease is not void; it is only voidable, at the election of the ward, as to the period beyond the term of the guardianship. The guardian has the power to make necessary repairs to the ward's property but not to make substantial improvements without an order of court. A guardian also has the power to sue or defend on behalf of the ward, to compromise or settle claims, and to submit claims to arbitration.

Powers with Regard to Investments

There may be a considerable difference between the investment powers of a guardian and those of a trustee. For example, in a state that has a mandatory list of investments for fiduciaries, investments made by a guardian must be confined to those on the mandatory list, whereas a trustee may receive special investment powers, either limited or broad, under the trust instrument. Some states make a distinction between legal investments for a guardian and legal investments for a trustee. Whereas in some states the prudent man standard may apply to the investments of both guardians and trustees (those of a guardian being subject to court approval), other states maintain legal lists to which a guardian's investments must be confined. Furthermore, in some states a guardian cannot make any investments without the approval of the court; however, a conservator may request and be given investment powers by the court.

With respect to the retention of original investments, there may be a difference between the power of the guardian of a minor and the power of the guardian of an incompetent. Normally the guardian of a minor is required to dispose of nonlegal investments within a reasonable time and to invest the proceeds in legal investments. The guardian of an incompetent, however, may have more latitude in retaining the original investments out of consideration for the incompetent, who may regain his legal competency and desire their return.

157

Powers with Regard to Out-of-State Property

An infant or an incompetent, like an adult or a competent person, may own property in several states. The guardian appointed by the court of the state in which the ward resides is regarded as the principal guardian, and the guardian appointed in another state is sometimes spoken of as the ancillary guardian. The ancillary guardian is charged with the care and management of the property located in the state in which it was appointed, and it must account to the principal guardian.

The question naturally arises: What authority has the principal guardian to take possession and assume control of the ward's property located in another state? The general rule is that an out-of-state guardian has no such authority until it has met the requirements of the state in which the property is located. Almost every state makes provision for out-of-state guardians. The usual procedure is for the out-of-state guardian to file a certified copy of its appointment in the state in which it wishes to take control of the ward's property, whereupon the local court will give it the right to exercise certain powers. The point to be noted is that a guardian appointed in one state has no authority to exercise the powers of a guardian in another state without first meeting the requirements of that state with regard to out-of-state guardians.

RESPONSIBILITIES

There is no need to dwell at length on the responsibilities of a trust institution as guardian. However, its responsibility with respect to contracts and the standard of care and skill required of a guardian should be mentioned.

Responsibility with Respect to Contracts

In executing a contract on behalf of its ward, the guardian may expressly exempt itself from personal liability to the other contracting party; otherwise it is personally liable. This does not mean that the guardian is necessarily out of pocket on all contracts it makes in connection with the guardianship. If the contract is a proper one, the guardian may reimburse itself from the ward's property. If the contract is shown before the courts to be an improper one, the guardian will have to suffer the loss.

This exacting responsibility is both logical and reasonable, since the ward cannot speak for himself. The guardian should know whether a contract is proper and in the best interests of the ward. As a matter of justice, the guardian should not be permitted, by signing a contract in its name as guardian, to impose on the ward's property an improper charge and, by contracting in a representative capacity, to relieve itself of liability for maladministration of its ward's property.

Standard of Care and Skill Required

Infants and incompetents are the objects of the solicitous care of the courts. The standard of care and skill required of a guardian in the management of its ward's estate is in all cases as high as the standard required of a trustee in the management of a beneficiary's estate and in some cases even higher. For instance, the creator of a trust may modify the requirements imposed on the trustee; but except in rare instances (which occur only in connection with testamentary guardianships), the guardian must live up to the exacting requirements of the general law governing guardianships. Since the court alone holds the guardian to strict accountability for the proper management of the property of the immature and the incompetent, such persons are frequently referred to as "wards of the court."

TERMINATION OF A GUARDIANSHIP

When the final accounting of the guardian has been formally approved by the court and the guardian has made delivery of the property to and taken receipts from the ward, from the successor guardian if there has been a change of guardians, or from the personal representative if the ward is deceased, the guardianship is terminated. Any surety on the guardian's bond is released.

Chapter 11

Personal Agencies

The Purposes of This Chapter:

1. To show the fundamental distinctions between a trust and a personal agency
2. To describe the personal agency services of a fiduciary nature that it is proper for a trust institution to render
3. To discuss the place of managing agencies in trust business

"An agent, as we know, in the broadest sense of the term, is anyone who acts for another by authority of the person for whom he acts. In this broad sense the kinds of agencies are absolutely numberless. All day long almost every day most of us as members of society are acting as agents for other persons. . . .

"Likewise, trust institutions are acting as agents for individuals, for corporations, for institutions, and even for units of government in many ways."[1]

There are three main groups of services to individuals: the settlement of estates, the administration of trusts, and the administration of agencies. The first two have been discussed in previous chapters. This chapter focuses on the kind of agencies commonly performed by trust institutions for individuals.

Creation of a Personal Agency

An agency is created when one person, called the principal, authorizes another person, called the agent, to act on behalf of and subject to the control of the principal. Since an agency arises from a contractual arrangement, it may be created by either an oral or a written agreement.

In accepting an agency, a trust institution usually requires a letter of instructions, an agency agreement, or a letter of attorney. Inasmuch as

---

1. Gilbert T. Stephenson, *Reflections of A Trustman* (New York: American Bankers Association, 1960), p.26.

an agency can be terminated at the will of either the principal or the agent, the agency agreement is sometimes less formal than a trust instrument. (Appendix C includes typical provisions of personal agency relationships that are common in banks.)

Distinctions Between A Trust and An Agency

There are five recognized distinctions between an agency and a trust.

1. An agent does not have title to the property of the principal, although he may have certain powers with respect to it. A trustee has title to the trust property.
2. An agent undertakes to act on behalf of and subject to the control of the principal. A trustee as such is not subject to the control of the beneficiary, except to the extent that he is required to deal with the trust property for the benefit of the beneficiary in accordance with the terms of the trust and can be compelled by the beneficiary to perform that duty.
3. An agent may subject his principal to personal liabilities to third persons. A trustee cannot subject the beneficiary to such liabilities.
4. An agency is created by the mutual consent of the principal and the agent. A trust may be created without the knowledge or consent of the beneficiary.
5. An agency can be terminated at the will of either the principal or the agent and is terminated by the death of either. A trust ordinarily cannot be terminated at the will of either the beneficiary or the trustee and need not be terminated by the death of either.

The two fundamental distinctions between a trust and an agency are commonly stated as follows: first, in a trust the title to the trust property passes to the trustee, whereas in an agency the title to the principal's property remains in the principal; and second, an agency must terminate on the death of either the principal or the agent, whereas a trust need not terminate on the death of the trustee or the beneficiary.

Kinds of Personal Agencies

Much confusion exists with regard to the terms used to designate the personal agencies performed by trust institutions. The terms "custodian," "agent," and "attorney in fact" are frequently employed interchangeably to designate the institution when it is acting in a single capacity. Very few trust institutions would define these terms in precisely the same way. This chapter attempts to employ a terminology that is to some extent descriptive of the services rendered. The principal kinds of agencies performed by a trust institution for individuals

162

are those in which the trust institution acts as safekeeping agent, custodian, managing agent, attorney in fact, and escrow agent.

SAFEKEEPING AGENCIES

The safekeeping of securities and other valuables is the simplest kind of personal agency performed by trust institutions. At one time it was performed by the commercial banking department of a bank or trust company without charge, as a service to customers. As time went on, the trust department of the bank or trust company was often called on to handle this work, also without charge, for customers of the banking department. Most free safekeeping agencies, whether in the banking or in the trust department, have been closed (except those performed for correspondent banks), and the securities have been placed by the owners in their safe deposit boxes or in custody accounts in the trust department, subject to the regular charges for custody service.

The duties performed by an agent under a safekeeping account are to receive securities and other valuables for deposit, to issue receipts for them, to keep them safely in the vaults, and to deliver them on demand to the principal or on his order. Such a safekeeping agency may include deposits of dividends and interest to an account, usually with information on the nature of the deposit and the amount. But a safekeeping account frequently develops into a custodianship or a managing agency, since securities need more care than mere safekeeping.

CUSTODIANSHIPS

Custodianship is one of the most common types of personal agency service rendered by trust institutions. A person may open a custodian account by addressing to the trust institution a letter of instructions, the form of which is fairly standardized (a sample appears in Appendix C). The letter and the custodian's receipt for the securities may constitute the agreement between the principal and the agent, or there may be a formal agreement. The chief duties of a custodian are as follows:

1. To receive, issue receipts for, and safely keep securities
2. To collect income and disburse it in accordance with instructions
3. To execute any ownership certificates required for income tax or other purposes
4. To collect the principal of matured bonds, called bonds, and matured mortgage notes and to report all such collections to the customer
5. To notify the customer of calls, subscription rights, defaults in principal or interest, and the adoption of protective measures
6. To buy, sell, receive, or deliver securities according to specific instructions from the customer

163

7. To render periodically a statement of collections, disbursements, and securities held

Not only does the custodian keep the securities safe; it also frees the owner from the routine details connected with the collection of income and of matured principal. Besides rendering safekeeping service proper, which merely saves the customer the cost of renting a safe deposit box, the custodian attends to the clipping of coupons and to receiving dividends and interest. This additional service relieves the customer of the need to make frequent trips to his safe deposit box to clip coupons and deposit them for collection and often saves him the loss incurred through failure to clip coupons promptly.

On collecting the income, the custodian either credits the amount to the bank account of the principal or pays it to him or on his order. The custodian presents matured bonds, called bonds, and matured mortgage notes for payment and notifies the principal promptly when payment is received. It reinvests the funds in accordance with the directions of the owner.

The custodian also notifies the principal promptly of defaults in the payment of bond interest or of matured bonds. It notifies him of any other events of interest to him in connection with the ownership of securities, such as appointment of receivers, adoption of protective measures, issuance of stock or bond conversion privileges, and issuance of rights or warrants to subscribe to new securities.

In addition to giving the customer detailed receipts for securities both when the account is opened and when additions are made to it, the custodian, at agreed intervals of time, renders statements of collections, disbursements, and securities held. It prepares all security ownership certificates required for income tax purposes.

The principal retains the full control and investment management of his property. The custodian buys, sells, and exchanges securities and sells or exercises rights and options only at the express direction of the principal; it also keeps an accurate record of all such transactions.

MANAGING AGENCIES

A managing agency represents a further enlargement of the agent's activities and responsibilities.

In its capacity as managing agent, whether for securities or for real property or for both, the trust institution provides, in addition to custodial services, a management and advisory service as complete as the customer may request and as the agency instrument may provide. The duties performed by trust institutions in the capacity of managing agent differ widely and are not yet fully standardized. A trust institution may perform all the duties listed in the next section, only one of them, or two or more of them in various combinations.

164

Usual Duties of a Managing Agent for Securities

A trust institution as managing agent for securities usually renders one or more of the following services:

1. It conducts periodic reviews and analyses of the securities in the account and makes recommendations for retention, sale, exchange, or conversion of present securities and for the purchase of new securities.
2. It gives advance notice of the pending maturities of bonds, notes, and mortgages.
3. At the end of each year, it prepares an annual statement of income for income tax purposes.
4. It pays personal property taxes and income taxes.
5. It sees that necessary renewals of insurance policies accompanying deposited mortgages are made and that taxes on the mortgaged property are paid.
6. It receives income from sources other than the deposited securities—for example, rents, royalties, or salaries.
7. It pays bills for the principal or makes other remittances if requested to do so.
8. It watches for advantageous opportunities to exchange convertible bonds for stock.
9. It watches for favorable opportunities to sell bonds to sinking funds.

The distinctive function of a managing agent for securities, and the one for which most managing agencies are created, is that of making recommendations for changes in investments based on reviews and analyses. The extent and frequency of those reviews and analyses, of course, are governed by the terms of the agency agreement.

Unless the agency agreement provides for only a limited service, a trust institution as managing agent gives the principal's securities the same degree of care and attention that it gives the securities in a trust. At the time the account is opened, the trust investment organization of the trust institution makes a complete review and analysis of the securities. The agent then gives the principal a comprehensive report on the investment status of the account, together with recommendations for the retention of some securities, the sale of others, and the purchase of new securities. The agent retains, sells, and buys securities according to directions given by the principal.

The managing agent makes reviews, analyses, and reports in accordance with the terms of the agency agreement. Important as are the original analysis, review, and recommendations, which are designed to improve the holdings in the account, they are no more important than the subsequent reviews, analyses, and recommendations, which are designed to keep the investments in the best possible condition.

A managing agency may extend over a brief or a long period of time. For example, a person who is going abroad for a few months may want his securities cared for only during his absence. A professional man or woman or a retired business man or woman may desire to be relieved permanently of the management of his or her property while at the same time retaining title to and full control of it. Unlike a living trust, which can continue by its terms, an agency terminates immediately at the death of the principal, and in some states in the event of his incompetency, whereupon the agent's functions are assumed by the conservator or guardian. Whether the agency is of short or long duration, it is the duty of the managing agent to give vigilant attention to the securities of the account.

As managing agent for securities, a trust institution would not normally accept an account that would necessitate departure from normal trust investment policy and procedure; nor should it conduct in the name of managing agency what in reality is a speculative or trading account. However, it might agree to an agency with special investment objectives, which might be referred to as aggressive or growth oriented.

Managing Agency Agreement for Securities

Since managing agencies for securities may represent a relatively important part of the personal agency business of some trust institutions, special attention should be given to the form and substance of the managing agency agreement. A managing agency may be created by word of mouth or by an informal letter of instructions followed by acceptance and action by the agent in accordance with the instructions; a formal agency agreement, which defines the duties and powers of the agent and is executed by both the principal and the agent, is preferred by many trust institutions.

Many of the paragraphs of a managing agency agreement are similar to those of a trust agreement, such as the paragraphs that state the names of the principal and the agent, refer to the property to be brought under the agreement, appoint the agent, provide for the agent's compensation, and close the agreement with the signatures and seals of the parties. (The essential provisions of a typical managing agency agreement relating especially to the agency functions are set forth in the various paragraphs of the sample form in Appendix C.)

Under one of the paragraphs in the sample in the Appendix, the agent assumes the responsibility for making recommendations as to investments. This, in substance, is the usual provision. Sometimes the agency does not contemplate such advisory service; in such a case, a provision that the agent shall be under no duty to review or examine the property held under the agreement or to make or submit recommendations as to sales or changes might be substituted.

The section of the agreement relating to the investment service of the agent must be adapted to individual cases. The agent may assume full responsibility for the supervision of investments or may act only at the direction of the principal, of a designated investment counselor, or of some other person.

Letter of Instructions

In managing agencies for securities, a considerable amount of individuality is required for different principals and situations. A management agency agreement in general use in some parts of the country is in the form of a printed letter of instructions to the agent. It contains a series of options as to investment management, payment of income, and income tax returns; by checking the options he wishes to exercise, the principal may easily and quickly prepare his letter of instructions to his agent. This form of agency agreement has two advantages: it calls the principal's attention to the various options he may exercise, and it encourages flexibility.

There are three options from which the principal may make a selection to indicate the degree of investment management he wishes the agent to perform for him:

1. The agent is authorized to have sole and complete management of investments. This authorization would usually be under an accompanying power of attorney with regard to investments.
2. The agent is authorized to purchase only certain specified kinds of investments—for example, legals or first mortgages on improved real property—without first obtaining the written approval of the principal.
3. The agent is authorized only to recommend and is empowered to buy, sell, or exchange securities only on the written order of the principal, who retains all authority and discretion over investments.

The principal has many options with regard to the disposition of the income derived from the property in the agency account. Thus the principal may direct the agent to dispose of the income in any of the following ways:

1. By crediting the income periodically to the principal's checking or savings account in the agent's banking department or to his account or accounts in some other designated bank or banks
2. By remitting the income periodically to the principal by check
3. By adding the income periodically to the principal's agency account for the purpose of investment

4. By retaining the income in the agency account for paying drafts drawn under letters of credit
5. By retaining the income for use in paying bills approved by the principal

Usual Duties of a Managing Agent for Real Property

As managing agent for real property, a trust institution may handle all the details connected with the management of real property (usually improved property). The following duties are typical:

1. To obtain tenants
2. To arrange and execute leases
3. To cancel or renew leases
4. To collect rents
5. To advise the principal as to the necessity of making repairs and alterations
6. To carry out instructions concerning repairs and alterations
7. To advise the principal as to the amount and kinds of insurance needed
8. To purchase the insurance
9. To pay insurance premiums, taxes, interest on mortgages, and assessments

The management of real property is described in greater detail in Chapter 18. Not all trust institutions are equipped to manage real property. An institution not so equipped may be able to effect an arrangement by which it accepts the managing agency for the securities and obtains the principal's consent to the use of a rental or real estate agency for the real property. When such an arrangement is made, the trust institution occupies the position of an owner supervising real property placed in the hands of a rental agency, and the rental agency performs only ministerial (delegated) functions, such as collecting rent and having repairs made. The rental agency as subagent may make reports and remit income to the trust institution as agent, an arrangement that would, of course, require the approval of the principal. Trust institutions that accept managing agencies for real property have duties and responsibilities comparable to those of a trustee in connection with trusteed real property.

ATTORNEYSHIPS IN FACT

On occasion, a trust institution may act as an *attorney in fact* for the same principal on whose behalf it is acting as custodian or managing agent. An attorney in fact is one who is given authority by his principal to do a particular thing not of a legal character. All attorneys in fact are agents.

Confusion in Terminology

In the following paragraphs an attorneyship in fact is considered in its technical sense. In this sense it embraces only a negligible portion of a trust institution's personal trust business.

An attorneyship in fact may arise in the following manner: a principal makes a trust institution his managing agent; to enable the agent to buy and sell and otherwise carry out the principal's instructions relating to his securities, he wishes to give the trust institution authority to draw checks, to execute assignments of stock certificates, registered bonds, or notes, and to execute notes and pledge securities as collateral. Therefore, in addition to executing a managing agency agreement in the usual form, he executes a separate power of attorney and in it specifies the powers that the attorney in fact may exercise. The attorneyship in fact is auxiliary to the managing agency, and the trust institution may or may not make an extra charge for its services as attorney in fact.

In practice, however, some trust institutions use the phrase "attorneyship in fact" in a nontechnical sense that is practically synonymous with "managing agency." Under letters of attorney, they handle accounts that other institutions would refer to as managing agencies or simply as agencies. In view of this confusion in terminology, it must be determined whether the term is used in a technical or in a nontechnical sense whenever attorneyships in fact are referred to.

Method of Creation

An attorney in fact is clothed with a power of attorney, which is a written authorization to an agent to perform specified acts or to act in general on behalf of his principal. The legal name of the document that evidences a power of attorney is *letter of attorney*, but the document itself is usually referred to as the power of attorney.

General Powers

Powers of attorney are either general or special. An attorney in fact with a general power of attorney is authorized to represent his principal in every way and in every business transaction that may arise. The following is typical of a general power:

> I authorize _____ generally to act as my attorney in fact in relation to all matters in which I may be interested or concerned, and on my behalf to execute all instruments and do all acts and things as fully and effectively in all respects as I myself could do them if personally present.

A trust institution would rarely be offered, and certainly would rarely accept, such a power. That is primarily because the trust offers a better vehicle for the services needed and functions with much less trouble and expense.

Special Powers

A special power of attorney is an authorization to an agent to do one or more specific things. Some of the powers that a trust institution as attorney in fact may be called on to exercise are the following:
1. To draw checks against an account in a named bank
2. To endorse notes, checks, drafts, or bills of exchange that may require endorsement for deposit in or for collection by the named bank
3. To borrow money from the bank and to execute, seal, and deliver any notes, bonds, or other instruments in writing required for obtaining the loan, and to assign as collateral security stocks, bonds, warehouse receipts, or other personal property
4. To endorse any paper that a named person may offer the bank for discount
5. To draw and accept all drafts or bills of exchange on behalf of the principal
6. To waive demand, protest, and notice of protest on all notes, checks, drafts, or bills of exchange on behalf of the principal
7. To receive and receipt for any stocks, bonds, securities, or papers to which the principal may be entitled
8. To endorse stock certificates or registered securities in the name of the principal
9. To execute deeds, conveyances, and leases in connection with real property

Termination of Attorneyship in Fact

As a general rule, an attorneyship in fact is terminated by the bankruptcy, insanity, or death of the principal or the agent unless it is coupled with an interest. In recent years some states have adopted legislation providing for the appointment of an attorneyship in fact (popularly referred to as durable) that may be continued in effect notwithstanding the incapacity or mental incompetence of the principal. Usually a member of the family is given the continuing power of attorney, and a corporate fiduciary plays the role of a substitute should the first attorney in fact be unable to perform his duties.[2]

ESCROW AGENCIES

An escrow agency is a type of personal agency that has been developed by trust institutions rather extensively in the Pacific Coast area but to a lesser extent in other sections of the country. Many trust institutions do not domicile all these agencies in the trust department but handle some in the banking department.

What Is an Escrow?

When two or more persons deposit money, securities, instruments, or other property with a third person, to be delivered on a certain contingency or on the occurrence of a certain event, such money, securities, instruments, or other property are said to be *in escrow*, and the person with whom they are deposited is termed the *escrow agent*. An escrow has four basic features:

1. A complete agreement between the parties to the escrow in the sense that there remains no essential difference of opinion between the contracting parties
2. A deposit of money, securities, instruments, or other property with the escrow agent
3. An intentional surrender by each party of dominion over the money, securities, instruments, or other property deposited by him (that is, the deposit must be made absolute)
4. Definite instructions to the escrow agent specifying the conditions on the performance of which or the event on the occurrence of which the escrow agent shall deliver the money, securities, instruments, or other property to the party entitled to receive them in accordance with the agreement between the parties.

As an example of a typical escrow, consider the following: A owns a house and lot that are valued at $30,000 but are at the moment subject to a first mortgage of $15,000, a second mortgage of $5,000, a judgment of $1,000, a tax lien of $500, and a paving assessment of $500, leaving A an equity of only $8,000 in the property. He lists the property for sale with B, a real estate agent, whose commission is to be 5 percent of the sale price. B finds C, who is interested in the property and is willing to pay $30,000 for it if he can obtain a clear title. A, B, and C call upon E, a trust institution, to take an escrow agency pending the working out of the details of the sale.

A makes a deed to C, delivers it to E, and joins in a letter of instructions to E. The letter directs E to deliver the deed to C upon receipt of

---

2. A sample of the approved language in a given state might be as follows: "This power shall not be affected by my disability or incompetency, and the authority conferred hereunder shall be exercisable by my attorney notwithstanding my disability or incompetency. All acts done by my attorney under this power during my disability or incompetency shall have the same effect, inure to my benefit, and bind me and my heirs, estate, and personal representative as if I were competent and not disabled."

171

$30,000 from C. It also directs E, upon receipt of the $30,000, to pay off the first mortgage of $15,000, the second mortgage of $5,000, the judgment of $1,000, the tax lien of $500, and the paving assessment of $500; to pay B's commission of $1,500; and to pay A the balance of $6,500 less any recording fees or other incidental charges. At the same time, C agrees to deliver $30,000 to E and joins in the letter that instructs E to pay the money to A, or to dispose of it as A directs, upon receipt of a title insurance policy showing title vested in C free of encumbrance.

Although this illustration pictures an escrow in connection with a real property transaction, escrows are by no means limited to such transactions. Under modern practice, instruments other than deeds and property other than real property may be the subjects of escrow arrangements. The instruments may be bills of sale, transferable licenses, mortgages, releases, bonds, notes, contracts, concessions, life insurance policies, licenses for the use of patents, certificates of stock, or stock rights. The property may be patent rights, formulas, or other choses in action[3] as well as stocks, bonds, or other intangibles.

Need for Escrow Service

The need for escrow service is apparent, particularly with reference to real property and increasingly with reference to other property. There is always an interval, from a day or two to several weeks or even months, during which the details of a real property transaction are being worked out. There must be time for drawing up the papers, searching the title, refinancing, clearing the records, and recording the papers. Anything may happen between the time the parties agree on the deal and the time the deal is finally consummated. One or both of the parties may die or become incapacitated. One or the other may change his mind about the sale. New liens such as judgments, taxes, and paving assessments may be attached. The title search and the title insurance policy must extend up to and include the moment of final settlement between the parties. The seller cannot be sure that he has sold or the purchaser that he has bought unless there is an escrow arrangement under which the rights of the parties vest and become enforceable on the date of the agreement, not on the later date on which the details are consummated.

Experienced escrow agents not only insist on a formal agency agreement setting forth their duties but also insist that the agreement

---

3. A chose in action is a right to personal property that has not been reduced to possession or enjoyment but is recoverable in an action at law. See *Glossary of Fiduciary Terms* (Washington, D.C.: American Bankers Association, 1976).

contain a definite termination date and thus ensure that this temporary agency is in fact temporary.

Agencies Improperly Called Escrows

People involved in trust business should be aware of certain types of agencies that are improperly called escrows. Some of them are less than escrows in that they lack one or more of the essential elements of an escrow; others are more than escrows in that they impose on the agent active duties in addition to those of escrow holding.

A kind of agency that is sometimes called an escrow is really more than that. The parties enter into a binding contract with each other; they deposit money, securities, instruments, or other property with the trust institution; and they issue a definite letter of instructions to the trust institution. Thus far the arrangement is an escrow. But the parties impose additional duties on the escrow agent. They charge it, for instance, with the duties of selling the property on certain conditions and applying the proceeds in a certain way, collecting the rents and otherwise managing the property, and investing the funds. It is not at all improper to impose such duties on trust institutions; but it is improper to burden an escrow agent with additional and to some extent extraneous agency duties, making the escrow arrangement appear much more complicated than it normally is.

The essence of a successful escrow agency is, first, to have definite, understandable instructions and, second, to carry out those instructions to the letter. The introduction of any additional agency services involving the exercise of discretion or the active management of property is unnecessarily confusing and may be detrimental to true escrow service. Inasmuch as many so-called escrow accounts are really more than escrow agencies involving additional duties, responsibilities, and potential liabilities not belonging to a true escrow account, a trust institution should make a thorough investigation of all the facts and circumstances before committing itself to the acceptance of a proffered escrow agency and should set its fee so that extra services are properly compensated for.

Chapter 12

Management of Personal Agencies

The Purposes of This Chapter:

1. To enumerate the basic duties and powers of an agent
2. To discuss the responsibilities assumed by a trust institution in undertaking a personal agency
3. To consider the standard of care and skill required of a trust institution as an agent

"Agency accounts under which the trust institution is to supervise investments should be accepted only (a) under a written agreement setting forth the powers and duties of the trust institution; (b) if the customer understands that the investment policy suggested by the trust institution will be substantially similar to that followed in trust accounts; and (c) if the trust institution, except in extraordinary circumstances, is to have custody of the securities." [1]

The responsibilities of agents discussed in this chapter are, for the most part, confined to those connected with the personal agencies considered in Chapter 11. The responsibilities of agents as they pertain to corporate agencies are covered in Chapter 16. In addition to presenting a detailed discussion of responsibilities, this chapter summarizes the duties and powers of an agent.

Duties

The basic responsibilities of an agent are determined and measured by its powers; and its powers, in turn, are determined and measured by its duties. The duties may range from endorsing a check to manag-

---

1. "A Statement of Principles of Trust Institutions (1933)", *Trust Principles and Policies* (Washington, D.C.: American Bankers Association, 1973). It should be noted that some of the larger trust institutions do offer investment counsel under an agency agreement under which the corporate fiduciary does not hold the securities.

ing an entire business or estate; there is no standard set of duties for a personal agent. There are, however, certain basic or general duties that are required of all agents, regardless of the type of agency.

LOYALTY TO THE PRINCIPAL

The first basic duty of every agent is to be loyal to its principal. The relation of an agent to its principal is ordinarily that of a fiduciary, and every fiduciary relationship involves a duty on the part of the fiduciary to act for the benefit of the other party to the relationship with respect to matters coming within the scope of the relationship. As a fiduciary, it is the agent's duty to act with good faith and loyalty for the furtherance of the principal's interests in all dealings affecting the property covered by the agency. It if fails to do so, the agent is responsible to the principal for any loss that results.

OBEDIENCE TO THE PRINCIPAL'S ORDERS

The second basic duty of an agent is to obey the orders of its principal, provided they do not require actions that are illegal or contrary to public policy. If an action would violate the law or contravene public policy, the principal himself could not properly do it; therefore he cannot delegate it to an agent, nor can he ratify it if done by an agent. With this exception, it is the duty of an agent whose authority is limited by instructions to adhere faithfully to them, regardless of its own opinion as to their propriety or expediency. If the agent exceeds, violates, or neglects such instructions, it will be liable to the principal for any resulting loss or damage.

EXERCISE OF CARE, SKILL, AND DILIGENCE

The third basic duty of an agent is to exercise ordinary care, skill, and diligence in the performance of its duties. If it fails to do so, it will be liable to its principal for any loss or injury suffered by him. The care, skill, and diligence required are such as should be exercised by a person of ordinary prudence in the conduct of his own affairs of like nature under similar circumstances or by persons of ordinary care and capacity who are engaged in the same business. What amounts to the exercise of ordinary care, skill, and diligence depends on the circumstances of the particular case, including the kind of agency and the nature of the property covered by it.

ACCOUNTING TO THE PRINCIPAL

The fourth basic duty of an agent is to account to its principal for all property or funds belonging to the principal that come into its hands by virtue of the agency or into the hands of a subagent appointed by the agent to receive them. Another duty of an agent is to account for property or funds received for application to a specific purpose; if the agent fails to apply them to the purpose for which they were received, the principal may recover them.

Powers

The powers of an agent are express, implied, and apparent. Unlike a personal representative. an agent has no inherent powers except the power to represent its principal as long as it acts within the scope of its authority and in the course of the principal's business.

EXPRESS AND IMPLIED POWERS

The express powers of an agent are those contained in the letter of instructions, letter of attorney, or formal agreement creating the agency. Its implied powers are those that grow out of its express powers. An express power to collect funds gives rise to an implied power to receipt for them, since it is not reasonable or customary for a debtor to make a payment without requiring a receipt, particularly if he is paying someone other than the creditor. Each express power gives rise to a number of implied powers.

APPARENT POWERS

The apparent powers of agents constitute a group of powers that are practically unknown in executorships, administratorships, and trusteeships. An apparent power may be defined as one that the principal permits the agent to appear to have, even though as between the agent and the principal the agent does not actually possess that power.

For example, A appoints B his agent to collect funds. B goes about the community collecting and receipting for funds and thus becomes generally known as A's collector. Later A gives B a note made by C to A's order, but *without* instructions to collect it. On his usual rounds, B presents the note to C, who pays it. B absconds with the money. A cannot compel C to pay the note again on the ground that B had no authority to collect it. A had permitted B to have apparent authority to collect the note, and C paid it in reliance on B's apparent authority, which was strengthened by possession of the note. As between the principal and the third party who relied on the apparent authority of the agent, the apparent authority has the effect of real authority.

AUTHORITY AND INSTRUCTIONS

An agent's authority is the sum total of its express, implied, and apparent powers. Instructions are the private orders given by the principal to the agent and not meant to be communicated to third parties. Thus a managing agent files with its broker a copy of its letter of attorney or agency agreement as evidence of its authority to buy and sell securities for its principal's account. At the same time, the agent may have in its possession a letter or memorandum containing instructions or restrictions about the quantity, price, or terms of purchase or sale but may not reveal that fact to the broker. In the absence of any circumstance that would put the broker on notice as to the existence of such instructions or restrictions, he may act in reliance on the agent's duties and powers as set forth in the letter of attorney or agency agreement filed with him. If, however, the broker knows of the instructions, they become as binding on him as they are on the agent.

In dealing with agents, third parties should keep clearly in mind the distinction between primary authority and private instructions. If instructions are communicated to third parties, they may become part of the agency relationship and may serve either to extend or to limit the agent's authority as far as those particular third parties are concerned.

Responsibilities

The following discussion applies the responsibilities of an agent to each of the kinds of personal agencies considered in Chapter 11. These include safekeeping agencies, custodianships, managing agencies, attorneyships in fact, and escrow agencies.

SAFEKEEPING AGENT

A trust institution has safekeeping responsibilities in connection with its custodian accounts, its managing agency accounts, and its escrow accounts, as well as its safekeeping accounts proper. The property placed in safekeeping usually consists of documents, such as deeds and contracts; securities—stocks, bonds, and notes; and formulas, secret processes, and patents. Although jewelry, keepsakes, and coins may be placed in safekeeping, in practice safekeeping as a function of the trust institution relates mainly to documents and securities.

The duties of a safekeeping agent for securities are to receive the securities, to keep them in the condition in which they are received (except for natural and unavoidable physical deterioration), and to deliver them to the principal on demand or to someone else on his order. In performing these duties, the agent must exercise proper care; and it receives adequate compensation for its services.

In its capacity as safekeeping agent, a trust institution has no responsibility with regard to property until it has actually received it. The act of *receiving property* sometimes takes place outside the office of the trust institution. In his own office, at home, or elsewhere, a customer may deliver securities or documents to a representative of the institution for safekeeping. In that case the institution's responsibilities as safekeeping agent begin at the moment the property is delivered to its respresentative, wherever he may be. There is one exception to this general rule. If a customer delivers property to a representative of the trust institution while that representative is off duty, with the request that the representative take it to the institution for safekeeping, the representative may be regarded as the servant of the customer, and the responsibilities of the trust institution may not begin until the property is actually delivered to its vaults.

The agent is responsible for the *safekeeping of the property* after it has been received. The agent must see that the property is not stolen, destroyed, mutilated, lost, or embezzled.

Under modern conditions, physical destruction or mutilation of property that has been committed to a trust institution as safekeeping agent can seldom occur without negligence on the part of the agent; thus the agent is usually held responsible for the loss. If property is left outside the vault or if the vault doors are left open and the property is destroyed by fire or water or any other means, the agent is liable for the loss incurred; but if the vault itself is destroyed by an earthquake and the property is destroyed or so mutilated as to lose its identity and value, the agent is not liable.

If tangible property or a security that passes by delivery is lost through negligence while in the agent's possession, the agent is responsible for the value of the lost property.

If tangible property is lost, the first responsibility of the agent is to recover the property itself. If the property cannot be recovered, the agent is responsible for making good its money value. If the property is an irreplaceable document, the agent is responsible not for the money value of the document itself (which might be negligible) but for the amount of loss sustained by the customer as a result of loss of the irreplaceable document. It if is a registered security, the agent may have a duplicate issued but must bear the cost of obtaining the duplicate.

Liability for embezzlement, as applied to a trust institution, relates to inside thefts committed by officers or employees. Trust and agency instruments sometimes provide that the trustee or the agent shall not be liable for the acts of its agents and employees, provided that it uses due care in selecting and supervising them. But a trust institution would suffer in public esteem and would be acting shortsightedly if it sought to escape responsibility for losses from inside thefts by setting up the claim that it had used due diligence in the selection and supervision of its employees and agents.

Property held in safekeeping is usually deliverable to the owner on demand or to someone else on his order. After *delivering the property*, the safekeeping agency is terminated. If the safekeeping agent delivers the property to the wrong person, it is liable for the value of the property wrongly delivered or for the loss sustained by the owner as a result of such wrong delivery, and the presence or absence of negligence is of little or no importance. Even though the safekeeping agent acts in good faith, wrong delivery furnishes no legal excuse for failure to return the property to the owner on demand. Wrong delivery is a departure from the terms of the safekeeping contract; therefore the safekeeping agent is responsible whether or not any negligence is involved. This rule has been carried to the extent of holding the safekeeping agent liable for delivery to the customer's wife when the instructions to the agent were not to deliver the property to any person except on the written order of the customer.

With respect to the responsibility of a trust institution as safekeeping agent, the question of *exercising care* frequently arises: Is there any difference between the standard of care required of a trust institution and that required of an individual agent? Although from time to time various courts have intimated that they would be disposed to hold a bank or trust company as safekeeping agent to a higher standard of care than they would an individual, nonprofessional agent, that higher standard has not been stated as a general principle of law. The *Restatement of the Law of Trusts* states that if the fiduciary "has or procures his appointment . . . by representing that he has greater skill than that of a man of ordinary prudence, he is under a duty to exercise such skill."[2]

The nature, as distinguished from the standard, of care required of a safekeeping agent varies with the kind of property placed in safekeeping. The care required of an ordinarily prudent trust institution in safekeeping a process whose value lies in keeping it absolutely secret would naturally be different from the care required in safekeeping a bulky heirloom. A safekeeping agent must give each kind of property the care required by that particular kind of property.

In most states, whether or not a trust institution receives compensation for its services as safekeeping agent makes no difference in its responsibilities. Most courts take the position that a bank or trust company that offers its services as a safekeeping agent and actually engages in the safekeeping business receives compensation, either directly or indirectly, for the service and should therefore be held to the standard of care of an ordinarily prudent man under the same circumstances. In the absence of direct fees or commissions paid for the service, the theory of compensation followed by some courts is that, by

---

2. *Restatement of the Law of Trusts*, 2nd ed. (St. Paul, Minn.: American Law Institute, 1959). Adopted and promulgated by the American Law Institute May 23, 1957.

offering free safekeeping service to its customers, the bank or trust company obtains or expects to obtain profitable business and thus is as truly compensated for the safekeeping service as if it charged fees or commissions.

The prevailing opinion of the courts—and the only one on which a trust institution can afford to rely—is that the responsibilities of a trust institution as safekeeping agent are not lightened when it accepts safekeeping accounts free of charge. If it makes a business of safekeeping, whether it is paid directly or (according to the courts) indirectly, it is held to the standard of care of an ordinarily prudent man and may be held to the standard of care of an ordinarily prudent trust institution engaged in the safekeeping business.

CUSTODIAN

As defined in Chapter 11, custodianship includes the essential functions of safekeeping—receiving, safekeeping, and delivering property. Each of the custodial functions discussed in the following paragraphs imposes on the trust institution definite and inescapable responsibilities.

The custodian is responsible for *collecting the income* from the property held in safekeeping and applying it as directed by the principal. If it fails to clip and deposit interest coupons, it is responsible for interest on the amount of the coupons between the due date and the date of presentation for payment; and if the coupons were collectible on their due date but became uncollectible on or before the time of actual presentation for payment, the custodian is responsible for both the full amount of the coupons and the interest on that amount after the due date.

If the custodian fails out of negligence to collect interest on mortgage notes, it is responsible for interest on the uncollected interest, and it may also be responsible for the amount of the uncollected interest if the interest becomes uncollectible.

If the custodian misapplies the income, even though acting in good faith, it is responsible for the loss. For instance, the principal directs the custodian to deposit the income to the credit of A, but the custodian deposits it to B's credit by mistake. The custodian is responsible for placing the same amount to the credit of A, even though it may be unable to recover that amount from B.

The custodian is also responsible for *collecting the principal of matured and called bonds*. If some bonds mature or are called and the custodian fails to deposit them for collection, the minimum amount for which it will be chargeable is the loss of interest and principal sustained by the owner because of the custodian's failure to deposit the bonds promptly.

Under its custodianship agreement, a trust institution sometimes contracts to *notify the principal* of all calls, subscription rights, defaults, and other matters in connection with securities in the account. If a custodian that has made such an agreement fails to notify its principal of such matters, the custodian is responsible for any loss sustained by the principal as a result.

Although a trust institution as custodian has no responsibility for changing the investments in a custody account on its own initiative, it has a responsibility, under the usual terms of the custody agreement, of *buying, selling, receiving, and delivering securities* on the order of the owner. If it fails to execute an order of the owner to buy, sell, receive, or deliver securities, it is responsible for any loss traceable to such failure, provided that it is able to execute the order at that time. If unreasonable delay occurs in the execution of an order, the custodian is responsible for the loss in profits attributable to the delay. In other words, the custodian is responsible for the prompt and faithful execution of its contractual obligations under the custody agreement.

When a trust institution as custodian accepts notes secured by mortgages or deeds of trust on real property, it *attends to certain mortgage details* in addition to its responsibilities connected with collecting and disposing of income and principal and, in fact, may be accepting a relationship that imposes on it all the responsibilities of a managing agency.

MANAGING AGENT FOR SECURITIES

A managing agent for securities contracts to supply investment management services in addition to performing the functions of a safekeeping agent and a custodian for the securities committed to its care. In agency agreements in general use, the managing agent contracts to analyze and review the securities and to make recommendations for changes in existing investments and for new investments with respect to cash added to the account or resulting from sales, called bonds, or matured bonds or notes.

According to the *Restatement of the Law of Agency*, an agent employed to make or manage investments has a duty to the principal, unless otherwise agreed:

1. To try to invest promptly
2. To invest only in such securities as would be obtained by a prudent investor for his own account, with a view toward both safety and income, in the light of the principal's means and purposes
3. To change investments in accordance with changes in the security of the investments or the condition of the principal, if his duties include management

The *Restatement* then comments on the analogy to trusts:

The duties of an agent who has authority to make and to

manage investments are similar to those of the trustee of a formal trust, except in so far as they are affected by the fact that the principal has control and may modify or determine the investments at any time. . . . There are no statutory or formal rules which can be stated in connection with the duties of an investing agent, since the purposes of principals are so varied. . . .

An agent to invest should not, if it is possible to make a suitable investment, let money lie in a bank without interest or even at a low rate of interest. If permanent investments are not available or desirable, it may be his duty to make such temporary investments as will secure the largest rate of interest commensurate with security.[3]

To what extent is a trust institution as managing agent responsible for basing its recommendations on actual analyses of securities and periodic reviews of the agency account as a whole? Suppose the trust institution does not have a statistical department. Suppose it does not make analyses of investment securities, tracing the history of the issuing company as to profits, assets and liabilities, management, affiliations, and prospects and studying all the other features that should enter into a proper analysis of investment securities. Suppose it does not subscribe to statistical services to keep itself informed on investment developments. Finally, suppose it does not have an investment committee to make reviews of the agency account as a whole, but a single officer or employee of the institution, without consulting his associates and without a systematic study of investments, makes recommendations about the investments, old and new, in the agency account. Although most of these are unlikely suppositions, they suggest that an inadequately equipped institution might not be exercising due care and skill in making investment recommendations.

The extent of the investment machinery required is determined in some measure by the size and location of the trust institution. As in the case of vaults and vault supervision, a trust institution in a small town would not be expected or required to have all the investment machinery that a metropolitan trust institution would have as a matter of course. Thus a small-town trust institution might be judged by the standard of the investment personnel and equipment of ordinarily prudent trust institutions in the community or in similar communities.

A point to be emphasized here is that investment recommendations for agency accounts impose responsibilities on trust institutions almost

---

3. *Restatement of the Law of Agency*, 2d ed. (St. Paul, Minn.: American Law Institute, 1958), Vol. 2, p. 291. Adopted and promulgated by the American Law Institute May 23, 1957.

as great as the responsibilities involved in selecting investments for trust accounts. In view of those responsibilities, every managing agency should be protected by a carefully considered and carefully prepared agency agreement or letter of instructions.

MANAGING AGENT FOR REAL PROPERTY

As managing agent for real property, a trust institution can expect to be offered all types of properties: undeveloped land, farms, shopping centers, income properties, and even condominiums. Although a larger portion of the institution's trust assets may be in the form of securities, real property requires as much—perhaps more—attention. Recognition of true income may sometimes be complicated by depreciation and obsolescence; often the true return is not readily perceptible.

In addition to the usual duties of paying taxes, collecting rents, and paying operating costs, the agent may be expected to negotiate leases, mortgages, and other agreements and to buy and sell on the principal's order.

INVESTMENT ADVISORY SERVICE WITHOUT CUSTODY

In some trust institutions there are a few agencies providing investment recommendations on securities not held in custody or safekeeping by the institution. Although the acceptance of such an account is sometimes said to be a feeder for regular services, in most cases this service is rendered to a special group composed of insurance companies, endowed institutions, and certain corporations. It has also been reported that the service is not profitable and should not be solicited and that acceptance can be justified only in special circumstances.

If a trust institution accepts such an account, it must keep complete records of the securities. When it does not control purchases and sales and other transactions, a considerable amount of staff time is required to ensure smooth operation and effective application of its policies and recommendations. While the customers often feel that the bank should reduce its fees when it does not have custody, under this arrangement as much or more time may be required in maintaining and reconciling the lists that are essential to the service.

ATTORNEY IN FACT

The question of what responsibilities a trust institution assumes when it accepts an attorneyship in fact cannot be answered definitely or specifically without exploring the whole field of the law of principal and agent, since it also involves answering the question: For what specific purpose is the trust institution made attorney in fact? The responsibilities of an attorney in fact depend wholly on its powers and duties in connection with the performance of the specific act or series of acts called for by the purpose for which the attorneyship in fact is created. Whatever the specific purpose, however, the trust institution is responsible for devoting to the performance of its agency the care, skill, and diligence of a reasonably prudent person in the performance of a similar service under similar circumstances.

ESCROW AGENT

What responsibilities does a trust institution assume when it accepts an escrow account? The answer to that question is confined to escrows proper (sometimes called pure escrows) and excludes agencies often improperly called escrows.

The main responsibility of an escrow agent is to carry out instructions, not to exercise discretion. In most instances in which escrow agents have been held liable for loss, they have failed to carry out instructions, although they have usually done so with the best of motives. An escrow agent should never deviate from the original instructions, even to the slightest degree. The deviation that most often leads an escrow agent into difficulty is the premature delivery of documents or money. An escrow agent assumes full liability for all losses resulting from deliveries not authorized by the instrument or by the consent of all the parties.

The first responsibility of an escrow agent is to see that it receives definite, written instructions that do not require the exercise of any discretion or independent judgment. If it does not receive such instructions, it should refuse to accept the account. An important element in the instructions is a definite statement of the time when delivery is to be made or some other action taken by the escrow agent.

A trust institution should never rely on the terms of the receipt issued to the principal but should obtain an independent instrument of instructions in the form of an escrow agreement or a letter of instructions. There should be a definite meeting of minds by all the parties—obligor, obligee, and escrow agent. As a practical matter, it is often advisable for the escrow agent to supervise the preparation of the instructions so that it may use language it unmistakably understands and put into the instrument the usual clauses that serve to protect the escrow agent and to notify the other parties of the extent and limit of the protection.

There is a kind of escrow, known as a closed escrow, that may prove a source of danger unless the escrow agent insists on having the proper protective clause incorporated into the escrow agreement. In a closed escrow, the documents are enclosed in a sealed package that is delivered to the escrow agent to be held unopened and then delivered in accordance with instructions. The escrow instrument should clearly state that the escrow agent will not be charged with notice of the contents of the sealed package and that its only duty is to deliver the sealed package exactly as received and in accordance with instructions.

Suppose one party to an escrow, in good faith, asks the escrow agent to change the instructions in some small way, and the escrow agent, in equally good faith, consents. In permitting a change in the instructions by one party without the knowledge or consent of the other, the escrow agent is guilty of breach of contract and renders itself liable for any loss sustained by the other party as a result of the change.

Chapter 13

Charitable Trusts and Agencies

The Purposes of This Chapter:

1. To explain the principal features of charitable trusts
2. To distinguish charitable trusts and agencies

"If a college or other charitable organization owns property outright or receives an absolute gift of property, it can create its own endowment trust with a bank or trust company. Or, if a property owner is so minded, he himself by will or agreement can create an endowment trust for the charitable institution or organization of his choice.

"But where the gift to the charitable organization is earmarked for endowment or some specified purpose, the organization itself becomes, in effect, trustee of the property for a specified purpose and cannot trustee already trusteed property. But what it can do is create an endowment agency, itself retaining title to property, and employ the agent to safekeep, protect and manage the property. . . ."[1]

Definition of a Charitable Trust

"A charitable trust is one created for the benefit of a legal charity." A legal charity is "an agency, institution, or organization in existence and operation for the benefit of an indefinite number of persons and conducted for educational, religious, scientific, medical, or other beneficent purposes."[2]

The following discussion relates to the services of trust institutions to charitable and other organizations and institutions created for the benefit of groups of persons as distinguished from individual persons. The

---

1. Gilbert T. Stephenson, *Reflections of A Trustman* (New York: American Bankers Association, 1960).

2. *Glossary of Fiduciary Terms* (Washington, D.C.: American Bankers Association, 1976).

functions of a trust department in rendering these services are sometimes those of trusteeships, including community and institutional trusteeships, and sometimes those of institutional agencies.

Community Trusts

A community trust is composed of gifts and bequests made by the citizens of a community for the benefit of the people of that community. In this definition the term "community" must be given considerable latitude in practice. A community may be a city, a town, a county, a state, a nation, or the world.

DEVELOPMENT OF THE IDEA

The first community trust, the Cleveland Foundation, was established in 1914. During the years since 1914, community trusts have been established in many large cities in the United States; and the volume of property under administration in these trusts, annual additions to them, and annual distributions from them for charitable, educational, and other public purposes constitute increasingly impressive totals.[3]

ADMINISTRATIVE FEATURES

There is considerable variation in the organization and operation of the many community trusts now in existence in the United States. However, most of them have certain fundamental features:

1. The property of the trust is trusteed. The trustee is authorized to receive, hold, and administer property of any kind, of any amount, received from anyone, and donated in any way in which property may be given.

2. Business management is provided for the trust property. The business administration of the property, which includes safeguarding, investing, managing, and accounting for it, is a fundamental responsibility of the trustee or trustees.

3. Many purposes are provided for. The resolutions, trust agreements, declarations of trust, or corporate charters creating community trusts include every kind of charitable or public service. Usually the trust instrument not only enumerates every such objective but also contains a general welfare clause to include pur-

---

3. For statistics on community trusts, refer to the annual reports of some of the larger trusts, such as the New York Community Trust, and to the combined figures for community trusts presented from time to time in *Trusts and Estates*, published monthly since 1904 by Communication Channels, Inc.

poses that may not have been thought of at the time the instrument was framed or that may come into existence afterward.

4. The trust affords flexibility in the application of gifts. Although the donor may specify the purposes for which he wishes his gift to be used and the terms and conditions on which it may be used or consumed, he nevertheless makes his gift with the understanding and on the condition that, if it should become impossible or even impracticable to use the gift for the purpose or in the manner specified, it will be used for some other purpose or in some other manner consistent with the general purposes of the community trust.

The wisdom of providing flexibility for gifts in trust for charity is amply borne out by experience. It is difficult to determine the exact number, but tens of thousands of charitable gifts in England and the United States have failed of their purpose and been rendered useless because of the inability of the donors to foresee or provide against the future obsolescence of the objects of their generosity.

5. Impartial distribution of funds by a distribution committee is provided for. The application of the funds available for beneficiaries, whether derived from income or, in some instances, from principal, is under the complete control of an impartial and representative distribution committee having from five to eleven members. Most of the members are appointed by some public official, such as the mayor of the city, the governor of the state, the judge of the highest court of the state, or the resident judge of a federal court.

ADVANTAGES

The advantages of a community trust to a community and the advantages to the citizens of making their gifts for charitable purposes through such a trust are many. The community trust safeguards the principal of all gifts (the smallest as well as the largest) for philanthropic purposes. It meets changing needs and guards against the influence of the dead hand, keeping abreast with ever-changing human needs. It accords large and small gifts equality of management. It masses property for beneficent purposes. Finally, it provides for economy of administration: funds can often be pooled for collective investment or placed in common trust funds.

TREND TOWARD MULTIPLE TRUSTEESHIP

In the early years of the community trust movement, it was common for one trust institution in a community to make the declaration of trust and to some extent preempt the field, since a single trust is generally deemed sufficient for a community. It is now the usual practice, however, for all the trust institutions in a community to act together in making a joint declaration of trust or contemporaneous, identical declarations of trust, in either case providing for the same distribution committee. In several instances what started as single trusteeships were later converted into multiple trusteeships. That was true of the Cleveland and Detroit community trusts, pioneers in the field.

Although most of the existing community trusts were created by declarations of trust made by trust institutions, a few have been established as charitable corporations. When a community trust (or its distribution committee) is incorporated, gifts may be made to or for the trust either directly to the corporation or to a trustee for the benefit of the corporation. If a gift is made directly to the incorporated trust, the corporation may arrange for the administration of the gift by a trust institution as agent or as trustee. If a gift is made to a trust institution in trust for the community trust, the trust institution will administer the gift and pay the income to the community trust.

FOUNDATIONS FOR SPECIAL PURPOSES

Another kind of trust, similar to a community trust but differing in various respects, is here referred to as a foundation for special purposes. It is a trust established by a religious denomination, a professional association, a fraternal order, a civic club, or some such group for the promotion of its special objects and for the benefit of its appointees. Examples would be a state or regional church foundation fostered by a particular denomination, a medical foundation sponsored by a state medical society, a Rotary foundation sponsored by a local Rotary club and devoted to making loans to boys and girls for their education, or a welfare foundation sponsored by a labor union for the benefit of the families of its members.

A foundation for special purposes is similar to a community trust in that its funds are received and invested by a trustee, its disbursements are made by a distribution committee whose personnel changes periodically, and that committee has discretion to divert gifts from specified objects to other objects of the foundation when it appears reasonable or necessary to do so to achieve the purpose of the gift, in substance if not in form. It differs from a community trust in that it is established by a particular group for a more or less specialized purpose connected in some way with the interests of that group, whereas a community trust is created for the entire community without regard to race, color, creed, or occupation.

Institutional Trusts

An institutional trust is created by or for a public institution for the benefit of the objects served by that institution. Institutional trusts are often used by colleges, hospitals, and charitable organizations.

In a typical institutional trust, the trust property is the endowment of a college, a hospital, or some other public institution. If the institution is the absolute owner of its endowment and not itself the trustee for its funds, it may create an institutional trust for its own benefit by delivering, transferring, and conveying its endowment to a trust institution, in trust, to administer in accordance with the terms and conditions set forth in the trust instrument. An individual benefactor may create an institutional trust by trusteeing funds and property for the benefit of a public institution.

Thus the test of whether a trust is an institutional trust is not who creates it but for whose benefit it is created. No matter who creates it, if the trust is created for the benefit of an association, a corporation, a fund, or a foundation organized and operated exclusively for religious, charitable, scientific, literary, or educational purposes or for the prevention of cruelty to children or to animals, and if no part of its net earnings inures to the benefit of any private shareholder or individual, it is an institutional trust. This description is substantially the same as the legal definition of a charitable institution and applies to funds and foundations as well as to institutions.

POTENTIAL FIELD

The potential field for institutional trusts is indicated by the immense amount of funds and property owned by charitable and other public institutions or held in perpetual trust for their benefit and by the rate at which those endowments usually increase annually. Almost every trust institution has within its trade area an endowed institution—a school, a college, a university, a hospital, an orphanage, a home for the aged, a philanthropic foundation, or another similar institution.

The large endowments of those institutions have usually been assembled over a long time from a multitude of sources (some local and some distant), through outright gifts made during the lifetimes of the donors, bequests under wills, and gifts in perpetual trust. In many instances the endowed institution receives unrestricted gifts aggregating millions of dollars and subject to no conditions or limitations whatsoever. It may use those funds for current expenses, for buildings or improvements, for endowment, or in any other way that it may wish in its uncontrolled discretion and acting through its governing body. In fact, it may trustee any part of or even all the funds of which it is absolute owner with as much freedom as an individual in the same circumstances.

FEATURES

The terms of an institutional trust are essentially the same as those of a personal trust and may be made either inflexible or fully as flexible as those of a personal trust. For example, the investment powers of the trustee may or may not be limited, and the trustee may or may not be required to obtain the approval of some committee or officer of the institution before making investment changes. The trustee administers the property of an institutional trust in the same way it administers the property of a personal trust, using similar records, equipment, and investment facilities. The chief difference is that the trustee of an institutional trust may sometimes be required to deal with several different persons representing the institution in connection with different matters—for example, the members of the finance committee in connection with investment changes, the treasurer in connection with payments of income, and the treasurer and the president or some other officer in connection with payments or deliveries of principal.

ADVANTAGES

An institutional trust relieves the institution's governing body of many business and investment responsibilities. An institution should be free to select its board of directors primarily for their fitness to promote and serve the main objectives of the institution, without undue emphasis on their ability to invest funds or manage property. An institutional trust imposes on a financially responsible and continuing corporation engaged in the business of managing other people's property the duties and responsibilities connected with the proper investment of the trust funds.

By relieving the governing board of investment responsibilities, the charitable or educational institution promotes the efficiency of the board and enables it to devote its full energy, time, and thought to the development of the objects for which the institution was established. Furthermore, such an institution is in a position to obtain the services of men and women who are qualified to serve on its governing board and direct its general policies but who would refuse to serve if they had to assume responsibility for the institution's financial affairs.

An institutional trust also encourages contributions to public institutions. Persons of means are more disposed to make gifts to the endowments of institutions (particularly local and smaller ones) if they are assured that the endowments are, or will be, trusteed with a well-known and highly regarded trust institution.

Institutional Agencies

Among the agency services of trust institutions to charitable and other organizations or institutions for the benefit of groups of persons are services as agent for endowments and as agent for financial secretary or treasurer. Though not covered in this text, trust institutions also serve as agents for municipal and state governments.

AGENT FOR ENDOWMENTS

In many cases an endowed institution holds its endowment property, or a large part of it, not as absolute owner but as trustee for objects specified in the various instruments creating the gifts. A gift may be made to a college in trust for the establishment and maintenance of a specified professorship; it may be a trust even though the word "trust" is not used in connection with the gift. In the many and varied instances in which an institution receives gifts in trust (formally or informally expressed), it cannot retrustee the property; but it may create an agency to handle the trust property. It is a well-settled principle of the law of trusts that a trustee may employ an agent if a prudent man would do so under the same circumstances. A managing agency for endowment property is adapted to the needs of institutions that hold such property in trust for specified purposes, since through a managing agency agreement such institutions may obtain the custodianship, income and principal collection, investment management, and accounting services of a trust institution without divesting themselves of title to the property.

AGENT FOR FINANCIAL SECRETARY OR TREASURER

There is a need for the services of a trust institution either as financial secretary or treasurer or as agent for the financial secretary or treasurer of religious, charitable, and other organizations and institutions. Such services may be limited to a few ministerial acts, or they may be as extensive as those of a managing agent.

One institution that has specialized in this field of trust service also acts as agent for the financial secretary or treasurer of schools, hospitals, homes for the aged or infirm, and welfare organizations. In performing its agency functions, it combines the services of safekeeping agent, custodian, and managing agent for securities and real property. In other agencies of this type, the duties of a trust institution as financial secretary or treasurer or as agent for the financial secretary or treasurer are more restricted.

Charitable Remainder Trusts

A charitable remainder interest in a trust following a noncharitable interest will not qualify for income, estate, or gift tax deduction unless the trust is a charitable remainder annuity trust, a charitable remainder unitrust, or a pooled income fund as these terms are defined in the Internal Revenue Code.[4] A brief discussion of each of these follows.

CHARITABLE REMAINDER ANNUITY TRUSTS

Under the Internal Revenue Code, a charitable remainder annuity trust is one that a person creates for himself or herself during life or for another under the terms of his or her will. The trust must pay out a specified amount each year, which may not be less than 5 percent of the property at the time the trust is established. For example, if the settlor or testator gives $100,000 to an annuity trust, retaining quarterly payments for life at the annual rate of 5 percent, the trustee will pay the annuitant $5,000 per year. At the death of the annuitant, the trustee delivers the property to the charity.

CHARITABLE REMAINDER UNITRUST

A charitable remainder unitrust (sometimes referred to as a variable annuity trust) is one in which the noncharitable beneficiary is to receive a fixed percentage—which cannot be less than 5 percent—of the net fair market value of the trust assets as determined each year. For example, if the contribution to the trust is $100,000, the assets are valued in the first two years at $100,000 and $110,000, and the settlor has reserved the right to receive annually 5 percent of the value of the assets, he or she would receive $5,000 in the first year and $5,500 in the second.

POOLED INCOME FUNDS

A third method by which a taxpayer can obtain a deduction for a contribution of a remainder interest in property is by way of transfer to a pooled income fund. A pooled income fund is nothing more than an investment fund maintained by a qualified charity and made up of commingled funds contributed by donors who have retained for life the income from the property contributed, the principal passing to the charity at the death of the donor. Usually the charity enters into an agency relationship with a corporate trust to manage the funds.

Private Foundations

As noted earlier in this text, the Tax Reform Act of 1969 severely restricted the operation of private foundations. As a result of the imposition of an excise tax on the net investment income and other regulations by government, many foundations have been terminated. An excise tax is imposed on acts of self-dealing. The tax can range from 5 percent of

---

4. Internal Revenue Code, Sec. 664; Reg. 1.664-1 (a) (1).

the amount involved imposed on the disqualified person and 2½ percent on the manager to 200 percent on the disqualified person and 50 percent on the manager.

Serving Charitable Needs

Granted that our larger, older, better established charitable, educational, and other beneficent institutions and agencies often handle their endowment property and handle it well, there are many thousands of colleges, universities, and small private and community foundations that greatly need the service of a corporate fiduciary. Even the larger and better established charitable institutions and agencies are finding that only the well-staffed trust institution has the expertise needed to cope with investments, taxes, and government regulations. Corporate fiduciaries not actively pursuing this area of business are probably overlooking at least "an acre of diamonds." With the use of the common trust fund for investments, the trust institution can serve the public both efficiently and economically.

Chapter 14

Employee Benefit Trusts

The Purposes of This Chapter:

1. To consider some of the distinguishing characteristics of employees' trusts
2. To study the impact of recent laws on employee benefit plans

"There was a time not so long ago when the services of a trust institution were thought to be confined largely, if not entirely, to people of wealth. Now, through these employees' trusts, the base of service has been broadened to include a vast host of retired employees of business corporations. These employees and their families now are looking to some bank or trust company as trustee for their former employing corporation to supply the funds which together with their Social Security payments are ample for their support and comfort."[1]

Possibly the fastest growing field of trust services is that of trusts established to provide employee benefits. The two most important types are pension plans, which are designed to provide a promised annuity to employees during their retirement, and profit-sharing plans, which may also provide such benefits but do so in relation to the profits to be shared.

Long before the first tax exemption was granted (in 1921), there were a number of pension plans in operation in major corporations. There were, of course, many organizations with informal traditional programs for their retired employees. Several factors stimulated the growth of pension plans: sharing of jobs, preservation of efficiency in industry, union programs, desire for the welfare of employees, and even the simple altruism of benevolent employers. However, tax exemption has unquestionably had a major effect on setting up em-

---

1. Gilbert T. Stephenson, *Reflections of A Trustman* (New York: American Bankers Association, 1960), p. 29.

ployee benefit programs, and inflation has had a great influence on their frequent revision and on the trend toward trustee funding.

Before the history of employee benefits—the story of tax exemption and the competitive activities of insurance companies and trust institutions—can be understood, the various kinds of plans and their funding should be described.

These trusts are sometimes referred to as employees' trusts, but that term is not exactly applicable to pensions resulting from union negotiations. The term "retirement plan" in the income tax area embraces pension, annuity, profit-sharing, and stock bonus plans. Sometimes the words "pension" or "employee benefit" convey the idea most conveniently, although they are technically inexact. The term "employee benefit" is used here to refer to any trust established to provide employee benefits.

Employee Retirement Income Security Act of 1974 (ERISA)

The Employee Retirement Income Security Act (generally referred to as ERISA) became effective on September 2, 1974. This new law impinges on every area of corporate and self-employed pension plans. It establishes new reporting and fiduciary requirements, the discussion of which is beyond the scope of this text. Indeed, it will take at least a decade and probably more for the full development of this law.

ERISA allows employees not participating in a qualified pension plan to establish an Individual Retirement Account (IRA) and expands the provisions for H.R. 10, or Keogh, plans (both discussed later in this chapter).

This text includes chapters on the management of trusts and agencies. In view of the severe complexities and ambiguities of ERISA yet to be reconciled, it has been decided to forego for this edition any coverage of the management of employee benefit trusts.

Establishment of Employee Benefit Trusts

All employee benefit arrangements begin with the establishment of a plan. The plan provides the details of the arrangement—eligibility, benefits, retirement age, administration, vesting, and so forth. A plan for a profit-sharing arrangement also provides the calculation of the share of profits that will be set aside, invested, and managed until retirement benefits are paid. If an insurance company is to issue a group annuity or individual policies or to administer the fund, it is an insured plan. If the funds are to be invested and managed by a trust institution as one of the trustees, it is a trusteed plan, and the plan provides for a trust. Although there may be two documents and two different groups responsible for the plan and the trust, the word "trust," as used here, embraces the whole arrangement and form of benefit under which the trust institution serves. Among the purposes for which corporations establish employees' plans and trusts are the following:

1. To provide for employees who have become incapacitated before reaching the age of retirement
2. To increase production by bringing in younger employees and to provide for the retirement of employees whose contributions to the productivity of the business are less than the compensation they are receiving
3. To enable employees to share in the profits of the enterprise
4. To enable employees to participate in the ownership of the enterprise.
5. To encourage habits of thrift and saving among employees through some plan under which they join the corporation in providing funds to meet the cost of benefits
6. To reward employees for outstanding service or distinctive contributions to the enterprise
7. To enable the employer and employee to reap the tax advantages provided when the plan is "qualified" under the law. If the plan meets the requirements of the law, the contributions of the employer are deductible, and such contributions are not taxable income to the employee in the year made.

Each of these purposes can be accomplished most satisfactorily by a trust. If a corporation wants to reward employees for their outstanding service, it can do so by starting an internal plan of the corporation or a life insurance annuity.

Kinds of Employee Benefit Trusts

The five principal kinds of employees' trusts are pension trusts, profit-sharing trusts, thrift or savings plan trusts, stock bonus trusts, and self-employed retirement trusts. There are many other trusts not discussed in detail here; their purposes include health and welfare, supplemental retirement benefits, supplemental unemployment benefits, vacations, and apprentice training.

PENSION TRUSTS

Pension plans may treat each employee separately, but they usually provide for employees as a group. The wage or salary of the employee after retirement may be continued at the rate received before retirement but is more often continued at a reduced rate as long as the employee lives. Permanent disability is often treated like retirement at a specified age. After having designed an employee benefit plan, a corporation creates a trust, usually but not necessarily with a trust institution as trustee.

There are three main types of pension trusts. In the first, the corporation makes payments to a trustee, and the trustee, in conformity with the terms of a trust agreement, immediately purchases individual annuity contracts from an insurance company for the participating employees. In the second, the corporation delivers cash or securities to a trustee to receive, hold, and administer under the terms of a trust agreement. The trustee invests and administers the cash and securities as a trust estate. As each participating employee reaches the age of retirement, the trustee purchases an individual annuity contract for him from an insurance company. The difference between the first and second types thus lies in the time when an annuity contract is purchased for the employee by the trustee.

These two types were popular in the first half of this century, and trust institutions served—and in some cases still serve—as trustees for them. In the 1950s, stimulated by collective bargaining and favorable tax laws, companies began to turn to the third type, which has been growing rapidly ever since.

Under the third type, the fully trusteed plan, the corporation delivers cash and securities to a trustee to be invested and administered, as in the second type. No annuity contracts are purchased at any time. As each participating employee reaches the age of retirement or becomes disabled, the trustee starts paying him an annuity out of the trust estate.

In both the second and third types, the trustee may have full investment responsibility, may serve the corporation in an advisory capacity, or may act only on instructions from the corporation. Contributions to the trust fund are based on calculations made by an independent actuary, who is retained by the corporation to appraise the liabilities of the fund periodically. The purpose of the appraisals is to keep the contributions to the fund in line with actual expenses (within tax-deductible limitations) and with changes in wages, salaries, and personnel.

Pension trusts may also be classified as contributory or noncontributory. A trust is contributory if the employees contribute to the fund, noncontributory if they do not.

Pension plans may be grouped in three general categories. Most common is the voluntary plan of the employee's company, which is unilateral. A second class is the plan negotiated as part of a union contract. In the third general category are multiemployer pension plans in which negotiations result in a promised rate per hour or percent of payroll rather than specified pension benefits; for this category the Taft-Hartley Law calls for the establishment of a joint union-management board of trustees who determine benefits and either invest or supervise the investment of funds.

Many pension plans provide that the employee may elect an alternative method of annuity payments that will enable his or her spouse or other dependent to receive the benefits after his death. If this method is elected, the regular annuity to which the employee is entitled is reduced (both for him and for his spouse) on an actuarial basis to compensate for the fact that the benefits are to be paid for the duration of two lives rather than one.

Although no attempt is made here to present a definitive discussion of employee benefit trusts, it should be noted that the requirements of ERISA and the Internal Revenue Code, along with the regulations, have a great impact on the design of every retirement plan. On the one hand, the code provides that a plan must not discriminate in benefits in favor of officers, stockholders, or highly paid employees. ERISA, on the other hand, provides that the eligibility of an employee for entrance into the plan cannot be delayed beyond the time the employee reaches the age of 25 and completes one year of service.

PROFIT-SHARING TRUSTS

A business corporation may use a trust to enable its employees to share in its profits. The corporation may place a certain amount or percentage of its net profits in trust for distribution in the future among all or some of its employees in accordance with the terms of a trust instrument.

Although a profit-sharing trust may be used as a means of accumulating a portion of the corporation's earnings for distribution to employees either during the time they are still employed or at their deaths, it is often used to provide extra benefits at the time of retirement. The essential difference between a pension trust and a profit-sharing retirement trust is that in the former the corporation sets aside the funds necessary to provide a previously determined amount of retirement income or benefit, whereas in the latter the amount of retirement income depends on the earnings the corporation is able to place in the trust from time to time before the participating employees retire and on investment results after those earnings or contributions are in the trust. Naturally, therefore, while a pension benefit has a certain dollar value as specified in the plan, profit-sharing benefits depend on the value of the share in the fund at the time the employee's interest is withdrawn or on his retirement.

The terms of a profit-sharing trust instrument are in many respects similar to those of a pension trust. The plan must, however, meet the terms of Section 401 of the Internal Revenue Code if it is to be qualified and the applicable provisions of ERISA. Except for the requirements of ERISA, the requirements concerning the eligibility of the participants tend to be much more flexible than those governing pension plans.

THRIFT AND SAVINGS PLAN TRUSTS

Instead of arranging for the receipt and investment of employee contributions in a pension plan, a company may combine a pension plan with a thrift plan to provide additional retirement benefits based on employees' savings and the company's added contributions. Under the thrift plan, of course—unlike the contributing pension plan—the employee has a choice as to how much he will contribute. The amount contributed by the employer is usually from 25 to 100 percent of the employee's contribution.

Thrift or savings plans are frequently more liberal than pension plans: they allow vesting some years earlier, sometimes permit withdrawal of the employee's contributions, are more liberal with respect to disability, and provide that all benefits will be available at the employee's death.

EMPLOYEE STOCK OWNERSHIP PLAN

An employee stock ownership plan (commonly called ESOP) is usually established for either or both of two purposes—to provide bonuses for outstanding service and to provide shares of stock for purchase by employees. Contributions may be in the stock of the employer company or in cash, or employees may borrow on the credit of the employer for investment in qualified securities and real property of the employer. ERISA defines ESOP as a qualified stock bonus plan or a combination qualified stock bonus plan and money purchase plan designed primarily to invest in the employer's securities. The regulations of the Internal Revenue Service define a stock bonus plan as a "plan established and maintained by an employer to provide benefits similar to those of a profit-sharing plan, except . . . benefits are distributable in the stock of the employer company."

This discussion would not be complete without mention of the Tax Reduction Act Stock Ownership Plans (TRASOPS). These were introduced in the Tax Reduction Act of 1975 and brought forward and expanded under the Tax Reform Act of 1976. A TRASOP is primarily designed to invest in employer securities. TRASOPS provide the employer a dollar-for-dollar tax credit rather than a tax-deductible contribution. TRASOP credits are scheduled to expire on December 31, 1980.

SELF-EMPLOYED RETIREMENT TRUSTS

In 1962, after 11 years of study, Congress passed the Self-Employed Individuals Tax Retirement Act, which eventually came to be known as H.R. 10, or Keogh. In so doing, it removed a glaring inequity from the law, which had long prevented the self-employed from enjoying the tax benefits of qualified pension and profit-sharing plans that were accorded to employed corporate stockholders. Under this law the self-employed person is permitted to establish a profit-sharing or qualified pension plan provided that any full-time employees in the company other than the owner are covered by the plan. A "full-time employee" is defined as one who works 1,000 or more hours a year.

Only about 1 million Keogh plans were established between 1964 and 1973. To encourage more, ERISA increased the annual contribution ceiling to $7,500 or 15 percent of income, whichever is less. In addition, the law puts a floor under the deduction by providing for a minimum annual deduction of up to the lesser of $750 or 100 percent of earned income, notwithstanding the limitation of 15 percent of earned income.

ERISA provides that lump-sum benefits will qualify for long-term capital gains treatment and ten-year averaging. However, death benefits paid on behalf of the self-employed individual must be included in the gross estate.

A self-employed person is entitled to deduct the full amount of a contribution made for the benefit of regular employees. Contributions to the plan may be in a bank-trustee, bank custodial accounts, face-amount certificates, government bonds, or insurance and annuity contracts.

Individual Retirement Savings

ERISA provides that an individual not otherwise covered may establish his or her own plan for retirement on a tax-deferred basis as of 1975. He deducts his contributions from gross income on his tax return, and the earnings on the investment of his contributions accumulate tax free.[2] Of course, the contributions and the earnings realized on the investment of them will be taxed as ordinary income when withdrawn from the account, when the employee will probably be in a lower tax bracket. A person may establish his individual retirement savings plan by making contributions to an individual retirement account, an individual retirement annuity, or a U.S. retirement bond.

Under law, an individual retirement account (IRA) requires the establishment of a trust or a custodial account. The trustee or custodian may be a bank or trust company or other qualified person or organization that demonstrates to the satisfaction of the Internal Revenue Service

---

2. The student should note that IRA contributions are based only on earned income and have nothing to do with dividend income.

that the account will be administered in accordance with law. The annual contribution generally must be made in cash and cannot exceed $1,500. Such assets cannot be invested in life insurance contracts. The value of the account is nonforfeitable, and the assets must not be commingled with other property of the contributor. Of course, distributions must be in accordance with law.

If he so desires, a contributor can invest his contribution in an individual retirement annuity purchased from a legally licensed life insurance company. The term "annuity contract" is interpreted to include endowment and retirement income contracts. Among the requirements of an individual retirement annuity plan are that the annual premium cannot exceed $1,500, the contract must be nontransferable, dividends must be used to purchase additional benefits or reduce future premiums, and the individual's interest must be nonforfeitable.

In addition to individual retirement accounts and individual retirement annuities, persons may establish individual retirement savings plans by purchasing U.S. retirement bonds. The maximum amount that can be purchased annually is $1,500. The bonds cannot be pledged and are nontransferable. All interest is accumulated and paid on redemption, and the bonds may be redeemed at any time.

Tax Exemption

Tax exemption was first granted under the Revenue Act of 1921 for qualifying profit-sharing and stock bonus trusts. Pension trusts were exempted in 1926, annuity plans in 1942. However, only qualified plans are exempted. There are many nonqualified plans in operation, but the vast majority achieve qualification by avoiding discrimination as to eligibility, contributions, or benefits in favor of employees who are officers, shareholders, supervisors, or highly paid.

Limits on deductions for contributions to all types of plans are necessary to qualify for tax exemption. Not only must the total compensation of the employee (wage or salary and benefit) be reasonable, but credits for past service or supplementary benefits must comply. Employee benefit trusts must also avoid transactions prohibited by the Internal Revenue Code.

There are four tax advantages associated with qualified employee benefit trusts. First, employer contributions are deductible, within liberal limits, for the year in which they are made. That of itself is not startling, because there is a comparable deduction for other types of compensation paid to employees. But where a qualified plan is concerned, the employer is permitted the deduction currently despite the fact that the employee may receive no benefit until much later. The employer is thus enabled to accumulate funds for his employees while suffering no current tax disadvantages.

The second advantage is that earnings and gains on the funds accumulated under the plan are wholly exempt from state and federal income taxes throughout the accumulation period. Thus the funds compound tax free and increase at a far greater rate than they would if they were subject to tax.

Third, the employees under the plan are not taxed while their benefit funds are accumulating. They are taxed only on benefits actually received or made available to them. If the funds are paid to the employee in a lump sum at retirement, a portion of the distribution may be taxed at capital gains rates, and a special averaging provision may be available as additional tax relief for the balance. Finally, if the monies represented by the company's contributions to the plan are paid to the employee's beneficiary after his death in more than one instalment, they are not subject to the federal estate tax.

Differences Between Pension and Profit-Sharing Plans

There are many differences between pension plans and profit-sharing plans. Under a pension plan, the amounts contributed by the employer are not related to profits but are actuarially necessary to provide the planned benefits. Under a profit-sharing plan, on the other hand, the employer's contributions are made from profits—usually before taxes—and vary with the size of the profit and the contribution formula of the plan. Under a pension plan, income provided after retirement is not based on company profits, whereas under a profit-sharing plan a share of those profits is provided as additional compensation, usually payable entirely or in part at retirement.

Another major difference is that company contributions to a pension plan for an employee are usually the actuarial instalments necessary to provide the planned benefits, generally based on compensation, age, and years of past service; while company contributions to a profit-sharing plan in any year are usually allocated among accounts of employees in proportion to their annual compensation, age and years of service usually being ignored. Benefits of a pension plan are usually payable only at retirement, death, disability or, if vested, termination of employment; cash disbursements from an employee's account in a profit-sharing plan can be made at prescribed occasions during employment (in addition to retirement, death, disability, layoff, discharge, or resignation).

Pension plan benefits are usually distributable in instalments, beginning at retirement age, whereas profit-sharing plan benefits are usually distributable as a lump sum (although other methods are also available). Pension plan benefits are fixed by the plan's benefit scale, while profit-sharing plan benefits at retirement, death, disability, layoff, and sometimes discharge or resignation are usually the amount in the employee's account. Severance benefits at discharge or resignation under a pension plan are usually in the form of retirement income deferred to normal retirement age, whereas under a profit-sharing plan they are usually in cash.

There are various other differences. Under a pension plan, for example, amounts forfeited must be applied to reduce the subsequent cost to the employer of maintaining the plan; under a profit-sharing plan, on the other hand, amounts forfeited by employees who leave before rights are fully vested are usually reallocated to increase the accounts of remaining employees. The rate of vesting is usually slower in a pension than in a profit-sharing plan.

Whether a trust is needed for a pension plan depends on the type of plan, whereas a trust is generally required to administer a profit-sharing plan. Finally, employees do not contribute under most profit-sharing plans but do contribute under some pension plans. Contributions are usually a prescribed percentage of compensation, periodically deducted from pay.

Procedure for Setting Up An Employee Benefit Trust

Several steps are involved in setting up an employee benefit trust by a corporation. The following is a typical procedure:

1. The corporation, often with the help of a specialist on employee benefit plans, designs the plan best suited to its needs and those of its employees.

2. A trustee for the plan is selected. The trustee may be an individual, a group of individuals, or a trust institution, but the prevailing practice is to select a trust institution.

3. The drafting of the plan and the trust agreement is extremely important. It is the function of the attorney for the corporation, usually in collaboration with the attorney for the trustee. Inasmuch as the trustee is a party to any agreement under which it is charged with certain duties and assumes certain responsibilities, its own attorney either collaborates in the drafting of the agreement or approves the instrument from a legal point of view before the agreement is executed by the trustee.

4. If the trust is to be contributory, a form of employee acceptance must be prepared. By signing this form, an employee accepts the terms of the plan and agrees to contribute to the trust fund, usually through

some form of salary or wage deduction. If the trust is to be noncontributory, this step is unnecessary.

5. The corporation presents the plan to its board of directors for adoption (the board has, of course, been previously consulted about the basic principles of the plan). The plan may be submitted to the stockholders for approval before being adopted by the board. The growing tendency seems to be to obtain the stockholders' approval even though the law may not require it.

6. It is customary for the corporation to prepare a summary description of the plan and submit it to all employees at the same time the plan is submitted to the Internal Revenue Service.

TRUST AGREEMENT

The trust agreement should contain provisions covering the receipt by the trustee of the property transferred by the company or the board of trustees, the duty of investment at the trustee's own discretion or under the policies or directions of the company or joint board of trustees, the payment of funds according to the directions of the authorized committee or group, and accountings by the trustee to company, committee, or joint board. It should also cover removal or resignation of the trustee, power of amendment (which, of course, cannot permit diversion of funds for any purpose other than the exclusive benefit of the employees, the retired employees, and their beneficiaries), and termination, which may not allow any funds to be returned to the company until all obligations under the plan have been satisfied.

OPERATION OF A PENSION PLAN

The amount of determinable pension benefit to be paid at retirement—and on such other occasions as are specified in the plan—is computed under the plan formula. With the aid of actuarial assumptions as to interest, mortality, turnover, and so forth, the company prefunds its promise by annual contributions. The two exceptions to the determinable aspect of the pension benefit are the variable benefit plan and the money purchase (accumulation) pension plan.

A fixed dollar benefit plan specifies the amount of monthly retirement pension that will be payable to all participants who satisfy plan requirements. The benefit may be expressed as a total dollar amount (for example, $100 monthly) or a stipulated monthly benefit for each year of the participant's service (for example, $2.50). Negotiated plans are frequently of the fixed dollar kind.

Under the career average plan, the participant earns a potential monthly pension during each year of his service with the company. The benefit is expressed as a percentage (1.5 percent for example) of his average monthly compensation during the year. Under such a formula, an employee earning $500 a month would accrue a monthly pension benefit of $7.50 multiplied by the number of years of service. The amount of the ultimate pension would be the cumulative total of his annual credits. Occasionally a ceiling is placed on the amount of the benefit.

Many plans provide benefits for service before the effective date of the plan (called past service benefits). Typically, in a career average plan, the employee's monthly compensation on the effective date of the plan is multiplied by the benefit percentage and by his credited years of past service to determine the accrued past service benefit. As a rule, the benefit percentage applicable to prior service is somewhat lower than that applicable to service after the plan's effective date.

Under the final pay plan, an attempt is made to adjust the pension benefit to a generally rising cost and standard of living. Thus some plans relate the amount of the pension to the participant's average monthly compensation during a selected period of service (for example, the participant's final five years of service or the five consecutive years of service that produce the highest average monthly compensation). For example, the formula might be "30 percent of final five-year average monthly compensation" or "1.5 percent of final five-year average monthly compensation per year of credited service." If the formula is of the former type, a minimum number of years of service is generally required before the participant is eligible for the full pension. A final pay formula is sometimes used as a minimum in a career average plan.

Pension plans may be correlated with Social Security benefits by eliminating a portion of the employee's monthly compensation from benefit consideration, providing a larger pension with respect to excess monthly pay than with respect to pay below the breakpoint, or offsetting the plan benefits by a portion of the primary Social Security benefits. If the plan provides preretirement death benefits, or the pension is payable on a years certain basis, or the participant retires with less than 15 years of service, the maximum allowable integrated benefits are decreased.

Each year the company contributes for the pension the credits accrued by the participants during that year (the plan's normal cost) plus an amount relating to past service credits. The cost of past service credits is determined by computing the value of all past service benefits as of the effective date of the plan. That past service liability may be amortized over a period of not less than 10 years; since the company is also liable for interest on the unpaid past service liability, the minimum period of amortization may extend to 11 or 12 years. Alternatively, the company may pay interest only on its past service liability, at the rate assumed in the plan.

ACTUARIAL ASSUMPTIONS

It should come as no surprise that the trust fund arrangement was the first method used to fund private pension benefits.[3] Trust fund plans cover the vast majority of employees receiving private pension benefits.

The annual contributions under a trust fund plan are not a matter of guessing. They are determined by periodic valuations by the plan actuary. Furthermore, the actuary is required to be enrolled under ERISA.

ERISA requires the actuary to choose actuarial assumptions and techniques that are reasonable for that particular plan. In computing the amount of contributions to be made, the actuary will choose assumptions that are more conservative than the experience actually expected. The value of the plan assets must be determined on a basis that takes fair market value into account.

Though not in a position to make the final decision, the employer can participate in decisions regarding the choice of actuarial assumptions, the cost method to be used in calculating the contribution payment, and the timing of the contribution.

Regulation of Employee Benefit Plans and Trusts

If the plan is to be qualified for the various tax benefits provided by law, it must meet the qualifications for tax exemption provided under the Internal Revenue Code. National and state banking authorities, the Federal Reserve System, the Federal Deposit Insurance Corporation, and state insurance departments all have an interest in employee benefit plans. The major factor, however, in administering such accounts is compliance with the regulations of the Department of Labor issued pursuant to the provisions of ERISA. Failure to conform to the provisions of ERISA and the applicable regulations may constitute violation of both civil and criminal law.

Under Regulation 9, the Comptroller of the Currency has authority over collective investment funds for pension and profit-sharing funds in national banks. Because of the impact of ERISA on the administration of employee benefit accounts, a special section has been included in the comptroller's questionnaire and the examination procedures checklist. The examination of employee benefit accounts should determine:

1. That the requirements of ERISA have been met
2. That the bank has taken the necessary action to protect itself from liability that might be imposed by the actions of others.

---

3. See Everett T. Allen, Joseph J. Melone, and Jerry S. Rosenbloom, *Pension Planning*, 3rd ed. (Homewood, Ill.: Richard D. Irwin, 1976), p. 195, for an excellent treatment of the subject.

As employee benefit business increases, there will probably be additional legislation designed to protect these funds. In view of the recognized fiduciary expertise of trust institutions and their excellent record of managing funds entrusted to them, the responsibilities of corporate trustees for the management of employee benefit funds may be expected to expand greatly in years ahead.

Rollovers

The student should be aware of the "rollover" provisions of the law, which permit the transfer of assets from one individual retirement savings plan to another. Furthermore, under the rollover provisions, an employee who receives a lump-sum distribution from a qualified pension or profit-sharing plan may transfer the amount to an individual retirement plan without the imposition of any taxes.

Not every distribution goes untaxed. If a person who is not disabled receives a distribution before reaching the age of 59½, the amount received is considered a premature distribution and must be included in the person's gross income in the year received. There is an additional tax of 10 percent of the amount of the premature distribution.

To escape taxation on a withdrawal from one individual retirement plan and a transfer to another, the following conditions must be met:

1. The full amount of the distribution must be reinvested in the new plan within 60 days after the date of distribution.

2. The new individual retirement plan must not contain any assets other than those received from the distributing plan.

3. After the first rollover, there may be no further rollovers for three years.

4. If property is received as part of the distribution, it must be reinvested in the new plan.

The law also provides for rollovers after age 70½. Such rollovers may not be made to U.S. government retirement bonds.

The law provides for rollovers from qualified pension and profit-sharing plans to individual retirement savings plans. There may also be a rollover from an H.R. 10 plan to an individual retirement savings plan. Once the transfer is made, however, such amounts may not subsequently be transferred to a qualified pension or profit-sharing plan.

Trends in Employee Benefit Plans

Investment trends and the trend toward collective investments are discussed in Chapter 17; in this chapter the word "trends" is used to refer to the amendments that have been made to many plans and to the pattern of newer plans.

In large companies there is a definite trend away from the insured plan toward the trusteed plan. Lower costs and greater flexibility are the key points. Continued inflation requires frequent upward revision of benefits, and corporate treasurers make more effective use of funds. There are no loading or sales charges. Trust institutions have become aware that their investment performance is a matter of vital interest to the companies that are placing funds in trust.

Generally speaking, there are definite trends in eligibility, employee contributions, age and service requirements for normal retirement, early retirement, disability retirement, vesting, preretirement death benefits, normal retirement benefits, and minimum and maximum pensions. Only a few of the more significant are mentioned here.

Eligibility requirements are being liberalized by the elimination or reduction of age and service requirements. Under ERISA, eligibility cannot be delayed beyond the time an employee reaches age 25 and completes one year of service. If, however, the plan provides for full and immediate vesting, a three-year service requirement, along with a minimum age requirement of 25, may be imposed. ERISA defines normal retirement as no later than age 65 or ten years of service, whichever is the last to occur. Formerly there was a trend toward retiring women at age 60 and men at age 65. Under Title VII of the Civil Rights Act that practice is declared to be discriminatory, and plans making the distinction have had to be amended, putting male and female employees on an equal footing.

Last but by no means least, there seems to be a definite trend toward the adoption of the trust fund arrangement for the management of private employee benefit plans. Already the assets of employee benefit plans constitute one of the largest sources of investment capital in the nation. By 1974 banks were administering $127 billion in assets for public and private pension, profit-sharing, thrift, and stock bonus plans. (Life insurance companies held about $56 billion in private pension plan assets.) About 70 percent of all pension fund assets were held in trust funds. Of the 33 to 40 million participants under private plans, about 25 million are current or future beneficiaries of bank-operated funds.

Chapter 15

Corporate Trusts

The Purposes of This Chapter:

1. To explain why corporate trusts are needed
2. To define some of the most important terms used in corporate trust business
3. To explain how corporate trusts are established and how bonds are used

"In considering the acceptance of a corporate trust or agency, the trust institution should be satisfied that the company concerned is in good standing and that the enterprise is of a proper nature."[1]

Although before the 1950s the number and volume of direct or private placement contracts were not large, debt financing has become very important. It has been estimated that during the 1960s 50 percent of the total capital debt financing of corporations came about through private placements. Thus what started as a small and insignificant service has become important and profitable for trust institutions that are staffed and equipped to manage the business. Not all corporate fiduciaries are engaged in corporate trust business. In that business the competition is keen, the exposure is almost unlimited, and the risk can be very great.

Inasmuch as corporate activities are found in the financial records the corporation must maintain, it is necessary for the corporate trust administrator to have a working knowledge of the usual financial statements prepared by management and audited by independent accountants. Among the statements the administrator works with are the balance sheet, the income and surplus statements, and statements showing the sources and uses of funds.[2]

---

1. "A Statement of Principles of Trust Institutions (1933)," *Trust Principles and Policies* (Washington, D.C.: American Bankers Association, 1973).

2. Robert I. Landau and Joseph C. Kennedy, *Corporate Trust* (New York: New York University Press, 1975), Chapter 10.

"A Statement of Principles of Trust Institutions" admonishes that "a new trust department should be established only if there is enough potential trust business within the trade area to justify the proper personnel and equipment."[3] To like effect is the declaration of the "Statement of Principles" concerning the rendering of corporate trust services.

Need for Corporate Trusts

The primary source of a corporation's capital is the funds supplied by stockholders, whose interests in the corporation are evidenced by certificates of shares of stock. If the equity capital supplied by the stockholders is not sufficient to meet the requirements of the corporation, the corporation may borrow money. If the corporation will not be in a position to pay back the borrowed money for several years, it may wish to borrow from the investing public by issuing bonds or other obligations. In connection with such borrowing, a corporate trust is set up; thus a demand is created for the services of a trust institution as trustee.

Those services are not the services of an investment banker. The trust institution does not purchase or underwrite the corporation's securities, nor does it attempt to find buyers for them. It does, however, perform useful—indeed essential—services in acting as trustee. The trustee acts as intermediary between the borrower and the lenders during the life of the loan, particularly as the representative of the lenders.

If a corporation could borrow all the funds it needed from a single lender or a small banking group, it might execute a mortgage or loan agreement, and a trustee would not be needed. But corporations frequently require larger amounts and for longer terms than can usually be obtained from commercial banks. Therefore they have to borrow from the investing public—that is, from hundreds or thousands of individual lenders.

It would be impractical for the corporation to enter into a separate mortgage or loan agreement with each of those lenders; so the corporation executes an agreement, called an indenture, with a trust institution, which acts as trustee for all the lenders. Bonds of the corporation are issued and delivered to the lenders, and the bonds are certified or authenticated by the trustee to show that they have been issued under a particular indenture. The indenture should set forth in great detail every part of the agreement the corporation makes to induce the public

---

3. "A Statement of Principles of Trust Institutions (1933)," *Trust Principles and Policies* (Washington, D.C.: American Bankers Association, 1973), Art. VI, Sec. 3.

to lend to it. In it the corporation pledges its full faith and credit to carry out the terms of the agreement. The most important term is the corporation's promise to repay the money borrowed, with interest. The corporation frequently secures that pledge by mortgaging its property to the trust institution that is to act as trustee.

The document that creates a corporate trust is variously called a mortgage, a trust mortgage, a deed of trust, a trust agreement, a debenture agreement, a collateral trust agreement, or simply an agreement or an indenture. Which of these designations is applicable in a given case depends largely on the kind of instrument involved. In this textbook the instrument is referred to as a trust indenture (sometimes merely as an indenture), regardless of whether it covers real property, personal property, both, or no property at all.

Equipment Trusts

In addition to the customary indenture and private placement contract, there is one indenture that is somewhat different: the equipment trust agreement and lease. It is a special form of contract used to finance the purchase of equipment first by railroads and more recently by major airlines.

Simply stated, the trustee has legal ownership of the property and leases it to the airline or the railroad. The obligations are in the form of trust certificates, the proceeds from the sale of which are used to purchase the equipment. The rental from the lease, which is usually for a period of 8 to 15 years, is sufficient to pay all the interest and principal on the certificates. Although the certificates are executed by the trustee, they carry a written guaranty of payment by the railroad company or airline, and the guaranty runs directly to the certificate holder. The administration of the trust is usually not difficult, but it can become so if there is a default by the corporation.

Revenue Bond Indentures or Resolutions

Another type of obligation is sometimes used to finance the construction of facilities to be used by the general public, such as bridges, tunnels, turnpikes, waterworks, and sewage disposal plants. The obligations may be those of a municipality or of a public authority. They are payable only out of revenues obtained from the facility.

Responsibilities of Trustee in Establishing the Trust

The duties of a trustee under a corporate trust indenture begin before the trust is created, before the indenture is executed, and before any bonds are issued. The trustee must first determine whether the trust is an acceptable one.

CONSIDERATIONS DETERMINING ACCEPTABILITY

The acceptability of a trust depends largely on the corporation that is to undertake the obligation, particularly on whether its management is experienced and reputable and whether, especially in the case of a new or an unseasoned venture, there is a reasonable prospect of success. Although the trustee does not in any sense guarantee the bonds issued under a trust indenture, the use of a responsible trust institution's name inevitably influences the investing public. The institution should therefore satisfy itself that its appointment as trustee is not motivated primarily by the obligor's desire to make speculative securities more salable by having them bear the authentication of a responsible trustee. The trust institution must also be qualified to act as a corporate trustee under the laws of the state or states in which the mortgaged property is located.

TRUST INDENTURE ACT OF 1939

The development of the Trust Indenture Act of 1939 is a good example of how government regulation developed in an effort to ensure adherence to uniform standards as private business corporations sought funds from the investing public.

In 1932 the United States was in the third year of a depression that had begun in the fall of 1929. The distribution and sale of securities were governed by the blue sky laws of the various states. Defaults under trust indentures, which had been developed with little or no government supervision, caused many investors to lose some or all of their life savings. The national financial disaster of the depression was followed by the passage of a number of securities acts designed to protect the investing public. The first of these was the Securities Act of 1933. The act required a corporation desiring to secure funds from the public to file with the Securities and Exchange Commission a registration statement with an issue of securities and publish a prospectus.

Next came the Securities Exchange Act of 1934, whose purpose was to regulate the national securities exchanges. It created the Securities and Exchange Commission to administer the law. The legislative activity of the period culminated in the enactment of the Trust Indenture Act of 1939 in August 1939, to become effective in February 1940. An amendment to the Securities Act of 1933, it was designed to aid investors by prescribing that certain provisions must be included in corporate trust indentures, that certain others might be included, and that still others must be excluded. In addition to setting minimum standards of responsibility and accountability for trustees under

216

indentures, the act requires the corporation to furnish financial data and other information to the trustee. Unless those conditions are met, the Securities and Exchange Commission will not qualify the indenture (that is, will not permit the registration statement regarding the securities to become effective), and the bonds cannot be offered publicly for sale. Not all indentures, however, need be so qualified. The notable exceptions are:

1. Indentures under which the securities of railroads (which are subject to regulation by the Interstate Commerce Commission) are to be issued
2. Indentures for securities that are not to be offered publicly (that is, private placements)
3. Indentures for security issues that do not exceed $1 million
4. Indentures under which securities of charities are to be issued

ESTABLISHMENT OF THE TRUST

The trust is established by execution of the indenture by the corporation and the trustee. Before that point is reached, however, the experienced trustee will have made a careful analysis of the indenture, particularly of the administrative provisions under which the trustee is to act. Although the indenture is not drawn up by the trustee or its counsel, both must give it their close scrutiny. The trustee's counsel must make certain that it is in satisfactory legal form, and the trust officer must detect any provisions that are unclear or unworkable or may give rise to unnecessary difficulties and complications in the administration of the trust. It is not within the province of the trustee to concern itself with terms of the trust indenture that are primarily matters for negotiation between the corporation and the purchasers of the bonds.

ELIGIBILITY AND QUALIFICATION

An essential step in qualifying any indenture under the Trust Indenture Act is to file with the Securities and Exchange Commission a document designed to show whether the trust institution is eligible and qualified to act as trustee under the standards set up by the act. The document is a questionnaire executed by the trustee, and the answers to the questions disclose any relationships between the trustee, the corporation, and the underwriters (who have purchased the bonds for sale to the public) that might constitute conflicting interests. Any existing defect in the trustee's eligibility and qualifications, under the strict standards of the act, will thus be brought to light in ample time to avoid later discovery and possible compulsory resignation, since the requirements as to the trustee's eligibility and qualifications continue throughout the lifetime of the trust.

ESSENTIAL DOCUMENTS

At the same time the trust indenture is executed, the trustee should be furnished with certain documents:

1. A copy of the corporation's charter or articles of incorporation, with all amendments, certified by the secretary of state or other appropriate officer of the state in which the obligor is incorporated.
2. A copy of the corporation's bylaws, with all amendments, certified by its secretary or other qualified officer.
3. A similarly certified copy of the stockholders' resolution authorizing the borrowing and the execution of the indenture (required by law in some states).
4. A similarly certified copy of the resolutions of the board of directors authorizing execution of the indenture, issuance of the bonds, and any other pertinent matter.
5. Evidence of the election of the corporation's officers, and specimens of their signatures.
6. A certified copy of the order or consent of any public body having jurisdiction over the proposed issue, such as the Securities and Exchange Commission (under the Public Utility Holding Company Act, the Securities Act, and the Trust Indenture Act), the Interstate Commerce Commission, or the public utility commission of the state concerned.
7. Opinion of counsel for the corporation to the effect that the indenture and the bonds are valid and binding, that all necessary corporate action has been taken, and that the indenture, when it has been properly recorded (if it is a mortgage), will constitute a valid and enforceable lien on the property pledged. The opinion states that the bonds have been approved by all necessary government authorities and includes evidence that the indenture has been qualified under the Trust Indenture Act and that the registration statement filed with the Securities and Exchange Commission has become effective (or that such qualification and registration are not necessary).
8. Opinion of counsel for the trustee to the effect that the trust indenture and the supporting documents are in satisfactory form and that it is proper for the trustee to execute and deliver the trust indenture. Sometimes the legal opinion is printed on the bond, and no separate document is required.

CLOSING

A corporate trust indenture is usually executed and delivered, and the bonds delivered by the trustee, at a meeting of the various interested persons—the obligor, the trustee, the purchasers of the bonds, and their counsel. This closing, which usually takes place at the office of the trustee, is necessary because the various steps in the financial transaction must logically be simultaneous. The bonds cannot be accepted and paid for by the purchasers until the indenture has been executed and the bonds authenticated and delivered by the trustee. The trustee cannot take those steps until the indenture has been executed and delivered by the obligor and the supporting documents have been duly filed with the trustee. The obligor is unwilling to proceed with the execution of the indenture and the delivery of the bonds unless it is assured that all arrangements are acceptable to those interested and that the sale of the bonds is to be carried through to completion.

Frequently, too, the issuance of bonds is predicated on the redemption of an old issue or the satisfaction of an old indenture, and funds for such redemption or satisfaction are to be derived from the new issue. In such instances simultaneous dealings are essential for the protection of all persons concerned in the transaction.

Essential Features of Corporate Trust Indentures

The provisions of the indenture that deal with the establishment of a corporate trust include introductory clauses, conveyance or granting clauses, and sections that detail the conditions under which bonds may be issued. Although different indentures have many similarities in the arrangement of material, in form, and even in substance, no two indentures are exactly alike. In the following discussion, therefore, it must be understood that some of the statements do not apply to all indentures or to all situations.

INTRODUCTORY CLAUSES

Nearly all indentures begin with brief recitals of the date of the indenture, the names of the parties, and the corporation's authority to borrow money, execute the indenture, and issue its bonds thereunder. The complete wording of the bond follows, in its registered as well as its coupon form (if both are to be issued), together with the form of the coupon.

A corporate bond should contain a promise to pay a fixed sum at a specified time and place and to pay interest thereon at a rate (except in the case of income bonds), time, and place also specified. It should recite the terms on which it may be redeemed before its stated maturity if there is provision for such early redemption. A bond is intended to be a negotiable instrument, and its attributes of negotiability should be preserved. The essential feature of negotiability—an unconditional promise to pay a sum certain in money at a fixed or determinable future time—must be retained.

219

The next item in the indenture is the wording of the trustee's certificate of authentication, which has become fairly standardized and usually reads substantially as follows: "This bond is one of the bonds, of the series herein designated, described in the within mentioned indenture." From this wording it is clear that the purpose of the certificate is to identify the bond as one of the stated issue. The trustee's certificate must, of course, be signed on each bond by an officer of the trustee.

GRANTING CLAUSES

In a mortgage, as distinguished from an unsecured indenture, the introductory clauses are followed by the important granting clauses. It is by the granting clauses that the property to be mortgaged is conveyed to the trustee. All the property owned by the corporation is usually included. The property is sometimes described in complete detail and sometimes in more general terms, depending on its nature. The real property of a manufacturing company, for instance, is probably described in full, whereas that of a railroad cannot be described in minute detail. The important point is that the description must be specific enough to permit a lien to be established against that particular property when the trust indenture has been recorded.

AUTHENTICATION OF BONDS

As a rule, nothing more is required for the authentication of bonds than a delivery order signed by specified officers of the corporation. A subsequent issuance of bonds under an open-end indenture, however, must be hedged in by definite restrictions, for the new bonds are normally entitled to the same rights in the security as those already outstanding; the result would be dilution of the security. To permit an increase in the amount of bonds secured by the mortgage without a stipulated increase in the security afforded by the mortgage would not be fair to the holders of the original bonds.

Consequently, all open-end mortgages contain specific, thorough, and sometimes complicated provisions aimed at maintenance of the security in connection with authentication of any additional bonds. Sometimes the issuance of additional series of bonds under supplemental indentures is provided for.

TRUSTEE'S RESPONSIBILITY IN AUTHENTICATION AND DELIVERY

In no phase of its duties is the trustee confronted with greater responsibility than in the authentication and delivery of bonds. By its authentication the trustee in effect declares publicly that the bonds, amounting to perhaps many millions of dollars, have been issued pursuant to the terms of a certain indenture. Those terms are probably very technical and complex and possibly difficult to interpret. Careful training, long experience, and a high degree of skill are required for the satisfactory performance of this special duty. A trustee cannot be too careful in matters involving the authentication and delivery of bonds.

ISSUE OF BONDS FOR REFUNDING

The issuance of bonds for refunding other bonds is essentially simple, but certain complications exist and numerous safeguards are necessary. It is usually impractical to turn over to the trustee all the bonds of the old issue before or simultaneously with the delivery of the refunding issue, and it is accordingly impossible for the trustee to deliver new bonds in direct exchange for the old ones. Therefore the trust indenture must provide some means of refunding and at the same time set up all the safeguards necessary to ensure that the old issue will not remain as a prior claim against the security to which the new issue is entitled. One way to accomplish that result is to issue the new bonds against the deposit with the trustee of an equal amount of cash, which may be released only when old bonds of an equivalent amount are redeemed or evidence is presented that they have been canceled.

Uniform Commercial Code

In addition to the Trust Indenture Act of 1939, the Uniform Commercial Code, which was first adopted in New York in 1962 and became effective there in 1964, has been adopted in all states except Louisiana and in the District of Columbia and the Virgin Islands. It is playing an increasingly important role in corporate trusts. For example, Article 8, in addition to making all investment securities negotiable, places the responsibility for administration on the fiduciary and defines the responsibilities of the trustee, the registrar, and the transfer agent.

Article 9 covers secured transactions and sets forth uniform rules for security transactions involving personal property. Inasmuch as a great deal of present-day financing involves equipment leases, receivables, chattel paper, and contract rights, the student should become familiar with the rules that provide for accounts receivable financing, subjection of after-acquired property to the security agreement, and mortgaging of inventory, stock in trade, or similar property by the debtor.[4]

---

4. Robert I. Landau and Joseph C. Kennedy, *op. cit.*, note 3, p. 37.

Chapter 16

Corporate Agencies

The Purposes of This Chapter:

1. To explain the duties and responsibilities of a stock transfer agent and a registrar
2. To emphasize the wide variety of services to business corporations that a trust institution may render as agent
3. To describe briefly how the need for these services originates and what duties the agent undertakes in their performance

"Since the need for trust and agency services to corporations outside the centers of population is much more limited than is that of trust and agency services to individuals, a trust institution should hesitate to enter the corporate trust or agency field unless an actual demand for such services is evident and the institution is specially equipped to render such service."[1]

In addition to serving as trustee of a corporate trust, the bank so designated may be appointed principal agent to service the indenture securities. It is not, however, uncommon and may sometimes be necessary to have one bank serve as trustee, protecting the security of the indenture and administering its provisions, and a second bank as principal agent to service the securities. For example, a bank that serves as corporate trustee for a secured bond issue will not be permitted to serve in the same capacity for an unsecured debenture issue.[2]

The various corporate agencies that a trust institution may be called on to handle may, for convenience, be divided into transfer agencies, registration agencies, paying agencies, exchange agencies, deposit agencies, and miscellaneous agencies.

---

1. "A Statement of Principles of Trust Institutions (1933)," *Trust Principles and Policies* (Washington, D.C.: American Bankers Association, 1973).

2. Robert I. Landau and Joseph C. Kennedy, *Corporate Trust* (New York: New York University Press, 1975), Chapter 9.

Transfer Agencies

Although the term "transfer agency" generally refers to the transfer of a corporation's stock, it may also relate to voting trust certificates, certificates of deposit, or any other security whose ownership is registered and does not pass by mere delivery of the instrument. The function of a bond registrar is essentially that of a transfer agent, for the bond registrar's basic duty is to record the ownership of bonds and transfers of ownership.

VOLUME OF STOCK TRANSFERS

In the early years of corporate organization, there were no stock certificates; the entire record of stock ownership was contained in the corporation's stock books. As time went on and changes in stock ownership became more numerous, stock certificates came into general use. However, no provision was made on those early certificates for assignment when ownership of the stock was transferred. If the registered holder of a certificate desired to sell or otherwise dispose of his stock, he had to surrender his certificate to the corporation and sign the book in which the transfer was recorded. Because that method of effecting transfers was inconvenient for stockholders, the present form of assignment on the back of the certificate, with authority to an attorney in fact to make the transfer, gradually evolved. Under current practice the name of the attorney in fact is ordinarily omitted, and the transfer agent (or an employee of the transfer agent) acts in that capacity.

During the early years, there were relatively few transfers of stock ownership; the work of transfer was not burdensome and was easily handled by the corporation. But in the course of time the volume of stock distributed to the public increased tremendously, and there was a great increase in the amount of stock bought and sold. As a result, many corporations found it advantageous to use the services of a trust institution as transfer agent.

Two other factors were instrumental in increasing the number of transfer agencies handled by trust institutions. One was a scandal involving the issuance of spurious and unauthorized stock certificates in large volume. The other was the requirement by certain stock exchanges that any stock listed on those exchanges be transferable at transfer agencies in the cities in which the exchanges are located.

The relationship between a corporation and the trust institution that transfers its stock is basically that of principal and agent. The corporation inevitably places a great responsibility on its agent and must therefore have full confidence in the agent's ability to perform the transfer functions so as not to impose liability on, or cause loss to, the principal. The agent, fully aware of the confidence reposed in it and conscious of its responsibility toward its principal, undertakes to perform its role as agent with the same scrupulous care that it would exercise if it were the principal.

APPOINTMENT AS TRANSFER AGENT

Before a corporation can issue any stock, certain government and corporate requirements must be met. A trust institution should undertake to act as transfer agent only after receiving a formal resolution of appointment by the corporation's board of directors and certain papers evidencing the corporation's authority to issue the stock.

DUTIES OF STOCK TRANSFER AGENT

The transfer of stock entails both issuing the stock certificate and recording the change in ownership. A trust institution may maintain the records of stock ownership in addition to serving as agent to effect transfers of the certificates, or the stock bookkeeping may be performed by another agent or sometimes by the corporation itself. The issuance of new certificates must always be accomplished expeditiously, anticipating peak loads and within the prescribed time limits, but bookkeeping can generally be completed at a more leisurely pace. In this connection a trust institution as transfer agent has a number of clearly defined duties.

Verification of Corporation's Signature

Stock certificates must generally be signed by officers of both the corporation and the transfer agent, as well as by an officer of the registrar if there is one. The corporation's signatures on stock certificates are usually permitted to be in facsimile form, provided that the certificates are manually signed by authorized officers of the transfer agent and the registrar.

Original Issue of Stock

The majority of the certificates issued and delivered by a transfer agent are in exchange for certificates representing shares already outstanding. But stock must, of course, be originally issued. An original issue may be based on money payments, on an exchange for property or other stock, on services rendered to the corporation, or on other conditions. The agent should have evidence that all government regulations have been complied with, that all taxes have been paid, and that the issuance of shares is duly authorized and not in excess of the limits set by the corporation's charter or articles of incorporation.

Transfer of Stock

The problems and responsibilities involved in the transfer of stock already outstanding are quite different from those involved in an original issue. The primary responsibility of the agent is to assure itself that the registered holder has duly assigned his ownership of the stock represented by the old certificates. The transfer agent obtains this assurance by establishing the identity of the transferor and his right to transfer the stock.

Establishment of Identity

Identity is more easily established than the right to transfer. If the transferor is an individual or a partnership, the identity of the person whose signature appears on the assignment is commonly proved by having his signature guaranteed.

Establishment of Right to Transfer

The right of a stockholder to transfer stock is not easily established if the transferor is a corporation or anyone acting in a fiduciary capacity or as an agent. The mere signature of an individual signing as trustee, executor, or attorney in fact or the signature of certain officers of a corporation may not be enough, even though such signatures are duly witnessed and guaranteed. The signature may be genuine, but the question of the assignor's right to assign remains. Although various laws protect the agent in many areas and special situations, the agent must determine the answers to such questions as: Has he the power to bind the corporation? Is the alleged trustee or executor actually the trustee or executor, and has he the power to sell or otherwise transfer ownership? Does the attorney in fact really have the right to act on behalf of his principal in so important a matter as the transfer of stock? Unless the law of his state or the corporation exonerates the agent, it must obtain satisfactory answers to all such questions before it can safely transfer the stock. The only way it can obtain the answers is by being supplied with duly authenticated documents to establish the facts. This responsibility requires that the transfer agent pass on difficult and intricate matters promptly. It may require:

1. Interpretation of wills, trust instruments, and powers of attorney
2. Knowledge of the powers of executors, administrators, guardians, and trustees with regard to the transfer of stock under the laws of the transfer agent's own state and of other states
3. Familiarity with the laws pertaining to the taxation of stock transfers and to estate and inheritance taxes

UNIFORM STOCK TRANSFER ACT

In 1909 the Uniform Stock Transfer Act was approved by the National Conference of Commissioners on Uniform State Laws. It was adopted, with slight variations, by all the states and the District of

Columbia. The act relates primarily to the rights of stockholders between themselves. It makes the transfer of a stock certificate operate as a transfer of the shares, whereas at common law it is the registry on the books of the company that actually effects the transfer. "The reason for the change," said the commissioners, "is in order that the certificate may, to the fullest extent possible, be the representative of the shares. This is the fundamental purpose of the whole act, and is in accordance with the mercantile usage. The transfer on the books of the corporation becomes thus like the record of a deed of real estate under a registry system."[3]

UNIFORM COMMERCIAL CODE

The Uniform Stock Transfer Act has been incorporated into the Uniform Commercial Code, which has been adopted by almost all states. There may, however, be variations in the code as adopted by each state. And since not all the provisions of the Uniform Stock Transfer Act were incorporated in the code, the student should ascertain the law in his or her state.

TAXES ON ORIGINAL ISSUES AND ON TRANSFERS

The transfer agent must keep itself informed about any stamp and transfer tax laws of the federal and state governments and the numerous estate and inheritance tax laws. At present there is no federal tax, but a number of state governments impose a transfer tax. Transfer taxes are usually payable by the transferor, and original issue taxes are payable by the issuing corporation. As the corporation's agent, the transfer agent is responsible for seeing that all transfer taxes are duly paid and that no stock belonging to a decedent's estate is transferred until the agent is furnished with evidence that all estate and inheritance taxes have been paid or provided for.

CO-TRANSFER AGENCIES

For the convenience of their stockholders or to comply with the regulations of stock exchanges on which their stock is listed, corporations often maintain two or more transfer agencies. The stock bookkeeping records are kept by one agent (called the principal agent), and the co-transfer agent sends to the principal agent a detailed report of its activities. That report, containing information regarding each certificate number issued and canceled, the number of

---

3. H. Noyes Green, ed., *Uniform Laws, Annotated,* Book 6, Uniform Stock Transfer Act (Northport, New York: Edward Thompson Company, 1922), p. 2.

shares involved, and the names and addresses of both old and new stockholders, enables the principal agent to post its bookkeeping records. A stock certificate may be transferred at either of the agencies, whether or not it was issued at the agency making the transfer. Each agent must have in its files evidence with respect to the appointment of the other agents and to the other agents' signatures that will enable it to verify the authenticity of any certificates presented to it for transfer.

MISCELLANEOUS DUTIES OF A TRANSFER AGENT

A transfer agent has certain duties in addition to the primary duties of effecting and recording transfers. They include custody of unissued certificates, disposition of canceled certificates, handling of replacements, stock bookkeeping, and dividend disbursing.

Custody of Unissued Certificates

Inasmuch as the transfer agent issues and delivers all stock certificates, it has the additional duty of holding unissued certificates and guarding them against theft, misuse, or unauthorized issuance. They are usually kept in vaults under a strict system of accounting and audit control.

Disposition of Canceled Certificates

Canceled certificates are generally retained by the agent for the time required by statute so that they may be available for verification of tax payments, either state or federal. Thereafter they are usually delivered to the corporation, which keeps them for several years, if not indefinitely. The principal object of keeping the old certificates is to preserve evidence of the propriety of the transfers in case the agent's action in effecting transfers is later attacked as improper.

Handling of Replacements

A transfer agent is sometimes called on to issue a new certificate to replace one that has been lost, stolen, or destroyed. Whatever the agent does in this respect must be based on formal authority given it by the corporation. The corporation gives either specific authorization and express approval of each duplication or a general authorization that is valid provided that certain conditions are met. In either case the transfer agent must obtain satisfactory affidavits as to the circumstances of the loss or destruction and a bond of indemnity in an adequate penal amount. Generally speaking, the amount of the penalty should be open rather than fixed, for the stock represented by the lost certificate may become much more valuable in subsequent years, and a fixed penalty of even double its market value may prove grossly inadequate.

Stock Bookkeeping

Detailed records of stock ownership are usually maintained by the transfer agent. Each transfer involves two entries on the stock bookkeeping records, one to post the new ownership and the other to post the cancellation of the old ownership. In addition, changes of address must be carefully recorded, and requests for special handling of dividends must be duly noted.

Dividend Disbursing

The function of dividend disbursing agent is usually performed by the principal transfer agent, since dividends are paid on the basis of data taken from the stock bookkeeping records. If a tax is payable, as on dividends to foreign stockholders, the tax must be withheld by the dividend disbursing agent and paid in due course to the proper government authorities. The corporation usually looks to the dividend disbursing agent to prepare and file with the federal and state governments, as required by law for tax purposes, separate information reports of dividend payments.

AGENCIES FOR TRANSFER OF BONDS AND OTHER SECURITIES

As indicated at the beginning of this chapter, a trust institution may act as agent to transfer ownership of securities other than stock certificates. The transfer of such registered instruments as certificates of deposit, voting trust certificates, and registered stock purchase warrants is not essentially different from the transfer of stock certificates. The transfer of bonds, however, has certain differences that deserve brief comment.

A trust institution that acts as agent for the registration and transfer of bonds is usually called a registrar, not a transfer agent. As agent for the corporation, its duties are to record changes in the ownership of bonds from bearer to a designated owner, from one designated owner to another, and from a designated owner to bearer. A bond registrar usually keeps complete ownership records for registered bonds rather than merely effecting their transfer, as sometimes happens in the case of a transfer agent for stock. The reason for this difference is that the bookkeeping records for registered bonds are usually far less extensive than those for stock. The number of a corporation's stockholders may reach tens or even hundreds of thousands, whereas the number of registered bondholders of any issue is usually small by comparison. Many trust institutions favor registration of bonds held in trust accounts, which eliminates the clipping and collection of coupons. This trend, together with the fact that the issuing organizations favor registration, may substantially increase the number of registered bondholders.

Securities Depositories

Much has been said and written about the need for a system to handle the projected volume of securities over the next 25 to 30 years. A stock is generally issued in the form of a paper certificate, which has to be transferred whenever the security is traded. But the physical transfer of millions of pieces of paper in today's fast-paced trading markets is costly and wasteful. Gradually a system for the transferral of ownership of securities is being developed that could eventually eliminate the need for the trust or stock certificate.

The Banking and Securities Industry Committee (BASIC) has recommended and helped to put in motion a securities depository system to act as custodian for large holders of securities. A securities depository attacks the "paper crunch" directly and moves a step closer to elimination of the paper stock certificate. Members of a depository (such as securities firms or banks) process trades with other members through the depository and settle their accounts by a book-entry system.

Some banks are placing increasing numbers of stocks in such depositories, and it is expected that the depositories will some day record transfers using a computerized, book-entry system of most participants' holdings. Although there are still many problems to be worked out, the benefits of depositories are inescapable, and there is every reason to believe that they will be able to deal with the unusually large trading volume in decades ahead.

Registration Agencies

Registration is not essential in handling stock in the same sense that transfer is essential. Many stocks are not registered. The primary function of a registrar is to guard against overissuance of stock. It is not charged with any duty to verify the propriety of the transfer or the payment of transfer taxes.

The New York Stock Exchange requires that all stock admitted to trading be registered; the registrar must be approved by the exchange and must be independent of both the corporation and the transfer agent. Furthermore, the registrar must enter into an agreement with the exchange not to register additional shares of listed stock until authorized by the exchange.

APPOINTMENT AS REGISTRAR

The registrar of a corporation's stock is appointed by a resolution of its board of directors. The resolution is similar to that by which a transfer agent is appointed.

DUTIES OF REGISTRAR OF STOCK

The registrar checks every new stock certificate prepared for issuance by the corporation or by its transfer agent against the old certificate being canceled in order to make sure that the number of shares represented by the certificate being issued and the number represented by the certificate being canceled are equal. If an original issue is involved, the registrar verifies the fact that only the authorized number of shares is issued. In this way the registrar acts as a check on the work of the corporation or its transfer agent, particularly with respect to willful or accidental overissuance.

OTHER REGISTRARSHIPS

Sometimes securities other than stocks are registered, in much the same manner and for much the same reasons. Most important among them are voting trust certificates and certificates of deposit.

Paying Agencies

A trust institution may act as a paying agent for dividends and as a paying agent for bonds and debentures.

PAYING AGENT FOR DIVIDENDS

As a corollary to the assumption of stock transfer responsibilities by trust institutions came the duty of disbursing dividends (a form of paying agency). As a result of the great increase in the number of stockholders, the prompt dispatch of dividend checks, the maintenance of accurate records, and the responsibility of paying the checks, trust institutions can now perform efficiently and economically periodic major undertakings that would be impossible for a company staff. Modern business machines can calculate the dividend, print the check, address the dividend, insert the check and supplementary reports in an envelope, and affix a metered stamp. Supplementary duties now being assumed by trust institutions include accumulating proxy data and designating employees to provide voting data before or at stockholders' meetings.

PAYING AGENT FOR BONDS AND DEBENTURES

In view of the many billions of dollars of bonds outstanding in the hands of the investing public, the payment of interest on the bonds and of the bonds when they become due constitutes an important function. That function is performed by paying agents. It can also be performed by fiscal agents and tax withholding agents.

Although corporations sometimes make interest and bond payments themselves, more frequently they use the services of a trust institution.

231

The trustee for a bond issue is often appointed paying agent as well; but since the functions are quite distinct, that is not necessary. A trust institution may also act as agent for the payment of interest on, and principal of, bonds issued by states, counties, towns, school districts, and other governmental units as well as revenue bonds of public authorities; it may not handle obligations of the federal government, which is done by Federal Reserve banks. Issuers of securities find that their obligations are accepted more readily if payments of interest and principal are made in more than one city.

Funds for Making Payments

A paying agent is not responsible for seeing that the funds necessary for making payments are provided (except in the case of bond issues qualified under the Trust Indenture Act), but the agent's task is greatly facilitated if it can have the funds on hand and in "collected" form no later than the date set for payment. Many agents therefore make a practice of giving their principals advance notice of payments falling due, especially in the case of municipal obligations.

Problems of Speed and Accuracy

If the bonds are fully registered, interest is paid by sending a check to each registered owner; otherwise interest is paid only on presentation of the proper coupons. The chief problem confronting the paying agent is that of paying all coupons promptly and without error. The amounts of money involved are usually large, the volume of coupons is great, and mistakes are likely to prove costly. Although counterfeits are rare, the agent must constantly be on its guard against them. Stop-payment orders, including such orders with respect to coupons from unredeemed bonds (previously called) on which interest has ceased, must also be watched.

Taxes and Government Regulations

A paying agent for interest must be familiar with all laws and government regulations (including reciprocal tax treaties) in connection with information returns, tax withholding, and other matters involving responsibilities imposed by state or federal governments. All taxes that are withheld must be paid to the government as required, and reports must be rendered to the government from time to time.

Payment of Bonds

Registered bonds are paid only when presented and only by check drawn to the order of the registered owner, except for bonds that have been assigned. The paying agent must see that all registered bonds it pays are submitted to the bond registrar for release from the registration records. If no assignment has been received, the agent must be prepared to certify that payment was made to the registered owner.

Exchange Agencies

An exchange agency is one in which the agent receives one or more kinds of securities and delivers other securities under some definite plan or arrangement. The principal types are:

1. Agent for stock splits
2. Agent for stock conversion
3. Agent for distribution of securities in a reorganization

In addition, the trust institution may sometimes be called on to accept subscriptions to shares or debentures.

AGENT FOR STOCK SPLITS

It usually happens that a corporation wants to split its stock by increasing the number of shares represented by the outstanding stock without actually selling any more stock. For instance, if a corporation splits its stock on a three-for-one basis, each old share represents three new shares. After such a split, the outstanding stock taken as a whole has no greater intrinsic value than it had before the split, because no assets have been added; therefore the new shares will sell in the market at about one-third the price of the old.

It is customary for the trust institution that acts as transfer agent to send out the notice and handle the exchange of certificates. That practice is not essential, however, because receipt of the old stock certificates and delivery (as distinguished from issuance) of the new certificates is generally looked on as an agency function separate from that of transfer agent.

An agency for handling a stock split is one of the simplest exchange agencies, but the performance of its duties is frequently complicated. Since the exchange may require that the entire body of stockholders take some action, it often results in numerous requests for changes in registration, reports of hitherto unnoticed losses of certificates, and questions from individual stockholders about many other problems. The volume of old certificates coming in and new certificates going out makes careful handling necessary to avoid costly errors. Moreover, since the corporation's entire stock is being handled, the values involved may run not merely into millions of dollars but into hundreds of millions or even into billions. The agent must be certain that the notice sent to all stockholders is clear in its instructions and that the letter of transmittal can be easily understood by them. It must arrange with the transfer agent for a mutually satisfactory and orderly procedure. It must check each lot of old stock certificates received not only as to amount, required endorsements, and transfer tax but also as to any special instructions concerning registration or delivery of new stock certificates.

The procedure described is not necessarily the one used by the agent in a stock split. When the stock has no par value or when there is to be no reduction in its stated par value, a corporation may want to accomplish the split simply by mailing the additional shares. For instance, if the split is on a three-for-one basis, the transfer agent may be instructed to mail to each stockholder a certificate for two additional shares of stock for each share registered in his name. The certificates previously held remain outstanding.

AGENT FOR STOCK CONVERSION

Securities are often issued with a provision that they may be converted, at the holder's option, into other securities—usually common stock of the issuing corporation. The conversion operation is essentially an agency function. It should be noted that bonds and debentures, as well as preferred stock, may be converted. The conversion price may have changed either because of lapse of time or because the common stock has been diluted in one way or another. Problems of dividend adjustments and of fractional shares must be solved, and a method for expeditious handling of the conversion must be devised.

AGENT FOR DISTRIBUTION OF SECURITIES IN A REORGANIZATION

The reorganization of a corporation's securities may be necessary in any of the following situations:

1. When a corporation is being reorganized (with or without actual bankruptcy) and the old securities must be exchanged for new securities of one or several kinds
2. When a corporation is being merged or consolidated with another corporation and its outstanding securities are to be exchanged for securities of the other corporation or partly for cash and partly for securities
3. When a corporation wants to adjust its capital structure by exchanging high-dividend preferred stock for stock carrying a lower dividend or by offering new securities in exchange for preferred stock on which dividend arrearages have accrued
4. When a company that holds substantial ownership in one or more other companies either wishes or is required to dispose of that ownership

Deposit Agencies

A deposit agency is one in which securities are received by the agent to be held for an indefinite period or for a prolonged period under an agreement of some kind. As evidence of the deposit of securities, a negotiable receipt or certificate is issued to the security holder by the agent. At the termination of the agreement, each holder of a certificate surrenders it to the agent and receives in return whatever is due him—cash, the securities deposited, or other securities.

DEPOSITARY FOR FOREIGN SECURITIES

The depositary for foreign securities provides American investors with a convenient means of investing in foreign securities, usually stock of important foreign corporations. A trust institution issues its receipts for a certain foreign stock (to be deposited with it or with one of its branches or correspondent banks in the country where the stock is issued). These receipts, generally called American depositary receipts (ADRs), are negotiable and possess most other characteristics of ordinary stock certificates. They are registered and entitle their holders to receive dividends paid on the foreign stock to the depositary, as the holder of record, after deduction of certain of the depositary's expenses and charges.

The holder may surrender his ADR to the agent with a request that the deposited stock be delivered to him in this country or to some designated person in the foreign country. As a practical matter, the holder generally handles such a transaction through a broker. The broker has available two different procedures: he may find a buyer for the stock in the American market and transfer the ADR to the buyer in the regular course of business, or he may have the agent cancel the ADR and arrange for delivery of the corresponding amount of deposited stock abroad to complete a sale made by him in the foreign market. The choice between the two procedures depends on which market offers the best net price.

Miscellaneous Agencies

There are many more agency functions that trust institutions are called on to perform; they cannot be classified into distinct categories because the agent's duties vary so widely in each case. Some of them are discussed in the following paragraphs.

AGENT FOR REDEMPTION OF PREFERRED STOCK

A preferred stock issue of a corporation is generally callable—that is, it can be paid off and retired either in part or as a whole, usually at a premium above its par value.

In addition to the provision for voluntary call of preferred stock, the charter or articles of incorporation sometimes provide for the retirement of a certain amount of stock each year. This is a sinking fund provision. Retirement of stock through the operation of a sinking fund is usually accomplished either by purchase of stock in the open market or by call of the required amount. The procedure is much the same for an optional partial call of bonds, except for the differences inherent in the fact that stocks are in registered form and bonds usually in bearer form.

The duties of a trust institution as agent for a corporation in connection with a preferred stock call are those contained in the corporation's letter of instructions, supported by a resolution of its board of directors. The agent must verify that those instructions are consistent with the requirements of the charter or articles of incorporation and will therefore need a certified copy of that document. It usually sends the necessary notices to stockholders whose certificates are called, receives the redemption money, and pays those funds against surrender of the called stock. The called certificates are canceled and delivered to the transfer agent for retirement.

AGENT FOR REINVESTMENT OF DIVIDENDS

An often overlooked service is that of agent for the reinvestment of dividends. In its role as dividend paying agent, the trust institution pays out dividends, which can be reinvested. Often shareholders are unaware of the availability of the reinvestment service. When it is called to their attention, many are quick to instruct the dividend reinvestment agent to purchase additional shares of the company whose dividend they are receiving.

SUBSCRIPTION AGENT

When a corporation contemplates raising new funds by the sale of stocks or bonds, it may wish (or may be required by law or by its charter or articles of incorporation) to give its present stockholders the first opportunity to buy the new securities.

A trust institution's function as agent in such operations is, briefly, as follows. It takes charge of the preparation and mailing of the warrants, splits the outstanding warrants into smaller denominations or groups them into larger ones on presentation and surrender by the holders, transfers warrants from one registered holder to another, accepts payment for new securities on surrender of a corresponding number of rights, arranges for issuance and delivery of the new securities to the subscribers, and accounts to its principal for all funds paid to it. Frequently, too, it handles the buying and selling of rights for the accounts of the holders. Those activities and others incidental to the agency are performed in accordance with detailed instructions received from the corporation.

Sometimes a subscription agency operates under a different arrangement. The trust institution may act as agent to receive subscriptions from a list of subscribers given to it by the corporation rather than on the basis of the surrender of subscription warrants. That is a simpler form of subscription agency, but it is handled in much the same way.

WARRANT AGENT

Similar in most respects to the agency in connection with subscription warrants or rights is the agency under purchase or option warrants. The fundamental difference is that the latter warrants are likely to be outstanding for several years, during which the holders may decide whether to exercise their options.

A trust institution's duties as warrant agent are usually to countersign the warrants when they are issued, to split and group warrants (if they are detachable from the securities in connection with which they were issued), and to accept subscriptions if the warrants are exercised. The agent accepts such subscriptions in much the same way as it does subscriptions based on short-term subscription warrants.

SCRIP AGENT

In connection with transactions that result in fractional units of stock, such as stock dividends or exchanges of securities in reorganizations or mergers, scrip certificates (commonly known as scrip) are frequently issued. From the standpoint of the issuing corporation and its transfer agent, scrip certificates are more convenient than fractional shares of stock. When sufficient fractions to make whole shares are assembled in the form of scrip, the scrip certificates may be exchanged for full-share stock certificates.

A trust institution commonly acts as agent to take care of all operational details in connection with scrip certificates. It either holds the stock corresponding to the outstanding scrip or arranges for an unissued reserve of such stock; it collects any dividends that accrue on the stock; it arranges for the issuance of full shares of stock to scrip holders who surrender certificates amounting to one or more full shares; it groups small fractions into larger ones or splits large fractions into smaller ones; it sells the underlying stock at the termination date of the scrip and pays the cash proceeds and any accumulated dividends as scrip is presented to it. It is often convenient if the trust institution that acts as transfer agent for a corporation's stock also acts as scrip agent, but the two functions are distinct and may be separated.

PURCHASE AGENT

At times a corporation finds it desirable to retire some of its securities, particularly common stock or bonds that are not callable by their terms. At such a time, the corporation may invite its security holders, either by written notice to each or by publication, to tender their securities for sale. A trust institution is frequently named as the agent to which such tenders should be sent. The notice usually specifies that the tenders made at the lowest prices will be accepted, up to an amount sufficient to exhaust the funds set aside for the purchase. Sometimes, however, the corporation provides that all tenders are to be made at a fixed price; in that case acceptance of the offers is usually pro rata if the tenders exceed the total funds available.

The agent's duties generally consist of the following: sending out or publishing the notices; receiving, examining, and classifying the tenders; sending out notices or rejection of tenders or of acceptance as a whole or in part; and arranging for the splitting of certificates if only part of the shares represented are purchased. The agent is also responsible for returning all shares tendered but not purchased, making prompt payment for shares purchased, maintaining the necessary records, and making appropriate reports to the corporation.

OTHER AGENCIES

A few trust institutions act for investment companies by serving as depositaries for funds on periodic or installment purchases of mutual fund shares, reinvesting dividends, and acting as redemption agent and as transfer agent. Mutual fund services can include acting as custodian of the assets of the company, serving as clearance agent for sales and redemptions of the company's shares, and establishing and maintaining daily pricing. A service performed by a few trust institutions is the issuance of commercial paper on behalf of corporations. Some trust companies also perform certain services for brokers; for example, executing orders made by dealers for sale or purchase of securities.

From time to time other corporate agency functions are performed by trust institutions acting as trustees. Among them are the sinking fund agency, the broad conversion agency, custodianships, managing agencies, and escrow agencies.

Even the extensive list of agency functions discussed in this chapter is far from exhaustive. The variety of services a trust institution may be called on to perform for corporations is almost without limit. A trust institution possesses the personnel and the mechanical aids required for the performance of such services; it possesses the confidence of the public, so necessary in connection with any service involving the handling and holding of securities; above all, it possesses the knowledge and experience required for the efficient, safe, and expeditious handling of whatever financial agency services a corporation may require.

238

Chapter 17

Investment of Trust Funds

The Purposes of This Chapter:

1. To present plans for the organization of trust investment work within a trust department
2. To suggest some of the facilities and equipment needed for analysis and review of investments held in trust accounts
3. To outline procedures for studying, selecting, and reviewing investments

"All that can be required of a trustee to invest is that he shall conduct himself faithfully and exercise a sound discretion. He is to observe how men of prudence, discretion and intelligence manage their own affairs, not in regard to speculation but in regard to the permanent disposition of their funds, considering the probable income, as well as the probable safety, of the capital to be invested."[1]

Investment Objectives and Policies

The investment management of trust funds and the analysis and review of investment holdings require an adequate organization, suitable trust investment equipment, and definite procedures for carrying out the duties of the department. Before discussing those requirements, this chapter briefly considers general investment objectives and policies.

As a general rule, the personal representative—administrator or executor—is not required to make investments. If, however, the estate is to be tied up in administration for more than a few months, consideration must be given to putting cash not otherwise needed in the settlement

---

1. Harvard College v. Amory, 9 Pick. 446 (Mass. 1830). Many states have adopted what is generally referred to as a "statutory prudent man rule." Generally such statutes, to remove all doubt as to the authority of the trustee to invest in all types of securities, provide that the fiduciary has the authority to invest in corporate stocks and bonds, including the authority to invest in securities of any management investment company or investment trust.

of the estate in a savings account or other short-term investment. More often than not, however, the personal representative is in the role of converting investments into cash to pay expenses, debts, and taxes. The personal representative's expertise is important if the decedent's estate is to escape undue damage. For example, selling the wrong property or the right property at the wrong time can, in the first instance, deprive the estate of a valuable asset and, in the second, produce serious tax consequences.

Both guardians and agents have investment responsibilities. Although a guardian is often restricted by law in the kind of investments he can make, investing the ward's money is a major concern of the court and guardian.

A managing agent usually does nothing more than recommend investments. It is up to the principal to make the final decision. Yet expertise is as important in recommending sound investments as in making them. If the agency agreement imposes on the agent the duty to invest rather than simply select investments, the duties of the trustee and the agent are essentially the same.

This chapter was introduced by the often quoted and usually followed guideline to investments laid down in the famous case of *Harvard College* v. *Amory.* Though originally applying only in Massachusetts, the so-called prudent man rule has been adopted in one form or another by practically all the states.

STATEMENT OF POLICIES

To the extent practicable, basic investment policies should be reduced to writing. In his *Handbook for National Trust Examiners,* the Comptroller of the Currency requires that in the examination of marketable securities, the examiner is:

1. To assess the policy of the bank with respect to the selection of investments which are to be purchased, retained or sold for accounts in which the bank exercises investment responsibility, review internal or external research data to ascertain that information pertaining to world, national and local economic conditions is considered in selecting industries to be researched and analyzed.

Notes.
   a. The above process is to be distinguished from that of tailoring investments for individual portfolios. . . .
   b. U.S. Government securities and those guaranteed by the U.S. Government are to be considered of trust quality.

2. Determine that the bank is receiving data with respect to the economy and specific industries which is based on reliable sources.

There are 14 other guidelines that the examiner is to consider. The 16 guidelines combine to require that investment policies be carefully thought out and reduced to writing.

If it is recognized that, no matter how carefully drawn, no written statement outlining investment standards can be wholly satisfactory in application, it should at least be possible to establish investment objectives. Variations from the established norms may be numerous, but they should be the result of conscious action. Carefully established general policies help define and fix responsibility and contribute to good organization and performance by separating routine matters from those requiring mature deliberation by senior officers or committees of directors.

Trust Investment Organization

The investment organization of a trust department varies greatly from one institution to another; there is no generally accepted plan in common use, in part because of wide differences in the size of trust departments, in part because of differences in the legal requirements of the jurisdictions under which trust departments operate, and in part because of variations in the problems that trust departments encounter. Even in neighboring trust institutions, departments of comparable size have distinctly different approaches to the organization of the group handling trust investment.

Whatever its size and location, the trust department has certain basic investment responsibilities; to deal with them, it must have an effective and efficient investment organization. That organization must be well grounded in the principles of trust investment and have a thorough knowledge of the investment policies of the institution so that both principles and policies can be carefully and consistently applied to the daily problems of individual trust accounts.

Regulation 9 (Fiduciary Powers of National Banks and Collective Investment Funds) of the Comptroller of the Currency, to which all national banks operating trust departments must adhere, has had and will continue to have marked influence on the procedures of all banking institutions exercising fiduciary powers. Even though the regulation has no direct application to state-chartered institutions (except for Section 18, Common Trust Funds, by provision of the Internal Revenue Code), trust investment policy should be thoroughly understood in conjunction with the regulation as amended.

TRUST INVESTMENT COMMITTEES

The adoption of sound investment policies is of little value unless provision is made for an organization that can carry them out effectively. Although the responsibility for determining investment policy rests with the board of directors, the board may delegate the discharge of this and other responsibilities to directors, officers, employees, or committees. For national banks, the delegation of authority is specifically provided for under Regulation 9, which states that the board, in discharging its responsibility for the investment and disposition of property held in a fiduciary capacity or the determination of policies, may assign such of the bank's fiduciary powers as it may consider proper to assign to such director(s), officer(s), employee(s), or committee(s) as it may designate.

The board is also required by Regulation 9 to ensure that at least once during every calendar year after the acceptance of an account and within 15 months of the last review, all the assets held in or for each fiduciary account where the bank has investment responsibilities are reviewed to determine the advisability of retaining or disposing of such assets. State-chartered institutions follow similar practices.

In large banks the duties may be divided by the board among teams of officers or employees or among several committees or may be delegated in part to junior committees (usually composed solely of officers) or subcommittees. There are also wide differences in the degree to which authority is delegated to individual persons.

The composition of any trust investment committee, subcommittee, team, or group of officers, the methods of procedure, and the orderly delegation of duties and responsibilities to the staff are of the utmost importance in obtaining a satisfactory investment result. In small banks it is good practice to have a small group, most of whose members are nonofficer directors. In large banks it is perhaps easier to find enough officers with the needed breadth of experience for such a group, but a relatively small unit with an "outside" majority still has much to recommend it. In any case, the members should be chosen on the basis of appropriate experience, capacity for public service, and open-mindedness in approaching new problems. If otherwise qualified, anyone who unselfishly serves the community in its social responsibilities is a likely candidate. Fortunately, no community is lacking in such persons. Because of the nature of the responsibility and the value of cumulative knowledge, continuity of membership is desirable. The value of a well-balanced group working conscientiously can hardly be overstressed.

In addition to being charged with the responsibility for developing and reviewing general investment policies, these groups pass on more detailed matters, such as the investment holdings of new accounts, the periodic review of old accounts (which should be at least annual and preferably more frequent), the review of individual investments, and the purchase and sale of securities. It is possible to simplify trust investment responsibilities somewhat by having subcommittees or teams perform certain tasks and submit their recommendations or actions for approval or by using an "approved list" of securities that have been carefully considered and approved as generally appropriate for trust investment. From this list securities that fit the investment needs of individual accounts are selected.

The number of committees or other groups and the degree of authority delegated to them is often dictated by the size and complexity of the bank's trust affairs. Some delegation of authority is generally desirable, for if the investment officer is in a position to speak for the bank, the bank can not only render better service and establish better public relations but also attract more broadly capable people to trust investment work. On the other hand, a department of considerable size can be effectively served by a single group that meets frequently and deals directly with all the investment and policy matters that arise, providing consistency and composite judgment that are helpful to the officers, yet leaving them proper scope for initiative. To be most effective, the administrative chart should be no more complex than the internal organization of the department requires.

Meetings should be held frequently on a regular schedule. At these meetings the following items should be considered:

1. New trust accounts
2. Investment review of trust accounts
3. Review of security holdings
4. Proposed sales, purchases, subscriptions, exchanges, and the like
5. Uninvested principal (cash) and unexecuted purchase and sale orders in compliance with previous committee votes
6. Review of general policy

If the bank is providing investment management or investment advice as agent, the simplest and most effective method is to deal with agency accounts as though they were trust accounts, using similar investment procedures. In some large banks or in special jurisdictions, there may be reason to segregate such accounts and provide different treatment for them.

INVESTMENT STAFF

The ability, diligence, and judgment of the working investment staff are probably most important to the investment result. The staff may consist of one person working part time or a large group of specialists. However small, the staff must study investment trends to provide background for policy, securities, and investment management of individual accounts. Formerly the application of policy to individual accounts was one of the general administrative duties of trust officers, but, with the growth of specialization, the preferred modern practice developed. It recognizes that this duty is a function of investment management and is best handled by investment-trained personnel. In the largest trust organizations, investment research groups are usually separated from portfolio or account management groups; but the liaison between the groups should remain close. It is desirable to have all matters relating to investment handled by personnel trained for that work and responsible to the chief investment officer. Under that system the knowledge and experience of noninvestment officers and their familiarity with the personal and administrative factors affecting particular accounts are utilized through their participation in meetings of junior and senior trust committees or subcommittees.

Equipment of Trust Investment Department

The investment organization obviously should have facilities and physical equipment to provide it with adequate information and to ensure a creditable performance. The facilities should include suitable records and services that supply information about securities.

In a small trust department, the principal accounting records can probably supply most of the information required. In large institutions, however, many of the records needed will to some extent duplicate the accounting records.

RECORDS OF SECURITY HOLDINGS

A complete index, alphabetically arranged, of all the assets held in all accounts is required. The index may be subdivided, if desired, for stocks, bonds, mortgages, real estate, and so on.

RECORDS OF ACCOUNTS

A complete set of records for each account, with a list of its holdings, is required and should be kept up to date as changes are made. There should also be a file for each account, including a copy or synopsis of the instrument under which the bank serves, a copy of the initial inventory of the account holdings, a copy of any initial review of the account, copies of subsequent reviews, and investment correspondence. Thus the file will provide a running historical record of the investment management of the account.

FILES BY COMPANY

A special folder should be maintained on each company or entity whose securities are held in the trust accounts. The smaller the amount of information available about those companies in published sources, the more important it becomes to maintain complete information in the file. The file should include the company's annual and interim financial reports, agency or brokerage reports, news items, written reports by the bank's analyst, correspondence and records of interviews, actions taken by the trust committee with respect to the company's securities, and all other pertinent data.

INVESTMENT SERVICES

A wide variety of investment services is available, some general and some specialized. A daily financial paper and a manual service are essential equipment. The purchase of additional services depends first on what services are needed and can be afforded and second on what services can be usefully employed. The best service is of little assistance if it is not used, but the purchase of all the good investment services that are needed should greatly reduce the research work that would otherwise be necessary.

TICKLERS

A tickler system is useful for timing the periodic reviews of companies and industries. It is also useful for noting the dates of conversion features of securities, subscription warrants, and the like, when those dates are not set up in the main accounting system of the department.

Procedures for Investment

Procedures in the trust investment division follow two distinct lines. One is analysis and review of assets as individual investments; the other is analysis and review of the asset composition of individual trust accounts.

There should be periodic reviews of securities to consider intrinsic merits and compare values. There should also be special reviews whenever unusual circumstances or additional information makes it appear desirable to have certain securities or groups of securities reviewed.

With respect to trust accounts, the reviewer should consider not only the basic merits of the various securities that make up the account portfolio but also the legal propriety and the appropriateness of holding them in the particular account. In doing so he should consider such factors as suitable diversification in the account, the length of time the trust is to continue, the tax bracket of the beneficiaries, the background of those having interests in the trust, proper recognition of the views of co-fiduciaries or investment consultants, and the general historical record of the account in light of its objectives.

There has been much progress in recent years in the new profession of investment analysis. Objective studies made by well-trained personnel in this field are now used by every trust institution in selecting and supervising investments. Other developments, such as the work of the Securities and Exchange Commission and the accounting refinements made by most corporations, have also helped. Electronic computers have processed data for statistical studies and are being used in identifying and selecting investments.

ANALYSIS AND REVIEW BY SECURITY

The analysis and review of trust investments by security includes periodic review of the securities held, usually classified by industry, review of specific securities because of unusual developments, and analysis of particular securities under consideration for investment.

Securities held in several or many trust accounts should usually be reviewed in connection with reviews of comparable securities in the same general field. If a security held in one trust is sold, other accounts holding the same security should be reviewed because the reason for the sale may apply equally to them. How frequently a particular security is reviewed depends on its quality and probably on the extent of the department's holdings of it. A constant effort should be made to reduce the number of different items held in trust accounts to make the most effective use of the time and effort devoted to review.

For periodic reviews trust investments are often classified by industry—for example, railroads, oils, banks—and each group is considered separately when the situation in that industry or class is under review. It is becoming increasingly difficult to place each company in a specific industrial category, but the basic classifications help in analyzing growth and profits. Thus general conditions affecting an industry or a particular security will be studied in relation to all such holdings in the trust department. If the department is large enough, the reviews may be prepared by analysts specializing in a single industry. The investment analyst must gather his information from industry and management sources, from special analyses by investment organizations and services, and from general reading. Original research involving direct company contacts is often desirable.

When special circumstances arise, good trust management does not delay review until a periodic review date. Information is swiftly assembled and presented to the individuals or groups having trust investment responsibilities with a list of all holdings of the securities in question. The problem may be broad and intangible, such as the consequences of a political development or of new competitive machinery or processes, or it may be specific, such as a flood, a merger, a reorganization, a request for subscription to additional securities, an exchange of stock, or a proposed ousting of corporate management. Timely attention to such matters, whether large or small, is the mark of alert investment management.

When new securities are offered or seasoned securities appear to be attractive investments for trust purposes, a careful study discussing and appraising their investment characteristics and their appropriateness for various trust uses is made and presented. Data presented for review of a particular security should include at least the following information:

1. The capitalization of the company and its history
2. The company's balance sheets
3. The company's operating record for several years (including earnings per share, dividends, and price range, as well as earnings coverage in the case of a bond or a preferred stock)
4. A description of the company's business and competition
5. Comments on recent developments and outlook

For stocks there should also be a study of the following factors:

1. Gross sales and the trend of sales
2. Earnings and the trend of earnings
3. Price-earnings ratio
4. Dividends—past, present, and projected

Bond and mortgage investments should be supported by information showing:

1. History of debtor
2. Appraisal of property mortgaged
3. Ability of debtor to retire obligation

APPROVED LIST

The approved list should always be based on the most suitable industries. When the list is being prepared, the top companies in each such industry should be considered.

Whether a formal approved list or a less rigid system is employed to indicate specific securities that are generally suitable for purchase, approval of a security is tentative in the sense that the security may not automatically be purchased for a given trust account. Full weight must always be given to the appropriateness of the security for the individual account and its market price at the time of contemplated purchase.

The approved list should be broad enough to provide diversification; it should be reviewed regularly and additions and deletions made as required. Generally the list should consist of stocks of companies with the following characteristics:

1. A fundamentally strong position
2. Experienced management
3. Established markets
4. Sound financial structure
5. Broad public ownership
6. Diversification of products or services
7. An upward trend in sales and earnings
8. Strong product development practices

A determined effort to adhere to an approved list and to conform accounts, when reasonably possible, to that list will minimize research and analysis, provide better supervision, and enable the trust department to serve its customers better.

INITIAL REVIEW

A well-prepared initial study of a new account and an orderly procedure for its systematic periodic review not only satisfy the basic requirements of Regulation 9 but also offer effective means of assuring the discharge of the institution's investment responsibilities. Since Regulation 9 is an accepted guide to trust investment review procedures, its stated requirement with respect to frequency of reviews should be regarded as establishing a minimum standard. In good trust practice, however, the frequency of review should be governed more by the composition and character of the assets of an individual account than by the necessarily fixed requirements of a regulation.

For the initial review, a questionnaire that covers the legal, tax, administrative, and investment details is desirable because it requires the investment section to gather full information at the outset. To abstract the information in usable form, the investment section should supply:

1. All the investment provisions of the instrument, including the degree of the bank's control of purchases and sales of account assets and any rights to determine allocations between principal and income and to distribute principal
2. Any provisions of the instrument granting special powers of retention or restricting the sale of closely held securities
3. Any opinion of counsel interpreting the bank's powers under these provisions
4. Wishes of donors, principals, and beneficiaries to the extent that they are germane
5. General background information about beneficiaries, such as ages, other income, income requirements, and tax position

For future use and easy reference, a simple summary sheet is frequently prepared. It contains such information as the title and nature of the account, the date of inception, the initial inventory, the income, the names of principals, life tenants, and remaindermen, the purpose of the trust, a brief statement of investment powers, and a statement of any unusual circumstances requiring special consideration.

DECISIONS ABOUT OBJECTIVES AND PROPORTIONS

As soon as possible after the acceptance of an account, the trust investment committee should determine the objectives to be accomplished and the investment policy to be followed in attaining those objectives. That determination should be recorded for future reference. It should serve as a plan for the trust department in the future administration of the account. The decision should set forth:

1. Whether the emphasis should be on income or preservation of principal
2. Whether investments should be handled individually or go into a common trust fund
3. Proportions of stocks, bonds, mortgages, and so forth
4. Frequency of review

A market valuation of the assets in the account by item and by class of security should be prepared, and the percentage of the assets held in securities, in industries, and in types of securities—such as common stocks, preferred stocks, and short- and long-term bonds—should be computed so that the diversification of the account can be carefully considered at the outset. Income by item and by group should be estimated.

The decision as to the proper proportions for a particular account is likely to be changed periodically. It depends on the objectives of the account, which may change from time to time. It also depends on broad investment policy, which is affected by business conditions. The policy on proportions must be fluid, and it is not unreasonable to have the investment committee determine a broad policy that is followed within limits by the staff.

Diversification can be wasteful if carried to extremes, not only in brokerage costs but in the expense of supervision. The saying is that diversification that can lead to mediocrity is a rule of caution, not a principle of investing. Legally there is no absolute duty to diversify, but the Restatement of the Law of Trusts requires the trustee to distribute the risk of loss by a reasonable diversification unless under the circumstances it is prudent not to do so.

The quality of each investment is examined, and a brief written report is prepared on holdings that are not well known or on which recent reports are not available. More attention may have to be given to large holdings or closely held securities, and more detail may be required for them.

When the investment section has assembled the information about the new trust, a detailed report should be prepared in which a complete picture of the asset holdings is presented and investment changes are recommended. That report provides a valuable background for periodic reviews of the trust throughout its duration. Those periodic reviews should not differ essentially from the initial review except in requiring less detail and perhaps in relying somewhat more on oral presentation.

REVIEW OF TRUST ACCOUNTS

The systematic review of the investment holdings of individual trust accounts is important because it provides a regular method of testing the application of broad investment policy to each account and of testing the effectiveness of other procedures in producing a good investment result. All the facilities of the trust department are coordinated to make investments serve the purposes for which the trusts were created.

All accounts, whether trusts or management accounts for individual persons, are the subject of formal periodic reviews as well as continuing informal consideration. The formal review, which may be annual or semiannual, subjects the list of securities—with necessary additional data on costs, responsibility, prices, and the like—to review by the officers' committee. The trust officer involved should be present and should be thoroughly versed in the objectives and the restrictions of the account. The primary function of the review is to determine whether the bank's investment policy is being followed in a manner appropriate to the particular account. The review need not lead to involved changes; in the majority of cases it should merely serve as a check on the activities of the account administrator or portfolio analyst. The formal review is also significant in that it records the attention being given to the account by the proper representatives of the bank's management.

From an operations standpoint, the more important reviews are those made as the situation changes within an account. Frequently those reviews arise from contacts between the man responsible for the administration of the account and the principal or beneficiary or co-trustee. There may be discussions about individual suggestions and changes in objectives, and changes within the portfolio may be executed. Other occasions that call for scrutiny of the account are the addition of cash by the principal, the calling of bonds, or the offering of rights on the stocks held.

Reviews are also triggered by decisions of the officers' committee on specific stocks. That is particularly true when an unfavorable rating is given to a stock already in an account. A system must be set up to call to the attention of all those involved the name of the particular account, the amount of stock held, and the degree of responsibility assumed by the trust institution at the time the account was established. The responsibility for action is placed on the shoulders of the man who is in charge of the account, and the committee, group, or team follows up in urgent cases.

RETENTION OF INVESTMENT RECORDS

From the trustee's standpoint, the keeping of adequate minutes and records of matters considered and actions taken with respect to trust investments is second in importance only to the rendering of irreproachable service. Although written material may be incorporated into the records, it is not good practice to attempt a detailed account of oral discussions and of reasons for the actions taken, because a written record can never do full justice to the relative weight of ideas and viewpoints.

There should be suitable procedures to determine that the actions taken or authorized are carried out. That is a matter not only of proper systems in the trust investment division but also of a point at which the auditing department should institute suitable controls and police them.

INVESTMENT FUNCTION OF THE TRUST ADMINISTRATOR

Ideally the trust administrator should have a working knowledge of investments and, if possible, should have spent some time in the investment department. He should also be familiar with the circumstances of the account and have a general knowledge of the kinds of investments best suited to it.

It is clear that, if the administrator is to fulfill his function properly, he must be thoroughly familiar with the investment provisions of the instrument under which he operates and the needs of the beneficiaries, both for life and in remainder. He should also know the local statutes and case law with respect to trust investments and the characteristics and purposes of the various types of securities with which he will be dealing.

He must also have a working knowledge of the elementary techniques of security analysis so that he can understand reports of the investment specialist and interpret decisions on trust investments. He should be familiar with the money markets and the influence of the Federal Reserve, basic economics and business trends, and the security markets— stock exchanges, over-the-counter trading, and private placements.

The financial section of a good newspaper and reports of the investment specialist will provide him with the basic information he needs. There are many other sources he can use; but it should be emphasized that although it is important to be well informed, it is equally important not to be overinformed. Any attempt to reconcile the mass of information and conflicting opinions available becomes a hindrance to the exercise of independent judgment that is expected of the bank by the grantor or testator.

The trust administrator should not usurp the authority and responsibility of the investment officers. In many banks the account administrator is given a good deal of latitude to operate within the framework laid down by the trust investment group, but an investment specialist should be consulted whenever unusual investment decisions are to be made, particularly in such cases as the determination of a price at which to sell inactive securities and the acceptance or rejection of offers for purchase or merger. The investment specialists must retain their authority if they are expected to retain their responsibility.

A decision on retention or sale should often not be made without an investigation. As a rule, the administrator does not have the time or the technical equipment to make such an investigation. He should therefore consult the investment specialist in such cases as the following:

1. When a new account contains securities that are not being followed by the bank
2. When there is considerable change in the market price of a security that the trust investment committee has approved for purchase or sale
3. When he is doubtful about the application of a particular investment decision to an account with restrictive investment provisions (an example would be a case in which there is a general decision "subject to account circumstances" to sell a stock that the trustee has a right to retain but, on reinvestment for that particular account, the bank would be confined to bonds)

The problem of cash requirements arises principally in executor accounts when funds must be raised within 6 to 18 months to pay taxes, debts, administrative expenses, and cash legacies. It is clear that in a rising market it is better to postpone liquidation of securities for those purposes until the last possible moment. It is also clear that if the administrator does this, he is speculating. Therefore, particularly when dealing with volatile securities, the better practice is to raise the necessary funds promptly. That is so even though the impact of a market decline is lessened by the right to reappraise assets as of the 6-month anniversary of the testator's death and thus reduce the federal estate tax. Where distributions of principal from a trust account are to be made at fixed future dates, it is obviously desirable to have bonds maturing on or about those dates so as to avoid having to liquidate long-term investments in a poor market.

Collective Funds

Another important development in investing has been the growth of collective investing.[2] While all investment departments should be staffed with a sufficient number of well-trained people with the initiative and intelligence to perform their assigned duties, some overworked investment staffs have insufficient time to give enough attention to the growing number of individual portfolios. Collective investing is not only better but less expensive.

Common trust funds have grown considerably in recent years, and collective funds have been emphasized in Regulation F and Regulation 9 since 1963. But not all trust institutions have such funds, nor are they

---

2. In 1955, 222 banks were operating common trust funds. By 1974, 2,416 banks had established common funds for employee benefit trusts or personal trusts.

required to under Regulation 9. Some institutions have established funds on a contractual basis before the passage of enabling legislation in the various states.

Many trust institutions have split their funds into segments of fixed and equity investments. Various other types—such as U.S. government bond, municipal bond, growth, and special situation funds—have been established. Because of certain technical problems related to capital gains, some institutions have started new funds of the same type they presently operate and used them for new trusts.

Collective funds must conform to state statutes as well as to regulations of the Comptroller of the Currency. State banks are not required to follow Regulation 9. Reference to the laws of an individual state will disclose any variations from the general practice of national banks.

Regulation 9 has removed the participation limit for any single trust or beneficiary but retained the 10 percent ownership limit of a fund by any single trust. Regulation 9 has also eliminated the restriction that bona fide trusts were the only type entitled to participate, since the term "bona fide" was difficult to define. Regulation 9 requires the annual preparation of a summarized audit report and upholds the right of any interested person to receive a copy. Forty percent of any common trust fund must be in marketable investments. A mortgage investment fund was eliminated by Regulation 9.

The student should note the difference between a collective investment fund for fiduciary accounts and an employee benefit fund. A collective investment fund is a pooled fund operated by the bank under well-established fiduciary principles and used for investments of the assets of its separate trust accounts. Employee benefit funds are held by the bank in both a fiduciary and an agency relationship.

After the permission to commingle trust funds in a common trust fund, a ruling of the Federal Reserve allowed a commingled fund for pensions, profit sharing, and other such trusts and agencies. Regulation 9 recognizes and regulates two kinds: the traditional common trust fund and the employee benefit fund.

All the investment principles and procedures discussed in this chapter apply to both the common trust fund portfolio and the individual portfolio. Although responsibility for a common trust fund may be placed with more senior officers, generally the same organization discharges the investment responsibilities, the same equipment is required, and the same procedure for selecting and supervising the investments that make up the fund is followed.

The law requires that each collective investment fund be established and maintained in accordance with a written plan, which must be approved by a resolution of the bank's board of directors and filed with the Comptroller of the Currency.

REACHING THE MASS MARKET

One has only to mention the extraordinary growth of trust business to realize that it is, directly and indirectly, finally reaching much of the mass market. Collective investment funds have enabled trust institutions to enlarge the base of their services and to handle economically, efficiently, and profitably modest accounts that they could not otherwise afford to accept.

COLLECTIVE INVESTMENT FUNDS AND THE COMPUTER

In handling corporate trust and agency accounts, the computer plays a vital role, particularly in investments. The portfolio manager in any department is paid to make investment decisions. He must have at his fingertips account investment objectives, performance measurement, security tax cost basis, up-to-date prices and posting, and no later than overnight access to needed reports and data. When provided with computer output relating to such matters, a portfolio manager can spend most of his time making important investment decisions rather than performing mechanical or updating chores.

Procedure for Investment in Real Property, Mortgages, and Miscellaneous Assets

The plans and procedures for the investment of trust funds described are designed primarily for the control of investments in stocks and bonds, which constitute only part of the trust property. Real property and first mortgages on real property often constitute a considerable portion of that property. Consequently it is essential that every trust institution have a plan and procedure for handling real property and mortgages. Private placements of securities, sale and leasebacks, oil and mineral interests, and family and close corporation stocks are beginning to appear with greater frequency in trust accounts.

Too often, review procedures adopted by the trust investment committee do not include consideration of assets other than marketable bonds and stocks. But investment responsibilities also extend to real estate and mortgages and a variety of other investments, such as interests in trusts and estates, oil royalties, interests in unincorporated businesses, and tangible personal property of various kinds. Review procedures should not neglect the review of those assets and should make recommendations for appropriate action.

Chapter 18

Real Property and Mortgages as Trust Investments

The Purposes of This Chapter:
1. To discuss some problems involved in handling real property
2. To suggest a plan of organization for the management of real property and mortgages
3. To discuss special problems in handling mortgages

"Property and law are born together and die together. Before laws were made, there was no property. Take away law, and property ceases."[1]

Real property and mortgages often constitute a considerable portion of the assets of trust accounts. The proportion held varies widely, depending on the policies of different trust departments. Recognizing the increasing importance and complexity of real estate and mortgages in the administration of trusts, the Comptroller's *Handbook for National Trust Examiners* provides an examination procedures checklist for determining the fiduciary's policies for the management of such property.

Although the management of real property and mortgages constitutes the second main division of the service activities of a trust department and can subject the fiduciary to serious liability, there is no uniform handling of such assets. Each trust department must determine for itself whether real estate and mortgages of the local area are sound trust investments. For example, a single-occupancy property in the right location may prove preferable to a multiple-occupancy dwelling in the wrong location; and a growing suburban residential area may provide an excellent investment opportunity, whereas a declining urban residential area may not.

Two critical areas of the management of mortgages and real property should be recognized. First, mortgages and real property lack the

---

1. Jeremy Bentham, *Theory of Legislation; Principles of the Civil Code,* Part 1 (Dumont edition, Hildreth translation, 1864), p.112.

marketability of more liquid investments, such as stocks and bonds. They should therefore be retained in the portion of a trust account that does not require ready liquidity. Second, they are more expensive to handle than stocks and bonds of large corporations or bonds of governmental units because of the greater need of personal supervision. It is thus necessary to make higher or additional charges to the accounts that hold mortgages and real property. The lowering of the costs of handling securities through computer applications underscores the higher costs of mortgages and real estate.

When held or acquired as investments, mortgages and real property should provide a greater yield than the current yield on stocks and bonds. In addition, the opportunity for appreciation in the value of real property should be a factor in decisions to acquire or hold it as an investment. In certain trusts such advantages could offset the advantages of easy sale and purchase of securities.

Real Property

Real property constitutes a large portion of the total economic wealth of the United States. It includes farms, woodlands, mines, houses, business houses, factories, office buildings, and apartment houses. From time to time, trust institutions may be responsible for the administration of every conceivable kind of real property.

Real property has potential value that may or may not be realized, depending on the kind of management it receives. If it does not receive proper attention, real property amounts to little more than acreage on a map or a number on a street; but if it is efficiently managed, it may often bring a high rate of return.

From the viewpoint of a trust institution, therefore, efficient management of real property means such scientific care and development of the property as will ensure an adequate, continuous income from it. It also means advantageous sale of the property when necessary or advisable.

Mortgages

Mortgages on real property may constitute a considerable portion of the trust assets of a trust institution. As used in this chapter, the term "mortgages" includes bonds and notes for which real property is pledged as security under a deed of trust or other form.

There is a difference between a mortgage and a bond or note secured by a deed of trust on real property. A simple illustration will make the difference clear. A borrows $10,000 from B; as security for the loan, he gives B a mortgage on his residence. A is the mortgagor, B is the mortgagee, and the instrument used to pledge the security is the mortgage. C borrows $10,000 from D by conveying his residence in trust to a trustee and executing and delivering to D one or more bonds or notes, aggregating $10,000, secured by the deed of trust. Such bonds or notes secured by real property are used in certain sections of the country instead of mortgages. Since deeds of trust require the same care and management as mortgages, this chapter makes no distinction between the two forms of obligation.

The attitude of trustees toward mortgages underwent radical changes during the first half of this century. In the early years, legal investments of trustees in some jurisdictions were limited largely to mortgages and government bonds. Mortgage investments, with their higher yields, were popular. However, in the depression of the 1930s the investment record of many mortgages was unfavorable, and there were numerous defaults and foreclosures. As a result of that experience, some trustees have avoided making new investments in mortgages.

With broad acceptance of the principle of continuous amortization, attributable in part to the amortization requirements of the various insurance plans of the federal government, that attitude began to change. Now many trustees invest in mortgages if the size of the debt is reasonably related to the fair value of the property, if there is provision for regular amortization to reduce the unpaid principal as value declines with normal depreciation, and if the borrower can be expected to pay his debts.

Real property and mortgages are treated together in this chapter because in most trust institutions they are handled in the same division of the trust department and by the same service and operative groups. The care and management of trusteed real property and of mortgages on real property require a trained and properly constituted organization, adequate equipment, and an efficient plan of procedure.

Real Property and Mortgage Organization

The methods and facilities for handling real property and mortgages vary considerably among trust institutions. The board of directors is responsible for setting the general policies of the institution as to real property and mortgages in trust accounts.

Although not every trust department has a separate real property and mortgage committee, every well-organized trust department has a committee of active officers who pass judgment on the problems arising in connection with real property and mortgages. The exercise of group judgment and the preservation of records that, if occasion arises, will prove to the satisfaction of the court that there was such exercise of group judgment are as essential in connection with real property and mortgages as with other trust assets.

Real property and mortgage officers should be experienced in every phase of management of the kinds of real property administered or held under mortgage by their trust department, as well as in selling, leasing, improving, repairing, converting, and adapting real property of all kinds. They should be thoroughly familiar with the many and varied requirements for the management of real property as diverse as farms, stores, offices, residences, tenements, warehouses, and commercial and industrial plants.

In a small trust department, the trust officer himself may be the real property and mortgage officer. In a medium-sized trust department, one real property and mortgage officer with assistants may manage and supervise all the real property and mortgages. But in a large trust department, there may be a corps of real property and mortgage officers (comparable in function to the trust investment officers), each charged with specific duties.

The real property and mortgage division performs the detailed clerical and technical work connected with the management of real property and mortgages, including collecting rents and interest, renting and selling property, making repairs, paying taxes, maintaining insurance, and purchasing, placing, and servicing mortgages.

In a small trust department, there is usually no need for a formally organized real property and mortgage division. In a large trust department, the activities relating to real property and mortgages may be so numerous and important as to require the services of 100 or more employees. But, whether the trust department is small, medium-sized, or large, efficiency requires that a specific person or group be charged with the duty and responsibility of caring for real property and mortgages.

Any basic plan of organization for the handling of a considerable volume of real property and mortgages is not essentially different from that for the management of other trust assets. The organization should be as well adapted to the handling of real property and mortgages as the investment organization is to the handling of other kinds of trust investments.

Equipment

Adequate equipment is an essential feature of the real property and mortgage division. Such equipment includes forms and records for all accounts that give the division complete information about all the property and mortgages in its care. Maps can also be valuable, and in large departments small computers are increasingly being used to maintain asset records.

RECORDS

Although the record systems of trust departments vary considerably, the forms used in connection with the management of real property and mortgages are fairly standardized and are designed to reveal the same kind of information. For example, there are detailed records of results (profit, loss, and yield on each parcel of real property), of the physical facts, such as photographs and inspection records, and of the terms of the trust as far as they need to be known by the real property and mortgage division. Other records relating to real property and mortgages constitute part of the account system of the trust department.

DEEDS, ABSTRACTS, POLICIES, AND DOCUMENTS

The real property and mortgage division must obtain all the deeds, abstracts of title or title insurance policies, and fire and liability insurance policies relating to every mortgage or parcel of real estate. In the case of a living trust, these documents are checked carefully with the owner if he is available; in the case of an executorship, they should be checked with a member of the decedent's family or some other person who is thoroughly familiar with the decedent's affairs. If such assistance is lacking or unsatisfactory, the necessary information may be obtained from a title company or by a search of the public records made by an attorney. This is the only safe course to follow in all cases in which the decedent was a trader or dealer in real property or mortgages or in which he appeared as the owner of numerous lots or tracts of land. A copy of the tax abstraction or tax returns on which the late owner listed his holdings or the income or expense of the property is useful in locating his holdings.

The emphasis on the importance of assembling the owner's maps, deeds, abstracts, and other documents of title should not convey the impression that their mere possession gave the owner a good title to the property or that the trustee may rely on them for its title. In the following section, in which the plan of procedure is described, the necessary additional steps to be taken by the trustee to perfect the title to real property in estates or trusts are discussed.

Special Procedure with Respect to Real Property

Information on which the real property and mortgage division may act is obtained from work sheets supplied by the administrative officers and their staff. The procedure for handling real property involves four activities, as follows:

1. Preliminary investigation of the property
2. Active management of the property
3. Determination of whether to retain or to sell the property
4. Conveyance of the property out of trust

PRELIMINARY INVESTIGATION

A thorough preliminary examination and inspection of the property and the establishment of proper contact with the tenants at the beginning of the trust will ensure smooth handling of the property thereafter. A tenant is disposed to size up a new trustee as he does any other new landlord, and his first impression, whether favorable or unfavorable, is likely to endure; hence it is important for the trustee to impress the tenant at the outset with the trustee's carefulness, thoroughness, businesslike attitude, and reasonableness. The trustee must:

1. Notify the tenant formally of the change in management or ownership of the property caused by the administration of an estate or the establishment of a trust
2. Check with the tenant the rent payments as revealed by the books of the trustor of testator, so that there will be no later misunderstanding on this point

The preliminary investigation includes:

1. Ascertaining how the title to the property passed to the trustee
2. Checking the condition of the title
3. Making a physical inspection of the property
4. Making an appraisal of the property

Ascertaining How Title Is Passed

In almost every state, the instrument of title to real property must be recorded in some public office (sometimes called the office of the register of deeds), where it is open to public inspection. In administering the estate, the trust institution must know the exact name in which the decedent held the property. There may be many variations of that name, all of which must be included in the record of the estate.

Placing real property in trust may call for special attention. Frequently it is preferred that the terms of the trust not be revealed by recording. Sometimes the title is conveyed to the trust institution with no trust indicated; the institution then makes a declaration of trust, which is not recorded. Sometimes the fact of a trusteeship is shown in the title and in the trust agreement with the trustor, or the declaration of trust is authority for the trustee to manage the property, fix the selling price, sell the property, and dispose of the proceeds of sale. It is important to remember that taking title without disclosure of the fiduciary capacity is not generally approved.

Checking Condition of Title

Having accepted an estate or a trust, the trustee should at once investigate the condition of the title, not only because this is the best time to remedy any possible defect in the title but also because if a defect should come to light at the time of a proposed sale or other disposition of the property, the delay or expense necessary to remedy the defect might defeat the transaction.

There are two ways in which the trustee may be assured that the title to the property is satisfactory. One way (the usual way, until quite recently, in many sections of the country) is to have the records searched and the title abstracted by an attorney at law, who issues a certificate that the title is good and indefeasible except for any such defects as he may specify. The other way is to have the title guaranteed by a financially responsible title insurance company. The insured is protected to the extent of the amount of the policy against the consequences of any defects in the title not revealed by the title examination. The title report will disclose any encumbrances on the property and any unpaid taxes or special assessments, enabling the trustee to give attention to the payment or other disposition of such charges. The trustee, for example, should not commit itself to a long-term lease of the property until it has had the title brought up to date or until the state of the title is satisfactory to the lessee.

Inspecting the Property

Inspection includes:
1. A study of the location and the kind of district in which the property is situated
2. A study of the character and condition of the buildings and other improvements on the land, including encroachments by overhanging eaves or fences (a written narrative description may be supplemented by photographs)
3. A determination of the kind and amount of insurance coverage required for the buildings and improvements, including public liability insurance
4. An inquiry into the occupancy of the property, that is, whether it is occupied or unoccupied, rented or unrented, and, if rented, the kind of tenants
5. An appraisal of the property

The inspection of the property is greatly expedited if the inspector is furnished with a work sheet that lists specific questions for him to answer.

Appraising the Property

The accurate appraisal of real property is important to the work of a trust institution. Values are placed on real property for many purposes. For example, real property in trust accounts is valued for estate and inheritance tax purposes and to determine whether assessments for tax and other purposes are fair and reasonable. The accurate appraisal of all buildings and improvements is necessary so that the real property and mortgage division may determine replacement values in case of fire or other damage and make certain that adequate but not excessive fire insurance is carried. When real property is placed on the market for sale or lease, an accurate knowledge of its value is important to obtaining the best possible terms of sale or lease.

Judging the value of real property is highly complicated, requiring an accumulated wisdom based on common sense, long experience, and a knowledge of underlying facts and principles. Even with those qualifications, an experienced appraiser readily admits that his opinion regarding the value of a particular piece of property is subject to correction.

In large cities there are independent professional appraisers whose services may supplement the knowledge and experience of the appraisers in the trustee's own real property and mortgage division. In all cases, of course, payment of their charges must be provided for. Such independent appraisals are especially useful and frequently recommended in connection with inheritance and estate tax returns, real property received in living trusts or successor trusteeships, the determination of profits and losses for income tax purposes, sales, and contests of assessed valuation.

ACTIVE MANAGEMENT

The trustee's active management of real property begins after its preliminary investigation. It includes:
1. Collection of rents
2. Execution of new leases and renewal of present leases
3. Making repairs
4. Making improvements
5. Payment of taxes and special assessments
6. Payment of interest on, and principal of, encumbrances
7. Maintenance of proper insurance coverage
8. Periodic inspection throughout the term of the trust

Collection of Rents

Rents are usually collected directly and promptly by the trustee or indirectly through a rental agency. In handling real property, as in other phases of trust administration, the trustee is held to the prudent man standard. The prudent trustee, like the prudent landlord, adopts all kinds of recognized methods of keeping property occupied. A rental agency may be employed and paid the usual commissions; particularly in connection with apartment houses and office buildings, a manager may be employed to attend to the property and collect the rents. Such agents as may be employed are, of course, paid from the funds of the trust account.

Execution and Renewal of Leases

In connection with the execution of new leases and the renewal of existing ones, the trustee must determine how long the lease may run. Must the duration of the lease be limited by the duration of the trust, or may it continue beyond the term of the trust? If the trust is to terminate on a fixed or determinable date, the lease may be made coterminous with the trust or for a shorter period. In many cases, however, the duration of the trust is not ascertainable. The trust may be one that is to continue for the lifetime of a beneficiary who may live 20 years or more or die in a few months or years. The laws of many states and many modern instruments, therefore, give the trustee authority to execute leases that may continue beyond the duration of the trust. Adult beneficiaries whose vested interests cover the whole trust estate often consent to the trustee's execution of a lease that may extend beyond the term of the trust. In the absence of such express authority or approval, however, the trustee would not execute a lease that might extend beyond the term of the trust without first obtaining the approval of the beneficiaries, or in some cases of the court; otherwise, at the termination of the trust, it would be requiring the principal beneficiaries to take over the real property encumbered by the lease—and this might not be to their liking.

The trustee must also determine what covenants, limitations, and waivers should be included in a new lease. In most communities standardized provisions have been worked out for leases of different kinds of real property. For example, leases peculiar to stores, offices, apartments, residences, warehouses, farms, pasturelands, and oil, gas, and mineral property have their own standard provisions, as do leases peculiar to farmlands leased for growing wheat, corn, cotton, tobacco, livestock, and truck crops. The trustee usually has on hand the standard forms of property leases in use in the community in which the real property is situated.

Similarly, the trustee adapts itself to the customs of the community in fixing both the amount and the basis of the rent; furthermore, it adopts the basis that, in its judgment, involves the least risk and produces the best results for the beneficiary.

Making Repairs

Repairs and improvements of real property are treated separately because the powers, duties, and responsibilities of the trustee may be different with respect to repair than with respect to improvements. For example, if part of the furnace of a residence is damaged, the trustee would unquestionably have it replaced as a repair essential to the upkeep of the property. But if the furnace itself is demolished beyond repair, the trustee must determine whether it is authorized to replace the furnace with a more modern one or with another of the same general character and whether the new furnace would legally constitute a repair or an improvement. These questions demonstrate some of the problems that confront the trustee in dealing with real property, and they must be answered in accordance with the law of each jurisdiction.

The upkeep of real property is one of the most important activities of the real property and mortgage division. Any neglect not only is bound to result in eventual vacancies and consequent loss of income to the estate or trust but also is detrimental to the community. Failure to repair buildings promptly is a principal cause of depreciation and obsolescence. Frequently a reserve from income is created voluntarily or in compliance with the terms of the instrument to permit repairs and replacements.

Like a silent partner, a trust department is vitally concerned with the tenant's success and cooperates with him in every reasonable way. If the tenant should fail in business, the trust estate might suffer a loss of income; if the tenant prospers, he may require additional space; if he is pleased with his relations with the trust department, he will consult its officers about his needs and thus give the trust department an opportunity to lease larger quarters to him. The experienced trust institution knows that repeat orders are the most profitable, that business transactions are frequently made with friends, and that to expand it must build and maintain a reputation for fair dealing.

Making Improvements

If the trustee decides that a proposed change in the real property constitutes a permanent improvement rather than a repair, it next determines:

1. Whether the trust instrument authorizes the trustee to make improvements
2. Whether the improvements will inure equitably to the benefit of the income beneficiaries and of the principal beneficiaries
3. Whether the estate is financially able to make the improvements

Many modern trust instruments give the trustee express authority to make reasonable improvements. In the absence of such authority, a trustee may be slow to make improvements, since they are in the nature of a trust investment, and the trustee may not be authorized to make that kind of investment. Even with such authority, the trustee always gives full consideration to the respective rights of the income beneficiaries and the principal beneficiaries.

The general rule is that repairs are paid for from income and improvements from principal; yet if too large an amount is expended on improvements, the income beneficiaries may profit unduly by the increased rentals, and the principal beneficiaries may ultimately suffer from having too large a proportion of the trust estate invested in real property. There is also a question whether improvements are imperative or justified by a probable increase in income.

If the improvements are inexpensive or the trust estate has ample ready cash in the principal account to pay for them, their financing presents no problem. Often, however, the improvements would be relatively expensive, and the estate, being fully invested, lacks ready cash. To make the improvements, the trustee would be obliged to sell some investments or borrow money. The trustee must decide whether the trust estate would gain more by having the improvements made than it would lose by selling good investments to pay for them. If, instead of selling the investments, the necessary funds were borrowed, is it likely that they could be repaid during the life of the trust? Or is it likely that the loan would still encumber the property when the time came for the beneficiaries to take it over? The trustee's only course, provided that it has the authority, is to make such improvements as a reasonably prudent man would make on his own property of a similar nature, conscientiously balancing the respective interests of the income beneficiaries and the principal beneficiaries.

Payment of Taxes and Special Assessments

All real property is subject to taxation by local government authorities. The taxes with which the real property and mortgage division is mainly concerned are the state, county, municipal, and local taxes levied against property within the jurisdiction of the levying authority.

The trust institution makes certain that all real property owned by its estates and trusts is valued fairly and equably by the various tax assessors. At each property listing or tax assessing period, it gives careful attention to checking the assessment values of the property under its management and makes any necessary revisions of values on its own records. If it believes that property has been assessed at too high a figure or that clerical errors have been made in computing the assessment, it should file a protest with the tax officials, stating the reasons for its request of a revised assessment. If its protests are overruled, counsel for the trust institution may appeal to a higher body and eventually to the courts for reconsideration of the claim.

The trust institution keeps copies of all tax abstracts relating to the property in each estate and trust and showing each item listed for taxation. Those abstracts are valuable work sheets for the real property and mortgage division, since they enable it to check and verify each new tax bill as it is received.

Assessments for improvements are a lien on the property and may be collected in the same way as taxes, although they are frequently made payable over a number of years to prevent too heavy a charge at any one time. In most instances the improvements are requested by means of a petition signed by a majority of the property owners affected. The trust institution must exercise great care in determining whether to join in the petition, since to do so would create a lien on trust property. It should consider the probable cost and the ability of the estate or trust to pay its share of the assessment. It may be wise and necessary for the trust institution sometimes to oppose a proposed improvement vigorously and at other times to initiate it.

Payment of Principal and Interest on Encumbrances

Sometimes the trustee takes over real property that is already encumbered by a mortgage. The trustee is responsible for having the mortgage renewed or refinanced to the best advantage of the trust estate. In very rare cases, when the encumbrance may amount to more than the value of the property, the trustee faces the question of whether or not to abandon the encumbered property.

Maintenance of Proper Insurance Coverage

Another important duty of the real property and mortgage division is the maintenance of proper insurance on the real property in its care. The kinds and amounts of insurance depend on the circumstances. The standard is that of a man of ordinary prudence under similar circumstances.

Many trust institutions effect blanket fire and extended coverage insurance for a period of 60 or 90 days for the protection of both the trustee and the trust estate to gain time to inspect the property and determine the amounts and kinds of permanent insurance necessary. All trust institutions should carry blanket public liability insurance providing automatic protection against damage claims filed by persons who may be injured on or by the trust property. Some also carry errors and omissions insurance as a safeguard against technical errors.

One of the first duties when taking over real property belonging to an estate or trust is to check the insurance policies against the various descriptions and appraisals of the property to make certain that adequate insurance is carried and that the policies correctly describe the property and all interests therein. It is, of course, a fundamental principle that the trust institution should restrict its policies to those of insurance companies that have a high rating and financial strength. The propriety of insuring trust property through a mutual company must be considered and determined in the light of local law and practice.

Periodic Inspection of Property

Fully as important as the preliminary physical inspection of the real property are the subsequent periodic examinations. The character of neighborhoods, the fortunes of tenants, and the physical condition of buildings change as time passes, and the trustee should keep fully abreast of all such changes. To this end the trust institution's tickler system or trust account review system operates to bring up for periodic inspection and reexamination every piece of real property under its care and to see that a signed and dated report is made, considered, and included in the property file.

WHETHER TO RETAIN OR SELL PROPERTY

Real property—whether it is improved, unimproved, farmland, ranchland, or the residence of the beneficiaries—may be either retained or sold. The duty of a trustee to convert all unsound trust investments into more desirable ones applies as much to real property as to other forms of investment. When the trust institution is serving as administrator or guardian, it may sell real property only by permission of the court. When serving as executor or trustee, it must obtain such authority from the court unless the trust institution is granted power of sale by the will or other trust instrument; it must then have the sale confirmed by the court if so required by the jurisdiction.

Some states have enacted laws under which real property passes to an executor or administrator on the death of the owner in the same manner as personal property; but in most states and under the common law, title to real property passes directly to the heirs and is subject to sale by the personal representative only when the will so provides or when all other resources for the payment of debts have been exhausted.

In all fiduciary capacities, the trust institution, since it is acting for others, is faced with a problem different from that of an individual owner, who is accountable to no one for his actions in managing his own property. When considering the sale of real property, therefore, a trust institution exercises unusual care with regard to both the time of sale and the price obtainable, whether or not the approval of the court is necessary. Before disposing of real property, it is advisable to check the appraisals made by the institution's real estate division against the valuations of independent appraisers who are well acquainted with the property and its value. The employment of inheritance tax or independent appraisers is required in most cases in which the approval of the court must be obtained for the proposed sale of property and in some states will be confirmed only if the sales price is not less than, for example, 90 percent of the appraisal.

Improved Property

In the case of improved property, the trustee decides:
1. Whether the net return is sufficient to justify retention of the property
2. Whether there is a reasonable prospect of increase in its value

267

3. Whether any present encumbrance and the difficulty in refinancing it may necessitate a sale
4. Whether the present condition of the property and the cost of rehabilitation may necessitate a sale

The trustee may find that by selling the property and investing the proceeds in some other form of investment it can obtain a larger and more dependable income for the trust than the present return.

Unimproved Property

In the case of unimproved property, the trustee decides:
1. Whether it should retain the property even though unproductive
2. Whether the probable increase in value justifies retention
3. Whether the property can or should be improved

As a general rule, vacant land is an improper trust investment—it generally does not produce adequate income, and taxes and other expenses create a constant drain on the funds of the trust account. If market conditions are such that the trustee can obtain a fair price for the property, it should be sold and the proceeds invested productively. As a general rule, development of unimproved property by a trustee is an unjustifiable speculation. The principal and income laws of each state should be reviewed, since certain allocations between income and principal are required in the event of sale that may be important in a particular case.

Farm or Ranch Property

In farming and ranching sections of the country, farm or ranch property constitutes a considerable portion of the trust assets, and the proper handling of it calls for a special organization or specialized knowledge on the part of the real estate officer.

Farms and ranches are not types of property in which a trustee would normally invest trust funds, for they are not liquid or readily marketable assets. If the beneficiaries are of legal age and competent, farmers or ranchers often leave their land outright and not in trust. Where it is not desirable to leave such property outright, the testator should be encouraged to give the executor and trustee a broad power of sale. In such estates and trusts, a considerable volume of farm or ranch property may be found that, for one reason or another, cannot or should not be left outright or sold immediately. Trust institutions in those sections do not decline to accept all accounts that involve the retention and management of farm or ranch property; they organize and equip themselves to handle such property economically and profitably.

The problem of management of farm and ranch property in trust accounts is usually met in one of two ways. In some sections of the country, there are farm management organizations analogous to rental agencies for town and city real property. Those organizations accept farm or ranch property for management from executors and trustees as well as from property owners. They undertake to manage the property as prudent farmers and ranchers handle their own property. According to the customs of the community or the exigencies of the particular situation, they operate the farm or ranch with hired labor and a manager or overseer, rent it for money or a specified share of the crop, or furnish all or part of the machinery, implements, seed, and fertilizer (thus assuming a portion of the risk) and receive in return a portion of the crop (sharecropping). As compensation for its services, a farm management organization usually charges a flat amount per acre or a percentage of the gross income of the farm or ranch.

In other sections of the country, especially where farm or ranch management has not been developed as a specialized occupation, some trust institutions have established farm or ranch management organizations in their own trust departments. At the head of such an organization is a farm or ranch management officer whose position is comparable to that of the trust investment officer. He and his staff give personal attention to the farms and ranches in the trust accounts, operating, overseeing, renting, or leasing them as best they can according to the customs of the community. In most cases, by provision in the trust instrument or by custom, the trust institution receives or is allowed additional compensation for farm or ranch management service.

Residence of Beneficiaries

Sometimes a trustee is empowered or directed by a will or trust instrument to retain or even purchase a residence for the use and occupancy of the family. The trustee should exercise particular judgment and foresight in such a case, because, on distribution of the trust (or even earlier on dissolution of the family by death or marriage), the trustee may be obliged to take over an unprofitable or even unmarketable investment.

During the continuance of the trust, the duties of the trustee with respect to the residence of the beneficiaries may be minor. The trustee is, of course, responsible for attending to taxes, insurance, and repairs.

CONVEYANCE OF PROPERTY OUT OF TRUST

Inevitably the time comes when the trusteed real property passes out of trust and into the hands of the ultimate owners. At that time the trustee should give special attention to the procedure by which the title passes. With the help of its attorneys, it must determine, in accordance with local law and practice, whether at the termination of the trust the legal title vests in the beneficial owners without a formal conveyance, what kind of deed should be used if a formal conveyance is required, what warranties are contained in the trustee's deed, and similar questions. In brief, the trustee exercises as much care in closing the trust as it did in accepting it.

Special Procedure with Respect to Mortgages

Real property and mortgages on real property are usually handled by the same organization in the trust department. The preceding section deals largely with the management of real property in trust accounts. This section is devoted to the procedure followed in selecting and retaining mortgages for trust investment and in servicing them.

ACQUISITION AND REVIEW

When investing in mortgage loans for trust accounts, trustees should follow certain well-defined procedures. They include receiving the application, appraisal, title search, review and reappraisal, insurance, and servicing. The procedures are similar to those carried out by the real estate section of the bank.

DEFAULTS

Most difficulties in the handling of mortgages arise when a mortgage goes into default; in this situation special skill and judgment become necessary. Defaults can result from failure of the mortgagor to make payments of interest or principal, to pay taxes that have become a lien, to pay insurance premiums, or to fulfill other covenants, for example, maintaining the premises in good repair.

If, after demand, the owner fails to correct defaults, the trustee explores the various alternatives. It may be that a forbearance agreement can be worked out or that an arrangement can be made for the acquisition of the title by purchase or by cancellation of the debt. On the other hand, a foreclosure proceeding or a sale by the trustee under the provisions of the deed of trust may be necessary, or a suit against parties on a bond or note. Any alternative presents numerous problems that the trustee must be competent to consider and pursue.

A forbearance agreement, which is essentially a covenant not to sue, may be suitable if the security seems to be of sufficient value to indicate no loss; but the distinction between a forbearance agreement and an extension agreement should be kept in mind. An extension agreement may be equivalent to the purchase of a new mortgage, and a mortgage that has been defaulted is not likely to meet the requirements demanded in an original investment. In an arrangement to acquire the property by purchase of the title or by cancellation of the debt, the trustee considers the financial condition of the debtor, the cost of a foreclosure proceeding, and the hazard of delay in getting title by foreclosure, which is substantial in many states.

When foreclosure is necessary, the trustee makes arrangements to provide the necessary funds for fees and expenses. It follows the various steps in the proceedings, watches the management during the legal proceedings, determines the amount it should bid at the foreclosure sale, ascertains that the title thus acquired is merchantable, and eventually takes over the property as a trust asset.

SPECIAL TYPES OF MORTGAGES

Mortgages insured or guaranteed by the federal government, as by the Federal Housing Administration (commonly known as FHA mortgages) under the National Housing Act, call for a somewhat specialized procedure. Most of the procedure is prescribed by the regulations under which the mortgages are issued.

TAXES

The income tax laws must always be taken into consideration when mortgages are held in a trust portfolio, particularly in cases of default. Questions of gain or loss, taxability of income during foreclosure proceedings, and other tax problems require great care and experience. The real estate and mortgage division keeps in close touch with the tax division of the trust department to be certain that tax problems affecting real estate and mortgages are promptly and properly solved.

APPORTIONMENT

When a piece of real property owned by a trust as a result of a mortgage foreclosure proceeding is sold, a fair division of the proceeds between principal and income accounts must be made if the trust has both income and principal beneficiaries. In most states the trustee may apportion the proceeds between such beneficiaries along certain well-established lines. The theory of apportionment is to provide equitable treatment to the income beneficiaries when the property held either is not income producing or produces less than a fair rate of return for trust investments as of the period in question and to provide fair treatment to the principal beneficiaries when the income, because of the hazardous nature of the holding, is so large as to be out of proportion.

The general rule is that the proceeds of the sale are apportioned by determining the sum that, with interest thereon at the current rate of return on trust investments from the day the interest on the mortgage ceased to be paid, would equal the net proceeds. The sum so ascertained is treated as principal and the rest of the net proceeds as income. The Uniform or Revised Principal and Income Act or a similar body of law, if adopted in the state, should be followed unless the instrument gives the trustee discretion.

The mechanics of apportionment are simple enough when the for-

271

mula has been determined. Different states, of course, have different laws concerning apportionment, and such laws should always be examined before action is taken.

Title-Holding Trusts

A state has the power to forbid corporations organized in another state (usually referred to as foreign corporations) to act within its borders. Although many states forbid foreign corporate fiduciaries to serve as executors or testamentary trustees within their borders,[2] others[3] expressly permit them to do so. Still other states[4] have adopted reciprocal statutes. Such statutes permit a foreign trust institution to exercise fiduciary powers within the state if the state's own corporate fiduciaries are permitted to exercise similar powers within the foreign state.

The prohibition on the right to act as executor or testamentary trustee in a foreign state does not prevent a property owner from conveying property, including real property, to a corporate fiduciary. Many trust companies hold real property in trusts under the terms of which little, if any, management is contemplated. Even though not permitted to serve as executor or testamentary trustee, the corporate fiduciary may be permitted to sell the property and pay taxes on it. The statutes of each state must be studied to determine the extent of the trustee's freedom to serve.

---

2. For a list of the states, see *Estate Planning—Wills, Estates, Trusts* (Englewood Cliffs, N.J.: Prentice-Hall), Sec. 16, 104.

3. Ibid., Sec. 16, 105.

4. Ibid., Sec. 16, 106.

Chapter 19

Trust Powers

The Purposes of This Chapter:

1. To show how a bank or trust company acquires trust powers
2. To show how a bank or trust company surrenders its trust powers
3. To discuss the trust powers of out-of-state banks and trust companies
4. To explain the effect of mergers and consolidations of banks and trust companies on their trust powers

"The creation of corporations specifically chartered to act as trustees is the most important American contribution to the growth of the modern trust."[1]

Trust Business in the United States

In the United States, trust business is confined largely to national banks and state banks and trust companies; however, some savings banks, safe deposit companies, and title guarantee companies have trust departments. The term "trust institution" is used to designate any corporation engaged in trust business, and the term "trust department" refers to the department of a corporation that renders trust services. Although an individual or a firm can engage in trust business, and in a few localities (notably Boston) individuals and firms have set up organizations for that purpose, in practice trust service is confined almost wholly to corporations.

At the present time about 98 percent of the trust institutions in the United States are banks with trust departments or trust companies with banking departments. Other types of corporations have gradually withdrawn from the trust field.

---

1. Louis S. Headley, "From Kings to Corporations—The Origins of Wills and Trusts," *Trusts and Estates* 93:230.

TRUST POWERS AND POWERS OF TRUSTEES

The term "trust power" or "trust powers" means the power of a corporation to engage in trust business. It refers to the various fiduciary capacities in which a corporation is authorized by law to act. The term "powers of trustees" means the things a corporation or an individual has the legal right to do or to refrain from doing while acting in a fiduciary capacity. These powers include the powers to sell, buy, borrow, mortgage, and lease.

Acquiring Trust Powers

A bank or trust company must follow a prescribed procedure to acquire trust powers. The procedure for national banks differs from that for state banks and trust companies.

NATIONAL BANKS

A national bank desiring to engage in trust business first applies to the Comptroller of the Currency. In passing on the application, the comptroller gives special consideration to these factors:

1. The sufficiency of the bank's capital and surplus to exercise the trust powers applied for (in no case may the capital and surplus be less than that required of state banks by state law)
2. The needs of the community for the trust services applied for and the probable volume of such business available to the bank
3. The general condition of the bank, particularly the adequacy of its net capital and surplus funds in relation to the character and condition of its assets and to its deposit liabilities and other corporate responsibilities, including the proposed exercise of trust powers
4. The general character and ability of the management of the bank
5. The nature of the supervision to be given to the proposed trust activities, including the qualifications, experience, and character of the proposed officer or officers of the trust department
6. The availability of competent legal counsel to advise the bank and to pass on trust matters whenever necessary

In addition to the factors the bank itself should consider in seeking trust powers, the Comptroller of the Currency thus takes into consideration the general character and ability of the bank's management as well as the qualifications, experience, and character of the proposed executive officer or officers of the trust department. That is, the comptroller considers the applicant as well as the application.

The Comptroller of the Currency is authorized to grant a national bank, when not in contravention of state or local law, the right to act as trustee, executor, administrator, registrar of stocks and bonds, guardian

274

of estates, committee of property of incompetents, assignee, receiver, or managing agent, or in any other fiduciary capacity in which state banks, trust companies, or other corporations that come into competition with national banks are permitted to act under the laws of the state in which the national bank is located. A national bank authorized by the comptroller to do trust business is subject to the laws of the state in which it is located.

STATE MEMBER BANKS OF FEDERAL RESERVE SYSTEM

A state-chartered corporation may receive its trust authority through a special charter granted by the legislature, or it may qualify to do trust business by meeting certain requirements of the general state statutes. In either case its trust authority comes as a direct grant from the state.

Under the conditions of membership in the Federal Reserve System, a state bank or trust company that was not exercising trust powers when it was admitted to membership must obtain permission from the Board of Governors of the Federal Reserve System before exercising trust powers.

STATE NONMEMBER BANKS OR TRUST COMPANIES

As far as the procedure to be followed by a state bank or trust company that is not a member of the Federal Reserve System in acquiring trust powers is concerned, the states fall into two main groups:

1. States in which the bank or trust company acquires its trust powers directly from an administrative body of the state
2. States in which the bank or trust company, as a corporation, obtains its right to engage in trust business from one administrative body or official and its license to begin acting in various fiduciary capacities from another administrative body or official

With respect to trust powers, in a few states a distinction is made between a bank and a trust company. In one state, reportedly, a state bank may not engage in trust business, but a trust company may engage in banking.

The method of acquiring trust powers may seem needlessly cumbersome and indirect, but one can think of many analogies from everyday life. An individual, though learned in the law, must nevertheless obtain a license before he can practice law in a given state. A lawyer would draw a distinction between legal *capacity* and legal *authority* and say that a bank or trust company receives legal capacity from its charter and legal authority from its license.

The right to grant trust powers has in most states been transferred from the legislative to an administrative branch of the state government. That transfer has not affected the status of a bank or trust company already exercising trust powers under a legislative charter previously granted. Some of the older trust institutions continue to operate under legislative charters, and others have sought and obtained a renewal or an amplification of their trust powers from the designated administrative body or official. It is not uncommon to find in the same state some trust companies and state banks carrying on trust business under legislative charters and others under administrative charters.

OTHER CONDITIONS

In most states a bank or trust company must meet two other requirements before it can acquire trust powers. Those requirements must also be met by a national bank exercising trust powers in such a state. One relates to capital, the other to a deposit of securities. A less frequent condition is that a bank or trust company must establish a separate trust department before it can engage in trust business.

Regulation 9 of the Comptroller of the Currency provides that the comptroller shall not issue a permit to any national bank having a capital and surplus less than the capital and surplus required by state law for state banks, trust companies, and other corporations exercising trust powers.

A distinction must be drawn between the capital requirements of a bank or trust company as a *bank* and as a *trust institution*. In some states there is no additional or special capital requirement connected with the acquisition of trust powers; in others there is such a requirement.

Regulation 9 provides that every national bank acting in a fiduciary capacity must preserve the separate identity of the trust department. As long as that separate identity is preserved, the trust department and other departments may use each other's facilities and personnel. It also provides that fiduciary records must be retained so as to furnish information or reports required by the comptroller and kept separate from other records. Those records must contain full information relative to each account.

A few states have similar provisions. Some provisions are stated in general terms; others are more specific and detailed. One state, for example, provides that before a bank or trust company can exercise trust powers, it must organize a separate trust department and place a trust officer in charge of that department. Another state provides that the bank or trust company shall have a trust department in which trust business is kept separate and distinct from its general business.

An important aspect of separation is the requirement that deposits of cash from trust department accounts in accounts in the commercial side of the bank be protected by the bank's placing in the control of its trust department securities of equal or greater market value. In determining the amount of those securities, the coverage of a savings account by federal deposit insurance is considered. This has proved to be a wise requirement; during the banking failures of the 1930s, losses to accounts in the banks' trust departments were virtually nonexistent.

Surrendering Trust Powers

There is a difference between surrendering and ceasing to exercise trust powers. Moreover, there is a distinction between the surrender of trust powers and the voluntary liquidation of a bank or trust company.

There is no fixed procedure by which a bank or a trust company ceases to exercise trust powers. It may do so simply by closing out, transferring, or otherwise getting rid of its present trust accounts and declining to accept new ones. Each bank or trust company would do this in its own way and in accordance with the law of its own state, dealing with each existing account on its merits. Many banks or trust companies, desiring to close their trust departments, would cease to exercise their trust powers without taking any formal steps to surrender them. In fact, they might desire to retain such powers for possible future exercise. However, sometimes the bank or trust company might desire formally to surrender its trust powers and, after such surrender, to have returned to it the securities deposited with the state banking authority.

This section deals with the procedure for the formal surrender of trust powers. The procedure for national banks and the procedure for state banks and trust companies must be discussed separately.

SURRENDER BY NATIONAL BANKS

The procedure for the surrender of trust powers by a national bank is prescribed in Regulation 9. It provides that any national bank desiring to surrender its fiduciary powers shall file with the Comptroller of the Currency a certified copy of the resolution of its board of directors signifying such a desire. If, on investigation, the comptroller is satisfied that the bank has been discharged from all the fiduciary duties it has undertaken, he issues a certificate to the bank certifying that it is no longer authorized to exercise such powers.

SURRENDER BY STATE BANKS AND TRUST COMPANIES

State laws outlining the procedure by which a state bank or trust company surrenders its trust powers vary widely. Generally the laws provide that any trust company desiring to retire from business shall furnish the superintendent or commissioner of banks satisfactory evidence of its release and discharge from all obligations and trusts. On receipt of the required proof, the superintendent of banks examines the trust company or causes it to be examined. If, after such examination, he is satisfied that the trust company has discharged all its obligations and trusts, he revokes its license and returns all securities on deposit with him.

277

After a bank or trust company surrenders and returns its license to engage in trust business, it is still liable for all existing obligations. In a state where no formal procedure for surrender of trust powers is provided by statute, it would seem, as a matter of course, that a state bank or trust company might return its license voluntarily and that thereafter, except as to existing obligations, it would be without trust powers.

DISCIPLINARY MEASURES

It is seldom necessary for either federal or state authorities to resort to disciplinary measures to induce a bank or trust company to surrender or cease to exercise its trust powers. In some cases the closing of a trust department would be accomplished simply by persuading the bank or trust company of the wisdom of its taking the step voluntarily. In rare and extreme cases the appropriate federal supervisory authorities might resort to such disciplinary measures as (1) forfeiture of the charter of a national bank, (2) forfeiture of the membership of a state bank or trust company in the Federal Reserve System, (3) removal of the directors and officers of a national bank or a state member bank or trust company, and (4) cancellation of the insurance of an insured bank. In some states the banking authorities have the disciplinary authority to remove directors, officers, or employees of a bank or trust company or even to close it for refusal to obey lawful orders, even though it is solvent. These disciplinary powers, though seldom exercised, are potent in inducing a bank or trust company to surrender its trust powers when the situation warrants such action.

Trust Authority of Out-of-State Banks and Trust Companies

What right has a bank and trust company located in one state, with a permit to engage in trust business issued by the Comptroller of the Currency, to exercise powers in another state? What right has a state bank or trust company, chartered and licensed to do trust business in one state, to exercise trust powers in another state? If a bank or trust company does not have such powers by virtue of its original permit or license, what steps, if any, can it take to acquire the right to engage in trust business in another state?

POWERS OF TRUSTEES

Banks or trust companies often settle estates or administer trusts that have among their assets real property or other property or interests situated in states other than the one in which the bank or trust company is located. In such cases the bank or trust company is frequently obliged to take action with regard to the out-of-state property or other interests.

In a number of states, there is a statute that specifies certain powers that an out-of-state bank or trust company may exercise. Among the powers specified are the following: (1) to sell real or personal property, (2) to foreclose mortgages, (3) to execute satisfactions or releases of mortgages, (4) to discharge and assign judgments, (5) to bring suits, and (6) to deliver property. These are powers that a bank or trust company may need to exercise in connection with the settlement of an estate or the administration of a trust. The statute is designed to authorize an out-of-state bank or trust company to go into the state and exercise those powers without having to qualify to do trust business generally in that state.

TRUST POWERS

To what extent may an out-of-state bank or trust company exercise trust powers in the sense of qualifying as executor, administrator, trustee, or guardian and taking all the steps necessary or appropriate for settling an estate or administering a trust or a guardianship?

Under the foreign corporation laws of most states, it is commonly held that an isolated or occasional business transaction by a foreign business corporation within the state does not constitute doing business in that state within the meaning of the law. Apparently an out-of-state trust institution cannot avail itself of the benefit of that doctrine to the extent of handling an estate or guardianship or trust account in its entirety even though it is only a single or occasional account. The theory is that the settlement of an estate or the administration of a guardianship is not a single act but the general exercise of trust powers so far as they apply to the particular account. However, the attorney general of at least one state has expressed the opinion that the administration of a single account is not doing business in the state within the meaning of the state's foreign corporation laws.

As to permitting out-of-state banks and trust companies to exercise trust powers within their borders, the states may be classified under four headings, as follows:

1. States in which out-of-state banks or trust companies may not exercise trust powers.
2. States that permit out-of-state banks or trust companies to exercise trust powers if they qualify as foreign corporations to do business in the state. As a practical matter, the requirements for qualifying (which may include payment of fees, deposit of cash or approved securities, and submission to examination by representatives of the state) may be so expensive and exacting that few out-of-state banks or trust companies would feel justified in undertaking to meet them.

3. A few states that permit out-of-state banks or trust companies to exercise trust powers without qualifying to do business. These jurisdictions usually permit qualification if the out-of-state bank or trust company meets relatively inexpensive and simple requirements, which usually include naming a local agent on whom a legal process may be served and giving a bond with surety on each qualification.

4. Reciprocal states. An out-of-state bank or trust company located in state A is permitted to serve in all or some fiduciary capacities in reciprocal state B if the laws of state A accord similar privileges to banks or trust companies located in state B. The statutes of the reciprocal states are not uniform. Some limit the reciprocity to executors and trustees named in the will; some do not reciprocate as to administratorships.

TRUST POWERS AND TRUST SERVICES DISTINGUISHED

A distinction must be made between exercising trust powers in a state and doing trust business for or rendering trust service to residents of that state. Although a state may prohibit an out-of-state bank or trust company from engaging in trust business within its borders, it cannot prohibit one of its citizens from opening a trust account with an out-of-state bank or trust company at its own office; nor can it prohibit one of its citizens from receiving payments or distributions from a trust account created for his benefit with an out-of-state bank or trust company. Thus state A cannot prohibit a bank or trust company in state B from doing trust business for or rendering trust service to citizens or residents of state A at its own place of business in state B.

Mergers and Consolidations

When two or more banks or trust companies merge or consolidate and one or both or all of them have trust powers, among the questions that arise are the following: Does the remaining or the new bank or trust company have the right to exercise powers of trustees (such as the power of sale or the power of foreclosure) in accounts already in one of the constituent banks or trust companies? Does it have the right to accept appointments under wills in which one of the constituent banks or trust companies has been named? Does it have the right to continue in the trust business without the acquisition of new trust powers? What is the necessary procedure for the continuance of trust authority or for the acquisition of new trust authority?

MERGERS AND CONSOLIDATIONS DISTINGUISHED

The legal difference between a merger and a consolidation may be stated thus: In a merger of two banks or trust companies, one of them is absorbed in the other and ceases to exist; in a consolidation, the two institutions are converted into a new bank or trust company, and both the original banks or trust companies cease to exist.

Another situation that may arise is the sale of its assets by one bank or trust company and the transfer of its assets and liabilities to another bank or trust company. Such a sale and transfer partakes of the nature of a merger; hence the situation is not treated separately. It should be stated as a general rule, however, that on the sale of the assets or the business of one trust institution to another, the trust accounts of the seller do not pass to the purchaser, and the trust accounts of the purchaser are not affected. Trust accounts are not articles of commerce subject to sale or purchase.

SUCCESSION OF TRUST POWERS

The question of succession of trust powers naturally arises more often in connection with consolidations than with mergers, since a consolidation puts both old corporations out of existence and brings a new one into existence, whereas a merger leaves one of the original banks or trust companies intact.

In this section, as in the preceding one, it is necessary to keep clearly in mind the distinction between trust powers and the powers of trustees. In respect to the succession of powers, three different situations must be dealt with. The first relates to estates in process of settlement and trust accounts in process of administration at the time of the merger or consolidation. Here the question of the survival of the powers of executors and trustees is raised. The second relates to the estate of a person living at the time of the merger or consolidation who has nominated one of the constituent banks or trust companies in his or her will as executor or trustee or both. That situation raises the question of the survival of trust powers. The third situation is that of the bank or trust company accepting new nominations and new trust accounts and continuing to engage in trust business generally; again the question of the survival of trust powers is raised.

Succession for a National Bank

When two or more national banks consolidate (one or more of which has trust powers, i.e., has received a permit from the Board of Governors of the Federal Reserve System or the Comptroller of the Currency to exercise fiduciary powers), the new national bank, by operation of law and section 9.4 of Regulation 9, succeeds to the trust powers of the constituent banks. If the name or charter number of the resulting bank differs from that of the bank to which the right to exercise fiduciary powers was originally granted, the Comptroller of the Currency will issue a certificate to that bank showing its right to exercise the fiduciary

281

powers previously granted to any of the national banks participating in the consolidation or merger.

When a national bank and a state bank or trust company consolidate to form a new national bank, the new bank, provided the original national bank had trust powers, may exercise trust powers in existing accounts without obtaining a new permit, accept appointments under wills in which one of the constituent banks has been named, and exercise trust powers generally. If the original national bank or trust company did not possess trust powers but the state bank or trust company did, the new national bank may exercise powers as to the specific trust accounts to which it succeeds; but it cannot accept appointments under wills in which the state bank or trust company has been named, it cannot act generally in fiduciary capacities, and it cannot accept any other trust business without obtaining a permit from the Board of Governors or the comptroller.

When a national bank and a state bank or trust company consolidate and the new corporation is a state bank or trust company, the survival of trust powers is determined by the laws of the state in which the state bank or trust company is located.

Succession for a State Bank or Trust Company

In about three-fourths of the states there are statutes pertaining to the merger or consolidation of banks and trust companies, but not all those statutes contain provisions relating directly to the survival or succession of powers affecting trust accounts or trust business.

Some of the statutes simply provide that in a merger or a consolidation the remaining or resulting bank or trust company shall possess all the rights, privileges, powers, and franchises of the predecessor banks or trust companies, no specific mention being made of fiduciary relationships. Whether the powers with respect to the trust accounts of the predecessor banks or trust companies survive under these general statutes is an unsettled point of law.

Many of the statutes deal definitely with the succession of powers: the powers of executors and trustees in estates already in process of settlement or administration, trust powers with regard to appointments under wills in which one of the predecessor banks or trust companies has been nominated, and the power to engage in trust business generally.

Chapter 20 **Government
Supervision
of
Trust Business**

The Purposes of This Chapter:

1. To trace the historical development of government supervision of trust business
2. To comment on the various government agencies that supervise banking
3. To offer a brief discussion of trust department examinations

"The goal of trust department supervision since the inception of the present-day comprehensive review process has been to provide an examination that is constructive in character and of the greatest possible service to corporate fiduciaries and to the public by assisting banks to formulate and adhere to sound practices in the administration of their fiduciary business."[1]

Who Examines Trust Departments?

State banks	State banking authority
State banks/members of Federal Reserve System	Board of Governors of Federal Reserve, through Federal Reserve banks
State banks/nonmembers of Federal Reserve System	Federal Deposit Insurance Corporation
National banks/some Washington, D.C., banks	Comptroller of the Currency

Regulation F—Trust Powers of National Banks

The passage of the Federal Reserve Act in 1913 and the issuance by the Federal Reserve Board on February 15, 1915, of its initial regulations opened the way for national banks to enter the trust field. In 1915 the National Metropolitan Bank of Washington, D.C., opened the first

---

1. Robert C. Masters, "Trust Examinations," *Trust and Estates* 93:280.

national bank trust department. The state-chartered trust companies strongly opposed the entrance of national banks into the trust field and tested the constitutionality of the Federal Reserve Act.[2] By 1925 the battle was over. In the now famous case of *State of Missouri* v. *Duncan*,[3] the Supreme Court of the United States upheld the right of national banks in any state to enter the trust field on a parity with the state banks of that state.

The collapse of the securities market in 1929 and the deterioration of real estate values that followed brought into question some of the practices and policies of trust administration. Although there were relatively few examples of maladministration of such a nature as to threaten serious capital impairment, those few received such publicity that the public became concerned about the quality of the services rendered by corporate fiduciaries. After the bank holiday in 1933, the Federal Reserve Board revised and in 1934 put into effect Regulation F, "Trust Powers of National Banks," and attached to it with its commendations "A Statement of Principles of Trust Institutions," which had been adopted in April 1933 by the Trust Division of the American Bankers Association and approved by its Executive Council.

Regulation F marked the beginning of comprehensive and effective government supervision of trust business. As adopted, it applied to national banks only. Fortunately the Federal Reserve Board prescribed for state banks applying for membership in the system requirements substantially similar to the regulations governing national banks. Soon state member banks were, as a rule, voluntarily operating their trust departments in harmony with Regulation F.

Regulation 9—Fiduciary Powers of National Banks and Collective Investment Funds and Disclosure of Trust Department Assets

On July 17, 1962, legislation was introduced in the U.S. Congress that would transfer the authority to grant and supervise the exercise of trust powers of national banks from the Board of Governors of the Federal Reserve System to the Comptroller of the Currency. The legislation was adopted, and on April 5, 1963, the comptroller published Regulation 9, entitled "Fiduciary Powers of National Banks and Collective Investment Funds." More recently the regulation has been broadened to require disclosure of trust department assets.

Banks seeking authority to do trust business must apply to the Comptroller of the Currency and pass six tests: sufficient capital and surplus,

---

2. First National Bank of Bay City v. Fellows, 244 U.S. 416 (1917).
3. 265 U.S. 17,21.

community need, sound bank condition, high caliber of bank management, qualified trust management, and available legal counsel.

Regulation 9 leaves no doubt that "the Board of Directors is responsible for the proper exercise of fiduciary powers by the bank. All matters pertinent thereto . . . are the responsibility of the Board. In discharging this responsibility, the Board of Directors may assign the administration of such of the bank's fiduciary powers as it may consider proper . . . to such directors, officers, employees or committees as it may designate."

Regulation 9 requires that a trust department be audited once a year by a trust committee, none of whom may be officers of the bank. Furthermore, trust funds awaiting distribution or investment must not be left idle any longer than reasonably necessary.

According to the regulation and by law, trust assets must be kept separate from the bank's assets. Where local law requires trust institutions to deposit securities with the state for the protection of customers, national banks must do the same. As a general rule, trust departments of national banks are subject to the same requirements as competing state banks.

Regulation 9 specifies that trust funds must be invested according to local law and the terms of the trust agreement. It prohibits self-dealing by banks operating trust departments. For example, the bank does not buy from nor sell to its estates, trusts, guardianships, or other fiduciary accounts any securities or other property in which it has a financial interest and does not purchase for itself from its fiduciary accounts any securities or other property. It does not engage in self-dealing in any manner whatsoever unless permitted by Regulation 9 and local law. Generally, it does not engage in self-dealing with any member of the board of directors or board of managers or with officers or employees of the bank unless a court of competent jurisdiction first determines that such a transaction is in the best interests of the trust estate.

A collective investment fund may not invest more than 10 percent of its assets in any single security, except for federal government securities or federally guaranteed instruments, where there is no limit.

Regulation 9 requires that a bank subject to the jurisdiction of the Comptroller of the Currency having total equity securities of $75 million or more reflected in its trust department annual report must prepare and file with the Comptroller of the Currency a report setting forth details concerning its buying and selling of securities. A similar report is required in respect to the purchase or sale of any equity security having a fair market value of $500,000 or more or involving 10,000 shares or more effected during the calendar quarter for any fiduciary accounts over which it has investment authority either alone or with others.

Exemptions are provided for any equity the aggregate holding of which is 10,000 shares or less and for the assets of any investment company, as that term is defined in the Investment Company Act of 1940. The Comptroller of the Currency may, at his discretion, exempt any reporting entity.

Glass-Steagall Act

The Glass-Steagall Act of 1933 established the Federal Deposit Insurance Corporation. In an attempt to prevent a repetition of post-1929 difficulties, it made other reforms. It separated investment banking and commercial banking. That separation was not complete; banks are permitted to purchase and sell securities on the order and for the account of customers. Banks may also deal in and underwrite U.S. bonds and general obligation bonds of states and municipalities.

It has been suggested that the Glass-Steagall Act creates artificial restrictions on competition and that it should be amended to permit banks to offer their customers such services as the underwriting of revenue bonds and the offering of commingled managing agency accounts.

Securities Acts Amendment

In 1975 Congress approved changes in the securities industry. It authorized the Securities and Exchange Commission to share with federal banking agencies jurisdiction over banks that act as transfer agents or securities depositories. The banking regulators retain primary enforcement jurisdiction over banks, while the Securities and Exchange Commission has primary jurisdiction over securities firms. The 1975 amendment also:

1. Extended federal securities regulations to securities firms and banks that underwrite and trade state and local government bonds
2. Established a Municipal Securities Rule-Making Board to set regulations for trading municipal bonds
3. Required institutional investment managers of more than $100 million in equity securities to disclose to the SEC their stock holdings in publicly owned companies
4. Allowed the SEC to require disclosure of holdings of debt securities (including tax-exempt securities), the voting authority of equity securities, and transactions of $500,000 or more (the SEC may lower the minimum transaction level)
5. Required fingerprinting of officers, directors, and employees of registered transfer agents
6. Required measures to cut theft and loss of securities

Government Supervision

In considering the principal relations of various government agencies with trust institutions during the period of their active operation, it may be well to bear in mind that those agencies are maintained as part of and a necessary incident to government supervision of banking in general. This function is performed by agencies that have the authority and responsibility to grant trust powers to banking institutions.

One significant development in trust business in the United States during the past 50 years is the changed nature and extent of government supervision of corporate fiduciary activities. Before 1933 examination of the banks' trust departments was sporadic and relatively superficial except in a few states where state banking departments had become vitally interested in the need for proper supervision.

There were few specially designated trust examiners—people trained and experienced in trust examination work—in the state and federal supervisory agencies. The comprehensive trust examination report form and the procedural techniques of trust examinations today had not yet been initiated. Statutory and regulatory provisions directly applicable to a bank's trust activities were either nonexistent or in need of considerable improvement and expansion to enhance their effectiveness.

For the purpose of this chapter, government supervision of banking means the activities of various government agencies concerned with the administration of banking laws and the regulation of banks with particular emphasis on bank trust departments. Before the period of business expansion in the 1920s, comparatively few banks engaged in the trust business. During that period some trust institutions were established, and many already established banks that had not previously operated trust departments obtained trust powers. Closer government supervision of trust business thus became necessary; and since the banking holiday in 1933, such supervision has generally been regarded as a normal part of the bank supervisory process.

AUTHORITY TO SUPERVISE

The authority of the various government agencies to supervise and regulate the banking business, including trust department activities, emanates from Congress and from the state legislatures. The principal federal statutes granting such authority are the National Bank Act, the Federal Reserve Act, the Federal Deposit Insurance Act, and the Trust Powers of National Banks Act. The banking laws of each state are the source of the regulatory power exercised by state supervisory agencies.

SCOPE OF SUPERVISION

Besides the power to license and close banks and to issue and revoke permits to transact trust business, government supervision of banking

287

includes visitatorial powers; power to promulgate, revise, or rescind regulations supplementing the banking law; and power to take steps to correct unsatisfactory conditions. It also includes the compilation, interpretation, and maintenance of comprehensive historical and statistical records of each bank and trust institution and of groups of banks and trust institutions.

REASONS FOR SUPERVISION

The principal reasons for government supervision of trust business are (1) that the government, having chartered the banks and permitted their entry into trust business, has been charged with some responsibility of seeing that the business is being properly conducted in the public interest and that the governing laws are being obeyed and (2) that defective operation of trust business might, if widespread and material, seriously disturb the entire banking system. Since the ability of the banking system to function properly has a direct effect on most types of enterprises and on the prosperity of the entire country, and since trust business has become an important activity of many banks, including most large banks, it is logical that trust business should be considered a proper subject of government regulation and supervision.

LIMITS OF SUPERVISION

Government supervision of banking was designed to protect and possibly strengthen the banking structure but not to operate or manage any bank or bank department. Conducting the business of a bank is the responsibility of its officers and directors. The responsibility of the supervisory authority is to keep itself informed about the condition and operations of the banks subject to its control and to help correct unsound situations. Government supervision cannot ensure efficient, sound, and profitable trust department operation; but it can point out weaknesses in organization and procedures and promote improved standards of administrative practice.

Trust Department Examinations

The entry of numerous banks into the trust business in the 1920s and developments preceding the banking holiday of 1933 focused considerable attention on trust department operations; as a result, virtually all supervisory authorities inaugurated regular and comprehensive examinations of trust departments. In 1934 the Board of Governors of the Federal Reserve System provided for one or more trust examiners at each Federal Reserve bank. Comparable action was taken by the Comptroller of the Currency, the Federal Deposit Insurance Corporation, and various state banking departments.

Banking institutions are subject to periodic, unannounced examination by trained and experienced examiners from the federal and state supervisory offices. The four supervisory offices that they represent are the office of the Comptroller of the Currency, the Federal Reserve bank of the district, the Federal Deposit Insurance Corporation, and the state banking department of the state in which the bank or trust company is located.

National bank examiners examine national bank trust departments; Federal Reserve bank examiners, state member banks of the system; Federal Deposit Insurance Corporation examiners, insured banks; and state bank examiners, state bank trust departments.

At one time there was a great deal of expensive overlapping of examinations by these four supervisory offices, but most of it has been eliminated, largely through the voluntary cooperation of the supervisory offices. State bank examiners do not, as a rule, examine the trust departments of national banks, but the state banking department has access to reports of examination by national bank examiners. State member banks of the Federal Reserve System are examined by both federal and state bank examiners, but examinations by the two are frequently made simultaneously and cooperatively. The FDIC examiners confine themselves to nonmember, insured state banks with trust departments.

In one way or another, needless overlapping of examinations is averted, and examiners of the several offices examine and closely supervise almost every one of the trust institutions of the United States.

OBJECTIVES OF TRUST DEPARTMENT EXAMINATIONS

The primary purpose of trust examination is to disclose to the supervisory authorities the condition of a trust department and to evaluate the findings in light of their relation to and effect on the condition of the bank. A collateral purpose is to improve the standards of quality of trust service in the interests of trust business and trust beneficiaries.

Trust department examinations have acquired an established place in the bank examination program. As examiners familiarize themselves with the administration and operation of highly developed trust departments, they are able to make constructive suggestions to departments that do not have the advantage of an extensive organization. Because they see many trust departments, the examiners are able to distinguish between good and undesirable policies and practices, and their suggestions are favorably received by most trust officers.

INSTRUCTIONS REGARDING PROCEDURE

The trust business is a business of rendering service. It involves the obligation to perform certain services faithfully and prudently, in accordance

289

with applicable laws, regulations, and governing instruments. It does not involve the assumption of liability similar to a bank's deposit liability. Therefore examination of a trust department is essentially an analysis of policies, systems, and functions and the disclosure of actual or potential liability arising from fiduciary activities.

To assist the trust examiner and to help give direction and uniformity to his examination, manuals and bulletins such as the comprehensive comptroller's *Handbook for National Trust Examiners* have been issued. These manuals and bulletins attempt to outline and explain the process of examining trust departments; and they review pertinent sections of laws, regulations, and court decisions. However, interpreting the data and information assembled in the examination and drawing conclusions from them require sufficient knowledge and experience on the part of the examiner to detect violations of applicable fiduciary law and regulations and weaknesses in trust department organization and methods. The manuals and bulletins, together with other available material, are intended in part to supply such knowledge and to stimulate further research on the part of examiners.

The forms on which the examiners for the various supervisory agencies report the results of their examinations are the same in most important respects. The basic form used by Federal Reserve bank examiners contains various topics related to organization, supervision, systems, safeguards, litigation, administrative and investment policies, and conflicts of interest. The comptroller's questionnaire on policies, practices, and controls for trust department examinations asks for the usual statistical data on such matters as organization, operations, administration, employee benefit accounts, internal and external audits, investment policies and practices, collective investment funds, and corporate trusts and agencies and includes questions on such subjects as conflicts of interest, self-dealing, and divided loyalty.

THE TRUST EXAMINER

Before beginning an examination, the examiner reviews the report and the work sheets from the previous examination. If he is not already familiar with the history, condition, and management of the bank or trust institution, he also reviews the information in the bank examination department's files. He determines in advance the scope of the examination, including the extent to which the assets are to be verified and the records proved.

Scope of the Examination

The scope of the examination varies according to the volume and kind of trust business handled. In small and medium-sized departments, the departmental accounting records are, as a rule, proved to the controls, and the assets are verified. In larger departments that are adequately supervised by independent auditing staffs, the proofs and verifications may be dispensed with or limited to test checks. Usually no audit is made of accounts or transactions, since the audit function is a primary responsibility of bank management, not a normal part of the bank examination process.

Trust examinations are concerned primarily with determining the effect, immediate and ultimate, of trust department administration on the solvency of the bank and collaterally with an attempt to disclose practices that may be detrimental to beneficiaries. In working toward these objectives, the examination seeks to determine whether operations and administrative practices conform to the requirements of governing laws and regulations and to the policies set forth in "A Statement of Principles of Trust Institutions." It also includes:

1. Various analyses and tests to determine the soundness and efficacy of fiduciary account administration
2. An appraisal of the character and ability of the management responsible for the conduct and supervision of the bank's trust business
3. An inquiry into administrative and investment policies to determine the effect they have had or may have on the condition of the bank
4. A constant effort to improve the standards of trust department operation and administration by offering constructive suggestions for correction of conditions disclosed or for improvement in practices and policies

The examination is concerned largely with questions of performance and administrative practice; it seeks to determine the quality of the service being rendered, to disclose conditions that have created or may create liability for the bank, and—through remedial measures suggested in examination reports—to help minimize the possibility of losses. A trust examination, therefore, unlike a commercial bank examination, is not concerned with appraisal of assets and determination of solvency; it is directed primarily toward a review of administrative performance and results.

Procedure of Examination

The comptroller's handbook recommends that the examiner, on entering the bank, obtain from responsible officers information on the system, character, and location of papers and records. All assets on hand are sealed and all records appropriately controlled by the examiner. Assets are released only when the examiner is satisfied that proper audit controls are in effect. A verification of assets by physical check may not always be necessary.

Ledgers are proved, and from these and other records the examiner may obtain information on new and closed accounts, changes in principal, overdrafts, and other matters of importance. Any errors detected are referred to the proper officers for correction, ideally during the examination.

Internal Controls and Audits

The examiner must observe and report on management supervision, as well as the audit required at least once each calendar year. The examiner will review the report of the audit to ascertain whether the trust department is being operated in compliance with law and according to sound fiduciary principles. The audit includes verifications of all accounts and records, as well as reconcilement of the bank's trust deposits. Assets and unissued securities in the corporate trust section must be safeguarded, joint custody maintained, and other verifications made.

Investment Policies and Practices

Several sections of Regulation 9 refer to such investment matters as funds awaiting investment or distribution, investment of funds held as fiduciary, custody of investments, conflicts of interest, self-dealing, divided loyalty, and questionable investments.

Funds must not be held uninvested or undistributed any longer than is reasonable for the proper management of the account. Investments must be in accordance with the instrument establishing the fiduciary relationship and with local law. Such investments shall not be in stock obligations of, or property acquired from, the bank, its officers or directors, or other persons connected with the bank.

Lists of the bank's fiduciary ownership of its own stock, as well as data on shares acquired and disposed of, must be included in the examination report. Particular note is made of any cases in which the total holdings exceed 10 percent of the shares outstanding. Such stock held by the bank cannot be voted unless there are directions in the instrument on this subject. Collective investment funds must be operated in strict compliance with regulations. Any variance from the regulations will be noted in the examination report.

Report of Examination

The examiners, whether federal or state, make detailed reports of their examinations to their supervisory offices. The reports are carefully analyzed, and the matters needing correction or action are called to the attention of the bank officers. The examination report is then presented to the board of directors of the bank; it is the duty of each director to review the report thoroughly and ascertain that management has adequately considered it and, where appropriate, has taken necessary corrective action.

Discussion of Report with Management

At the end of the examination, the examiner discusses his findings with the executive management of the institution. If the examiner has reported matters requiring attention, he sometimes adds a statement from the management concerning the corrective action to be taken. This procedure obviates much correspondence and, as far as the supervisory authority is concerned, readily disposes of matters requiring attention or correction. It also guards the examiner from drawing hasty conclusions and making impractical recommendations.

In the case of national banks, the Regional Administrator of National Banks is responsible for the preparation and submission of letters to banks on matters requiring attention revealed in the examination report. For this reason, all matters commented on in the report must be supported by a clear and complete statement of all pertinent facts.

Chapter 21

Trends in the Development of Trust Business

"O wad some power the giftie gie us
To see oursels as ithers see us!
It wad frae monie a blunder free us,
An' foolish notion."[1]

As we come to the close of this introduction to the study of trust business, it seems wise to look at some of the trends in the development of one of the nation's most dynamic businesses. At the same time we should try to determine how the public views trust officers, trust institutions, and their relationship to their customers, the bank, the court, and the various administrative agencies of government.

Notwithstanding the dramatic growth of trust business, there is every reason to believe that we are in the morning hours of that growth. There is no reason to believe, however, that the years ahead will be any less demanding than those of the past. Indeed, faced with such problems as increased competition, government regulation of securities and employee benefit plans, the increased activity of administrative agencies and the courts, and the rise of consumerism, the task ahead could be more challenging than any yet faced by corporate trustees.

Self-Dealing and Undue Control

One of the most damaging charges to evolve in recent years is the allegation that corporate trustees give only lip service to the rule against self-dealing. Some persons seemingly believe that trust departments exist primarily to protect the commercial bank. It has been alleged that officers of the bank and officers of the trust department swap inside

---

1. Robert Burns, "To a Louse," 1786, *Literature of England,* 5th ed., George K. Anderson and William E. Buckler, eds. (Scott Foresman and Co., 1966), Vol. 2, p. 122.

information that is likely to leave the customer at the mercy of those bent on wrongdoing.

In addition, banks and trust departments have come under congressional fire as having endangered, so it has been charged, the capital market by channeling their wealth into a relatively few corporations. Although no one wants unjust criticism and much of what has come has been unjust, it demonstrates a clear lack of public, and in some instances regulatory, understanding of the safeguards and restraints thrown around trust business.

As the number of trust departments increases despite all the mergers and consolidation, with a resulting increase in assets, the charge of overconcentration of economic power is likely to be made more frequently. It will be necessary to face such charges with patience, good humor, self-restraint, and a willingness to educate the public about the principles and policies of trust business.

Changing Relations with the Judiciary and Administrative Agencies

Whether well-founded or not, the conflict-of-interest criticism of banks and their trust departments has stimulated greater judicial and administrative activity. Courts that have in the past been reluctant to substitute their judgment for that of the fiduciary are losing that reluctance. Furthermore, the extension of the Sherman Anti-Trust Act and the impact of such administrative agencies as the Securities and Exchange Commission and the Labor Department on trust business will make the administration more complex and more expensive as the corporate trustee will have to meet ever-increasing demands for additional information.

The Changing Law of Trusts

Few will disagree with Maitland, the great historian of English law, that the development from century to century of the trust idea is the most distinctive achievement of Englishmen in the field of jurisprudence. The American lawyer, both in and outside trust business, can take much pride in his contribution to this development.

Although many of the legal principles surrounding the administration of trusts are still found in court cases, the adoption of a number of uniform acts, usually with local modifications, has done much to clarify the law relating to the creation and administration of trusts. With the possible exceptions of the Uniform Principal and Income Act, the Uniform Probate Code, and the Uniform Gift to Minors Act, which needed clarification, the uniform acts have been incorporated into the existing framework of trust law with relatively few difficulties. Indeed, such acts as the Uniform Powers Act, the Uniform Act for Simplification of Fiduciary Security Transfers, the Revised Uniform Principal and Income Act, the Uniform Testamentary Additions to Trusts Act, and the Prudent Man Rule stand as evidence to the good work done by legislatures.

Taken as a group, the legislative acts mentioned combine with the Internal Revenue changes and Regulation 9 to indicate that corporate fiduciaries are well respected and accepted by the general public. It is reasonable to assume that other legislation, probably equally favorable to corporate trustees, will be forthcoming in the years ahead. If that is to occur, however, the public must be made to understand that corporate trustees have used responsibly their voting powers of stock held in trust and such devices as nominee registration and street names.

Profitability

Much has been written and said about the profitability of trust business. Trust business must be made—and, once made, kept—profitable. Trust compensation must be based on the costs of the services provided and the risk and responsibility assumed. More attention will have to be given to the development of systems to aid in determining the costs of services. Among the things that will have to be considered are the logging of time and schedules of compensation that can be applied to individual accounts, remembering always that the size of the account does not necessarily determine the complexity of administration or the risks assumed.

Imaginative Management

Perhaps the greatest compliment paid to corporate fiduciaries has come from the broad powers of administration that have been granted under the terms of wills, trusts, and agency agreements and by state legislatures. It is not enough, however, to have the powers; the executor or trustee must be prepared to use them in the interest of the beneficiaries.

With an increase in litigation in every area of business and professional life, trustees will have to be careful if they are not to become subconsciously preoccupied with possible suit for maladministration. Considering the vast number of accounts handled and the few successful suits, corporate fiduciaries should put away undue apprehension and give the estate or trust the imaginative and individual management that only they can give. Only then will corporate fiduciaries be able to avoid slipping from being prudent conservators to being deadweight conservationists.

That is not to imply that every estate or trust will lend itself to innovative management. In some cases the executor will liquidate the estate, pay the taxes and debts, put the family on a stringent budget, and invest in a manner that offers little prospect for growth. In others the owner will want his property managed in a very restricted way. In still others the property owner will not be especially concerned with the mere preservation of principal or the protection of a remote generation; the corporate fiduciary will be expected to extend the owner's productive management and keep the assets of the estate appreciating at a rate at least equal to the rate of inflation.

Personal Service

Whether in the bank, the trust department, the corporate office, or the college campus, mechanization and automation are inevitable. The most important question for the trust institution is how to mechanize without losing personal touch with beneficiaries. In designing products, systems, and reports, the emphasis must be on meeting the needs of customers and keeping them informed. Surveys seem to show that the average trust customer is more concerned with prompt and sensitive personal attention to his needs than with investment performance. In other words, the future development of trust business will in large measure be determined by the willingness of corporate fiduciaries to place as much emphasis on "people problems" as they do on profitability and innovative management.

Meeting the Challenge

It comes as no surprise that the growth of trust business has greatly stimulated competition. Investment counselors, brokerage firms, insurance companies, mutual funds, and lawyers are competing for the business that until just a few years ago was considered almost the exclusive domain of trust institutions. If trust departments are to continue the growth that has characterized their efforts in recent years, they will have to develop and market new services, such as financial planning for executives and asset management for charitable organizations. These two groups have had, often to their detriment, little or no external investment counsel or management.

Looking at the past and present, one has to be "bullish" about the future of trust business. Corporate trustees have earned the respect of the public. Furthermore, no competition has yet emerged that can match the efficient and economic personal and financial service of the corporate trustee operating at its best. When one realizes the great advances made since the opening of the Farmer's Fire Insurance and

298

Loan Company in 1822 (now the First National City Bank of New York), it is not difficult to understand why bank trust departments control the world's largest pool of investment money.

A former president of the Trust Division has observed: "I have no doubt that, in 1984, as now, and as then, our trust industry—howsoever it may change in form—will remain faithful to the spirit as well as to the letter of the fiduciary relationship. This has been the keystone of our stability and our growth. As long as we remain true to the tradition, we have little to fear from the future—and much to gain in the new challenges that force us to innovate, to expand, to strengthen our structure and our services in ways hardly imaginable, a short generation ago."[2]

---

2. Chalkley J. Hambleton, "The Trust Industry Looks Ahead to 1984," *Trusts and Estates* 113:816.

Appendix A

Will

I, Jasper Paul Wilson, a resident of Dunn, Harnett County, North Carolina, declare this to be my last will and revoke any will or codicil heretofore made by me.

FAMILY

Item I. My immediate family consists of my wife, Vivian Lewis Wilson, who is forty years of age; a son, James Paul Wilson, who is sixteen years of age; and a daughter, Mary Harmon Wilson, who is twelve years of age. In addition to these members of my family, James Martin Wilson, my nephew and son of my deceased brother John, is ten years of age and has resided with my family since he was five years of age. It is my hope to be able to adopt my nephew in the near future, but whether or not he has been adopted at the time of my death, he shall be considered as one of my children for the purposes of this will.

Throughout this will, when I say "my wife," I mean my present wife, Vivian Lewis Wilson; and when I say "my children" or "our children," I mean the children named above, including my nephew James Martin Wilson, and any children of mine hereafter born or adopted.

PAYMENT OF DEBTS

Item II. I direct that all of my just debts (including unpaid charitable pledges whether or not the same are enforceable obligations of my estate), my funeral expenses (including the cost of a suitable monument at my grave), and the costs of administration of my estate be paid out of the assets of my estate as soon as practicable after my death.

I further direct that any obligations of mine secured by a mortgage on any real estate (whether owned by me as a tenant by the entirety or individually) and any obligation secured by pledge of or lien against any of my personal property or life insurance be paid out of the principal of my residuary estate; and that no part of such debts be charged to or paid by any devisee, legatee, surviving tenant by the entirety, or beneficiary.

PAYMENT OF TAXES

Item III. I direct that all estate and inheritance taxes and other taxes in the general nature thereof (together with any interest or penalty thereon) which shall become payable upon or by reason of my death with respect to any property passing by or under the terms of this will or any codicil to it hereafter executed by me, or with respect to the proceeds of any policy or policies of insurance on my life, or with respect to any other property (including property over which I have a power of appointment) included in my gross estate for the purpose of such taxes, shall be paid by my executor out of the principal of that portion of my residuary estate which is not included in the gift qualifying for the marital deduction, and I direct that no part of any of such taxes be charged against (or collected from) the person receiving or in possession of the property taxed or receiving the benefit thereof, it being my intention that all such persons, legatees, devisees, surviving tenants by the entirety, appointees, and beneficiaries receive full benefits without any diminution on account of such taxes.

PERSONAL EFFECTS AND HOUSEHOLD GOODS

Item IV. Section 1. I bequeath to my wife, if she shall survive me, all of my personal effects, household furniture, library, jewelry, works of art, chinaware, silverware, automobiles, owned by me and held for personal use, and all other tangible personal property in, around, about, and used in connection with my main residence, but excluding cash on hand or on deposit, stocks, bonds, choses in action or other intangible personal property, and tangible personal property (although in, around, or about my residence) used for business purposes. The decision of the executor as to what property shall be included in this bequest shall be conclusive.

Section 2. If my wife shall not survive me, I bequeath all of the above-described property, share and share alike, to my children, with the issue of a deceased child representing and taking their deceased parent's share. In the division into equal shares, if any of my children or issue of deceased children shall be a minor, such child's share may be delivered to the person with whom such child is residing, or to such child's legal guardian, or my executor may represent such minor. The receipt of the person with whom such minor resides, or the receipt of such minor child, shall constitute a full acquittance of my executor with respect to the legacy so delivered. If in the making of such division there should be any disagreement among my children or issue of deceased

302

children, I direct that the executor shall determine and put into effect the method of settling any such disagreement, and the result of the method so determined shall be conclusive.

SPECIFIC LEGACY

Item V. I bequeath the portrait of my father, James Paul Wilson, painted by Joseph Wallace Johnson and now hanging in the living room of our residence in Dunn, North Carolina, to my son, James Paul Wilson, if he shall survive me; if not, I bequeath the same to my daughter, Mary Harmon Wilson, if she shall survive me; if not, to the next of my children who shall survive me in the order of his or her age; hoping thus to keep this portrait of my father in our family.

SPECIFIC DEVISE

Item VI. I devise to my daughter, Mary Harmon, if she shall survive me, the building lot, 100 feet front and 300 feet deep, shown on the map of Dunn as Number 207 Morehead Street. If she shall not survive me, I direct that this gift shall lapse and become a part of my residuary estate as hereinafter set out.

PECUNIARY LEGACY

Item VII. I bequeath the sum of two thousand dollars ($2,000.00) in cash to my former teacher Miss Ernestine Cherry, if she shall survive me.

DEMONSTRATIVE LEGACY

Item VIII. I bequeath the sum of five thousand dollars ($5,000.00) in cash to my longtime business associate and personal friend Robert F. Clodfelter, if he shall survive me. This gift is to be paid from my savings account in the Dunn Bank and Trust Company; but if my savings account shall not be sufficient to satisfy this legacy, I direct that any deficiency shall be made up out of my general estate.

GIFT TO CHARITY

Item IX. I bequeath the sum of $5,000.00 to the Dunn-Harnett County Foundation, a community trust created by the Board of Directors of the Dunn Bank and Trust Company of Dunn, North Carolina, on the fourteenth day of October, 1919. This is intended to be an undesignated gift to the foundation.

RESIDUE TO EXECUTOR

Item X. I bequeath and devise the residue of the property which I may own at the time of death, real and personal, tangible and intangible, of every nature and wherever situated, including all property which I may acquire or become entitled to after the execution of this will and including all lapsed legacies and devises and property over which I may now or hereafter have a general power of appointment by will, to my executor, and I direct that my executor shall administer and dispose of the residuary estate in accordance with the terms and provisions set forth and contained in the succeeding Items of this will.

MARITAL DEDUCTION TRUST

Item XI. Section 1. If my wife shall survive me, my executor shall ascertain and set aside for the benefit of my wife a sum which together with the total of any other amounts allowed as a marital deduction in the federal estate tax proceeding relating to my estate shall equal the maximum allowable marital deduction; provided, that this sum shall be reduced by an amount, if any, needed to increase my taxable estate to the largest amount which, after allowing for the unified credit against the federal estate tax, and any other allowable credits, will result in no federal estate tax being imposed on my estate. In computing the maximum allowable marital deduction for purposes of the preceding sentence, all transfers as to which I am the "deemed transferor" under the generation-skipping provisions of the Internal Revenue Code as amended, or the corresponding provision of any federal tax law, shall be disregarded.

Section 2. I direct that the sum provided for in this Item shall be satisfied only out of assets that qualify for the marital deduction under the provision of the Internal Revenue Code applicable to my estate or out of the proceeds of such assets, and that this sum shall not be reduced by any estate, inheritance, transfer, succession, legacy, or similar taxes paid out of property passing under this will. To the extent, also, that other assets qualifying for the marital deduction are available, said sum shall not be satisfied by the distribution of: (a) assets with respect to which a credit for foreign taxes paid is allowable under the federal Internal Revenue Code; (b) rights to income deemed "income in respect of a decedent" under the federal Internal Revenue Code; or (c) United States Treasury Bonds eligible for redemption at par in payment of federal estate tax.

Section 3. The sum provided for by this Item, as well as any other pecuniary bequest or any other distribution made of assets constituting the residue of my estate, may be satisfied in cash or in specific property, real or personal, or an undivided interest therein, or partly in cash and partly in such property; and in instalments or all at one time; and without regard to the income tax basis of specific property allocated to any beneficiary (including any trust); provided, that any assets so distributed in kind shall be valued at their date or dates of distribution values. In making such distributions, I request (but do not direct) that to the extent deemed advisable or practical, my executor do so in a manner which will result in the property to be sold to satisfy obligations of my estate (or of any trust) having an aggregate income tax basis as close as possible to its aggregate fair market value and, to the extent consistent with this primary objective, that my executor do so in a manner which will result in maximizing the increase in basis for federal and state estate and succession taxes attributable to appreciation.

So long as any part of the bequest provided for by this Item shall remain unpaid, my said wife shall be entitled to receive from my executor all of the net income of my estate.

Any such income to which my wife is entitled under the provisions of this Item shall be paid over as hereinafter provided at such time or times as may be determined by my executor during the settlement of my estate, but not later than at the time of the satisfaction in full of the sum provided for in this Item.

Subject to the foregoing, the decision of my executor as to which assets shall be distributed in satisfaction of the bequest given by this Item; as to whether my estate shall be valued under the optional valuation provisions of the federal estate tax law; as to what tax elections should be exercised; and as to what proceedings are necessary to complete the ascertainment of the federal estate tax, shall be conclusive and binding on all persons, and no compensating adjustments between income and principal or between the marital and other bequest shall be made as a result of such tax elections exercised by my executor.

Section 4. (A). I direct that my executor shall deliver and convey the sum ascertained and constituted as aforesaid to the Dunn Bank and Trust Company, N.A., in trust for the following uses:

(B). During the lifetime of my wife, all the income derived from this trust shall be paid to my wife, or applied for her benefit, in convenient instalments, but no less frequently than annually.

(C). If the income payable to my said wife in accordance with the provisions of paragraph (B) above, supplemented by income (other than capital gains) available to her from other sources, shall not be sufficient to meet the reasonable needs of my wife in her station in life—as to all of which the judgment of my trustee shall be conclusive—then, and in that event, I authorize my trustee to pay to or apply for the benefit of my wife so much of the principal of this trust as my trustee in its sole discretion shall from time to time deem requisite or desirable to meet the reasonable needs of my wife, even to the full extent of the entire principal of this trust.

Section 5. During her lifetime, my wife shall have the right to appoint at any time and from time to time part or all of the principal of the trust as she may determine to and among one or more or all of my children, their spouses, more remote issue, and their spouses. The trustee may pay to my wife such amounts from the principal of the trust as represent any gift tax which may become due because of the exercise of this power.

If at any time during the administration of this trust, the trustee in its absolute discretion deems the continuation thereof to be uneconomic or not in the best interests of my said wife, the trustee, in its absolute discretion, is authorized to terminate the same and to distribute the assets, free of the trust, to my wife, absolutely.

Section 6. So much of the principal of this trust as shall remain in the hands of my trustee at the time of the death of my wife shall be transferred and delivered, discharged of the trust to such appointee or appointees of my wife (including my wife's estate) and in such amounts or proportions and upon such terms and provisions as my wife shall appoint and direct in an effective will or codicil specifically referring to this general power of appointment. The trustee may rely upon an instrument admitted to probate in any jurisdiction as the last will of my said wife, but if it has no written notice of the existence of such a will within a period of three months after her death, it may be presumed that she died intestate and the trustee shall be protected in acting in accordance with such presumption. If this general power of appointment shall not be effectually exercised as aforesaid as to all or any portion of such principal, so much of the principal as shall not have been disposed of by the effectual exercise of such general power of appointment shall pass as a part of the remainder of my residuary estate and be disposed of in accordance with the provisions of Item XII hereunder, as if I had died on the date of my wife's death.

Section 7. On the death of my wife, the trustee shall be authorized to withhold distribution of an amount of property sufficient, in its judgment, to cover any liability that may be imposed on the trustee for estate or other taxes until such liability is finally determined.

Section 8. I hereby declare: (1) that it is my intent and purpose that the trust provided by this Item for my wife shall qualify for the marital deduction; (2) that in the establishment and administration of such trust, my executor and my trustee shall be vested with all the discretionary powers herein conferred, but that neither my executor nor my trustee may exercise any of such discretionary powers in any manner which would disqualify such trust for the marital deduction; and (3) that all other provisions of this will, or of any codicil to it hereafter executed by me, shall be subordinate to the qualification of such trust for the marital deduction.

Section 9. I hereby authorize my wife to disclaim all or any portion of my estate herein provided for her, and I authorize and direct my trustee to join in any such disclaimer if my trustee shall deem its joinder necessary or desirable under the law in order to make such disclaimer fully effective. To be effective, such disclaimer shall be made in writing and shall be delivered to my executor within the sixty-day period following the date of qualification of my executor as such. Any portion of my estate so disclaimed shall pass as a part of the remainder of my residuary estate and shall be distributed in accordance with the provisions of Item XII as if my wife had predeceased me.

FAMILY TRUST

Item XII. I direct that after satisfying all legacies and devises hereinabove set out and after payment or provision for payment of all administration expenses and all death taxes, my executor shall deliver and convey all the remainder of my residuary estate to my trustee for the following uses and purposes:

Section A. During the lifetime of my wife, to accumulate or to pay over or apply the net income—that is, net after the payment of all expenses including the maintenance and upkeep of the family home— as my trustee in its absolute discretion shall from time to time determine, according to one or more of the following optional methods of disposition:

(1) To pay over or apply the net income for the benefit of my wife in such manner and at such intervals as the trustee in its uncontrolled discretion shall from time to time determine; or

(2) To pay over or apply the net income for the benefit of my children or the issue of any deceased child of mine in such manner and at such intervals as the trustee in its uncontrolled discretion shall from time to time determine; or

(3) To accumulate all or any portion of the net income as the trustee in its uncontrolled discretion shall determine; provided, however, that any income so accumulated may subsequently be used in any manner authorized in the above subsections (1) and (2).

Section B. In addition to the net income, to pay to or apply for the benefit of any income beneficiary of this trust so much of the principal of the trust as the trustee, in the exercise of its uncontrolled discretion, shall deem needful or desirable for the beneficiary's comfortable support and maintenance and education and for the medical, surgical, hospital, or other institutional care of such beneficiary.

Section C. After the death of my wife, the trust estate, including any accumulated income, shall be apportioned in equal shares to such of my children as shall then be living and to the living issue *per stirpes* of such of my children as shall be dead; and I direct that the several equal shares shall be administered and disposed of as follows:

(1) The share apportioned to each child of mine who shall have attained twenty-five years of age shall thereupon be delivered and conveyed to such child, discharged of trust.

307

(2) The share apportioned to each child who shall be under twenty-five years of age shall be held in trust for the benefit of such child and all or any part of the net income derived from the trust for such child and all or any part of the principal of the trust shall be paid to or applied for the benefit of such child in such manner and at such intervals and in such amounts as the trustee in its uncontrolled discretion shall deem needful or desirable for the child's comfortable support and maintenance and education and for medical, surgical, hospital, or other institutional care of such child. As each child shall attain twenty-five years of age, the principal and accumulated income then constituting the child's separate trust shall be delivered and conveyed to the child, discharged of the trust.

(3) If a child shall die prior to the termination of his trust, at his death the principal and accumulated income constituting the trust for such child shall thereupon vest in and be delivered and conveyed to such child's surviving issue *per stirpes* (subject to the provisions in Section D hereunder); or if such child shall leave no issue surviving, the principal and accumulated income shall inure in equal shares to the benefit of my living issue *per stirpes,* and their respective shares or portions shall be administered and disposed of in accordance with the terms and provisions of the trust herein created for their benefit.

(4) The share apportioned to the living issue *per stirpes* of a deceased child shall vest in and be delivered and conveyed to such issue *per stirpes,* subject to the provisions in Section (D) hereunder.

Section D. If any of the issue of a deceased child or any of my issue shall be under twenty-five years of age at the time that his share of the trust estate becomes distributable, then although his share shall vest immediately, I direct that the trustee shall continue to hold his share in trust and administer it as a separate trust and pay to or apply both income and principal as the trustee in its uncontrolled discretion shall deem needful or desirable for the comfortable support and maintenance and education and for medical, surgical, hospital, or other institutional care of such issue until he attains twenty-five years of age, and then deliver or convey to such issue his portion of the trust estate, discharged of trust.

SPENDTHRIFT PROVISION

Item XIII. If any income beneficiary of any trust, other than the beneficiary of my marital deduction trust, shall attempt to anticipate, pledge, assign, sell, transfer, alienate, or encumber his or her interest, or if any creditor or claimant shall attempt to subject such interest to the payment of any debt, liability, or obligation of such beneficiary, then thereupon the absolute right of such beneficiary to the income shall terminate, and thereafter the trustee shall pay such income to or apply

308

same for the maintenance and comfort of one or more of the following persons, namely: (1) such beneficiary, (2) his or her spouse, (3) his or her issue, and (4) those who would be entitled to receive the principal of the trust had the beneficiary died immediately prior to the receipt of such income by the trustee, in such manner and proportions as the trustee in its sole discretion may determine, regardless of equality of distribution; but in no event shall the trustee be required or compelled to pay any part of the income to or for such beneficiary.

RULE AGAINST PERPETUITIES

Item XIV. Anything in this will to the contrary notwithstanding, each trust (other than a trust of a vested interest) created under this will shall in any event terminate twenty-one years after the death of the last survivor of those beneficiaries who were living at the time of my death; and upon the expiration of such period all trusts shall terminate and the assets thereof shall be distributed outright to such persons as are then entitled to the income therefrom and in the same proportions.

APPOINTMENT AND SUCCESSION OF EXECUTOR AND TRUSTEE

Item XV. Section 1. I appoint the Dunn Bank and Trust Company of Dunn, North Carolina, the executor and trustee of the several trusts created under my will and request that it be permitted to serve without bond.

Section 2. If the Dunn Bank and Trust Company, either before or during the settlement of my estate, shall (by sale, merger, conversion, consolidation, reorganization, or otherwise) be changed into another corporation, under the same or another name, whether a state bank or a national bank, authorized to serve as executor and trustee, such successor or resulting corporation shall succeed to all of the powers and be entitled to all of the compensation of the Dunn Bank and Trust Company.

COMPENSATION

Item XVI. For its services as executor and as trustee, the Dunn Bank and Trust Company, or its successor, shall be entitled to receive the compensation stipulated in its regularly adopted schedule of compensation in effect and applicable at the time of the performance of such services; provided, however, that such compensation shall not exceed the maximum commissions then allowable by law for such services.

POWERS OF EXECUTOR AND TRUSTEE

Item XVII. Without distinguishing between its powers as executor and as trustee, and in addition to any inherent or implied or statutory powers it may have now or hereafter in either capacity, I grant to my executor and trustee and its successor, the continuing, absolute, discretionary power to deal with any property, real or personal, held in my estate or in any trust, as freely as I might in the handling of my own affairs. The power may be exercised independently and without the prior or subsequent approval of any court or judicial authority, and no person dealing with the executor or trustee shall be required to inquire into the propriety of any of their actions. Without in any way limiting the generality of the foregoing, I hereby grant to my executor and my trustee the powers set forth below. None of these powers, however, shall be exercised in a manner to defeat my intention regarding my marital trust.

Section 1. *Postpone Distribution.* If, in the judgment of the executor, additional time is needed for the payment or collection of debts, for the determination of questions concerning taxes, or for the orderly reorganization or liquidation of any business, including farming operations, in which I shall be engaged or financially interested at the time of my death, or for any other purpose, the settlement, distribution, and accounting with respect to my estate may be postponed for a period of five years from the date of its qualification as executor.

Section 2. *Retention of Original Investments.* To retain any security or other property owned by me at the time of death, so long as such retention appears advisable, to exchange any such security or property for other securities or properties, and to retain such items received in exchange. I am of the opinion that any securities which I may own at the time of my death will be of investment quality and worthy of retention by my trustee. My opinion shall not be binding on my trustee and shall not impair the power of sale or exchange or any other powers or discretion given the trustee; however, if the securities or other properties are retained by my trustee for the duration of the trust or any shorter period of time, my trustee shall not be responsible or liable for any loss or decrease in the value of the trust, by reason of such retention.

Section 3. *Retention and Acquisition of Trustee's Stock.* In addition to any inherent or implied or statutory powers it may have now or hereafter, I authorize my executor and trustee (a) to retain any stock that I may own in the Dunn Bank and Trust Company, or its successor, until it shall determine that there exists some circumstance or condition (other than desirability of diversification) which shall cause it to decide that the sale or other conversion of all or any portion of the stock is in the best interests of the trust estate; (b) to acquire by purchase, exchange, or otherwise additional shares of stock in the Dunn Bank and Trust Company.

Section 4. *Make New Investments.* To invest and reinvest in stocks (common and preferred), bonds, notes, property, or mortgages on property in or outside the State of North Carolina; in participations in common trust funds established and administered by the Dunn Bank and Trust Company or its successor; in insurance contracts on the life of any beneficiary or annuity contracts for any beneficiary; in real property, even though unproductive at the time of the purchase; and generally to invest in such property and in such proportion of such property as the trustee deems to be in the best interests of this estate.

Section 5. *Carry On Business.* To continue and operate any business which I may own or in which I may be financially interested at the time of my death and to do all things needful or appropriate, including the power to incorporate or to participate with others in the incorporation of the business; to invest other estate or trust assets in the business; to borrow and to pledge other assets of the estate or trust as security for loans made to the business; to control, direct, and manage any business; to delegate all or any part of its power to supervise and operate a business to such person or persons as it may select, including any associate, partner, officer, or employee of the business; to hire and discharge officers and employees, fix their compensation, and define their duties; to sell or liquidate all or any part of any business at such time and price and upon such terms and conditions as to it shall seem best; and the executor or trustee shall not be held liable for any loss resulting from the retention, operation, or liquidation of any business except for its own negligence.

Section 6. *Carry On Farm.* To continue and carry on any farming operation in which I am financially interested at the time of my death or which may be acquired after my death by my executor or trustee and to operate such farming operations as a corporation or corporations, partnership, or sole proprietorship, and by way of illustration and not limitation of its powers, to operate the farms; to lease the farms for cash or a share of the crop; to purchase farm machinery or livestock; to construct, repair, and improve farm buildings including the homes of the tenants; to manage and improve the timber and forest on the farm and sell the same, when in its uncontrolled discretion it deems it in the best interests of my estate; to engage in livestock production or dairying; to install irrigation systems; to employ the recognized and approved soil conservation practices, and in so doing to obtain loans or advances at the prevailing rate of interest and to pledge assets of the estate or trust as security for such loans.

Section 7. *Manage, Lease, and Develop Real Property.* To improve and manage any real property in my estate or trusts; to make repairs, replacements, and improvements, structural or otherwise, to such property; to mortgage or encumber any such property; to lease the property for such term or terms and upon such conditions and rentals and in such manner as it may deem advisable, although the period or periods of the lease may extend beyond the duration of the trust in which the property is held; to subdivide the property; to dedicate it to public use and to grant easements as it may deem proper; and, generally, to deal with the property in the same manner as it would be lawful for any person owning the same to deal with such property.

Section 8. *Receive Property.* To receive additional property from any source, including any living trust or insurance trust created by me or some other person, and to administer the property as a portion of the appropriate trust under my will. If the receipt of additional property imposes additional or different duties on the trustee, it shall be entitled to additional compensation.

Section 9. *Sell and Exchange Property.* To sell, exchange, assign, transfer, and convey any security or property, real or personal, held in my estate or in any trust, with or without an order of court, at such times and upon such terms and conditions as to the executor or trustee shall seem advisable; and the purchaser shall be under no duty to follow the proceeds of such sale.

Section 10. *Deal with Other Trusts.* To sell or exchange property with the trustee of any trust I or my wife or any of our children shall have created, or shall create, without an order of court, at such times and upon such terms and conditions as to sale price, payment, and security as to the executor or trustee shall seem advisable.

Section 11. *Borrow Money.* To borrow money for such periods of time and upon such terms and conditions as to it shall seem advisable, including the power to borrow from its own banking department or from any trust created by me or my wife or any of our children, and to mortgage and pledge estate and trust assets as security for the repayment of the loan.

Section 12. *Nominee Registration.* To register and carry any or all of the trust property in my name, in its own name, in the name of any other person, partnership, or corporation, in bearer form, or in the name of its nominee, with or without disclosing its fiduciary relationship, and its liability shall not be increased or decreased.

Section 13. *Vote Shares.* To vote in person or by special, limited, or general proxy, but without power of substitution, any securities held in my estate or trusts; and to vote my shares of stock in the Dunn Bank and Trust Company in the election of directors in the manner determined by my wife, and, except for the election of directors, to vote or not vote such bank stock in such manner as it deems to be in the best interests of my estate and trusts.

Section 14. *Sell or Exercise Options, Rights, and Privileges.* To sell or exercise all options, rights, and privileges to convert stocks, bonds, notes, mortgages, or other property into other stocks, bonds, notes, mortgages, or other property; to subscribe for other or additional stocks, bonds, notes, mortgages, or other property; and to hold such property acquired so long as it deems it to be in the best interest of my estate or trusts.

Section 15. *Reorganizations.* To consent to and participate in any plan for the liquidation, reorganization, consolidation, or merger of any corporation, company, or association, the securities of which may form a portion of the estate or trusts.

Section 16. *Reduce Interest Rates.* To reduce the interest rate at any time and from time to time on any mortgage or other indebtedness constituting a part of my estate or trusts.

Section 17. *Modify or Release Guaranties.* To consent to the modification or release of any guaranty of any mortgage in my estate or trusts or in which my estate or trusts have a partial interest.

Section 18. *Renew and Extend Mortgages.* To continue mortgages upon and after maturity with or without renewal or extension upon such terms as may seem advisable to the executor or trustee, without reference to the value of the security at the time of such continuance.

Section 19. *Foreclose and Bid In.* To foreclose, as an incident to collection of any bond or note, any mortgage or deed of trust securing such bond or note and bid in the property at such foreclosure sale, or to acquire the property by deed from the mortgagor or obligor without foreclosure; and to retain as a trust investment property so bid in or taken over without foreclosure. However, in any foreclosure action, it will not be necessary to make the decedent's heirs a party thereto.

Section 20. *Insure.* To insure the property of my estate and trusts, for such hazards and in such amounts, either in stock companies or in mutual companies, as the executor or trustee shall deem advisable.

Section 21. *Compromise.* To compromise, settle, or adjust any claim or demand by or against my estate or any trust and to agree to any revision or modification of any contract or agreement.

Section 22. *Employ Agents.* To employ accountants, attorneys, rental agents, investment brokers, tax specialists, and such other agents, assistants, and advisers as deemed by my executor and trustee to be needful in the proper settlement of my estate and the administration of my trusts; and to pay reasonable compensation for their services and to charge the same to (or apportion the same between) income and principal as it may deem proper.

Section 23. *Consolidate Funds.* To hold the principal of two or more trusts in one or more consolidated funds until division shall become necessary in order to make distributions; to hold, manage, invest, and account for the several shares or parts of shares by appropriate entries in the trustee's books of account; and to allocate to each share or part of share its proportionate part of all receipts and expenses. In no event shall the carrying of several trusts as one estate defer the vesting of the interest of any share or part of share of my estate or trusts.

Section 24. *Establish Reserves.* Out of rents, profits, or other income received, the trustee is authorized to set aside and accumulate as a reserve fund as the trustee, in its uncontrolled discretion, shall deem requisite or desirable in providing for the general maintenance, preservation, and improvement (including provision for depreciation, obsolescence, replacement, taxes, assessments, insurance premiums) of buildings or other property; and to set up reserves for the equalization of payments to or for beneficiaries of the trusts.

Section 25. *Distribute in Cash or Kind.* Whenever required or permitted to divide and distribute my estate or any trust created hereunder, to make such division or distribution in money or in kind or partly in money and partly in kind; and to exercise all powers herein conferred, after the termination of any trust until the same is fully distributed.

Section 26. *Pay to or Apply for Minors.* To make payments to or for a minor in any one or more of the following ways:

(1) directly to such minor;
(2) directly by the trustee itself in payment for the support, maintenance, education, and medical, surgical, hospital, or other institutional care of such minor;
(3) to the legal or natural guardian of the minor; or
(4) to any other person, whether or not appointed guardian of the person by any court, who shall, in fact, have the care and custody of the person of such minor.

The receipt of the person who receives the payment shall constitute a full acquittance to my trustee if the person to whom payment was made was selected with due care.

Section 27. *Administration Expenses—Income or Estate Tax Deduction.* To claim administration and other expenses as deductions either in the income tax returns of my estate or in the estate tax return, whichever will result in the smallest combined taxes being paid, although such expenses may be payable from income or principal; and, my executor is directed not to make adjustments between income or principal or between the property interests passing to the beneficiaries under my will which may be substantially affected as a result of its election. I exonerate my executor from all liability for any such election and direct that no beneficiary shall have any claim against my executor or my estate by reason of the exercise of my executor's judgment.

Section 28. *Apportion and Allocate Receipts and Expenses.* To determine what is principal and what is income of any trust and to allocate or apportion receipts and expenses as between principal and income, in the exercise of its uncontrolled discretion.

Section 29. *Rely upon Evidence.* To rely upon any affidavit, certificate, letter, notice, telegram, or other paper writing, or upon any telephone conversation believed by it to be genuine, and upon any other evidence believed by it to be sufficient.

EXECUTION

In witness whereof, I sign, seal, publish, and declare this instrument to be my last will this the seventh day of November, 1977.

(Signed) Jasper Paul Wilson

ATTESTATION

Signed, sealed, published, and declared by Jasper Paul Wilson, the testator, to be his last will, in our presence, and we, at his request, and in his presence and in the presence of each other, have hereunto subscribed our names as witnesses.

Robert Thomas Byrd, 200 North Street, Dunn, North Carolina
Randolph Gale Johnson, 105 South Street, Dunn, North Carolina
William Alston Godwin, 210 Sprague Street, Dunn, North Carolina

Appendix B

Trust Agreement

This agreement, made this eighth day of September, 19___, and executed in duplicate, between Jasper Paul Wilson of Dunn, North Carolina, hereinafter referred to as the settlor, and Dunn Bank and Trust Company of Dunn, North Carolina, a corporation of the State of North Carolina, hereinafter referred to as the trustee, witnesseth that:

ARTICLE I

The settlor, in consideration of ten dollars paid to him by the trustee, receipt of which is hereby acknowledged, has delivered to the trustee the property itemized on Schedule A, attached hereto and made a part of this agreement, which, together with other property that hereafter may be added to this trust, is to be held by the trustee or its successor in trust for the purposes hereinafter set forth.

ARTICLE II

Section 1. The trustee shall receive, hold, manage, convert, sell, assign, alter, reinvest, and deal with the trust property and additions thereto or substitutions therefor as it, in its discretion, shall deem to be for the best interests of the beneficiaries hereunder to the same extent that the settlor, as the absolute owner of the property, himself might do.

Section 2. By way of illustration but not of limitation of the trustee's powers, the settlor hereby authorizes the trustee as follows:

a. *To retain original property.* To retain, without liability (except for its own negligence) for loss or depreciation resulting from such retention, original property, real or personal, at any time received by it from the settlor, for such time as to it shall seem best, although such property may not be of the character expressly approved by law or authorized by the terms of this trust for the investment of other funds of this trust and although it represents a large percentage of the total property of the

317

trust; to dispose of such original property by sale, exchange, or otherwise as and when it shall seem advisable to the trustee and to receive and administer the proceeds therefrom as part of the trust estate; and if unproductive property is retained, then upon the sale, exchange, or other disposition thereof, to make a reasonable apportionment (in the judgment of the trustee) of the proceeds between the income and the principal of the trust estate.

b. *To invest funds.* To invest and reinvest funds in such common stocks, preferred stocks, common trust funds, bonds, debentures, notes, mortgages, life insurance, or other property as it shall deem advisable even though they may not be of the character expressly approved by law for the investment of trust funds.

c. *To purchase from or lend to the general estate.* To acquire at a fair price by purchase, exchange, or otherwise, property belonging to the settlor's general estate, with power to retain property so acquired as part of the trust estate so long as the trustee shall deem advisable, and to make secured or unsecured loans to the settlor's general estate.

d. *To exercise options and rights.* To exercise all options, rights, and privileges to convert stocks, bonds, debentures, notes, mortgages, or other property or to subscribe for additional or other stocks, bonds, debentures, notes, mortgages, or other property; to make such conversions or subscriptions and to make payments therefor; to advance or to borrow money for that purpose; and to hold such stocks, bonds, debentures, notes, mortgages, or other property so acquired as investments of the trust estate.

e. *To participate in reorganizations.* To unite with other owners of securities or other property similar to the securities or other property which may be held at any time in this trust estate in carrying out any plan for the merger or consolidation, dissolution or liquidation, foreclosure, lease, or sale of the property, or incorporation or reincorporation, reorganization, or readjustment of the capital or financial structure of any corporation, company, or association the securities or other property of which may form a portion of the trust estate; to deposit any such securities or other property in accordance with such plan; to pay any assessments, expenses, and sums of money which it may deem expedient or which may be required for the protection or furtherance of the interests of the trust estate with reference to any such plan; and to receive and retain as investments of the trust estate any new securities or other property issued as a result of the execution of such plan, whether or not such new securities or other property may be of the character expressly approved by law or authorized by the terms of this trust for the investment of other funds of this trust.

f. *To sell property.* To sell any and every kind of property, real or personal, publicly or privately, for cash or on time, without an order of court, upon such conditions as to it shall seem best, without liability on the part of the purchaser to see to the application of the purchase money.

g. *To lease property beyond the duration of the trust.* To lease real property for periods within or beyond the duration of the trust.

h. *To set up reserves.* Out of income received, to set up reserves for taxes, assessments, insurance, repairs, depreciation charges, and general maintenance of buildings or other property.

i. *To borrow money.* To borrow money for the benefit of the trust estate for such periods of time and on such terms or conditions as it shall deem advisable and to mortgage or pledge such part of the trust estate as may be required to secure such loan or loans.

j. *To compromise claims.* To compromise, arbitrate, abandon, and otherwise adjust claims in favor of or against the trust estate.

k. *To vote by proxy.* To vote at corporate meetings in person or by special, limited, or general proxy.

l. *To hold securities in the name of a nominee.* To cause the securities or other property (other than assessable securities) which may constitute the trust estate or any part thereof to be registered in its name as trustee hereunder, or in the name of its nominee without disclosing the trust, or (in the case of securities) to take and keep the same unregistered and to retain them or any part of them in such manner that they will pass by delivery; but no such registration or holding by the trustee shall relieve it of liability for the safe custody and proper disposition of such trust property in accordance with the terms and provisions hereof.

m. *To allocate or to apportion stock dividends.* To allocate stock dividends and other extraordinary dividends to income or principal of the trust or to apportion them between income and principal in its absolute discretion, and the decision of the trustee shall be conclusive and binding upon all persons interested in the trust.

n. *To allocate or to apportion premiums on securities.* To charge the premiums on securities purchased at a premium either to principal or to income or partly to income and partly to principal, as to the trustee may seem advisable.

o. *To allocate or apportion expenses.* To determine what expenses, debts, and charges shall be charged against income and what against principal, and its decision with respect thereto shall be conclusive and binding upon all parties at interest.

p. *To pay accrued income to the next successive beneficiary.* To pay to the beneficiary entitled to the next successive estate dividends declared but not paid and income accrued but not received at the time of the termination of any estate hereunder.

q. *To make distribution in cash or in kind.* To make distribution of principal in cash or in kind or partly in cash and partly in kind, not

319

necessarily ratably but on the basis of equal value, according to the trustee's judgment.

ARTICLE III

The trustee shall administer this trust estate for the following uses and purposes:

a. *Income to wife for life.* The trustee shall pay over the net income monthly or quarterly or as often as, in the judgment of the trustee, her needs shall require, but at least once a year, to the settlor's wife, Vivian Lewis Wilson, during her lifetime for the support of herself and for the support and education of the settlor's minor children or of any minor issue of deceased children of the settlor, without requiring her to make an accounting; and the trustee shall not be required to see to the application of funds for the benefit of the settlor's minor children or grandchildren.

b. *Distribution of principal.* Upon the death of the settlor's wife, Vivian Lewis Wilson, or upon the death of the settlor in the event that his said wife shall have predeceased him, the trustee shall pay over, transfer, and convey the trust estate in equal shares to those of the settlor's children who shall then be living and to the descendants, *per stirpes,* of any children of the settlor who shall then have died leaving descendants then living; provided, however, that the share or shares of any of these beneficiaries who are minors shall be retained by the trustee, which shall, from time to time, expend for the support and education of the several beneficiaries, and for such other purposes for their benefit as the trustee shall consider desirable, such part of the income and principal of their respective shares or parts of shares as the trustee in its discretion shall deem best, and shall accumulate any income not so expended and shall add it to the principal of their respective shares or parts of shares until each beneficiary, in turn, shall attain the age of twenty-one years, at which time the share or part of a share, as the case may be, of each such beneficiary shall be paid over, transferred, and conveyed to him or her, discharged of the trust. If upon the death of the settlor's said wife, or upon the death of the settlor in the event that his said wife shall have predeceased him, no children of the settlor or descendants of deceased children of the settlor shall be living, the trustee shall pay over, transfer, and convey the trust estate to Doeville University, a corporation of the State of North Carolina, discharged of the trust.

c. *Trustee's power to use principal.* In the event that, during the lifetime of the settlor's wife, Vivian Lewis Wilson, the trustee shall deem it necessary or desirable to do so, because of illness or accident or misfortune or need of any kind, or even on account of diminution of income yield, having in mind the size and nature of this trust estate and the beneficiaries' other resources, the trustee is authorized, in the exercise of its uncontrolled discretion, from time to time to pay to the settlor's said wife or to expend for her benefit, or with her written consent, unless she shall be incapable of giving such consent, to expend for the benefit of the settlor's children or their descendants (including their college, professional, or technical education), so much of the principal of the trust estate as the trustee shall deem necessary or desirable under the conditions then existing. Any such payment to or expenditure for the benefit of any of the settlor's children or their descendants shall not be treated as an advancement and shall not diminish the proportionate share or shares of the trust estate to which such children or their descendants may eventually become entitled.

d. *Protective provision.* If any beneficiary hereunder shall attempt to assign, transfer, convey, or encumber the principal or income payable to him, or if any person by any proceeding at law shall attach or seize the same by any execution or proceeding in equity which would otherwise attach the same, then, while such attempted assignment, transfer, encumbrance, or proceeding shall remain unremoved, so much of the income as the trustee, in its uncontrolled discretion and without any obligation so to do, shall deem best, shall be applied for the support and maintenance of such beneficiary; and the remainder, if any, of the income shall be applied from time to time to the use of the person or persons who presumptively would be entitled to the trust estate if such beneficiary were deceased.

ARTICLE IV

Rights reserved by the settlor. The settlor reserves the right to withdraw from the operation of this agreement any of the property held in trust, to add other property, to change the beneficiaries, their shares, and the plan of distribution, and to modify, amend, add to, or revoke this agreement, provided that the duties or the compensation of the trustee shall not be changed or fixed without the consent of the trustee.

(or) ARTICLE IV

Trust declared irrevocable. The settlor hereby declares that he has been fully advised as to the legal effect of the execution of this trust agreement and informed as to the character and amount of the property hereby transferred and conveyed, and, further, that he has given consideration to the question of whether the trust hereby created shall be revocable and that it shall stand without power in the settlor at any time to revoke, change, or annul any of the provisions herein contained.

ARTICLE V

Right of the trustee to resign. Any trustee acting hereunder may resign at any time during the lifetime of the settlor by an instrument in writing addressed to him, and may resign after the death of the settlor by an instrument in writing addressed to the beneficiaries not under legal disability then receiving the income from the trust estate. Any trustee acting hereunder may be removed by the settlor if he be living or by a majority of the beneficiaries not under legal disability then receiving the income from the trust estate if the settlor be not living. In the event of the resignation or the removal of the trustee, the settlor, if he be living, or a majority of the beneficiaries not under legal disability then receiving the income from the trust estate, if the settlor be not living, may appoint a successor by an instrument in writing lodged with the trustee, having endorsed thereon the acceptance of such successor; and the trustee which has resigned or has been removed shall convey and assign to the successor so appointed all cash, securities, or other property then held hereunder, and an accounting by the trustee which has resigned or has been removed, submitted to and approved by the settlor if he be living or by the beneficiaries not under legal disability if the settlor be not living, shall be a full and complete acquittance and discharge of the trustee which has resigned or has been removed; *provided* that any successor in trust appointed after the death of the settlor shall be a bank or a trust company doing business in North Carolina and having a capital and surplus of not less than ———— hundred thousand dollars.

ARTICLE VI

Successor trustee. If the trustee shall, during the term of this trust, by sale, merger, consolidation, or reorganization, be merged or consolidated with any other corporation authorized to do trust business, including a national banking association organized under the laws of the United States, the merged or consolidated corporation (whether it be one of the merging or consolidating banks or a new corporation or national banking association formed by means of such sale, merger, consolidation, or reorganization) and the corporate successors of the merged or consolidated corporation shall thereupon, without further act or deed, succeed as the trustee hereunder and be vested with all the trust estate rights, obligations, powers, discretions, immunities, privileges, and compensations herein conferred upon the Dunn Bank and Trust Company of Dunn, North Carolina. This is supplementary to and not in limitation of any law on the subject that now exists or may hereafter be enacted.

ARTICLE VII

Accounting by the trustee. The trustee shall render at least annually to the settlor during his lifetime, and at least annually after his death to each beneficiary not under legal disability and to the guardian or legal representative of each beneficiary under legal disability, a statement of account showing in detail receipts, disbursements, and distributions of both principal and income of the trust estate.

ARTICLE VIII

Trustee's compensation. As compensation for its services, the trustee shall receive the usual compensation provided for such services under published schedules in use by the trustee at the time such compensation becomes payable; in the absence of such published schedules at that time, the trustee shall receive reasonable compensation for the services rendered.

ARTICLE IX

Construction of the agreement. This trust is established under and its validity shall be construed according to the laws of the State of North Carolina. Its administration shall be pursuant to the laws of the State of North Carolina.

In witness whereof, the settlor has hereunto set his hand and affixed his seal; and the trustee has caused these presents to be signed by one of its vice presidents and has caused its corporate seal, duly attested by its assistant secretary, to be affixed on the day and year stated above.

Appendix C

Letter of Instructions: Investment Management Agency

(Full discretion—no approval required)

Date_____

_____, _____

The Dunn Bank and Trust Company is hereby appointed Agent to render INVESTMENT MANAGEMENT AGENCY service in accordance with the following provisions:

With respect to the securities subject to this Agency, schedule "A" attached, you shall:

1. Review, analyze, and appraise the specific securities as often as you deem advisable.
2. Render periodic reports, analyses, and appraisals of the account or individual items thereof, as you may deem advisable.
3. Confer, upon my request, as to such reports, analyses, and appraisals.
4. Purchase, sell, exchange, or otherwise dispose of such securities as you may deem advisable.

With respect to the securities subject to this Agency, you shall provide care and custody thereof, collect, remit, or otherwise, as I shall direct herein, dispose of all interest or other income from and principal of such securities and notes; you shall notify me of any items affected by redemption, exchange, issuance of rights and stock dividends, calls, reorganization, etc., and perform such other services with respect to such securities as I may from time to time direct you in writing. I reserve the right to give you specific instructions with reference to the purchase of securities or to the sale, exchange, or other disposition of the securities subject to this Agency.

All payments to be made by you as provided herein, including your fees and expenses, shall be made from the income, or should that be

325

insufficient then from the principal, received by you. You shall have full authority to set aside out of such income or principal such amounts as in your judgment may be advisable as a reserve fund for such payments, and to hold any such reserve as a cash fund without interest; but you shall not have any duty to advance any of your own funds for the purpose of making any such payments. After making the payments and providing for any reserve fund as set forth above, you shall hold or disburse the balance of such income, from time to time, in accordance with my written directions to you; and you shall from time to time, after first obtaining my written approval, invest the balance of such principal funds in such securities or other property as you may deem advisable, unless you are otherwise directed in writing by me. You shall send me periodical statements of your receipts and disbursements. [General provisions are at the end of this appendix.]

Letter of Instructions: Investment Management Agency

(Advisory—written approval required)

Date_____

_____, _____

The Dunn Bank and Trust Company is hereby appointed Agent to render INVESTMENT MANAGEMENT AGENCY service in accordance with the following provisions:

With respect to the securities subject to this Agency, schedule "A" attached, you shall:

1. Review, analyze, and appraise the specific securities as often as you deem advisable, and submit written recommendations for investment and reinvestment.
2. Confer, upon my request, as to such recommendations.
3. Render periodic reports, analyses, and appraisals of the account or individual items thereof, as you may deem advisable.
4. Purchase, sell, exchange, or otherwise dispose of such securities as you may deem advisable, after first obtaining my written consent.

At all times I shall be at liberty either to follow or disregard either wholly or partially any information, advice, or recommendation as to the investment and reinvestment of the securities. It shall be my responsibility to communicate with you as to my decision regarding your advice or recommendations.

With respect to the securities subject to this Agency, you shall provide care and custody thereof, collect, remit, or otherwise, as I shall direct herein, dispose of all interest or other income from and principal of such securities and notes; you shall notify me of any items affected by redemption, exchange, issuance of rights and stock dividends, calls, reorganization, etc., and shall follow any instructions specified herein or which I may otherwise give to you with reference to such items, and perform such other services with respect to such securities as I may from time to time direct you in writing. I specifically reserve the right to give you instructions with reference to the purchase of any securities, or to the sale, exchange, or other disposition of the securities subject to the Agency.

All payments to be made by you as provided herein, including your fees and expenses, shall be made from the income, or should that be insufficient then from the principal, received by you. You shall have full authority to set aside out of such income or principal such amounts as in your judgment may be advisable as a reserve fund for such payments, and to hold any such reserve as a cash fund without interest; but you shall not have any duty to advance any of your own funds for the purpose of making any such payments. After making the payments and providing for any reserve fund as set forth above, you shall hold or disburse the balance of such income, from time to time, in accordance with my written directions to you; and you shall from time to time, after first obtaining my written approval, invest the balance of such principal funds in such securities or other property as you may deem advisable, unless you are otherwise directed in writing by me. You shall send me periodical statements of your receipts and disbursements. [General provisions are at the end of this appendix.]

Letter of Instructions: Real Estate Management Agency

Date_____

_____, _____

The Dunn Bank and Trust Company is hereby appointed to render REAL ESTATE MANAGEMENT AGENCY service in accordance with the following provisions:

With respect to the real estate subject to this Agency, schedule "A" attached, you are authorized to act as Agent and Attorney-in-Fact, to take possession of, manage, and maintain the property subject to this Agency.

With respect to such real property subject to this Agency, you shall rent, lease, and manage such real property in such manner as you may deem advisable; collect all rents and notify me in writing within a reasonable time of any such rents that may be delinquent; maintain insurance of such types and in such amounts as in your judgment may be advisable, including insurance for your own protection; pay all taxes, assessments, and encumbrances and all costs of any repairs, replacements, or other maintenance expenses in connection with such real property which you may determine to be advisable for its proper maintenance and upkeep; and perform such other services with respect to such real property as I may from time to time direct you in writing.

All payments to be made by you as provided herein, including your fees and expenses, shall be made from the income, or should that be insufficient then from the principal, received by you. You shall have full authority to set aside out of such income or principal such amounts as in your judgment may be advisable as a reserve fund for such payments, and to hold any such reserve as a cash fund without interest; but you shall not have any duty to advance any of your own funds for the purpose of making any such payments. After making the payments and providing for any reserve fund as set forth above, you shall hold, disburse, or dispose of the balance of such income and principal funds, from time to time, in accordance with my written directions to you. You shall send me periodical statements of your receipts and disbursements. [General provisions are at the end of this appendix.]

Letter of Instructions: Custodianship of Securities

Date_____

_____, _____

The Dunn Bank and Trust Company is hereby appointed Custodian, in accordance with the following provisions:

With respect to the securities subject to this Custodianship, schedule "A" attached, you shall hold all such securities deposited with you subject at all times to the instructions of the undersigned and subject to the terms and conditions set forth herein, these instructions to remain in force until expressly revoked or amended in writing.

You shall provide care and custody of the securities and other property, collect and dispose of all income and principal as herein directed, purchase and sell such securities as I shall direct you to purchase or sell, and shall send me periodical statements of receipts and disbursements.

With respect to the securities and funds subject to this Custodianship, you shall hold, disburse, or invest the income and principal funds received by you, in accordance with my written directions to you; effect such sales and purchases of securities through such brokers as I may direct you in writing, on a regular delivery basis, accepting broker's receipt for cash pending receipt of securities purchased and for securities sold pending receipt of the proceeds; hold all registered securities in my name or in the name of your nominee as I may in writing direct you; notify me in writing within a reasonable time of all maturing or called obligations, and of the issuance of rights or stock dividends on all stocks, of which you shall receive actual notice in writing at your office where this Custodianship is being administered; and perform such other services with respect to such securities and funds as I may from time to time direct you in writing. [General provisions are at the end of this appendix.]

Letter of Instructions: General Provisions

Your fees for this service are to be in accordance with your letter of this date accepted by me.

Each of us shall have the right to terminate this Agency at any time upon written notice to the other. This Agency shall terminate upon the death or incompetence of any Principal, but all acts performed by you prior to your receiving written notice of such death or incompetence, at your Trust Department where this Agency is being administered, shall be valid and binding upon all Principals and their successors in interest. Upon termination of this Agency, you shall deliver all funds and other property then held by you to any surviving Principal, the guardian or conservator of the estate of any incompetent Principal, and the personal representative of any deceased Principal, jointly, after your fees and expenses have first been paid.

You shall be under no duty to take any action other than as herein specified with respect to any securities or other property at any time deposited hereunder unless specifically agreed to by you in writing, or to appear in or defend any suit with respect thereto unless you are requested to do so by the Principal in writing and indemnified to your satisfaction.

The Principal shall be responsible for all expenses, taxes, and other charges or liabilities incurred by you in connection with this account, and you are hereby authorized to charge this account therefor.

If in this Letter of Instructions two or more individuals are named as Principals, the right of the Principal to give directions or approvals to the Agent and to terminate this Agency, as provided herein, shall be exercised jointly by all of the Principals, unless otherwise specifically provided herein; and all other references herein to the Principal shall apply to all of the Principals, unless the context of the particular provisions otherwise requires.

This Agreement shall be governed by, and construed under, the laws of the State of North Carolina.

S.S. or T.I. No.: ———————————   ———————————————————
                                                Principal

Legal Residence: ——————————

Citizenship: ————————————

S.S. or T.I. No.: ———————————   ———————————————————
                                                Principal

Legal Residence: ——————————

Citizenship: ————————————

The Dunn Bank and Trust Company hereby acknowledges receipt of the foregoing Letter of Instructions and accepts its appointment as Agent for the purposes and in accordance with the provisions set forth therein.

DATED_____,19_____.

Dunn Bank and Trust Company, Agent

By_____

By_____

Appendix D

Features of Insurance Trust Agreements

1. Collection of Insurance

The following is a typical section of an insurance trust agreement setting forth the duties of the trustee as to the collection of insurance:

As soon as practicable after the death of the insured, the trustee shall make proper proofs of death and shall collect all moneys due under the policies then within the operation of this agreement and then payable to the trustee.

Likewise, as soon as practicable after the occurrence of some event after the death of the insured which may cause any policy or policies then within the operation of this agreement to become payable to the trustee, the trustee shall make proper proofs and shall collect all moneys then due under such policy or policies; provided, however, that the trustee is specifically authorized, upon the death of the insured and likewise upon the occurrence of some event after the death of the insured, to exercise any option, right, or privilege granted to the trustee in or with respect to any policy then payable to the trustee. By way of illustration but not of limitation, the trustee is authorized to exercise the privilege of taking the commuted value of any policy contract providing for future payments, such as a family income or family maintenance contract, if such privilege is granted by the insurance company, and the trustee is likewise authorized to exercise the privilege of receiving such future payments, if such privilege is granted by the insurance company, instead of taking the commuted value of such future payments.

The trustee may institute any proceeding at law or in equity in order to enforce the payment of any policy and may do and perform any and all other acts and things which may be necessary for the purpose of collecting any sums which may be due and payable under the terms of such policy; but the trustee shall not be required to maintain any litigation to

331

enforce the payment of any of the policies unless it is indemnified to its satisfaction against all expense and liability arising from such litigation. If the trustee shall elect to demand indemnity, it shall make such demand in writing upon each of the beneficiaries under this agreement by mailing or delivering the same to his last known address. If satisfactory indemnity is not furnished within thirty days thereafter, the trustee shall assign its rights under the policy in question to the beneficiaries under this agreement and thereupon its liability with respect to such policy shall cease.

The trustee is authorized to compromise and adjust claims arising out of the insurance policies, or any of them, upon such terms and conditions as it may deem just, and the decisions of the trustee shall be binding and conclusive upon all persons interested therein.

A trustee of life insurance should have the same power of compromising and adjusting claims against the insurance company that an executor should have with respect to claims in favor of or against the general estate (this matter is discussed in Chapter 6).

2. Rights Reserved by the Insured

This agreement shall be operative only with respect to the net proceeds of such policies as may be due and payable upon the death of the insured and with respect to the net proceeds of such policies as may be due and payable to the trustee upon the occurrence of some event after the death of the insured; and during the lifetime of the insured all rights of every nature accruing solely to him are hereby reserved by him to be exercised in accordance with the terms of the respective policies; but if the consent of the trustee is necessary at any time, the trustee agrees to give its consent, which consent shall bind all the beneficiaries of this trust.

By way of illustration but not of limitation of the rights reserved by the insured, the insured reserves the following rights:

(a) To add other insurance to the trust by making the policy payable to the trustee either upon the death of the insured or upon the occurrence of some event after the death of the insured;

(b) To receive or apply dividends or distributive shares of surplus, disability benefits, surrender values, or the proceeds of matured endowments;

(c) To obtain and receive from the respective insurance companies such advances or loans on account of a policy as may be available;

(d) To exercise any option, right, or privilege granted in a policy;

(e) To sell, assign, or pledge a policy;

(f) To change the beneficiary of a policy;

(g) To withdraw a policy contract in order to exercise a reserved right or for any other purpose;

332

(h) To change the beneficiaries under this trust agreement, their respective shares, and the plan of distribution; and

(i) To revoke this agreement and to amend it, provided that the duties and responsibilities of the trustee shall not be enlarged or the compensation of the trustee changed by any amendment without its consent.

3. Payment of Premiums—Unfunded Trust

The insured shall pay all premiums, assessments, and other charges required to continue all policies in force at any time within the operation of this agreement, and the trustee shall be under no duty or obligation to pay any of these charges or to keep itself informed with respect to them or with respect to the performance of any act necessary to keep the said policies in force.

The trustee shall not be liable to anyone if for any reason the policies, or any of them, shall lapse or otherwise be uncollectible.

The trustee shall have no duties or obligations hereunder until the death of the insured and until the proceeds of the said policies shall have come into its hands.

4. Payment of Premiums—Funded Trust

Out of the net income of the trust estate and out of the principal to the extent to which it may be necessary, the trustee shall pay the premiums and assessments and other charges on the above described policies and additions thereto as they fall due. Unless hereinafter otherwise provided, any surplus income shall be added to and reinvested as a part of the principal of the trust estate. The trustee may apply the dividends on such policies or may use the loan or other values under the policies for the payment of premiums, assessments, and other charges, all in accordance with the terms of the respective policies.

If, however, the trustee shall not have in the trust estate sufficient income or principal, including the above-mentioned dividends and loan and other values under the policies themselves, to pay the premiums, assessments, and other charges then due upon the policies or any of them, it shall proceed to take the necessary steps to divest itself of all rights under the policies, whether by release or assignment or otherwise, and then shall mail the policy or policies to the last known address of the insured, whereupon the trustee shall be relieved of all liability for lapse of the policy or policies for failure to pay the premiums, assessments, or other charges thereon, and the trust shall thereupon terminate with respect to such policies.

Glossary

Abatement. The reduction of a gift under a will because of insufficient assets to satisfy all the gifts after the legal obligations of the estate (debts, taxes, charges, and claims) have been paid in full. The general rule is that all gifts of the same class shall abate proportionately.

Absolute gift. A gift of property by will that carries with it possession of and complete dominion over the property; as opposed to a conditional gift.

Active trust. A trust under which the trustee has some active duty to perform; as opposed to a bare, dry, naked, or passive trust.

Actuary. A person who calculates insurance and annuity premiums, reserves, and dividends.

Adjudication. The decision of a competent court with regard to matters in dispute; to be distinguished from arbitration.

Ad litem. For the purpose of the suit.

Administration. The care and management of an estate by an executor, an administrator, a trustee, or a guardian.

Administrator. An individual or a trust institution appointed by a court to settle the estate of a person who has died without leaving a valid will. If the individual appointed is a woman, she is known as an "administratrix."

Administrator cum testamento annexo (administrator with the will annexed, abbreviated to administrator c.t.a.). An individual or a trust institution appointed by a court to settle the estate of a deceased person

---

The student should also have available to him a copy of the *Glossary of Fiduciary Terms* (Washington, D.C.: American Bankers Association, 1976).

in accordance with the terms of his will when no executor has been named in the will or when the one named has failed to qualify.

Administrator cum testamento annexo de bonis non (administrator with the will annexed as to property not yet distributed, abbreviated to administrator c.t.a.d.b.n. or d.b.n.c.t.a.). An individual or a trust institution appointed by a court to complete the settlement of the estate of a deceased person in accordance with the terms of his will when the executor or the administrator with the will annexed has failed to continue in office.

Administrator de bonis non (administrator as to property not yet distributed, abbreviated to administrator d.b.n.). An individual or a trust institution appointed by a court to complete the settlement of the estate of a person who has died without leaving a valid will when the administrator originally appointed has failed to continue in office.

Administrator pendente lite (administrator pending the continuance of litigation). *See* Temporary administrator.

Affinity. Relationship by marriage; to be distinguished from consanguinity.

After-acquired property. Property acquired by a corporation after the execution of a mortgage.

After-born child. A child born after the execution of the parent's will; to be distinguished from posthumous child.

Agency. A type of accounts in trust institutions. The main distinguishing characteristic of an agency is that the title to the property does not pass to the trust institution but remains in the owner of the property, who is known as the principal.

Agency coupled with an interest. An agency in which the agent has a legal interest in the subject matter of the agency. Such an agency is not terminated, as are other agencies, by the death of the principal but continues until the agent can realize on his legal interest.

Agent. A person who acts for another person by the latter's authority. The distinguishing characteristics of an agent are (1) that he acts on behalf and subject to the control of his principal, (2) that he does not have title to the property of his principal, and (3) that he owes the duty of obedience to his principal's orders.

Alienation. The transfer of title to property by legal conveyance. *See also* Restraint on alienation of property.

Allocation. The crediting of a receipt in its entirety or the charging of a disbursement in its entirety to one account, as to the principal account or to the income account; to be distinguished from apportionment.

Allowance. The sum or sums awarded a fiduciary by a court as compensation for its services; to be distinguished from charge, commission, and fee. *See also* Widow's allowance.

Ancestor. One who precedes another in the line of descent. At common law the term "ancestor" applies only to a person in the direct line of ascent (parent, grandparent, or other forebear), but by statute it has been broadened to apply also to a person of collateral relationship (uncle or aunt, for example) from whom property has been acquired.

Ancillary. Subordinate or auxiliary; used in such terms as "ancillary administration," "ancillary administrator," and "ancillary guardian."

Annuitant. The beneficiary of an annuity.

Annuity. A stated amount payable annually or at regular intervals for either a certain or an indefinite period, as for a stated number of years or for life.

Appointment. *See* Power of appointment.

Apportionment. The division or distribution of a receipt or a disbursement between or among two or more accounts, as between principal and income; to be distinguished from allocation.

Appreciation. Increase in value; as opposed to depreciation.

Appurtenance. Something belonging or attached to something else and passing as incident to the principal thing; as, a right of way (the appurtenance) over land (the principal thing).

Arbitration. The hearing and determining of a controversy by a person or persons mutually agreed on by the parties or chosen by the court or by someone under statutory authority; to be distinguished from adjudication.

Attest. To bear witness to; as, to attest a will or other document.

Attestation clause. The clause of a document containing the formal declaration of the act of witnessing; in the case of a will, the clause immediately following the signature of the testator and usually beginning, "Signed, sealed, published, and declared by the said . . . ."

Attesting witness. One who testifies to the authenticity of a document, as the attesting witness to a will; to be distinguished from a subscribing witness.

Attorney at law. A person who is legally qualified and authorized to represent and act for clients in legal proceedings; to be distinguished from an attorney in fact.

Attorney in fact. A person who, as agent, is given written authorization by another person to transact business for his principal out of court; to be distinguished from an attorney at law. *See also* Power of attorney.

Authenticated copy. A copy of a document the similarity of which to the original has been evidenced in the manner required by law, as by the certification and seal of a specified public official.

Authentication. The signing, by the trustee, of a certificate on a bond for the purpose of identifying it as being issued under a certain indenture, thus validating the bond.

Authorized investment. An investment that is authorized by the trust instrument; to be distinguished from a legal investment.

Award. A decision of an arbitrator; to be distinguished from a decree and a judgment.

B

Bailment. The delivery of personal property by one person to another for some specific purpose, such as use, repairs, or safekeeping, but without passing title to the property. The person delivering the property is known as the "bailor"; the person receiving it is called the "bailee."

Beneficiary. The person for whose benefit a trust is created. Also the person to whom the amount of an insurance policy or annuity is payable.

Bequest. A gift of personal property by will; the same as a legacy.

Betterments. Improvements to real property that add to its value otherwise than by mere repairs.

Blanket bond. A bond the security for which is a mortgage not on a specific asset but on all the assets of the issuing corporation.

Bona fide (adj.). In good faith; as, a bona fide transaction.

Bona fide purchaser. One who purchases property in good faith, without notice of any defect in the title, and for a valuable consideration.

Bona fides (noun). Good faith, honesty; as, the bona fides of the transaction.

Bond discount. *See* Discount on securities.

Bond of indemnity. *See* Indemnity bond.

Bond power. A form of assignment executed by the owner of registered bonds that contains an irrevocable appointment of an attorney to make the actual transfer on the books of the corporation. *See also* Power of attorney.

Bond premium. *See* Premium on securities.

Breach of trust. Violation of a duty that a trustee owes to a beneficiary.

Burden of proof. The duty of proving a particular position in a court of law. Failure in the performance of that duty calls for judgment against the person on whom the duty is imposed. Thus the burden of proof that the paper and writing is not the valid will of the testator is placed upon the person who contests a will.

Business insurance trust. A trust of life insurance policy contracts created in connection with a business enterprise. The term is applied both to a trust created for the liquidation of business interests and to a trust created for credit purposes or otherwise for the benefit of a business enterprise.

C

Canon. A rule or law. Under civil law the rules by which the title to real property is traced are known as canons of inheritance; under common law such rules are known as canons of descent.

Causa mortis. *See* Gift causa mortis.

Cemetery trust. A trust that has as its purpose the upkeep of a grave, burial plot, or cemetery.

Cestui que trust (pl., *cestuis que trust*). A person for whose benefit a trust is created; the same as a beneficiary.

Charge. As applied to trust business, the price fixed or demanded by a trust institution for a trust department service. It is compensation that a trust institution has a legal right to fix (in the form of either a commission or a fee), in contrast to an allowance granted by a court. *See also* Allowance; Commission; Fee.

Charitable bequest. A gift of personal property to a charity by will. *See also* Charity.

Charitable devise. A gift of real property to a charity by will.

Charitable trust. A trust created for the benefit of a community, ordinarily without a definite beneficiary; as, a trust for educational purposes. The same as a public trust; as opposed to a private trust.

Charity. A gift of real or personal property (or both) to be applied, consistently with existing laws, "for the benefit of an indefinite number of persons, either by bringing their hearts under the influence of education or religion, by relieving their bodies from disease, suffering or constraint, by assisting them to establish themselves in life, or by creating or maintaining public buildings or works, or otherwise lessening the burden of government."

Chattel. Any property, movable or immovable, except a freehold estate in land. *See also* Chattel personal; Chattel real; Freehold estate.

Chattel mortgage. *See* Mortgage.

Chattel personal. An article of personal property, as distinguished from an interest in real property.

Chattel real. An interest in land, such as a leasehold, that is less than a freehold estate. *See also* Freehold estate; Tenancy at sufferance; Tenancy at will; Tenancy for years.

Chose (thing). Anything that is personal property.

Chose in action. A right to personal property that has not been reduced to possession or enjoyment but is recoverable in an action at law—for example, a patent right, a copyright, a royalty right, a right growing out of a contract or out of damage to person or to property, or a right under a life insurance policy. While the right itself is the chose in action, the evidence of the right, such as the life insurance policy, is sometimes referred to as if it were the chose in action; to be distinguished from a chose in possession.

Chose in possession. Any article of tangible personal property in actual, rightful possession, such as a watch, an automobile, or a piece of furniture; to be distinguished from a chose in action.

Civil law. The legal system prevailing in the European, Asiatic, Central American, and South American countries that inherited their legal systems from Rome—in other words, in practically all but the English-speaking countries. *Compare* Common law.

Closed mortgage. A corporate trust indenture under which bonds have been authenticated and delivered (as an original issue) to the extent authorized under the indenture. *Compare* Open-end mortgage.

Cloud on title. A defect in the owner's title to property arising from a written instrument or judgment or from an order of court purporting to create an interest in or lien upon the property and therefore impairing the marketability of the owner's title, although the interest or lien may be shown by evidence to be invalid.

Codicil. An amendment or supplement to a will. It must be executed with all the formalities of the will itself.

Collateral. Specific property, commonly securities, given by a borrower to a lender as a pledge for the payment of a loan or other obligation.

Collateral heir. A person not in the direct line of the decedent from whom he inherits real property. A nephew of the decedent who receives a share of his aunt's estate is a collateral heir. *See also* Direct heir; Heir.

Collusion. A secret agreement between two or more persons to defraud another person of his rights or to obtain an unlawful object.

Commission. A percentage of the principal or of the income (or of both) that a fiduciary receives as compensation for its services; to be distinguished from allowance, charge, and fee.

340

Committee for incompetent. An individual or a trust institution appointed by a court to care for the property or the person (or both) of an incompetent; similar to a guardian, conservator, or curator.

Common law. The legal system prevailing in the English-speaking countries—that is, the United States and the countries making up the British Empire and Commonwealth of Nations. It originated in England, and its form of development was different from that of Roman (civil) law. *Compare* Civil law.

Common trust fund. A fund maintained by a bank or trust company exclusively for the collective investment and reinvestment of money contributed to the fund by the bank or trust company in its capacity as trustee, executor, administrator, or guardian and in conformity with the rules and regulations of the Comptroller of the Currency pertaining to the collective investment of trust funds by national banks, as well as with the statutes and regulations (if any) of the several states.

Community property. Property in which a husband and wife have each an undivided one-half interest by reason of their marital status; recognized in all civil law countries and in certain states of the Southwest and Pacific coast areas of the United States.

Community trust. A trust ordinarily composed of gifts made by many people to a community for educational, charitable, or other benevolent purposes. The property of the trust is trusteed; and distribution of the funds is under the control of a group of citizens who act as a distribution committee. There may be one trustee or, as is more often the case, several trustees (usually trust institutions of the community), each serving under identical declarations of trust in the administration of the property committed to its care and management. *See also* Foundation.

Compensation. As applied to trust business, this general term covers four specific terms—"allowance," "charge," "commission," and "fee"—which should be differentiated. *See* each of these terms for definitions.

Conditional gift. A gift of property by will that is subject to some condition specified in the will or in the trust instrument; as opposed to an absolute gift.

Condominium. Individual ownership of a unit in a multiunit structure (such as an apartment building); also, a unit so owned.

Consanguinity. Blood relationship; to be distinguished from affinity.

Conservator. Generally, an individual or a trust institution appointed by a court to care for property; specifically, an individual or a trust institution appointed by a court to care for and manage the property of an incompetent, in much the same way that a guardian cares for and manages the property of a ward.

341

Constructive trust. A trust imposed by a court of equity as a means of doing justice, without regard to the intention of the parties, in a situation in which a person who holds title to property is under a duty to convey it to another person; to be distinguished from an express trust and a resulting trust.

Contest of a will. An attempt by legal process to prevent the probate of a will or the distribution of property according to the will.

Contingent interest. A future interest in real or personal property that is dependent on the fulfillment of a stated condition. Thus the interest may never come into existence; to be distinguished from a vested interest.

Contingent remainder. A future interest in property that is dependent on the fulfillment of a stated condition before the termination of a prior estate; to be distinguished from a vested remainder.

Contribution. A sum paid by an employer to an unemployment or group insurance fund or for retirement benefits for employees; also, a sum paid by employees under such a plan.

Conversion. In law, wrongful appropriation to one's own use of the goods of another. In equity, the change of property from one form to that of another (as from real property to personal property, or the reverse) that is considered to have taken place even though no actual exchange has been effected. For example, when a trustee has been directed to sell real property and purchase bonds but has failed to do so, the real property has become personal property in the eyes of the law. Conversion in this sense is known as "equitable" conversion.

Convertible. Capable of being exchanged for a specified equivalent (such as preferred stock into common stock).

Corporate depositary. A trust institution serving as the depositary of funds or other property. *See also* Depositary; Depository.

Corporate fiduciary. A trust institution serving in a fiduciary capacity such as executor, administrator, trustee, or guardian.

Corporate trust. A trust created by a corporation, for example a trust to secure a bond issue.

Corporate trustee. A trust institution serving as trustee.

Corporation sole. A one-person corporation, the authority, duties, and powers of which are attached to and go with the office, not the natural person who for the time being holds the office.

Corporeal hereditament. *See* Hereditament.

Corpus (body). The principal or capital of an estate, as distinguished from the income.

Court trust. A trust coming under the immediate supervision of the court, such as a trust by order of court or, in some states, a trust under will.

Covenant. A promise, incorporated in a trust indenture, to perform certain acts or to refrain from the performance of certain acts.

Curator. An individual or a trust institution appointed by a court to care for the property or person (or both) of a minor or incompetent. In some states a curator is essentially the same as a temporary administrator or a temporary guardian.

Curtesy. The interest or life estate of a widower in the real property of his wife who died without leaving a valid will or from whose will he has dissented. At common law curtesy took effect only if a child capable of inheriting the property had been born of the marriage. In many states common law curtesy has been abolished by statute or has never been recognized. *See also* Dissent; Dower.

Custody account. An agency account concerning which the main duties of the custodian (agent) are to safeguard and preserve the property and to perform ministerial acts with respect to the property as directed by the principal. The agent has no investment or management responsibilities; to be distinguished from a managing agency account and a safekeeping account.

D

Death taxes. Taxes imposed on property or on the transfer of property at the owner's death; a general term covering estate taxes, inheritance taxes, and other succession or transfer taxes.

Debenture. An obligation that is not secured by a specific lien on property. As the term is usually employed, a debenture is an unsecured note of a corporation.

Declaration of trust. An acknowledgment, usually but not necessarily in writing, by one holding or taking title to property that he holds the property in trust for the benefit of someone else.

Decree. The decision of a court of equity, admiralty, probate, or divorce; to be distinguished from the judgment of a court of law.

Deed of trust. A sealed instrument in writing duly executed and delivered, conveying or transferring property to a trustee; usually but not necessarily covering real property. *See also* Trust agreement.

Defeasible. Capable of being annulled or rendered void; as, a defeasible title to property.

Deferred compensation. The postponement of payment for services presently rendered until a future time.

Deficiency judgment. A judgment for the balance of a debt after the security has been exhausted; as, a deficiency judgment following the foreclosure of a mortgage. *See also* Judgment.

Definitive bond. A permanent bond issued by a corporation; to be distinguished from a temporary bond issued pending the preparation of the definitive bond.

Demise. The conveyance of an estate, usually one for life or for years; death.

Demonstrative gift. A gift, by will, of a specified sum of money to be paid from a designated fund or asset; as, a gift of $1,000 payable from a specified bank account.

Deposit administration. A form of group annuity in which the contributions are held by the insurer, usually at a guaranteed rate of interest, until an employee's retirement, at which time an annuity is purchased.

Depositary. One who receives a deposit of money, securities, instruments, or other property.

Deposition. The written testimony of a witness, under oath, before a qualified officer, to be used in place of the oral testimony of the witness at a trial.

Depository. A place where something is deposited; as, a safe deposit vault where valuables are stored.

Depreciation. Decrease in value; as opposed to appreciation.

Descendant. One who is descended in a direct line from another, however remotely (for example, child, grandchild, great-grandchild); the same as issue.

Descent. The passing of property by inheritance. *See also* Devolution.

De son tort (of his own wrongdoing). *See* Executor de son tort; Guardian de son tort.

Devise. A gift of real property by will. A person who receives such a gift is called a "devisee."

Devolution. The passing of property by inheritance; a general term that includes both descent of real property and distribution of personal property.

Direct heir. A person in the direct line of the decedent; as, father, mother, son, daughter. *See also* Collateral heir; Heir.

Disbursement. Money paid out in discharge of a debt or an expense; to be distinguished from distribution.

344

Discount on securities. The amount or percentage by which a security (a bond or a share of stock) is bought or sold for less than its face, or par, value; as opposed to premium on securities.

Discretionary trust. A trust that entitles the beneficiary to only so much of the income or principal as the trustee in its uncontrolled discretion shall see fit to give him or to apply for his use.

Dissent. The act of disagreeing. Thus a widow's refusal to take the share provided for her in her husband's will and assertion of her rights under the law is known as her dissent from the will. *See also* Curtesy; Dower.

Distributee. A person to whom something is distributed; frequently applied to the recipient of property under intestacy.

Distribution. In law, the apportionment by a court of the personal property (or its proceeds) of one who died intestate among those entitled to receive the property according to the applicable statute of distribution; to be distinguished from disbursement.

Distributive share. The share of a person in the distribution of an estate.

Divest. To annul or take away a vested right.

Domicile. The place in which a person has his permanent home and principal establishment; the place to which, whenever he is absent, he has the intention of returning. A person's domicile may or may not be the same as his residence at a given time. *See also* Residence.

Donor. *See* Settlor.

Dower. The interest or life estate of a widow in the real property of her husband. At common law a wife had a life estate in one-third (in value) of the real property of her husband who died without leaving a valid will or from whose will she dissented. In many states common law dower has been abolished by statute or has never been recognized. *See also* Curtesy; Dissent.

Dry trust. *See* Passive trust.

Duress. Compulsion or constraint by force or fear of personal violence, prosecution, or imprisonment that induces a person to do what he does not want to do or to refrain from doing something he has a legal right to do. Sometimes the word is used with reference to the making of a will, as that it was made under duress.

E

Easement. An acquired right of use or enjoyment, falling short of ownership, that an owner or possessor of land may have in the land of another; as, A's right of way over B's land.

Election. The choice of an alternative right or course. Thus the right of a widow to take the share of her deceased husband's estate to which she is entitled under the law, despite a contrary provision in the will, is known as the widow's election.

Eleemosynary. Pertaining or devoted to charity; as, an eleemosynary institution.

Eminent domain. The inherent sovereign power of the state over all the private property within its borders that enables it to appropriate all or any part of the property to a necessary public use by making reasonable compensation. This power is termed "the right of eminent domain."

Employee benefit trust. A trust established by an employer (usually a corporation) for the benefit of employees.

Entity. That which exists as separate and complete in itself. A corporation is an entity separate and distinct from its stockholders.

Equipment trust. A corporate trust established for the purpose of financing the purchase of equipment; commonly resorted to by railroads for the purchase of rolling stock.

Equitable charge. A charge on property imposed by and enforceable in a court of equity, as distinguished from a charge enforceable in a court of law. A conveyance of real property, absolute on its face but intended only as security for a loan, may constitute an equitable charge on the property.

Equitable conversion. *See* Conversion.

Equitable ownership. The estate or interest of a person who has a beneficial right in property, the legal ownership of which is in another person. A beneficiary of a trust has an equitable estate or interest in the trust property.

Equitable title. A right to the benefits of property that is recognized by and enforceable only in a court of equity; to be distinguished from legal title.

Equity. A system of legal principles and rules developed to supplement and correct a system of law that had become too narrow and rigid in scope and application. Its characteristic is flexibility and its aim is the administration of justice.

Equity annuity. *See* Variable annuity.

Escheat. The reversion of property to the state (in the United States) in case there are no devisees, legatees, heirs, or next of kin; originally applicable only to real property but now applicable to all kinds of property.

Escrow. Money, securities, instruments, or other property deposited by two or more persons with a third person, to be delivered on a certain contingency or on the occurrence of a certain event. The subject matter of the transaction (the money, securities, instruments, or other property) is the *escrow;* the terms on which it is deposited with the third person constitute the "escrow agreement"; and the third person is termed the "escrow agent."

Estate. The right, title, or interest that a person has in any property; to be distinguished from the property itself, which is the subject matter of the interest. It may also be the property of a decedent. *See also* Fee simple; Fee tail; Freehold estate; Life estate; Real estate; Remainder; Residuary estate; Tenancy in common.

Estate in common. *See* Tenancy in common.

Estate tax. A tax imposed on a decedent's estate as such and not on the distributive shares of the estate or on the right to receive the shares; to be distinguished from an inheritance tax.

Estoppel. The legal principle that precludes a person from alleging in an action contrary to his previous action or admission or that bars him from denying a misrepresentation of a fact when another person has acted upon that misrepresentation to his detriment. The person so precluded or barred is said to be estopped.

Executor. An individual or a trust institution nominated in a will and appointed by a court to settle the estate of the testator. If a woman is nominated and appointed, she is known as an "executrix."

Executor de son tort. One who, without legal authority, assumes control of a decedent's property as if he were executor and thereby makes himself responsible for what comes into his possession.

Exemplified copy. A copy of a record or document witnessed, sealed, or certified to as required by law for the purposes of a particular transaction.

Express trust. A trust stated orally or in writing, with the terms of the trust definitely prescribed; to be distinguished from a resulting trust and a constructive trust.

F

Failure of issue. Failure, by nonexistence or death, of lineal descendants (children, grandchildren, and so on).

Fee. In trust terminology, a fixed amount that a trust institution receives as compensation for its services; to be distinguished from allow-

347

ance, charge, and commission. Also an estate of inheritance in real property, sometimes referred to as an estate in fee.

Fee simple. An absolute fee, that is, an estate of inheritance without limitation to any particular class of heirs and with no restrictions upon alienation; sometimes known as fee simple absolute; the largest estate a person may own.

Fee tail. A limited fee, that is, an estate limited to a person and the heirs of his body: fee tail male if male heirs; fee tail female if female heirs. In most states, estates in fee tail have been abolished, generally by converting them into fee simple estates.

Fiduciary. An individual or a trust institution charged with the duty of acting for the benefit of another party as to matters coming within the scope of the relationship between them. A guardian and his ward, an agent and his principal, an attorney and his client, one partner and another partner, a trustee and a beneficiary are all examples of fiduciary relationships.

Fiscal agent. An agent for a corporation to handle certain matters relating to taxes in connection with an issue of bonds. Also an agent for a national, state, or municipal government or governmental unit to pay its bonds and coupons or to perform certain other duties related to financial matters.

Foreign corporation. A corporation organized under the laws of a state other than the state in which it is doing business. Also, a corporation organized under the laws of another country, although such a corporation is more frequently referred to as an alien corporation.

Foundation. A permanent fund established by contributions from one source (as the Carnegie Foundation) or from many sources (as the Cleveland Foundation) for charitable, educational, religious, or other benevolent uses or purposes. *See also* Community trust.

Freehold estate. A legal estate in land, commonly referred to as an estate of inheritance. There are three freehold estates: fee simple, fee tail, and life estate.

Funded insurance trust. An insurance trust in which, in addition to life insurance policies, cash and securities have been placed in trust to provide sufficient income for the payment of premiums and other charges on or assessments against the insurance policies. *See also* Unfunded insurance trust.

Future estate or interest. Any fixed estate or interest except a reversion, with the right of possession and enjoyment postponed until some future date or until the occurrence of some event. *See also* Remainder; Reversion.

G

General gift. A gift by will of personal property that is not a particular thing as distinguished from all others of the same kind.

Gift causa mortis. A gift of personal property made by a person in expectation of death, completed by actual delivery of the property, and effective only if the donor dies; to be distinguished from gift *inter vivos*.

Gift inter vivos. A gift of property between living persons. To make such a gift effective, there must be actual delivery of the property during the lifetime of the donor and without reference to his death.

Grantee. A person to whom property is transferred by deed or to whom property rights are granted by means of a trust instrument or some other document.

Grantor. A person who transfers property by deed or grants property rights by means of a trust instrument or other document. *See also* Settlor.

Ground rent. A price paid each year, or for a term of years, for the right to occupy and improve a piece of land. As the term is used in certain states, a rent charge reserved to himself and his heirs by the grantor of land in fee simple out of the land granted.

Group annuity. A pension plan providing annuities at retirement to a group of persons under a master contract. It is usually issued to an employer for a group of employees.

Guardian. An individual or a trust institution appointed by a court to care for the property or the person (or both) of a minor or an incompetent. When the guardian's duties are limited to the property, he is known as a guardian of the property; when they are limited to the person, he is known as a guardian of the person; when they apply to both the property and the person, he is known merely as a guardian. In some states the term "committee," "conservator," "curator," or "tutor" is used to designate one who performs substantially the same duties as a guardian.

Guardian ad litem. A person appointed by a court to represent and defend a minor or an incompetent in connection with court proceedings; sometimes called a special guardian.

Guardian de son tort. One who, though not a regularly appointed guardian, takes possession of an infant's or an incompetent's property and manages it as if he were a guardian, thereby making himself accountable to the court.

H

Heir. A person who inherits property; to be distinguished from next of kin and from distributee. An "heir of the body" is an heir in the direct line of the decedent. A son, for example, is the heir of the body of his father or mother. *See also* Collateral heir; Direct heir; Distributee; Next of kin.

Hereditament. Any kind of property that is capable of being inherited. If the property is visible and tangible, it is a "corporeal" hereditament; if it is not, it is an "incorporeal" hereditament—for example, a right to rent or a promise to pay money.

Holographic will. A will entirely in the handwriting of the testator.

Hypothecation. Originally, a pledge to secure an obligation without delivery of title or possession; now, any pledge to secure an obligation, such as the hypothecation of securities for a loan.

I

Immediate beneficiary (also called present beneficiary and primary beneficiary). A beneficiary of a trust who is entitled to receive immediate benefits from the trust property, whether or not limited to income; as opposed to ultimate beneficiary.

Income. The returns from property, such as rent, interest, dividends, profits, and royalties; as opposed to principal, capital, or corpus.

Income beneficiary. The beneficiary of a trust who is entitled to receive the income from it.

Income bond. An obligation in which the promise to pay interest is conditional upon the earnings of the obligor. Usually interest is to be paid in any year only if it is earned.

Incompetent. One who is legally incapable of managing his affairs because of mental (not physical) deficiency.

Incorporation by reference. Reference in one document to the contents of another document in such a manner as to give legal effect to the material to which reference is made.

Incorporeal hereditament. *See* Hereditament.

Increment. That which is gained or added.

Indefeasible. Incapable of being annulled or rendered void; as, an indefeasible title to property.

Indemnity. Protection or exemption from loss or damage.

Indemnity bond. A written instrument under seal by which the signer, usually together with his surety or bondsman, guarantees to protect another against loss. An indemnity bond in which the obligation assumed by the surety is not a fixed amount is known as an "open penalty form" of indemnity bond.

Infant. A person not of legal age, which at common law was twenty-one years but which in some states has been changed by statute; the same as a minor.

Inheritance tax. A tax on the right to receive property by inheritance; to be distinguished from an estate tax.

In loco parentis (in the place of a parent). A phrase referring to a person who takes the place of a child's parent. While the term sometimes refers to a guardian, a person who has not been legally appointed guardian may also stand *in loco parentis.*

Insurable interest. An interest in the subject matter of life or property insurance that will entitle the person possessing the interest to obtain insurance on it.

Insurance trust. A trust composed partly or wholly of life insurance policy contracts.

Intangible property. Property that cannot be touched or realized with the senses, such as a legally enforceable right. The right possessed by the holder of a promissory note or a bond is intangible property, the paper and writing being only the evidence of that right.

Inter vivos (between living persons). In the term "trust *inter vivos*" or "*inter vivos* trust," the same as a living trust. *See also* Gift inter vivos.

Intestacy. The condition resulting from a person's dying without leaving a valid will.

Intestate (adj.). Not having made and left a valid will. (noun) A person who dies without leaving a valid will.

Irrevocable trust. A trust that by its terms cannot be revoked by the settlor.

Issue. All persons who have descended from a common ancestor; a broader term than children.

J

Joint tenancy. The holding of property by two or more persons in such a manner that, upon the death of one joint owner, the survivor or survivors take the entire property; to be distinguished from tenancy in common and tenancy by the entirety.

Judgment. The decision or sentence of a court of law; to be distinguished from a decree.

Judicial settlement. The settlement of an account in accordance with the order, judgment, or decree of a proper court, the effect of which in many states is determined by statute.

Jurisdiction. Legal right, power, or authority to hear and determine a cause; as, the jurisdiction of a court.

K

Keogh plan. A self-employed retirement plan; so called for Representative Keogh, who sponsored the enabling legislation in the House of Representatives.

Key man insurance. Protection of a business firm against the financial loss caused by death or disability of a vital member of the firm; a means of protecting the business from the adverse results of the loss of an individual possessing special skills or experience.

Kin. Persons of the same blood or members of the same family.

Kind. In the phrase "distribution in kind," distribution of the property itself and not the cash value of the property.

Kindred. Persons related by blood.

L

Lapse (noun). The falling of a gift into the residuary estate by reason of the death of the legatee or devisee during the testator's lifetime. Such a gift is known as a "lapsed legacy" or "lapsed devise."

Last will. The will last executed by a person. Since all former wills ordinarily are revoked by the last one, the term is used to emphasize the fact that it is the latest, and therefore the effective, will of the maker.

Laws of descent. Laws governing the descent of real property from ancestor to heir; to be distinguished from laws, rules, or statutes of distribution governing the disposition of personal property.

Laws of distribution. *See* Statutes of distribution.

Leaseback. The sale of property to a financial or eleemosynary institution that leases it to the vendor for a period of years at a rental that will give a return and amortize the investment.

Leasehold. Land held under a lease.

Legacy. A gift of personal property by will; the same as a bequest. A person receiving such a gift is called a "legatee."

Legal investment. An investment that conforms to the requirements of the statutes. A term used principally with reference to investments by trustees and other fiduciaries and by savings banks; often abbreviated to "legals"; to be distinguished from an authorized investment.

Legal ownership. An estate or interest in property that is enforceable in a court of law; to be distinguished from equitable ownership.

Legals. *See* Legal investment.

Legal title. Title to property recognized by and enforceable in a court of law; to be distinguished from equitable title.

Letter of attorney. A written document that evidences a power of attorney.

Letters of administration. A certificate of authority to settle a particular estate issued to an administrator by the appointing court; to be distinguished from letters testamentary.

Letters testamentary. A certificate of authority to settle a particular estate issued to an executor by the appointing court; to be distinguished from letters of administration.

Life beneficiary. The beneficiary of a trust, usually for the term of his own life, but sometimes for the term of another person's life.

Life estate. Either an estate for the life of the tenant alone or an estate for the life or lives of some person or persons other than the tenant. If the estate is for the life of a person other than the tenant, it is known as an estate *pur autre vie*.

Life insurance trust. *See* Insurance trust.

Life tenant. One who owns an estate in real property for his own life or for another person's life or for an indefinite period bounded by a lifetime.

Limited open-end mortgage. An indenture under which additional bonds may be issued, but which establishes certain limits, or measures, of maximum amounts that may be issued.

Lineal descendant. A person in the direct line of descent, as child or grandchild; as opposed to collateral heir.

Lives in being. Lives in existence at a given time. *See also* Rule against perpetuities.

Living trust. A trust that becomes operative during the lifetime of the settlor; as opposed to a trust under will. The same as a trust *inter vivos*.

M

Managing agency account. An agency account concerning which the agent has managerial duties and responsibilities appropriate to the kind of property and in conformity with the terms of the agency; to be distinguished from a safekeeping account and a custody account.

Massachusetts rule. A term frequently applied to a rule for the investment of trust funds enunciated by the Supreme Judicial Court of Massachusetts in 1830; now commonly referred to as the prudent man rule. *See also* Prudent man rule for trust investment.

Massachusetts trust. An unincorporated organization created for profit under a written instrument or declaration of trust, by the terms of which the property held in trust is managed by compensated trustees for the benefit of persons whose legal interests are represented by transferable certificates of participation or shares; also called business trust.

Minor. A person under legal age, that is, under the age at which he or she is accorded full civil rights; the same as an infant.

Mixed property. Property that has some of the attributes of both real property and personal property, such as fixtures and keys to a house.

Mortgage. An instrument by which the borrower (mortgagor) gives the lender (mortgagee) a lien on property (commonly real property) as security for the payment of an obligation. The borrower continues to use the property, and when the obligation is fully extinguished the lien is removed. If the subject matter of the lien is personal property other than securities (such as machinery, tools, or equipment), the mortgage is known as a "chattel mortgage."

Mutual fund. A popular expression for an open-end investment company. A company that sells shares to the public, pools the proceeds, and invests in different types of securities. It thus offers the small investor the advantages of diversification and reduction of investment risk. The company is obligated to redeem or repurchase its shares on request.

N

Natural guardian. The parent of a minor; originally the father but now either the father or the mother. Natural guardianship relates only to the person of a minor.

Negative pledge clause. A covenant in an indenture to the effect that the corporation will not pledge any of its assets unless the notes or debentures outstanding under the particular indenture are at least equally secured by such pledge; also called the "covenant of equal coverage."

Negotiated plan. A pension, profit-sharing, or other employee benefit plan that has been bargained for with an employer by a group of employees, usually through a union as bargaining agent.

Next of kin. The person or persons in the nearest degree of blood relationship to the decedent. As the term is usually employed, those entitled by law to the property of a person who has died without leaving a valid will (such persons do not include the surviving spouse except where specifically so provided by statute).

Nomination. The naming or proposal of a person for an office, position, or duty; to be distinguished from appointment. Thus the testator nominates but the court appoints the executor under a will.

Nominee. A person named for an office, position, or duty; in trust business, usually the person, firm, or corporation in whose name registered securities are held.

Non compos mentis (not of sound mind). A term that includes all forms of mental unsoundness.

Nonlegal investment. An investment that does not conform to the requirements of the statutes; a term used principally with reference to trust investments; to be distinguished from unauthorized investment.

Notice to creditors. The notice in writing by posting in public places or by notice in newspapers to creditors of an estate to present their claims for what the executor or administrator owes them; it is usually also a notice to debtors to come in and pay what they owe the estate.

Nuncupative will. An oral will made by a person on his deathbed or by one who is conscious of the possibility of meeting death in the near future. It is declared in the presence of at least two witnesses and later reduced to writing and offered for probate in the manner prescribed by statute.

O

Obligee. One to whom an obligation is owed, such as a bondholder.

Obligor. One who has an obligation to discharge, such as a corporation that issues bonds.

Open-end mortgage. A corporate trust indenture under which bonds in addition to the original issue may be authenticated and delivered by the trustee from time to time. *Compare* Closed mortgage.

Ordinary court. *See* Probate court.

Original investment. An investment received by the trustee as part of the decedent's estate or from the settlor of a living trust.

Orphan's court. *See* Probate court.

Overt act. An act done openly in pursuance of an avowed interest or design; as opposed to a threat without any act to carry it out.

P

Part service benefit. Credit toward a pension, provided by the employer, for all or part of a participant's years of service with the company before the adoption of a pension plan.

Passive trust. A trust regarding which the trustee has no active duties to perform, being merely a titleholder; the same as a bare, dry, or naked trust; as opposed to an active trust.

Pecuniary legacy. A gift of money by will.

Pendente lite. During the continuance of a suit at law or in equity.

Pension trust. A trust established by an employer (commonly a corporation) to provide benefits for incapacitated, retired, or superannuated employees, with or without contributions by the employees.

Per capita (by the head). A term used in the distribution of property; distribution to persons as individuals (per capita) and not as members of a family *(per stirpes)*. For example, "I give my estate to my son A and to my grandsons C, D, and E (the sons of my deceased son B) per capita." C, D, and E take as individuals (not as the sons of B), each taking the same share as A, namely, one-fourth of the estate.

Perpetuity. Duration without limitation as to time. *See also* Rule against perpetuities.

Person. Either a human being or a corporation, unless the context shows that one or the other is intended.

Personal effects. Goods of a personal character, such as clothes and jewelry.

Personal property. All property other than real property.

Personal representative. A general term applicable to both executor and administrator.

Personalty. Personal property.

Per stirpes (by the stalk). A term used in the distribution of property; distribution to persons as members of a family *(per stirpes)* and not as individuals (per capita). Two or more children of the same parent take *per stirpes* when together they take what the parent, if living, would take. For example, "I give my estate to my son A and to my grandsons C, D, and E (the sons of my deceased son B), my grandsons to take *per stirpes*." C, D, and E take as the sons of B (not as individuals), each receiving one-sixth of the estate (one-third of the one-half to which B would be entitled if living), while A receives one-half of the estate. Taking *per stirpes* is also known as taking by right of representation.

Posthumous child. A child born after the father's death; to be distinguished from after-born child.

Pour-over. A term referring to the transfer of property from an estate or trust to another estate or trust upon the occurrence of an event as provided in the instrument.

356

Power. Authority or right to do or to refrain from doing a particular act, as a trustee's power of sale or power to withhold income; to be distinguished from trust powers.

Power of appointment. A right given to a person to dispose of property that he does not own. A power of appointment may be general or special. Under a "general" power the donee may exercise the right as he sees fit. A "special" power limits the donee as to those in favor of whom he may exercise the power of appointment. A wife who is given the power to appoint among her children has a special power of appointment.

Power of attorney. A document, witnessed and acknowledged, authorizing the person named therein to act as attorney in fact for the person signing the document. If the attorney in fact is authorized to act for his principal in all matters, he has a "general" power of attorney; if he has authority to do only certain specified things, he has a "special" power of attorney. In financial transactions, the power of attorney is usually special. *See also* Bond power; Letter of attorney; Stock power.

Premium on securities. The amount or percentage by which a security (a bond or a share of stock) is bought or sold for more than its face, or par, value; as opposed to discount on securities.

Present beneficiary. The same as immediate beneficiary.

Pretermitted child. A child to whom a will leaves no share of the parent's estate without affirmative provision in the will showing an intention to omit. It may be an after-born child, a posthumous child, or a child erroneously believed to be dead.

Pretermitted heir. An heir not included in the devolution of a decedent's estate.

Primary beneficiary. The same as immediate beneficiary; as opposed to secondary beneficiary.

Principal. 1. One who employs an agent to act for him. 2. One who is primarily liable on an obligation. 3. The property of an estate other than the income from the property; the same as capital.

Principal beneficiary. The same as ultimate beneficiary.

Private trust. 1. A trust created for the benefit of a designated beneficiary or designated beneficiaries; as, a trust for the benefit of the settlor's or the testator's wife and children; as opposed to a charitable (or public) trust. Also a trust created under a declaration of trust or under a trust agreement; as, a living trust or an insurance trust; as opposed to a trust coming under the immediate supervision of a court. *See also* Court trust.

Probate court. The court that has jurisdiction with respect to wills and intestacies and sometimes guardianships, adoptions, and the like; also

357

called court of probate (Connecticut), surrogate's court (New York), ordinary court (Georgia), orphan's court (Delaware, Maryland, New Jersey, and Pennsylvania), and prefect's court (New Mexico).

Probate of will. Formal proof before the proper officer or court that the instrument offered is the last will of the decedent, as it purports and is alleged to be.

Profit-sharing trust. A trust established by an employer (usually a corporation) as a means of having the employees share in the profits of the enterprise.

Proxy. A person empowered by another to act as his agent in voting; the instrument evidencing the authority of the agent to vote.

Prudent man rule for trust investment. A term applied to a rule laid down by statute or by judicial decision that authorizes a fiduciary to apply the standard of a prudent investor instead of selecting investments according to a list prescribed by statute or by some governmental agency under authority of law; formerly known as the American rule or the Massachusetts rule.

Public administrator. In many states, a county officer whose main duty is to settle the estates of persons who die intestate, when there is no member of the family, creditor, or other person having a prior right of administration who is able or willing to administer the estate.

Public trust. The same as a charitable trust; as opposed to a private trust.

Purchase. A term applicable to every method of acquiring property except by descent—that is, by right of blood.

Q

Qualified plan or trust. A pension, profit-sharing, or other employee benefit plan or trust that meets the requirements of Section 401(a) of the Internal Revenue Code of 1954. The major requirements are that it be written, permanent, for the exclusive benefit of employees or their beneficiaries, and not discriminatory in favor of officers, stockholders, supervisors, or other higher paid employees.

R

Ratable distribution. The distribution of an estate according to a proportionate rate. For example, if all the legacies cannot be paid in full and each of them is reduced by the same percentage, there is ratable distribution.

Real estate. The right, title, or interest that a person has in real property, as distinguished from the property itself, which is the subject matter of the interest.

Real property. Land, buildings, and other kinds of property that legally are classified as "real" as opposed to personal property. *See also* Real estate.

Receiver. An officer appointed by a court to receive the rents, issues, and profits of land or a business; to manage a personal estate; or to perform other duties under the court's guidance during the pendency of a suit.

Reciprocity. A mutual exchange of courtesies between two states or institutions; specifically, recognition by each state or institution of the validity of licenses or privileges granted by the other to its citizens or members.

Recordation. In connection with a mortgage, the recording of the fact that a lien has been created against certain property, described in the mortgage, such entry usually being made in the appropriate public record of the county or other jurisdiction in which the particular property is located.

Register of wills. In some states (Delaware, for example), the name of the officer before whom wills are offered for probate and who grants letters testamentary and letters of administration.

Registrar. In connection with stock, the agent that affixes its signature to each certificate issued, the object being the prevention of over-issuance; in connection with bonds, the agent that maintains the record of ownership of registered bonds.

Registration statement. A statement that sets forth certain facts as prescribed by statute and by rules and regulations issued thereunder and (with certain exceptions) must be filed with the Securities and Exchange Commission before a public offering of new securities.

Remainder. A future estate in real property that will become an estate in possession upon the termination of the prior estate created at the same time and by the same instrument as the future estate. For example, A conveys Greenacre to B for life and upon B's death to C in fee simple. C's interest is a remainder. The term "remainder over" is sometimes used in such phrases as "to B for life, with remainder over to C," calling attention to the fact that there is a prior estate or interest; to be distinguished from reversion.

Remainder beneficiary. The beneficiary of a trust who is entitled to the principal outright after the prior life beneficiary or other prior beneficiary has died or after his interest has been terminated.

Remainderman. The person who is entitled to an estate after the prior estate has expired. For example, "I devise Greenacre to A for life, remainder to B." A is the life tenant; B, the remainderman. Originally, the term applied (and in many states still applies) to real property only.

Remoteness of vesting. *See* Rule against perpetuities.

Renunciation. As the term is employed in trust business, an act, in accordance with prescribed procedure, by which an individual or a trust institution named in a fiduciary capacity declines to accept the appointment.

Res (thing). In the phrase trust *res,* the same as trust property.

Residence. The place where one resides, whether temporarily or permanently. *See also* Domicile.

Residuary devise. A gift, by will, of the real property remaining after all specific devises have been made.

Residuary estate. The property that remains after the testator has made provision out of his net estate for specific, demonstrative, and general gifts. Those who take the residuary estate are known as residuary legatees (as to personal property) and residuary devisees (as to real property).

Restraint on alienation of property. A limitation on the right of a person to transfer title to property or property rights.

Resulting trust. A trust that arises in law from the acts of the parties, regardless of whether they actually intend to create a trust—as when a person disposes of property under circumstances that raise an inference that he does not intend that the person taking or holding the property shall have the beneficial interest in it; to be distinguished from an express trust and a constructive trust.

Reversion. The interest in an estate remaining in the grantor after a particular interest, less than the whole estate, has been granted by the owner to another person; to be distinguished from remainder. The reversion remains in the grantor; the remainder goes to some grantee.

Revocable trust. A trust that by its terms may be terminated by the settlor or by another person; as opposed to an irrevocable trust.

Revocable trust with consent or approval. A trust that by its terms may be terminated by the settlor or by another person, but only with the consent or approval of one or more other persons. For example, A creates for his son B a trust that may be revoked by B with C's consent (in this case C is B's mother).

Rule against accumulations. The limitation imposed by common law or by statute on the accumulation of income in the hands of a trustee.

360

Rule against perpetuities. A rule of common law that makes void any estate or interest in property so limited that it will not take effect or vest within a period measured by a life or lives in being at the time of the creation of the estate plus twenty-one years. In many states the rule has been modified by statute. In some states it is known as the rule against remoteness of vesting.

S

Safekeeping account. An agency account concerning which the duties of the agent are to receipt for, safeguard, and deliver the property in the account on demand of the principal or on his order; to be distinguished from a custody account and a managing agency account.

Schedule of distribution. A list showing the distributive shares of an estate.

Seal. An impression, device, sign, or mark recognized by statute or by judicial decision as having the legal effect of a common law seal. The letters "L. S.," a scroll made with a pen, a seal of wax or gummed paper, or a mark embossed on the paper itself are all recognized seals.

Secondary beneficiary. A beneficiary whose interest in a trust is postponed or is subordinate to that of the primary beneficiary.

Securities. Literally, things given, deposited, or pledged to assure the fulfillment of an obligation. In this narrow sense, a mortgage is a security; but the term is now generally used in a broader sense to include stocks as well as bonds, notes, and other evidences of indebtedness.

Self-employed retirement plan. A pension or profit-sharing plan established by a self-employed individual or a partnership pursuant to the Self-Employed Individual's Tax Retirement Act. The act, sponsored by Congressman Keogh, grants self-employed people (for example, doctors, lawyers) tax advantages in the establishment of their plans similar to qualified corporate retirement plans. Also called H.R. 10 plan. *See also* Keogh plan.

Separate property. The property that one person owns free from any rights or control of others; as, the property that a married person owns independently of his spouse.

Settlement. The winding up and distribution of an estate by an executor or an administrator; a property arrangement frequently involving a trust.

Settlor. A person who creates a trust, such as a living trust, to become operative during his lifetime; also called "donor," "grantor," and "trustor." *Compare* Testator.

Special administrator. An administrator appointed by the court to take over and safeguard an estate pending the appointment of an executor or administrator; sometimes known as a temporary administrator or as a curator.

Special guardian. A guardian appointed by the court for a particular purpose connected with the affairs of a minor or an incompetent; sometimes a guardian *ad litem* is known as a special guardian.

Specific devise. A gift, by will, of a specific parcel of real property.

Specific legacy. A gift, by will, of a specific article of personal property, such as a watch.

Spendthrift provision. A provision in a trust instrument that limits the right of the beneficiary to dispose of his interest, as by assignment, and the right of his creditors to reach it, as by attachment.

Spendthrift trust. A trust in which the interest of a beneficiary cannot be assigned or disposed of by him or attached or otherwise reached by his creditors.

Statute of frauds. A statute, first enacted in England in 1676, designed to prevent "many fraudulent practices by requiring proof of a specific kind, usually in writing, of the important transactions of business, declaring that no action shall be brought or that no contract shall be allowed to be good when the transaction is not so evidenced." For example, the original statute declared that all trusts of land shall be in writing. While each state has its own statute of frauds designed to serve the same general purpose as the original statute, many of these statutes differ greatly from the original.

Statute of limitations. A statute that bars suits on valid claims after the expiration of a specified period of time. The period varies for different kinds of claims. In most states there is a 20-year limit on judgments; contract claims ordinarily expire in six years; and claims for torts (injuries to persons or property) expire within a shorter time. Each state has its own statute or statutes of limitations.

Statute of uses. An English statute enacted in 1535 that provided that the legal as well as the beneficial title to land held for the use of a person vested in that person. There were certain exceptions to this vesting under the statute that opened the way for the development of the law of trusts.

Statutes of descent. Laws, rules, or statutes governing the descent of property under intestacy.

Statutes of distribution. Laws, rules, or statutes governing the distribution of personal property under intestacy.

362

Statutes of mortmain. Several early English statutes, dating back as far as 1279, restricting the alienation of land to a corporation, particularly an ecclesiastical corporation. Mortmain means "dead hand." In the early English law, an ecclesiastic was deemed civilly dead; hence the origin of the term "dead hand."

Statutes of wills. Statutes (the first one was passed in 1541) providing that no will shall be valid and no devise or bequest shall be valid unless the will is in writing, signed and attested in the manner provided by the statute.

Stock bonus trust. A trust established by a corporation to enable its employees to receive benefits in the form of the corporation's stock as a reward for meritorious service or as a means of sharing in the profits of the enterprise.

Stock power. A form of assignment executed by the owner of stock that contains an irrevocable appointment of an attorney to make the actual transfer on the books of the corporation. *See also* Power of attorney.

Stock purchase trust. An insurance trust under which a surviving stockholder of a close corporation may purchase the stock of a deceased stockholder.

Subscribing witness. One who sees a document signed or hears the signature acknowledged by the signer and signs his own name to the document, such as the subscribing witness to a will; to be distinguished from an attesting witness.

Substituted trustee. A trustee appointed by the court (not named or provided for in the trust instrument) to serve in the place of the original trustee or of a prior trustee; to be distinguished from a successor trustee.

Succession. The act or fact of a person's becoming entitled to property of a deceased person, whether by operation of law upon his dying intestate or by taking under his will.

Successive beneficiaries. Beneficiaries who take one after another in succession. Thus under a will in which property is left to A for life, then to B for life, and then to C outright, A, B, and C are successive beneficiaries. The term is also used to denote the inheritance of property by descent or transmission to the next in a succession—as from parent to child and so on down the direct line.

Successor trustee. A trustee following the original or a prior trustee, the appointment of whom is provided for in the trust instrument; to be distinguished from a substituted trustee.

Surcharge (noun). An amount in excess of the value of the property held by a fiduciary, or in excess of the proceeds thereof constituting a loss from the value of the property when originally acquired by the fiduciary, which the fiduciary is required by law to make good because of negligence or other failure of duty. The term is also used as a verb; as, the court surcharged the trustee.

Surety. An individual or a company that, at the request of another, agrees to be responsible for the performance of some act in favor of a third person in the event that the principal fails to perform as agreed; as, the surety on an administrator's or a guardian's bond.

Surrogate's court. *See* Probate court.

T

Tangible property. Property that can be touched or realized with the senses, such as a chair; as opposed to intangible property.

Temporary administrator. An individual or a trust institution appointed by a court to take over and safeguard an estate during a suit over an alleged will, over the right of appointment of an executor or administrator, or during the period that probate is delayed for any reason, such as difficulty in finding or citing missing heirs.

Tenancy. The holding of property by any form of title.

Tenancy at sufferance. A tenancy in which the tenant comes into possession of real property under a lawful title or interest and continues to hold the property even after his title or interest has terminated.

Tenancy at will. A tenancy in which the tenant holds the property at the will or pleasure of the grantor.

Tenancy by the entirety. Tenancy by a husband and wife in such a manner that, except in concert with the other, neither husband nor wife has a disposable interest in the property during the lifetime of the other. At the death of either, the property goes to the survivor; to be distinguished from joint tenancy and tenancy in common.

Tenancy for years. A tenancy for a definite period of time—for example, a year or 99 years. It cannot be terminated by either party alone except at the expiration of the time agreed upon.

Tenancy in common. The holding of property by two or more persons in such a manner that each has an undivided interest that, at his death, passes as such to his heirs or devisees and not to the survivor or survivors; the same as an estate in common; to be distinguished from joint tenancy and tenancy by the entirety.

Tenant. One who holds or possesses real property.

Testament. Under early English law, a term that referred to the disposition of personal property at the death of the owner. The words "and testament" are no longer necessary, since a will now relates to both real and personal property.

Testamentary capacity. Mental capacity to make a valid will.

Testamentary guardian. A guardian of a minor or of an incompetent named in the decedent's will.

Testamentary trust. A trust established by the terms of a will.

Testate. Having made and left a valid will; as opposed to intestate.

Testator. A man who has made and left a valid will at his death. *Compare* Settlor. *See also* Trustor.

Testatrix. A woman who has made and left a valid will at her death.

Title insurance. Insurance against financial loss resulting from claims arising out of defects in the title to real property that are existent but undisclosed at the time the policy is issued by the title company.

Tort. Any wrongful act or omission that causes damage to the person, property, or reputation of another. Commonly spoken of as a private wrong, as opposed to a public wrong, which is called a crime.

Transfer agent. An agent of a corporation to effect the transfer of the corporation's stock or bonds (or both) from one owner to another. A transfer agent for bonds usually is known as a "registrar."

Trust. A fiduciary relationship in which one person (the trustee) is the holder of the legal title to property (the trust property) subject to an equitable obligation (an obligation enforceable in a court of equity) to keep or use the property for the benefit of another (the beneficiary).

Trust administrator. A person in the employ of a trust institution who handles trust accounts in the sense of having direct contacts and dealings with trust customers and beneficiaries.

Trust agreement. A written agreement setting forth the terms of a trust. *See also* Deed of trust.

Trust authority. The legal right of a corporation to engage in trust business.

Trust by declaration. *See* Declaration of trust.

Trust by order of court. A trust created by an order of a competent court.

Trust charges. The charges made by a trust institution for its trust and agency services. *See also* Allowance; Commission; Fee.

Trust committee. A committee of directors or officers (or both) of a trust institution charged with general or specific duties relating to its trust business.

Trust company. A corporation that engages in trust business for both individuals and business organizations.

Trust costs. The costs to a trust institution of rendering trust and agency services; as opposed to trust charges.

Trust deed. *See* Deed of trust.

Trustee. An individual or a trust institution that holds the legal title to property for the benefit of someone else, who is the beneficial owner.

Trust estate. All the property constituting a particular trust account.

Trust for support. A trust that provides that the trustee shall pay or apply only so much of the income or principal as in its judgment is necessary for the support or education of the beneficiary.

Trust function. A fiduciary capacity in which an individual or a trust institution may act, such as executor, administrator, guardian, or trustee.

Trust fund. Technically, only money held in trust; but frequently applied to all the property held in trust—the trust estate.

Trust institution. A trust company, state bank, national bank, or other corporation engaged in trust business under authority of law. It is a trust institution if any department is engaged in trust business, although other departments may be otherwise engaged.

Trust instrument. Any writing—will, trust agreement, declaration of trust, deed of trust, or order of court—under which a trust is created.

Trust investment committee. A committee of directors or officers (or both) of a trust institution charged with specific duties relating to trust investments. The general trust committee sometimes goes by this name.

Trust investments. The property in which trust funds are invested; a broad term that includes all kinds of property, not securities alone.

Trust officer. A title given to certain officers of a trust institution.

Trustor. A person who creates a trust; a broad term that includes both settlor and testator.

Trust powers. As the term is used in the Federal Reserve Act, authority to engage in the trust business; to be distinguished from the powers of a trustee.

Trust receipt. A formal receipt issued by a trustee for property held in trust; used in certain commercial transactions.

Trust under agreement. A trust evidenced by an agreement between the settlor and the trustee; the same as a trust *inter vivos* or a living trust.

Trust under decree. A trust evidenced by a decree of a court of equity.

Trust under deed. A trust evidenced by a deed of conveyance as distinguished from an agreement; originally confined to real property but now frequently applied to personal property as well.

Trust under will. A trust created by a valid will, to become operative only at the death of the testator; the same as a testamentary trust; as opposed to a living trust.

Tutor. Under civil law, one who has been legally appointed to care for the person and the property of a minor; the equivalent of a guardian.

U

Ultimate beneficiary (also called principal beneficiary). A beneficiary of a trust who is entitled to receive the principal of the trust property in final distribution; as opposed to immediate beneficiary and income beneficiary.

Unauthorized investment. A trust investment that is not authorized by the trust instrument; to be distinguished from a nonlegal investment.

Undivided interests. *See* Tenancy in common; Joint tenancy; Tenancy by the entirety.

Undue influence. The influence that one person exerts over another person to the point where he is prevented from exercising his own free will.

Unfunded insurance trust. An insurance trust in which the premiums on the policies are to be paid by the insured or by some third person and not by the trustee; to be distinguished from a funded insurance trust.

Use (noun). The beneficial ownership of property the legal title to which is in another; the forerunner of the modern trust.

V

Variable annuity. An annuity that pays income in units the dollar value of which fluctuates in relation to the underlying securities, primarily common stocks. Also called an equity annuity. To be contrasted with the guaranteed fixed-dollar payments of the conventional annuity.

Vest. To confer an immediate, fixed right of immediate or future possession and enjoyment of property.

Vested interest. An immediate, fixed interest in real or personal property, although the right of possession and enjoyment may be postponed until some future date or until the occurrence of some event; to be distinguished from a contingent interest.

Vested remainder. A fixed interest in property, with the right of possession and enjoyment postponed until the termination of the prior estate; to be distinguished from a contingent remainder.

Vesting. As applied to pension and profit-sharing plans, vesting is a term that indicates the attainment by a participant of a benefit right, attributable to employer contributions, that is not contingent upon his continued employment. Vesting may be total and immediate, graduated over a period of years, or may occur on completion of stated service or participation requirements.

Voluntary trust. A trust created by the voluntary act of the settlor and not conditional on his death; the same as a living trust; to be distinguished from a trust under will or a testamentary trust.

W

Waiver. The voluntary relinquishment of a right, privilege, or advantage. The instrument evidencing the act is often known as a waiver.

Ward. A person who by reason of minority, mental incompetence, or other incapacity is under the protection of the court either directly or through a guardian, committee, curator, or conservator.

Waste. Spoil or destruction of real property done or permitted by the tenant in possession, to the prejudice of the heir or owner of the remainder or reversion.

Wasting trust. A trust composed of property that is gradually being used up.

Widow's allowance. The allowance of personal property made by the court or by statute to a widow for her immediate requirements after her husband's death.

Widow's election *See* Election.

Will. A legally enforceable declaration of a person's wishes regarding matters to be attended to after his death and inoperative until his death. A will usually, but not always, relates to the testator's property, is revocable (or amendable by means of a codicil) up to the time of his death, and is applicable to the situation that exists at the time of his death.

Writ. An order or mandatory direction in writing, under seal, issued in the name of a state, a court, or a judicial officer, and commanding the person to whom it is addressed to do or not to do some specified act.

Index

U

W